The March to Hougoumont

ALEXANDER GEORGE FRASER, LORD SALTOUN
IN LATER LIFE

The March to Hougoumont
Lord Saltoun & the First Guards from Sicily, Walcheren and the Peninsular War to Waterloo, 1805-15

ILLUSTRATED

John H. Lewis

The March to Hougoumont
Lord Saltoun & the First Guards from Sicily, Walcheren and the Peninsular War to Waterloo, 1805-15
by John H. Lewis

ILLUSTRATED

FIRST EDITION

Leonaur is an imprint of Oakpast Ltd

The author, John H Lewis asserts his rights for copyright purposes
© 2020 Oakpast Ltd

The illustrations of Hougoumont which appear in this book are copyright John H Lewis/Leonaur.2020 and all rights are reserved.

ISBN: 978-1-78282-978-2 (hardcover)
ISBN: 978-1-78282-979-9 (softcover)

http://www.leonaur.com

Publisher's Notes

The views expressed in this book are not necessarily those of the publisher.

Contents

Introduction by the Author	9
Acknowledgements	15
Lord Saltoun & His Regiment	21
The Expedition to Sicily, 1805-1807	30
The First Guards on Sicily	37
The Invasion of Portugal, 1807	51
The Peninsular Campaign of 1808	55
The Brigade of Guards in Spain, 1808	63
The Retreat to Corunna, 1809	73
The Battle of Corunna	80
The Return to Portugal, 1809	88
The Walcheren Expedition, 1809	95
The Siege of Cadiz, 1810	107
The Guards at Barrosa, 1811	114
Operations in the Peninsula, 1811-12	126
The Advance from Cadiz to Seville, 1812	130
The Siege of Burgos and the Retreat, 1812	137
The Decline of the Empire of the French, 1812	149
The Remote Courtship of Lord Saltoun, 1813	157

The Investment of San Sebastian, 1813	167
The Pyrenees—The Bidassoa, 1813	181
The Nivelle, 1813	191
The Nive & St. Pierre, 1813	203
The Forcing of the Adour	213
The Investment of Bayonne, 1814	225
Napoleon's War in the North, 1814	235
The Sortie from Bayonne, 1814	240
A Brief Interlude	249
The Gathering Storm	255
Saltoun's Letters from Belgium, May, 1815	268
The Affairs of Early June, 1815	291
The Drums Begin to Beat	299
The Battles of Ligny & Quatre Bras	310
Belgium, June 17th, 1815	328
The Battle of Waterloo—Morning	338
The Struggle for Hougoumont	351
The Battle of Waterloo—Afternoon	361
The Battle of Waterloo—Evening	372
The Pursuit to Paris	384
The Occupation of Paris	406
Epilogue	418
Appendix No. 1	425
Appendix No. 2	432
Appendix No. 3	434

Dedications

First there is Patsie, wife, ally, partner and editor,
Because first there is always Patsie
And no one I know would begrudge her that place.
Secondly, to Jim Goddard, contributor,
Enduring friend, collaborator and confederate
And my sister-in-law, Sylvia the dependable,
Who marches the extra mile.
Finally, but not least, to Charles 'Charlie' Radford,
Officer and gentleman, first among Leonaur supporters,
Who regularly and willingly steps up to the line
And beyond for us.

✶✶✶✶✶✶

*Destiny itself is like a wonderful wide tapestry
In which every thread is guided
By an unspeakable tender hand,
Placed beside another thread and held
And carried by a hundred others.*
                    Rainer Maria Rilke

Introduction by the Author

Converging paths. Intersecting events and lives. These are the weft and warp of the fabric of history. Some are momentous in their effects, some are seemingly insignificant, but all are interdependent and in their connections are carried the destinies of the affairs of humankind.

This book, of course, concerns only a very small portion of that huge and fascinating cloth. It is the story of a premier infantry regiment of the British Army; the First Regiment of Foot Guards, which in due course became the Grenadier Guards, during a particularly active and significant period of its own long and illustrious history. It is also the story of a young man who joined that regiment and served with it as an officer growing in experience and distinction as his career progressed, principally revealed in this book through his journals and correspondence.

It is a story of wars and campaigns which have become among the most notable among the history of the warfare of comparatively modern times for they were fought, from the perspective of that soldier and his regiment, against the First Empire of the French under the inspirational leadership of one of the most outstanding military figures in history, the Emperor Napoleon. He created an epoch, the spirit of which has endured to perennially fascinate historians and, of course, it therefore inevitably concerns the military career of the Duke of Wellington, who became the emperor's nemesis. It also transpired to be, perhaps quite unexpectedly from the author's perspective, a love story.

These elements were inexorably drawn together, travelling for a decade on roads that ran through Sicily, Iberia, France and the Low Countries until they eventually arrived at a cataclysmic rendezvous during which, over a three day period between the 16th and 18th of June, 1815, were fought two of the most renowned engagements in the annals of conflict; The Battle of Quatre Bras and The Battle of Waterloo.

Our principal character, having seen long service during the Peninsular War and other conflicts, fought in both of those battles, in part commanding two light companies of the First Guards tasked with the defence of the orchard and wood of Hougoumont. This *château*-farm had been transformed into a bastion and was the key of the extreme right of Wellington's defensive line, so had essentially to be held against the attacking French troops under the command of Napoleon's brother, Prince Jerome Bonaparte, to prevent a flanking manoeuvre in that direction. He then took his place with his regiment, in its principal position and with it withstood the great cavalry charges against the beleaguered squares of infantry, thereafter playing his part in the final action of the battle which brought the Imperial Guard to ruin.

How the book you are holding came into being is another story of converging lines and intersecting events, though it is, of course, a far more prosaic tale. That said it is one worth the telling, for it is not without some interest. The beginning of that story came about not long after two hundred years had elapsed from the time of the Battle of Waterloo though, quite genuinely, on the field of that very conflict in the farmlands beyond the city of Brussels in Belgium.

Since it remains a working farm in private ownership the ordinary visitor can (at the time of writing) only safely gaze wistfully at the buildings of the farm of La Haye Sainte, in front of the centre of the British line, from the other side of a usually busy road. Likewise, Hougoumont was until recently privately owned and although there was access to it for special interest groups, for most of my time, as a very ordinary visitor, one could not enter this legendary position which became, 'a battle within the battle'.

My wife and partner, Patsie and I (in company with one of our grandsons) visited the newly renovated Hougoumont, now at last open to the public, at the first opportunity available to us. This is not the place to describe Hougoumont or the engagement that was fought there, for that will eventually appear in the course of this book. In any event that first visit, for us, was less about historical detail than about atmosphere. We were, simply put, overwhelmed to be walking on the cobbles and within the space of such iconic, evocative and familiar events. It is true that one can experience similar sensations practically anywhere on the field of Waterloo, but these impressions are surely nowhere (currently accessible) more profound than within Hougoumont.

The paintings of the scenes of the battle for Hougoumont have long been very familiar to those who have an interest in military art and these events. Hillingford's scene in the courtyard, Dighton's action beyond the south gate, Gibb's iconic image of the north gate being shouldered shut by the Guards as the French infantry try to burst through and perhaps above all, for me, Ernest Crofts' wonderful painting from the perspective of the attacking French infantry. Brutal and appalling as all warfare undeniably is, it is virtually impossible not to be romantically swept away under the influence of these images (which was the idea of them, of course) when one stands upon the locations, readily and infallibly identifiable, where these dramas took place.

Since the Hougoumont visitor centre curators have constructed steps and a wooden platform for the purpose, Patsie and I found our way to the defenders' side of the garden wall beyond the south gate, which appears to the right of Crofts' painting and, returning in the imagination two hundred years, peering over it for a moment, indulged in our reveries. That moment was short lived.

It was a warm afternoon and so we were both wearing short-sleeved shirts, our forearms resting on the brick parapet. Before long, an extraordinarily large flying insect, not immediately identifiable to us, but attired in the yellow and black striped uniform ominously associated with wasps, flew up to Patsie, boldly alighted on one of her exposed arms and without preamble, slowly extended a long 'bayonet' from its nether region, presumably with the intention of sinking it into her flesh. It had selected entirely the wrong target.

Not one to panic, a familiar (to me, anyway) expression of combined vexation and determination crossed over my wife's usually pleasant countenance. The creature was then promptly and decisively 'batted for six' by Mrs. Lewis with a severe, 'Get off, you *blank*!' reprimand to accompany a really impressive trajectory as it spiralled away to cross some far away boundary. I laughed aloud, the gravitas of the history of the place notwithstanding, since, unbidden, it immediately occurred to me this was not the first time an affronted English voice had said those words at that point, on that wall with much the same outcome. Whilst Patsie is some way (and many inches) from a guardsman of any era, I had read similar phrases several times spoken by British soldiers upon different battle-grounds in various campaigns among the many personal military narratives that have come my way.

It was then, believe it or not as you will, that I began to contemplate how a book could be created that included the struggle for Hougoumont in a way that had not necessarily been covered before by other writers within other books. This does not admittedly amount to much by way of serious academic motivation for the creation of a work of history, but we are in the business of making books in quantity and one inspiration or epiphany serves fairly as well as any other. So, there it is.

My first thoughts for the model of the enterprise were not so very far from the kind of book that has ultimately come to fruition. That was it should combine the career of one of the notable personalities of the Guards who fought in the Battle of Waterloo in or around Hougoumont, within a narrative that embraced his own regiment's service during the Napoleonic Wars; a march which inexorably led to Hougoumont and, as it transpired, beyond.

When I considered the potentials of Lord Saltoun (pronounced Salton), by the time of Waterloo, a 30-year-old captain/lieutenant-colonel of the Third Battalion, First Guards, initial investigations were not promising. I knew nothing about him other than in accounts of the action at Hougoumont in which his name appeared regularly so I apologise if, in the light of what follows, my ignorance seems peculiar to the better informed. There did not seem to have been a biography published concerning his life. He had not written an autobiography, so far as I could discover, nor indeed a published volume of recollections confined to his military career. It then occurred to me that Saltoun, since it is a title, might not necessarily be the name under which such a volume might have been written. Lord Saltoun, (the 16th of that title, incidentally) was in fact Alexander George Fraser of the Fraser's of Philorth.

I began, therefore, to make further investigations in that direction which was when, in the parlance of those who dig in hope of discovering treasure, 'I hit pay-dirt', for another Alexander Fraser, (the 17th Lord Saltoun and our subject's nephew) had served posterity particularly well by becoming the author, archivist and presumably publisher (since the work is a privately circulated, numbered limited edition from 1879) of a substantial three volume work chronicling the extraordinarily long history of his Scottish family and there, to keep this introduction no longer than it need be and to avoid repetition, in volume three was the correspondence of his uncle, written during his service with the First Guards (and latterly Grenadier Guards) in the course of the Napoleonic wars and, of course, including the Waterloo Campaign. I subsequently discovered more valuable biographical material was included in volume one.

It may be that this correspondence has been published elsewhere specifically within the context of these campaigns, but I can only report that if that is the case, then in the course of my fairly extensive reading on this subject, it has slipped by me. So, this was a 'Eureka' moment. Indeed, my enthusiasm was about to exponentially increase, since my first recourse was to investigate the number of Peninsular War bibliographies in my possession and, having done so, found within them no reference to these letters. This was reassuring for discoveries like this do not come one's way very often or in my case, more accurately, to this date, ever.

So, I was thrilled and motivated for I had found my subject or, dependent on one's perspective, it had found me. That pleasure was enhanced by the fact that Alexander Fraser, Lord Saltoun was no stranger to the section of wall and garden that had inspired the creation of a book that became this book. Converging paths and intersecting events had become a theme. What agency sent the intersecting insect responsible for all of this, I cannot say nor dare venture to speculate. All the afore written is true though, I do assure you, as indeed to the best of my ability to judge and relate, is what follows.

John H. Lewis, 2020

Acknowledgements

My first acknowledgements must be that I am not an academic of history or any other subject and I have never been a soldier. I do not profess, likewise, to be an expert on the subject of the Peninsular War or indeed the Waterloo Campaign, notwithstanding that I can honestly claim to have read many works on both subjects for pleasure, as an editor and as a publisher. My own career was in the media, firstly as a journalist followed by several decades in creative marketing. So, my first instinct as an author is to entertain by telling a good story and my hope is that, in its company, the reader will spend some rewarding and pleasurable time. I have ploughed through my share of books on interesting historical subjects, crammed with essential, well researched information which were, nevertheless, something of an endurance course to read, much less complete. Their authors did not, demonstrably, have the recreation of others highly placed on their agendas. However, from my own perspective, my worst disservice in the recounting of Saltoun's fascinating and eventful story would be that I made it appear dull.

That I have employed Lord Saltoun's papers published within, 'The Frasers of Philorth', published in three volumes by Alexander Fraser, The 17th Lord Saltoun, printed in Edinburgh for private circulation in 1879, may be acknowledged with little emphasis, since he is the principal character in this story and these papers were not only the inspiration for this book, but also comprise a significant portion of its content. I have also been extensively guided by 'The Origins & History of the First or Grenadier Guards', by Lieutenant-General Sir F.W Hamilton in three volumes published by John Murray, London in 1871. Hamilton was formerly a Grenadier Guards officer, who served actively with the regiment during the Crimean War.

I am persuaded—on the whole—that it is reliable to follow the detail provided in these kinds of books, written in the nineteenth century, as to matters concerning regimental movements etc., because the authors certainly have had access to regimental records and diaries together with memoirs and manuscripts. In Hamilton's case, he may have been able to speak directly with some of the people who took part in the events here related or to their immediate families, since he was born in 1815—in fact, just 10 days before the Battle of Waterloo was fought.

One cannot take the entire contents of these kinds of volumes as completely dependable for several reasons. They invariably reveal a bias on the part of their authors with regard to their principal subjects, since these kinds of books (this one, as revealed, being no exception) are frequently written by former members of the regiment in question. So not only can they be guaranteed to contain only favourable views of their subjects, but one may discover that more emphasis has been placed on the role of the regiment or regimental individuals than may have been—in sober judgement—the case. This habit also tends to minimise or relegate to obscurity those who were also involved in the same events, but who were not associated with the author's regiment. For example, Hamilton's account of the conflict for Hougoumont does not mention the name of the officer in command of the post who was not a First Guard, but, at the time, a Coldstreamer. Since that omission cannot be ascribed to any other account on the subject, one must consider MacDonnell's absence from Hamilton's narrative to be intentional. In fact, there are a number of differences between Daniel Mackinnon's account of the Coldstreams at Hougoumont and the Grenadier Guards' history on the same subject by Hamilton.

I have taken some pains to briefly mitigate these kinds of shortcomings, for without doing so it is impossible for the reader to have an understanding of all the events which were taking place in the same location and period of time. That having been said, the First Guards (later Grenadier Guards) do intentionally appear in this book as the particular focus and perspective, because it is not intended to be a general history of the events featured within it and Saltoun was always, during this period of his life, an officer of that regiment and their stories are, therefore, inextricably entwined.

Secondly, the authors of these kinds of books have a tendency to be diplomatic to the point of servility concerning the influential characters of society who appear in their pages, whether for reasons of good form or self-preservation, it is difficult to evaluate; something of both factors was probably the case, though for the historical record, accuracy and candour are the perpetual casualties. If the better-informed reader discovers that I have failed to be diligent with regard to any of those erroneous assertions that required rectification, then I offer my unreserved apologies.

It was also never my intention to deal with battles and campaigns fully in military detail—orders of battle, casualties etc. In fact, I have also deliberately only sketched the assault on Bergen-op-Zoom in 1814, because only a small number of First Guards were actually involved in the assault itself and Saltoun was not involved at all. Similarly, events in the Peninsular War that did not include the Guards are only mentioned in their chronological place. A work which embraced all of these details would be huge and the thread of the intended narrative would have been inevitably submerged.

That kind of information is available, in any event, elsewhere so I decided, in the interests of keeping matters simple and the book something smaller than the dimensions of a house brick, to take my military and political cues, concentrating on the 'broad brush-strokes' in the main, from the extremely thorough and accessible writings of Professor Charles Oman and Sir John Fortescue. I have supplemented these with reference to Captain William Siborne's invaluable, 'History of the War in France and Belgium in 1815,' (Fourth Edition) T & W Boone, London, 1848 and, of course, his collated 'Waterloo Letters' written by British officer participants in some of these events and collated into book form by his son, since in these, it seems to me, will be found information—closest coming from 'the horse's mouth'—which has the likelihood of being both authentic and comparatively accurate.

That having been said, one can never be entirely certain of these matters concerning events two centuries in the past, of course, so where there have been inconsistencies I have undertaken some further research from various other sources including Daniel Mackinnon's, 'Origin & Services of the Coldstream Guards', Volume 2, Richard Bentley, London, 1833. The author was present within Hougoumont during the battle. Similarly, and for the same reason, I have accessed Rees Howell Gronow's anecdotes which appeared in several volumes of reminiscences and recollections.

Gronow was an officer of the First Guards who served during the Peninsular War and during the Campaign of 1815. He was within the regimental position at Waterloo and on the march thereafter to Paris and he brings a sensitive, humane and occasionally humorous aspect to these events. Of course, as a brother officer, he knew Saltoun well, enabling the reader to see him as others saw him and I have valued his contribution more from the perspective of his impressions than his accurate reportage of the military facts. I have discovered several other letters and journal extracts written by First Guards and have utilised them at points in the narrative for much the same reason as the inclusion of the Gronow extracts.

Common accord is, however, often hard to find, as anyone who has cross-referenced a quantity of written history very well knows. Definitive 'truth', in my view, stands on a peak too steep for me to scale and too tenuous to stand upon indefinitely, even if one reaches the summit. So, I make no claims of planting my flag upon it. Rather than coming to conclusions in those cases where broad agreement remains elusive, I have assumed the role of an impartial reporter of versions rather than misrepresenting myself as a new authority.

Nevertheless, I have been unable to resist the selfish temptation to editorialise and that is because notions have occurred to me in the course of my extensive reading of different versions of the same events during the period covered by this book and indeed, as a consequence of editing both Oman's and Fortescue's writings on the Napoleonic era . If I am in error or provoke disagreement in those instances where I have let my opinions or imagination run free, I have only my own hubris to blame, which as anyone who is likely to read this book knows, is a time-honoured cause of personal downfall.

It is traditional to thank people who have given assistance on these kinds of projects and, whilst I trust I am given to a generosity of spirit, I cannot make a list of mine very long for Leonaur is a small publishing imprint and we keep pretty much to ourselves. Everyone associated with it knows who they are and what they contribute to it. They also know what I feel about them, because we are in the most part related in one way or another or have been comrades for a long time.

I must, on behalf of Leonaur, acknowledge the contribution made by the graphic designer and artist, Glyn Staves, in the creation of the illustrations of Hougoumont. It has been my privilege to know and work with Glyn for many years in several capacities including, in this case, as his client. It is worth emphasising that the motivation behind the commission of this 3D image was to give the reader an *impression* of the *château*-farm and its environs. It is also intended to assist in the identification of the locations of events which took place around the buildings, roads and pathways, gardens, orchards and woods, described in the text. We have achieved that objective by the examination of a plethora of available material (including satellite images) and, where there were gaps of information we could not readily fill, we have employed some considered imagination and artistic licence. The author is well aware of the significant volume of serious research that has been undertaken at the site and which, indeed, is ongoing at time of writing. Though proportions and relative distances are more or less accurate, these illustrations were never intended to be considered in a remotely academic way. However, in keeping with the spirit that guided the writing of this story I trust, since I have seen nothing quite like them myself in the past, that perusing them will give others some enjoyment.

Two other people stand clear in my mind and they are Charles 'Charlie' Radford, former C.O of the 16th/5th Lancers and the veteran historian, Ian Robertson. Both men have always made me feel we were doing something worthwhile. So, thank you both, that encouragement has always been appreciated, whether you were aware you were giving it or not. In Charlie Radford's case he must also be thanked for eliciting approvals and assistance from the families of several authors whose work we have published and so, accordingly, all of those very kind people must be thanked for their open-hearted generosity and cooperation. Finally, I must acknowledge the support of everyone who has purchased a Leonaur imprint book, most especially Kevin Jones who has, to date, diligently collected every Leonaur Napoleonic subject title in a hardback edition.

J. H. L

CHAPTER ONE

Lord Saltoun & His Regiment

The First Guards (today and as of 1815, The Grenadier Guards) regiment was raised by Charles II in 1656 as Lord Wentworth's Royal Regiment of Guards, whilst he was in exile in Bruges, in modern Belgium, following the English Civil War, which was, at that time, within the Spanish held Netherlands. The regiment first went into action at the Battle of the Dunes, near Dunkirk in 1658. This was a peculiar baptism of fire since the royalist regiment, among Spanish allies, was fighting not only the French under Turenne, but also their allies; troops from the British Commonwealth under Lockhart. The battle was a French victory and the soldiers who had remained loyal to their king suffered severely. However, their time of exile was soon to come to an end and the survivors accompanied Charles II to England in 1660 upon the restoration of the monarchy following Oliver Cromwell's death and the collapse of the Commonwealth.

During the remainder of the 17th century the regiment saw its share of action, fighting in the capacity of marines aboard Royal Navy ships during the Dutch Wars 1665-7, most notably off Lowestoft and in the Battle of Sole Bay. It was during this period that John Churchill (later the Duke of Marlborough) joined the regiment as an ensign.

More conventional infantry service followed at Tangier on the North African, Mediterranean coast (which had come to Charles II as part of the dowry of his wife, the Portuguese princess, Catharine of Braganza) against the Moors in 1680. Notwithstanding the English king's claims, made without their consent and probably their knowledge, the local inhabitants took some exception to the incursive presence of *infidels* on their lands and hostilities inevitably broke out. The Guards were awarded their first battle honour, 'Tangier', for their service, which was also the first battle honour (Honorary Distinction) of the modern British Army.

The Battle of Sedgemoor in 1685 saw the regiment fighting on English soil to defeat, Charles II's illegitimate pretender son, the rebellious Duke of Monmouth. Foreign service came again in Flanders during the War of the League of Augsburg, 1689-97, though matters did not begin auspiciously for the regiment, which suffered a defeat at the Battle of Steenkirk in 1692 and again in 1693 at the Battle of Landen. The assault of the fortress of Namur in 1695 brought about a restoration of the regiment's fortune for the enemy position was successfully carried, a French Marshal was captured, and 'Namur' became the regiment's second battle honour.

With the first years of the 18th century came a new war against the French which brought to the fore the superlative generalship of the Duke of Marlborough, placing him in the pantheon of his nation's outstanding military men. During the War of Spanish Succession, 1701-14, the First Guards initially saw action at the fortified hill-top position of The Schellenberg, overlooking Donauworth, in July,1704. This desperate action cost the lives of three quarters of the First Guards grenadiers who led the assault, though the battle delivered Marlborough his first victory of the campaign and gave the French their first battlefield defeat in approaching half a century. The renowned victory at the Battle of Blenheim followed in the following month and, during the subsequent five years of the war, the regiment added battle honours which resound to this day including, 'Ramillies', 1706, 'Oudenard', 1708 and 'Malplaquet', 1709. Additionally, between 1704-5, 200 soldiers of the First Guards successfully contributed to the defence of Gibraltar earning the regiment yet another battle honour for its colours.

Another issue of European royal succession created a pretext for war and once again the British Army was in conflict with the old enemy; the France of the Bourbons. The War of Austrian Succession, 1740-48, brought forth two notable engagements which involved the First Guards. The first was the Battle of Dettingen, 1743 which was the last occasion a British monarch commanded on the field of battle. The second was the Battle of Fontenoy, 1745; a hard-fought affair which was probably concluded in a stalemate, but is not regarded as a British victory since the French force held the field of conflict at the close of the engagement.

Meanwhile, the Jacobite Rebellion was breaking out in Scotland. Guards were employed on horseback as mounted infantry to move swiftly northwards and although four hundred First Guards assisted in the relief of Carlisle, they did not take part in the final battle on Culloden Moor which brought the aspirations of Charles Stuart and his highlanders to ruin. The regiment suffered defeat in the abortive Raid on St. Malo on the northern coast of France, 1758 and, despite gallant service, in the disastrous (for the British cause) American War of Independence, 1775-83.

******

The Frasers of Philorth are a lowland Scottish family whose clan chieftains are representative peers of Scotland; the Lords Saltoun. The family seat is Castle Fraser at Sauchen in Aberdeenshire and they should not be confused, therefore, with the highland Frasers of Lovat, centred about Inverness. The first Lord Saltoun, in the fifteenth century, was Lawrence Abernethy and there followed nine Abernethy, Lords Saltoun in succession until the seventeenth century when Margaret Abernethy became the 10th Lord Saltoun. However, her position is not traditionally counted and thus, henceforth a Lord Saltoun could be referred to as (for example) the 17th and the 16th Lord Saltoun. From Margaret Abernethy the title transferred to the Fraser family name and to date, eight Lords Saltoun have borne Alexander as their Christian name.

ALEXANDER FRASER.
FIFTEENTH LORD SALTOUN.
BORN 1758, DIED 1793

MARJORY FRASER, LADY SALTOUN.
WIFE OF THE FIFTEENTH LORD. ÆTAT INTER 80-90.
DIED NOV. 15TH 1851, ÆTAT. 97.

By the closing decades of the 18th century war with the old enemy, France, was again looming. This enemy was no longer, of course, the France of the Bourbons for the age of revolution had dawned, the head of the Bourbon king, Louis XVI had fallen into the basket of the guillotine in Paris in January, 1793. The established orders of continental Europe were then under no illusion that they entering into a period of dire instability and threat.

In the same year, the early and unexpected death of the fifteenth (by traditional styling) Alexander Fraser, Lord Saltoun, in September 1793, meant his eldest son, Alexander George Fraser, the subject of this narrative, who was born on the 22nd of April 1785, succeeded to the title when he was between eight and nine years of age. In this book he is principally referred to as Saltoun, since that is the name, he used himself, even when corresponding to close family members. The impact of the loss of a father on a young boy requires no elaboration, though he, of course, received the abiding support of his mother, Margery and that of his maternal grandfather, Simon Fraser of Ness Castle.

******

The French Revolutionary Wars, 1793-1802 heralded more than a contest for territory and resources, for the tricolour of republicanism championed an ideology which proposed to eradicate the power of monarchs, aristocracies and the church wherever it could prevail.

In the first year of the war the First Guards, as part of a small force of just over a thousand troops under the command of General Gerard Lake, (who would earn laurels in India against the Marathas in concert with the soldier who would one day become the Duke of Wellington), marched upon the fortified hill-top village of Lincelles in Flanders which was occupied by 5,000 of the enemy. The successful assault, against artillery and massed musket fire, was carried out with great gallantry and in consequence, 'Lincelles' was awarded to the First Guards as another battle honour.

******

Alexander Fraser was sent to the public school at Eton, where, as an extraordinarily bold and fit young man, he soon earned a reputation among his schoolfellows for deeds of daring. He was the first Etonian to jump into the Thames from the parapet of the centre arch of Windsor Bridge. A junior contemporary said that he remembered, upon first attending Eton, that the whole school was 'ringing with the description of a fight that had just taken place between Lord Saltoun and a champion of the bargemen', or *bargees* as they were termed. The young Saltoun apparently triumphed on that occasion. In another encounter with the *bargees* he had a very narrow escape, for tripped up by the prone body of a friend, he fell on his back whereupon one of the *bargees* stabbed at him with a pitchfork. He was found stunned by the fall, but uninjured, the prongs having passed, one on each side of his neck, pinning him into the ground.

******

Six years after Lincelles was fought, in 1799, the First Guards took part in their final campaign of the century in the expedition to the Helder. Against all expectations, and much to the surprise of all those who opposed it, the inexperienced army of the new republic of France frequently fared well on the field of conflict. France's determination to spread republicanism throughout Europe had, by this time, already created six minor republics including the Batavian Republic of Holland and Belgium. The great powers including Russia, Austria, Prussia and Britain determined to decisively defeat the French revolutionary armies, for they were by this time, thinly spread whilst engaged in several campaigns and so considered to be particularly vulnerable. The Second Coalition of nations to oppose France was formed and hostilities commenced, delivering some initial success for the allies, principally because they possessed significant numerical superiority.

A joint Russian and British force was formed for an expedition to the Low Countries to ensure the French concentrated defences on a hitherto unthreatened frontier. The plan was then to capture a number of valuable military arsenals, the ships of the

Dutch naval fleet and re-establish the power of the Stadtholder. Furthermore, it was hoped that the people of the new republic (including those under arms in the service of the enemy) would stand aside from the conflict and, in due course, join the allies. The campaign was launched by a landing in North Holland near to the Helder since this location provided a secure anchorage for the fleet and placed the army within striking distance of Amsterdam.

Poor weather delayed the landing giving notice of its arrival to the French, who could see the invasion force at sea, allowing them the time to concentrate their own forces. The landing transpired to be unopposed, but the advance guard had hardly begun to move forward before it was hotly engaged by the enemy. Nevertheless, the Helder was secured, the enemy garrison withdrew and two line-of-battle ships, five frigates and thirteen Indiamen immediately fell into British hands. The Dutch navy crews, as had been hoped, refused to fight, which soon delivered more valuable enemy vessels into the hands of the invaders.

The campaign on land, before long however, began to founder and the British commander, Abercromby, aware that the terrain between his force and the enemy was latticed with canals and ditches would not risk an advance until he was reinforced. His counterpart, Brune, perceiving his opponent's procrastination, struck pre-emptively, employing his entire force on the 10th of September. Two brigades of Guards under Burrard were well placed to defend the village of Pettin on the left of the line and despite being sorely pressed threw back the attacking force, inflicting losses of approaching 1,000 men, whilst suffering very few casualties themselves. Burrard's career, alas, would not continue so promisingly.

Soon after this action the Duke of York arrived with reinforcements and assumed command of the British Army which, in concert with its Russian allies, began an advance towards Bergen. The minute details of this brief and entirely unsuccessful campaign are not germane to the principal theme of this account, though it is worth noting that from a position of strength the allies very soon found themselves at such a disadvantage that not only was success acknowledged as impossible, but a fighting evacuation was also considered untenable. The Duke of York therefore entered into negotiations with the republicans which would allow the unhindered departure of his command and this arrangement was ratified towards the end of October. Sir James Pultney, the final senior British officer to depart from the continental shore, embarked with his last remaining troops on the 19th November, 1799. The French re-occupied the Helder on the same day.

The turn of the new century was just weeks away and Revolutionary France was making its presence and potentials felt in ways that guaranteed the nineteenth century would, for the coalition nations, begin in strife and uncertainty which showed very little indication of abating or improving. Indeed, by the close of the same year, the brilliant General Napoleon Bonaparte had, following a short military career, risen in power to establish himself as the First Consul of France.

★★★★★★

In 1802, at seventeen years old, Lord Saltoun entered the British Army, receiving his commission of ensign (by purchase) in the 91st, (Argyllshire Highlanders) Regiment of Foot in which his uncle, Major General Duncan Campbell of Lochnell, held the rank of colonel. By the Autumn of the same year he had become a lieutenant in the second battalion of the 35th Regiment of Foot which at that time bore the territorial title of 'Dorsetshire', (it was retitled the 35th (Sussex) Regiment of Foot in 1805) and from which he was put on half-pay in 1803 when the battalion was reduced. Subsequently he obtained a lieutenancy in the 42nd Highlanders, The Black Watch, remaining in that regiment until he attained the rank of captain in 1804, when, on the 23rd of November, he exchanged into the First Regiment of Foot Guards. In the British Army the First Guards was, among the infantry and household regiments of foot, the pinnacle of the military elite and a fitting regiment in which to serve for a young man of Saltoun's social status.

★★★★★★

Such was Napoleon's meteoric rise in power that by 1805 he had crowned himself Emperor of France. The nations of Europe had only just begun to see the consequences of this remarkable man's lust for power which would dominate politics and embroil them in war on the continent for another turbulent decade. In England, the young Saltoun was initially established in the First Battalion, First Guards, but in January 1805 he was transferred to the third battalion, with which he took the first steps of his military career on active service abroad and with which he would during his time with the regiment, henceforth, be associated.

CHAPTER TWO

The Expedition to Sicily, 1805-1807

Since the regiment's service during the expedition to the Helder, no battalions of the First Guards had been sent for service overseas. The government's priority had been the safety of Britain and the security of its coastline from an expected invasion by the French. So, the maintenance of military resources at close quarters to oppose such an incursion, should it arise, entirely influenced the deployment of the regiment during the first years of the nineteenth century. However, in 1805, the third and first battalions, First Guards, were selected to be part of the reinforcements sent to the Mediterranean island of Sicily.

For the purposes of this narrative, the Expedition to Sicily is significant, though it has, together with the peculiar battle of Maida in Calabria on the Italian 'toe peninsula' (July 4th 1806) with which it is associated, taken a subordinate position in the complete account of Britain's campaigns against France at this time. In France, the Revolution and Consulate periods had come to an end and Britain was about to embark on the long wars with the First Empire of the French under the autocratic influence of Napoleon Bonaparte. Furthermore, it was from Sicily that the first of Saltoun's letters, which form the focus of this account, were written and despatched to his family.

Nelson's great final naval victory off Cape Trafalgar in October 1805, had established the Royal Navy's dominance in seapower to the extent that Napoleonic France could never again aspire to compete with the British anywhere on the seas and oceans. Indeed, the Royal Navy ruled the waves in the absence of any serious challenge from any nation for over a century, until the Battle of Jutland during the First World War. At the turn of the 18th and 19th centuries however, the double blow of the Battle of the Nile, (1798) and the subsequent Battle of Trafalgar, meant the Royal Navy effectively controlled the waters of the Mediterranean Sea, which was of vital significance, strategically and logistically, for nations at war across continental Europe.

Perhaps more importantly for immediate events, the Royal Navy's blockade of the English Channel neutralised the French, 'Army of the Ocean Coast', or as it was more optimistically titled, 'The Army of England', waiting to invade Britain from its camps around Boulogne in Northern France. Once again, and not for the last time, the English Channel, though not wide in miles, demonstrated itself to be quite wide enough. As a French invasion of Britain ceased to be a viable proposition for him, Napoleon, never done with his machinations, turned his attentions elsewhere and in directions where his great armies might march unimpeded to accomplish victories crafted by his undeniable military genius.

On the 20th of November, 1805, a combined allied force of Russian and British troops, under the command of General Sir James Craig, landed at Naples to contribute to the defence of this small Italian kingdom positioned usefully on the shores of the middle sea. The Neapolitan, King Ferdinand (who was also King of Sicily), had decided to ally himself, principally with Austria, though in consequence with the alliance of nation states which formed the Third Coalition opposing Napoleon's France. These states included the Holy Roman Empire, Russia, Britain, Sweden and the union Kingdom of Sicily. The diminutive Kingdom of Naples was incapable of making a significant contribution to the greater war effort, so its own future security was in peril in the absence of support by foreign troops.

The Treaty of Amiens between Britain and France, signed in March 1802 as a 'definitive treaty of peace, friendship and understanding' had endured for just thirteen months, only to be

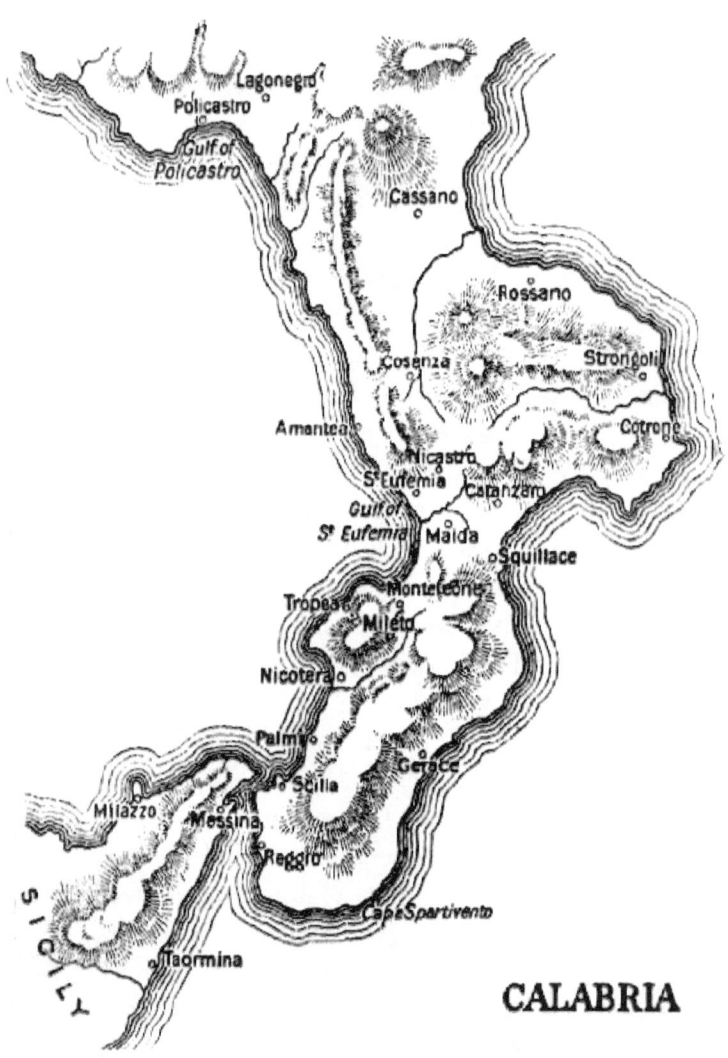

terminated by Britain with a declaration of war, since it could no longer disregard Napoleon's flagrant advances in Switzerland, Germany, the Netherlands and Italy. Whilst the Royal Navy had ensured that the armies of France would turn away from the continental shore of the English Channel, British good fortune meant ill fortune at the hands of Napoleon would befall someone before much time had elapsed and so it was that the road from Boulogne led to Austerlitz. That battle, which inflicted a severe defeat upon the Austrians and Russians on the 2nd of December, 1805, shook continental Europe to the core, for it seemed that Napoleon was possessed of an insuperable will and ability to conquer whomever and wherever he chose to deploy his armies.

Napoleon was perpetually aware of the ideal times to play his advantages and that there was never a better time than immediately following the delivery of a severe military object lesson. Furthermore, never one to be influenced by a deterrent he had calculated had neither the resources or determination to abide by its intentions, he unilaterally declared, on the 27th of December, 1805, that 'the dynasty of Naples had ceased to reign.' The French Army marched to take possession of Naples and Napoleon's unexceptional older brother, Joseph, implausibly re-profiled as Giuseppe I, was nominated to place his accommodating bottom on the Neapolitan throne.

Having seen both the mighty Holy Roman Empire and Russia humbled, the Neapolitan royal family could think of nothing but that they had backed the wrong side and, indeed, that view was at the time understandable for the defeat at Austerlitz effectively put an end to the Third Coalition of allies that had opposed the French. Perhaps, more in hope than any expectation of reprieve, King Ferdinand and his queen, Maria Carolina of Austria (sister of the executed Marie Antoinette), pleaded with Napoleon for forgiveness, but their entreaties predictably availed them nothing. The Neapolitan king's discomfort was exacerbated by the fact that he had previously entered into a treaty with Napoleon concerning southern Italy, upon which he had demonstrably reneged. The emperor was reliably never one to pass by the opportunities presented by an excellent pretext.

In January, 1806 without disputing the matter with the usurpers by force of arms, the Neapolitan court quit mainland Italy and fled (or retreated, dependent on perspective) to Sicily accompanied by the British contingent, while the Russian troops who had formed a portion of the foreign Neapolitan defence force, embarked for Corfu in the Ionian Islands. Joseph Bonaparte entered Naples as sovereign on the 15th of the following month. The forces of the Kingdoms of Naples and Sicily subsequently offered resistance, but were defeated at Campo Tenese in early March.

In the spring of the year 1806, Sir James Craig resigned the command of the British Army on Sicily and the defence of the island was transferred to the command of Sir John Stuart. Given the less than advantageous circumstances which had placed his force on an island in the Mediterranean in close proximity to the enemy, it was obvious to Stuart that the French would not long tolerate his position and that he could, in all likelihood, expect a French invasion of Sicily, for the narrow Strait of Messina, between the toe of the Italian boot and the island, was no English Channel.

Stuart concluded that his best option was a pre-emptive offensive which, if it was successful, would fulfil three objectives. Firstly, he might 'wrong foot' the French before they launched their own attack, thereby destroying some of their preparations whilst giving the enemy sobering notice of what they could expect from an engagement with a British Army. Secondly, a decisive strike would inspire and inflame the spirit of insurrection which yet burned among the people of Calabria, and finally a demonstration of the will to take the fight to the enemy might encourage the besieged coastal garrison of Gaeta, though it remained defiant in a position of undeniable isolation, far from his own comparatively small force and some distance north of Naples itself. The hoped-for relief of the Gaeta garrison by Stuart (which in any event was not his brief) was problematic to the point of unlikely.

Setting sail with an army of British regulars with artillery and supported by Swiss, Corsican and Sicilian troops, Stuart crossed over to Italy, on the 1st of July with about 5,000 men who came ashore, landing without resistance on the Gulf of St. Euphemia (Golfo de Santa Euphemia) approximately 100 miles north of the northern coast of Sicily. The enemy was already close at hand near the town of Maida under the command of General Jean Reynier, with in the region of 5,500-6,000 French troops, which constituted the bulk of the enemy in that part of Calabria, under his command.

Though the details of the Battle of Maida fought on the 4th of July are interesting, they are not pertinent to the principal narrative of this book. Suffice it to note that the engagement was a short and decisive British victory which some commentators have gone so far as to term a 'drubbing', since allied casualties amounted to 327 and those of the enemy were in excess of 2,000. Stuart mopped up pockets of French troops positioned in garrisons south of the battlefield towards his Sicilian base, but these actions could not assist the isolated besieged Neapolitans of the Gaeta garrison, which was forced to capitulate to Masséna on the 18th of July, releasing up to 12,000 more French troops for duty elsewhere.

Stuart established himself for a time at Silla (Scylla) at the mouth of the Gulf of Messina on the Italian mainland, but towards the end of the year withdrew his forces once again to Sicily. He was shortly afterwards transferred to Malta, and was succeeded in Sicily by General Henry Fox, an obese man in clearly poor health who, in fact, died in 1811 aged just 56 years. However, during his time in Sicily his incapacities meant that placed reliance on his able second in command, Sir John Moore, who would shortly make a notable appearance in the conflict which would soon erupt on the Iberian Peninsula.

Some months before this change of generals, the British Government had already determined to substantially reinforce the army in the Mediterranean, and to put into action initiatives intended to prevent Napoleon from taking possession of Sicily.

The Battle of Maida

CHAPTER THREE

The First Guards on Sicily

In 1806, two battalions of the First Guards, the first and the third, under Colonel F. G. Lake and Colonel Moore Disney, which formed the First Brigade of Guards under General Wynyard, were in their barracks at Chatham on the Medway. The area contained valuable naval dockyards (Nelson's flag ship *'Victory'* had been launched there) and extensive defensive works to protect them from potential continental raids or invasions; considered a very real threat as the Dutch raid on the Medway of the later 17th century had demonstrated.

Orders were received by the Guards in early July, at about the time Stuart and his force were crossing over to Italy to fight at Maida, to ensure that there were 120 able bodied men available per company and to prepare for immediate foreign service. A fortnight later, on the 26th of July, the brigade set out upon its 40-mile march to the port at Ramsgate, whereupon arrival both the first battalion and the third battalion embarked on board their transport ships.

Also, on board this fleet anchored in the Downs was a brigade of the infantry of the line. Bad weather delayed sailing on two occasions until the ships at last set sail in mid-August, coasting down the English Channel to anchor in Plymouth Sound, where another brigade of line infantry supported by cavalry boarded. All seemed finally ready to leave for the southward voyage, when naval priorities necessitated an immediate disembarkation of the army and in the first days of September, after a month of delays, the Guards marched to Bickleigh Down, some 5 or 6 miles from Plymouth, where they went into camp. In the meantime, six flank companies of the two Guards battalions had been formed into a separate unit. Among the officers of the Third Battalion, First Guards embarking on this expedition was Lieutenant-Captain, Lord Saltoun, then in his twenty first year.

In the prestigious Guards, officers held two ranks—a regimental one which was lower than their army rank, since the former was required to correspond with the command structure of a regimental unit. This peculiar arrangement meant that, at this time, the regimental majors and the senior captains were all major-generals in the army, whilst two others were brigadier-generals and all these officers, by virtue of high rank, returned to staff duties.

Accordingly, the Guards reinforcements bound for Sicily were constituted as follows: The flank battalion of 725 men was commanded by Clinton. The first battalion of 919 men was commanded by Lake. And the third battalion of 915 men was under Moore Disney. The total strength of the brigade was 2,559 men under the command of Wynyard.

The brigade embarked once again in mid-September, under the protection of the Royal Navy's 100-gun war ship, *Royal George*. The fleet then set sail, though it was not until late October, in consequence of perpetual bad weather, that it anchored in the Bay of Tangiers, arriving in Tetuan Bay on the first day of November.

Among the transports carrying part of the light infantry battalion of the First Guards, was a collier brig, *Christopher*, which lost her foremast during a gale in the Bay of Biscay and becoming separated from the convoy, then lost her way. The ship's captain sailed for three weeks by his own reckoning, but had no idea where he was. One evening as night drew in, Sergeant-Major Colquhoun noticed the sea had much changed colour, which he knew was an indication that the vessel was close to land. Colquhoun passed on his observations to his commanding officer who in turn spoke to the vessel's captain.

The *Royal George*, (right) at Chatham

The sailor laughed, declaring they were more than 100 miles from any coast. However, on gauging his depth he discovered, to his surprise, no more than ten fathoms under the keel and, as the light improved the following morning, nearby land appeared. The transport was anchored, and the Guards, as a precaution, were served with ammunition. Before long, boats were sighted setting out from the shore and their occupants brought news that they were off the mouth of the Spanish river, Guadalquivir, north of Cadiz, close under the guns of the batteries of Rota. *Christopher* was towed further out to sea during the night and put in charge of a brig-of-war, which guided them safely to Gibraltar. The progress of the main fleet, though unimpeded by misadventures, had been painfully slow and it was not until December that the Guards finally entered the Bay of Messina, nearly three months after they had left England.

In later life, Saltoun wrote to his friend 'Charley' Ellis, who joined the First Guards in 1811 as an ensign and became, in due course, Saltoun's subaltern. He was still by Saltoun's side four years later at Waterloo and was wounded during the action at Hougoumont.

> We reached Sicily about the middle of December 1806, having coasted along the whole island, from the little island of Marstino to the town of Messina at the head of the strait of that name, having sailed along a most beautiful mountainous country, in many places, particularly near Messina, studded with villas, having Etna in view the whole time; and one of the finest sights was to see the sun strike the top of Etna on rising, which it did about five minutes before you saw it, and lit the mountains down by degrees till you were aware that the sun was up, also the snow on the top, when first struck by the sun, looking like an immense ball of fire.

Instead of landing immediately, the transports carrying the brigade were ordered to Catania, some miles to the south on the island's eastern coast and to disembark their men there. The First Guards, including the flank companies, disembarked on the 6th of December at the port of Catania, which sits at the foot

of the volcano of Mount Etna. Once ashore six companies of the third battalion, under Colonel Disney, were temporarily sent 40 miles farther down the coast to the ancient city of Syracuse. Troops moved occasionally to different locations, but essentially the battalions of the First Guards were distributed in the principal posts along the east coast of Sicily, extending from Messina to Syracuse, for about eighty or ninety miles.

Major-General Wynyard placed his headquarters at Catania which enabled him to readily command the district. General Fox, as Commander-in-Chief, resided at Messina with Captain John Colborne as his military secretary. Colborne, a soldier of whom it was said, 'had a singular talent for war', was destined to become a notable figure in the Peninsular War and upon the field of Waterloo where, in command of the 52nd as part of Adams' Brigade, he would deliver the *coup de grace* to the flanks of advancing columns of Napoleon's Imperial Guard at the close of the battle

Despite their role as protectors of the island and its royal family, the British troops were viewed by the population at large as unwelcome interlopers and were generally unpopular. At the beginning of the year 1807, the British forces on the island, including Wynyard's brigade of Guards, amounted to 18,000 men, and there were also about 14,000 Neapolitan troops available for deployment in the event of an attack.

In northern Europe, Napoleon's campaigns brought about political consequences which were the British Government's principal concerns. Defeats of the previous year had overturned the Prussian monarchy and the disheartened Russians had retired to the Niemen, but the *Tsar* had refused to ratify a peace and rumours spoke of some Russian successes in Poland. Ready to grasp at any straw which might make the restoration of the Neapolitan throne more probable, the exiled queen lobbied for an attack upon Naples to be undertaken with the support of the British Army at hand. General Fox, however, had no confidence in the prospects of this initiative and though resolved to keep a firm hold on Sicily, would not risk the army operating farther afield.

In the spring of 1807, the British Government removed the option of an expedition onto the Italian mainland by seconding 5,000 men of the regiments of the line stationed in Sicily for an ill-fated expedition to Alexandria, while at the same time it sent a fleet to the Dardanelles in an attempt to dissuade the Turks from going to war against Russia at Napoleon's behest. Desperation drove the Neapolitan queen, despite the hopelessness of the enterprise, to launch an unsupported invasion of Calabria, but her troops were inevitably defeated by the French in late May. The much-depleted ranks of the expedition to Alexandria returned to Sicily in October.

Although there was no actual fighting for the Guards stationed on Sicily, the fact the enemy lay perilously close across the narrow Strait of Messina, meant a strict watch had to be kept upon French movements to be in readiness to meet any hostile attempt to cross over to the island.

Lord Saltoun was involved in an incident at this time, the details of which were recorded in a memorandum, and which, to use his own words, showed 'how little attention your English soldier pays to anything, unless long service and severe experience has driven something like observation into him.' This incident is interesting in its own right and though Saltoun describes his own part in these events in a matter of fact manner, his narrative, all be it unintentionally, gives the reader an insight into this very young officer's physical strength and determination, especially bearing in mind the fates of others who were involved.

> We had been some months at Contessa, when the French, who since the Battle of Maida had remained in upper Calabria, suddenly marched a large force down to the straits of Messina, commenced a sort of siege of the Castle of Scilla, where we had a garrison, and taking possession of Regio, a town on the coast, nearly opposite our cantonments, began collecting boats and making preparations to invade Sicily. A party of an officer and 30 men was established at a place called Milia, about six miles from our cantonments, in order to give the alarm should any landing take place about there; and we communicated by small posts of a corporal and three men at certain distances all along

20TH LIGHT DRAGOONS, SICILY, 1806-7

the line, to a particular point from which it was about 3 miles to Milia, which post was visited every night by the captain on duty, and a patrol of a corporal and file of dragoons went from Messina to Milia twice during the night.

It had rained most of the evening, and I had started a little later than usual to go my rounds, and I had met the first patrol on its return from Milia, a little before I came to the great *fiumara* or watercourse, which ran from the mountains into the strait; in summer this was in general dry, or at most very small, but in heavy rains often impassable, and on the Milia side of this *fiumara* was situated our extreme corporal's picquet on the right, our left one communicating with the Citadel of Messina.

When I crossed the *fiumara* it was running a strong stream, but nothing dangerous. I proceeded on to Milia and visited the post there, stayed a short time, and smoked a cigar with the officer. According to the time of the patrol, I ought to have met it between the *fiumara* and Milia, but I did not, and when I came to the *fiumara* I at once saw that it was utterly impassable; it was raging with a force that would have carried away an elephant, and in the current of the burn, from the stones it covered at the sides, must have been more than ten feet deep. I made no doubt but that the patrol finding it in this state had returned.

This ford was about 200 yards above the junction of the *fiumara* with the sea, which is so deep, close to land all along that part of the straits of Messina, that a man-of-war could tack with its bowsprit over the land.

As I had no inclination to stay there in the rain I coasted the torrent down to its junction with the sea, and being an excellent swimmer myself, as well as in the constant habit at that time of swimming my horse, I at once put him into the deep water, and without any difficulty reached the other side, and proceeded on my rounds. I found that the patrol had visited all the posts on its way out as usual, and on reaching the cavalry post at Messina, as I was obliged to mention in my report the circumstance of my not having met the patrol, I inquired of the officer about it, and found that it had not returned.

I mentioned my fears for it to the officer, but as it was possible that they had taken some shelter to wait till the *fiumara* should run off, a sergeant was sent to look for them and bring them back, but they were never heard of afterwards, and as desertion was impracticable, at least with their horses, and moreover a crime not at all prevailing in the English part of the army at that time, there can be no doubt but they were carried away in trying to ford the *fiumara*.

During their comparatively uneventful stay in Sicily, the officers who could procure leave, assembled shooting parties and a pack of hounds also enabled them to engage in their favourite pastime. Exploring expeditions took place all over the island, visiting the ancient temples, Girgente, and others, describing them in 'a true antiquarian spirit'. The young Saltoun was no exception to the rule and in his letters large sections are dedicated to descriptions of the ancient ruins of Sicily which, since they bear little on the focus of this account, have been excised from this edition.

Saltoun's letter to his mother, Margery, (sometimes spelled Marjory), Fraser, Lady Saltoun, written during this period and a month before his 22nd birthday illustrates that the Sicily Expedition was unlikely to offer the opportunity of active soldiering and we have the impression that he was fairly much a young man at liberty for leisure. Nevertheless, this letter is included at this point, notwithstanding it reads more like a traveller's excursion report than anything other because, devoid of action though it is, it describes from a personal perspective the experience of serving in Sicily for the officers and men of the First Guards in 1807.

>18th March 1807.
>Catania, Sicily,

Dear Mother,
I wrote you by the last pacquet from Messina, informing you that I was fortunate enough to receive your letters at Palermo, where I was on a tour round the island.

I say fortunate, as most likely I should not have received them for some time, if at all, as Palermo is three days' journey from this place by the nearest road, and the country post so badly regulated that one-half of the letters are lost, and we have no correspondence by means of dragoons with that side of the island, which is entirely under the government of the King; so if you wish me to get any letter punctually, do not send it that way, but if it does not signify how soon I receive it, they may as well go there as anywhere else, as Mr. Drummond will keep them till he has some safe conveyance for them either to this place, or indeed to this side of the island, as there is a regular military post twice a week from Malazzo (*Milazzo*) to Cape Passero.

I have obeyed your instructions in every particular, and sent the letters enclosed in two separate packets, as it was impossible to get them conveyed in one to Messina, where the mail for England is made up. The circular letters I have signed on the inside, but not on the back, as I do not know their separate destinies. The letters to the Dukes of York and Cumberland I have put in a cover and directed; those to the other peers I have directed on the back, and you can put them in covers and send them. They are all open, in order that they may be sealed with my arms. *(Refers to his candidature for election as a Representative Peer.)* Our tour to Palermo was delightful. We had the finest weather possible; the country very beautiful; but as to the accommodation on the road you can have no idea of anything so bad. We were obliged to carry our beds with us, and, as it was *starvation* time, our provisions also; and the inns were so bad that we slept more than once in *lettigas*, (horse-litters for journeys) rather than go into them, notwithstanding which I got my bed so full of fleas and bugs that I was obliged to boil the mattress as the only way of getting them out of it.

Our first day's journey was to Calata Girone, 43 miles. Our way led over the plain of Catania, through Palagonia, a pretty little village. We reached Calata Girone at six at night. It is situated on an immense hill, and is the largest inland town in Sicily, and as dirty. The only thing worth seeing is the view from the top of the great church; and at the Franciscan convent, about half a mile from the town, on the road to Terra Nova, there is a most beautiful figure of a Madonna and child in marble, which is the best bit of sculpture I have yet seen in the island. They do not know who made it, but tell you some cock-and-bull story of the Virgin having made it a present to St. Francis when he was doing Peñance in a wood near the convent.

We left Calata Girone at nine, and after seeing the Madonna, proceeded on to Terra Nova through a most beautiful country, and across the forest of Calata Girone, the second in size in Sicily, I got a shot at a partridge, the only one I had seen in the island, and killed him. He was a very fine bird of the red leg kind, but not half so good eating as our sort of partridge.

We got to Terra Nova at three, probably so called from the flat on which it stands having been gained from the sea, as it has very much that appearance. We found the way very hot, and so went into the sea, which so astonished the natives, that they turned out one and all—men, women, and children—to see us bathe, and could not conceive how we could bathe in the winter, and confessed to us that when it was very cold they did not even wash themselves.

Terra Nova has a small port, at which there is some importation of corn, but very trifling, as the exportation laws of this country are, as far as regards corn, so very nefarious that the farmer cannot afford to send the corn out of the island except at the free ports, for which liberty they pay some tax to the king.

From Terra Nova we went the next day to Alicata, a well-built town and a free port. There is a castle here from which you have a fine sea view—they call it a garrison—which consists of fifty old men who can hardly stand, without arms or ammunition.

The next day we reached Girgenti; on our road there we breakfasted at Palma, a place which Swinbourne mentions as being notorious for rascals, so much so, says he, that not a jail in the country is without more than one Palmanese in it for murder or for theft. The present generation are not far behind them in that science, as they contrived to steal a couple of bottles of wine from us, and our meat-basket; however, we found them out before they could get away, and on producing our pistols they produced the meat.

The approach from Palma to Girgenti is beautiful, through the most fertile country in Sicily, and close by the ruins of the ancient temples. Girgenti, old Agrigentum, is, generally speaking, the best place worth seeing in the world for antiquarians, as the remains of the Greek antiquities are more perfect there than at any other place. However, the temple of all others that one would wish to have seen is that one of Jupiter Olympius, the columns of which were of a most gigantic size, and the fluting of them large enough to contain a man. This temple, I am sorry to say, is no longer in existence; but from what remains, the enormous size of the pillars is clearly to be perceived. Two capitals, which are the only remains of them, are broken in four pieces; and in the small part of the pillar still attached to one of them, Montgomery, who is rather a thin man, could get into the flute with all ease.

In the great church at Girgenti there is a very fine picture of the Virgin and Child by Guido Reni, and also a beautiful antique, a representation of the story of Hippolytus and Phaedra; there is also another singular circumstance, which is, that a person getting up above the altar, can hear anything said at the other end of the church even in a whisper. This is said to have been discovered in the following manner:—A carpenter was up there one day mending the figure of a dragon, and saw his wife come in to confess. He was surprised at so plainly hearing the priest speak to her, and therefore listened and heard the whole of her confession. On returning home he gave her wholesome correction for what he had overheard, and made a regular practice of mending the dragon whenever any rich person went to confess, by which means he got together a good deal of money. We left Girgenti, and the third day after reached Palermo. The packet has arrived, but I have received neither letters nor papers. I conclude they are to come by Palermo. We are all in perfect health, and some of the men talk of going home to be married, or, in other words, to go out;—the more the better! With best love to all at home, I am, dear mother, your dutiful son,

Saltoun.

Catania, 2nd April, 1807

In the course of the summer of 1807 the possibility of an invasion of Naples by a combined British and Neapolitan force from Sicily re-emerged as a suggestion from the British Government, though the practicability of this proposal was left to General Fox's judgement. However, irrespective of the general's opinion, the idea was so poorly greeted among the population that the initiative was soon abandoned. It is probable that the Sicilians had little reason to have faith in the success of such an enterprise, based on the outcomes of previous military engagements, believing that 'awakening the sleeping dog' would only bring the weight of the enemy down on the island. Ill feeling ran high and civil disturbances were expected which, were they to escalate, would require already unpopular foreign troops to suppress them, which would have certainly exacerbated antipathy towards the British presence, notwithstanding the support they were providing to the Sicilian Government.

General Fox resigned his post in Sicily in July, 1807, and returned to England whereupon the command devolved upon Sir John Moore. News arrived in August of another French victory in the wider theatre of the war; the defeat of the Russians at Friedland. More than ever, there seemed no impediment to discourage a French Army from marching anywhere it wished in Europe. Moore was left with no illusions as to the tenuous position of his command isolated in Sicily and so began to make preparations for what he believed would be an inevitable and imminent attack from the French on the island. To make matters worse, in the hot weather sickness swept among the troops. Many men were soon in hospital, and still more of them were pronounced unfit for duty. Colonel Salisbury of the First Guards died in the middle of September and was buried in the church of San Filippo.

The First Guards had not much longer to serve on Sicily and the fortunes of the Kingdom of Naples were not destined to soon revive. After Joseph Bonaparte had departed the throne (undergoing another tragicomic change of national identity to become King Jose I of Spain), he was replaced by the flamboyant commander of Napoleon's cavalry, Joachim Murat who had married one of the emperor's sisters, Caroline. His reign of the Kingdom of Naples was destined to end fatally before a firing squad comprised of his less than enamoured 'subjects'. The dispossessed Neapolitan royal family would only regain a measure of its former position after the end of the Napoleonic era in 1815, though the queen by this time had already died in Austria.

Chapter Four

The Invasion of Portugal, 1807

Since Spain remained a monarchy, the French Revolution was justifiably seen, as it was by all the monarchies of Europe, as a threat of cataclysmic proportions. However, for Spain the situation was particularly acute for the spirit of insurrection was an infection which would take little encouragement to spread across the Pyrenees to pollute an impoverished Iberia. The Spanish monarch had agreed, therefore, to join the First Coalition in an attempt to put an end to the French Republic and restore a Bourbon to the throne of France. Despite encouraging beginnings on land and sea, the French forces proved irresistible and the Peace of Basel in 1795 forced a weakened Spain to quit the coalition. Spanish national status was about enter decades of sharp decline.

The following year brought forth an extraordinary *volte-face* when a Franco-Spanish alliance was formed and Spain found itself at war with Britain as an ally of the new republic. This war, which concluded in 1802, also did not go well for Spain, principally because the Royal Navy succeeded in establishing an economically damaging blockade, though the numerical superiority of the Spanish Mediterranean fleet forced the British from the islands of Corsica and Elba. The Treaty of Amiens provided a short lull in hostilities, but when the British reacted to French provocations, the Royal Navy came back into action and in 1804 attacked and captured most of a treasure fleet of Spanish frigates.

As has been explained, this was the time of Napoleon's proposed invasion of Britain, the success of which required a period of naval superiority and the participation of the Spanish navy was an essential element in the acquiring of an advantage at sea. Nelson, by defeating the Franco-Spanish fleet at Trafalgar, not only put an end to that scheme forever, but arguably provoked the catalyst by which Napoleon ceased to see Spain as a useful, if temporary, ally. The emperor, with his insatiable desire for conquest, determined to subjugate the whole Iberian Peninsula and he built his gambit, as he had done so often, upon the foundations of a grand deceit.

Following the Battle of Friedland, Napoleon had signed an armistice with the Emperor of Russia, which resulted in the signing of the Treaty of Tilsit (7th of July, 1807). This treaty required Russia, among others, to adhere to the emperor's ruling of the 'Continental System,' which was intended to ruin the commercial capabilities of Great Britain by excluding her ships from all the ports of Europe. The Portuguese at first acceded to the emperor's demands, but when the British responded by sending a fleet to blockade the Tagus, reversed that policy, refusing after motivated reconsideration, to take exclusive measures against their ally.

Napoleon could not allow such a defiance to go unpunished and proposed a treaty, couched in terms which promised many attractive material gains for Spain, by which it was agreed that the combined armies of the two nations should over-run and divide Portugal between them. A substantial French Army was assembled at Bayonne, and, in 1807, Napoleon decreed, in his typical imperious fashion, that 'the reigning House of Braganza had ceased to exist in Portugal'. General Junot at the head of 'The First Corps of Observation of the Gironde' comprising some 25,000 men, was then directed to march towards Lisbon; a route, that hardly requires emphasis, which which would necessitate large numbers of French troops on Spanish soil initially, and given success, indefinitely.

Orders arrived in Sicily early in October, 1807, directing Sir

John Moore to immediately embark 7,600 men of his army to Gibraltar, where he would receive further directions as to their ultimate destination. Among their number was the Brigade of First Guards, together with other regiments of the line. Moore boarded the *Queen*, a 98-gun three-tiered ship of the line, and the fleet sailed for Gibraltar at the end of the month, leaving Sir John Sherbrook with 6,000 men to protect Sicily. The unpredictability of sail once again influenced the journey, so the fleet did not arrive at its destination until the first day of December. Moore here discovered the disheartening news that the frigate, *Volage* had carried out a dispatch for him, whilst he had been *en route,* ordering him not to leave Sicily. Colonel Disney's appointment as brigadier-general was also confirmed, with orders that he should return to Sicily.

Sir John Moore now learned the details of his original orders which were that he should proceed to Lisbon, where he was to have been joined by 8,000 men under the experienced General Brent Spencer, to support the king and the Prince Regent of Portugal. By this point, however, the time for intercession was past, for the French had almost arrived in Lisbon and the Portuguese royal family, believing it impossible to resist them, had already quit the capital with the rest of their supporters, and had set sail for South America. General Junot's force, in consequence, marched into Lisbon without opposition. For Napoleon there was nothing discouraging about the outcome of his stratagems which appeared, at the time, to be not only to be not only well founded as to their immediate outcomes, but also particularly promising for further easily achieved objectives in the Iberian Peninsula.

Moore, nevertheless, considered it was worthwhile to personally go to Lisbon, since a Royal Navy presence under Sir Sydney Smith lay off-shore, to determine whether a landing would be of any advantage, but discovered upon his arrival there that any intervention by him would be futile. He therefore returned to Gibraltar, and leaving two line regiments on the rock, set sail again for England in mid-December with the Guards and remainder of his troops.

In a letter to a fellow officer, Saltoun wrote a slightly different perspective of the confused state of affairs at this time.

> We left Sicily in the autumn of 1807, forming part of a force of 10,000 men, with Sir John Moore. Our first instructions were to take Ceuta, (on the North African coast.) but they thought it too strong. We were then (in the event of the King of Portugal submitting to the French) to have gone to the Brazils, and taken that; but as the King of Portugal abandoned his kingdom, and went to the Brazils himself, Sir John Moore brought us to England.

The first and third battalions, First Guards landed at Portsmouth and marched to their barracks, arriving in the first days of 1808. In consequence of his promotion to lieutenant-general, in May, 1808, General Wynyard, the second major of the regiment, who had commanded the First Brigade for five years departed. Major-General Warde, the senior captain and lieutenant-colonel, succeeded him and Major-General Henry Campbell was appointed to command the Second Brigade of Guards until the return of Major-General Moore Disney from Sicily.

Saltoun took the opportunity offered by this hiatus to visit his family. His widowed mother was living at this time in Dartmouth House, Blackheath, south of the River Thames in order to be near her father. In fact, Saltoun's earlier years had been spent in England, and it is doubtful whether he had ever, since his succession to the title, visited his paternal estates. So, in the autumn he travelled northward to Philorth and Fraserburgh and thereafter took a tour of Scotland to visit relatives and friends.

CHAPTER FIVE

The Peninsular Campaign of 1808

In late November of 1807, the French 'Second Corps of Observation of the Gironde' under Dupont and some 30,000 men strong began to filter into northern Spain ostensibly *en route* for Portugal, whilst making little discernible progress in that direction. Several more 'corps of observation' followed, crossing the Franco-Spanish border and spreading out over the country, securing vital positions as they went. By the time 'The Army of Observation of the Eastern Pyrenees', under Duheseme had moved into Catalonia on the Mediterranean coast in the middle of February it was obvious to all that these armies had not come to 'observe' and were definitely not going to Portugal.

A rift in the Spanish royal family between Charles IV and his son, Ferdinand, exacerbated by the politicking of First Secretary, Manuel Godoy brought matters to a head. Napoleon removed the troublesome and weak Spanish royal family having lured them into France. Joseph Bonaparte's obliging posterior once again became useful and his brother placed it on the throne of Spain. Madrid was quickly taken, but the populace rose up in aggrieved indignation and slaughtered numbers of their occupiers which provoked a brutal reprisal by the French. Though Napoleon did not understand it at the time, for he was ignorant of the Spanish character, this was the first indication that he had 'grasped the tiger by the tail'.

The Spanish people maintained a jaundiced view of their aristocracy and had little faith in their politicians or military com-

BLACKHEATH, WITH A VIEW TOWARDS LONDON, EARLY 19TH CENTURY

PHILORTH HOUSE, EARLY 19TH CENTURY

manders. Indeed, Spanish military resources were very low and the poorly organised Spanish troops were incapable of offering more than feeble resistance to the veterans of France. However, they were certain of their identity as Spaniards and that the country they knew to be their own was invaded by a foreign army which could never be tolerated or allowed to abide. This will to endure in spite of any defeats or consequences is in itself a most powerful opponent and one impossible to master.

The flame of patriotism and resistance, within armies, guerillas and peasants alike, was kindled throughout the land and grew into a conflagration of passion which, despite many reverses, refused to be extinguished. Genuine hatred escalated the number and degree of atrocities on both sides until their horrors became emblematic of the entire conflict. Napoleon had inadvertently created the 'Spanish Ulcer', a 'war to the knife' that would fatally drain his resources more than any of his wars.

Nevertheless, by the close of May 1808, the French emperor had marched in excess of 100,000 troops into Spain. The Spanish Supreme Junta, in June 1808, realising the nation's peril, appealed to Britain for succour. The British Government, applying the principle of, 'my enemy's enemy is my friend', put aside past antipathies, ratified a peace with Spain in London on the 6th of July and the two nations became allies. But that this alliance would prove to be as straightforward in practice as it was in its creation.

The French and Spanish continued to fight localised campaigns and battles, but the campaign that primarily concerns this narrative was that undertaken by Junot who, with a force of 28,000 men in Portugal, was holding down the centre of the country and sending out flying columns in the month of June to suppress the uprisings that had flared up all about him.

It is worth noting that Spain soon gave Napoleon further notice that it was not prepared to be submissive, for at the Battle of Baylen fought on July 19th, 1808, its army beat a French Army, which threw Joseph into a panic.

The days of the stalwart Spanish *tercios* were long past, so had the emperor been asked to nominate a candidate who would deliver the first open-field defeat upon his armies in any of his conflicts, he would probably not have chosen a Spanish Army for the laurels. As it transpired, this victory came about less as a result of Spanish military acumen than by the incompetence of the French commander, General Dupont. The details of that battle are less germane to this narrative than that the news of it swept through a cowed Europe and rekindled hope in the hearts of nations which previously could see no future that did not include a virtually omnipotent Napoleon. That inspiration contributed, in due course and among other factors, to persuade the emperor to turn away from a retreating British Army in Spain when it was almost within his grasp.

On the 12th of July, an army (which included no Guards battalions) of about 10,000 men, under the command of Sir Arthur Wellesley, set sail from England, landing on the Portuguese coast at Mondego Bay in the first days of August. Wellesley already had something of a reputation as a '*Sepoy* General', following his victories in India. Indeed, it was his own understanding that he would command the expedition to Portugal, but his family had enemies in the government and so, unknown to him since he had already embarked, he would be at the point they arrived in the field, subordinate to two senior officers. These were Sir Hew Dalrymple, Governor of Gibraltar and Sir Harry Burrard who formerly commanded the First Brigade of Guards, and was still the lieutenant-colonel of the First Guards.

Readers will recall Burrard during the Expedition to the Helder. Though he had done well in defence of Pettin, neither he or Dalrymple were noted as commanders of larger forces or had particularly notable battlefield accomplishments to their credit, particularly compared to Wellesley. However, though few fully appreciated it at this time, Sir Arthur Wellesley's abilities as a commander would set a bar impossibly high for any British general of his day (and few, if any, generals of other nations), for he would become, in due course, the Duke of Wellington and Napoleon's nemesis.

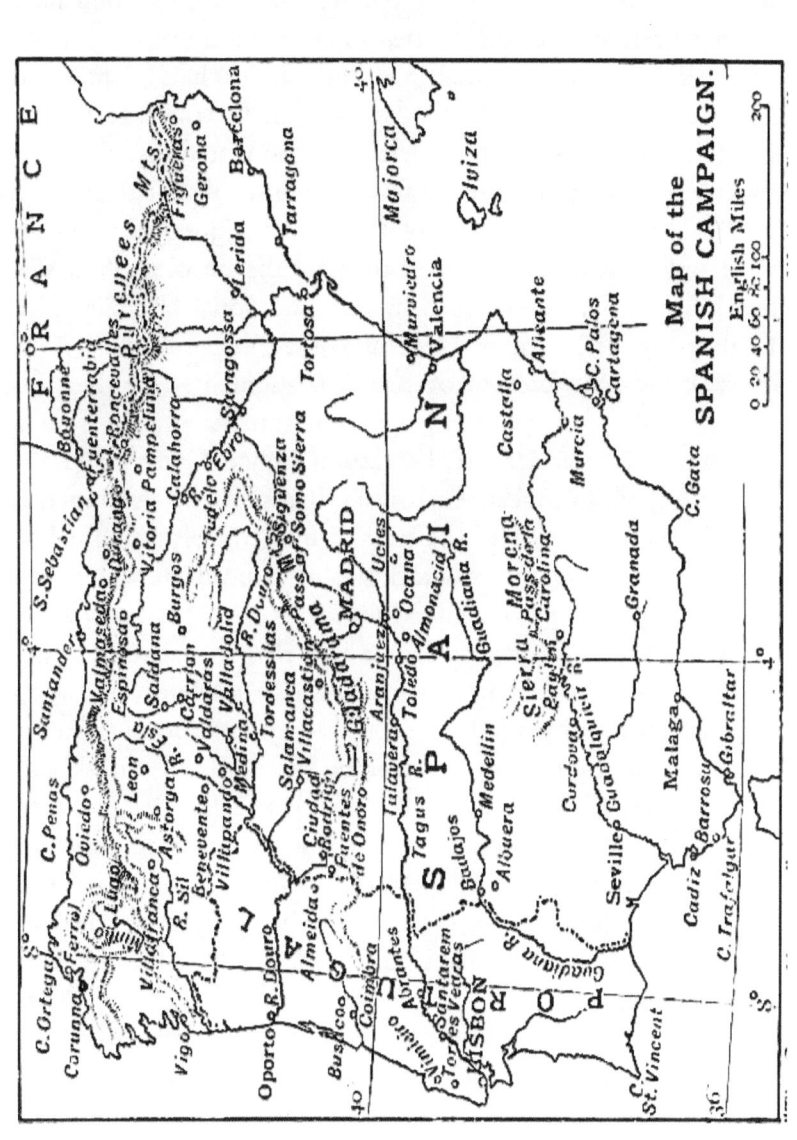

The plan of the British Government was first to drive the French out of Portugal, and then advance into Spain to co-operate with Spanish armies. On the 17th of August, Wellesley, whose command was now in the region of 13,000 men having been reinforced from home, attacked and drove the French force, under Laborde, which had been despatched by Junot to delay him, from a strong defensive position at Roliça. This was a small but promising beginning, for from lamentations of despair, the cry of victory was for the first time raised in Portugal.

Upon hearing the news of this reverse, Junot came north from Lisbon with 13,000 men to meet the invasion. Wellesley had by now been reinforced by two additional brigades from England, under Brigadier-Generals Anstruther and Ackland, increasing his own force to over 16,000 augmented by the support of 2,500 men from Portuguese regiments and insurgents, including 41 members of the Lisbon Police Cavalry. On the 21st of August, Junot came across the British Army encamped at Vimeiro with its back to the sea and immediately launched an aggressive and impetuous attack against a position which was well placed on a line of rolling hills.

Simply put, this battle would be an early lesson, taught by the master, of the maintenance of a well-situated defensive position with the ideal troops for the purpose and Junot's poorly coordinated assault columns were promptly thrown back with severe losses inflicted by the volleys of the British line. Years hence, Wellington would comment of Waterloo, 'They came on in the same old way and we saw them off in the same old way'. It is tempting to imagine he was tacitly praising the prowess of British soldiers, though justifiably, he was as likely to be speaking quite literally.

At the moment, as Wellesley was about to unleash his reserves to follow up his advantage, matters in Portugal turned sour. Sir Harry Burrard arrived upon the field and stopped the pursuit, apparently for the purpose of waiting for the large reinforcements expected with Sir John Moore who had also been called to the theatre and would, therefore, upon his arrival also be superior to Wellesley. The following day, Sir Hew Dalrymple arrived from Gibraltar and as senior officer assumed overall command of the army. Any impetus that had been created in this campaign now ground to a halt.

Wellesley was, predictably, for marching on Lisbon, inflicting a trouncing and exacting an unconditional surrender from the enemy. Junot, quickly acknowledging that he was about to be beaten, sued for an armistice and proposed a treaty; the infamous Convention of Cintra, which stipulated that the French army of 25,000 men would evacuate Portugal to be transported unmolested by the British back to France together with all the spoils they had plundered during their stay in the country as invaders. Sir Hew Dalrymple agreed to this ostensibly outrageous proposal; a decision which elicited gasps of astonishment and indignation in the British Government and throughout the home country.

Dalrymple's pragmatic arrangement meant, emotive sentiments aside, Portugal had been won cheaply and quickly (so far as the British were concerned) given that time was of the essence and that the policy objective was to liberate Spain. However, seen in the best light, his was a 'statesman's victory' providing meagre satisfaction in the wake of the unambiguous soldier's victory of Vimeiro. Moore, by contrast, had no time for Dalrymple's resolution, abilities or intelligence, so it is possible that this outcome came about more by accident than design. Certainly, many people believed the French had got off unnecessarily lightly and there were numerous complaints from serving officers and from the Portuguese provisional government which would have preferred to see a good deal more French blood spread on the ground.

Dalrymple, Burrard and Wellesley were recalled to England and sent before a court of enquiry which concluded that none of them were to blame for any wrong doing, 'acting to the best of their judgement and with the proper zeal' and so all three of them had the satisfaction of being exonerated. For Dalrymple and Burrard this vindication of their actions meant, in practice, that they were never again sent on active service, whereas Wellesley was returned to Portugal the following Spring as commander-in-chief. In the meantime, the army in Portugal came under the command of Sir John Moore.

CHAPTER SIX

The Brigade of Guards in Spain, 1808

Early in August, as Sir John Moore's command advanced from Lisbon towards central Spain, the British Government decided to send out a further reinforcement of 10,000 men, including a Brigade of Guards, to operate in the north of Spain within a British Army of in the region of 30,000 infantry and 5,000 cavalry. This army would include the first and third battalions (in which Lord Saltoun served with the light company) of the First Guards, commanded respectively by Lieutenant-Colonels Cocks and Wheatley, which formed the First Brigade under Major-General Warde.

These battalions had been quartered at Deal, on the English coast between the North Sea and the English Channel since their return from Sicily and they now marched some twelve miles to Ramsgate and embarked on the 8th of September. The first battalion amounted to 1,511 men of all ranks and the third battalion stood at 1,243 men. Following embarkation, they sailed for the general rendezvous at Falmouth, dropping anchor on the 22nd of September.

The assembled troops, numbering 13,000, under the command of Sir David Baird, were now organised into four brigades. These were the first and third battalions, First Guards under Warde, the 1st, 26th, 27th, and 31st regiments of Foot under Manningham, the 51st, 59th, 60th, 76th and 81st regiments under Mackenzie and Craufurd's 14th, 23rd, 43rd regiments and the second battalion of the Rifles—the 95th. The fleet sailed on the 8th of October, anchoring off Corunna, at the northwestern tip of Spain on the 13th of the same month.

Early in October the main body of the army under Sir John Moore had advanced from Lisbon in Portugal and, as if in a portent of things to come, its affairs had gone awry almost immediately. Moore had acted upon what proved to be very bad advice concerning the difficulty of the terrain the army would traverse. This led him to split his force, sending the cavalry and artillery on an unnecessarily circuitous route, on the understanding that the direct way would be problematic for them. Meanwhile, he marched his 16,000 infantry over the mountains, with no apparent difficulty, *via* the fortified town of Almeida on the border with Spain, to Ciudad Rodrigo, where he made his headquarters for a short period, before reaching Salamanca in mid-November. This inauspicious start meant his full force did not come together until early December. Simply put, Moore was in unfamiliar territory, both literally and figuratively, and, it might be fairly suggested that he remained so until his last day.

Moore's first objective had been to join forces with and so offer assistance and cooperation to Spanish armies, but he found them to be disorganised and depleted, for they had paid dearly whenever they engaged the enemy in battle. In the course of the autumn the Spanish Army of the north, under Blake, had been defeated at Espinosa. Another large force had been dispersed by Soult near Burgos and the Spanish generals, Palafox and Castanos, were routed at Tudela.

By early December, Napoleon was in the capital, Madrid having comprehensively thrashed Spanish armies on his way in several battles, for he had realised that to bring about the desired outcome in Spain he could not depend on the talents of his brother, Joseph and that his own intercession was required. To ensure his objectives might be achieved in a timely fashion the emperor had, by this time, little fewer than 300,000 men at his disposal within Spanish borders.

Moore was not long in understanding that any expectation of concerted military operations with the Spaniards was hopeless for several reasons, including a seemingly natural inclination to be uncooperative with their British ally, their perpetual organisational disarray and the fact that their armies were beaten and in retreat. Furthermore, since the French in Spain were now in overwhelming numbers, the position of his own unsupported small army was becoming increasingly more tenuous.

In the meantime, the regional *Junta* of Corunna had astonishingly refused to allow Sir David Baird's division, which had arrived there (as indicated) on the 13th of October (and included the Guards), to land to aid the war effort without the approval of the Central Junta, and that authority did not arrive for several days. Saltoun wrote a letter to his mother at this time which not only reflects the delay and confusion in which British forces in the peninsula found themselves, but also revealed the lack of information, exacerbated by the rumour mill, which is the perennial lot of the regimental soldier. However, much of what appears in the second paragraph of this letter, given it was written some time before the fact, demonstrated his judgement was remarkably astute.

> Corunna, Spain
> 26th October 1808
>
> Dear Mother,
> We have been so bothered with orders, counter orders, and reports, that till this morning nothing certain has been known. The Rifle Corps and the Forty-Third Light Infantry have disembarked this morning, and our brigade begins tomorrow.
> We have a march of at least 600 miles before we can reach the enemy, and by all accounts are not likely to be very well off on the way, as the only thing the *Junta* can provide for us is black bread and sour wine, which John *(Bull—presumably, meaning the rank and file,—JHL)* will not relish much; and on our arrival we may expect to be in snow during the greatest part of the time, as our position will be on the left of the Spanish Army, and on the left bank of the Ebro between Bilboa and Pampeluna which is the strongest post the French have at present, and it is whispered is to be the first affair that the British will be employed on. Should we succeed in driving out the enemy, which

THE BRITISH PENINSULAR ARMY IN CAMP

is not so easily done as you have settled it in the city, I dare say we shall proceed to Italy, which will be rather better than Spain. There are at present no less than eight people packing up in the cabin, and the noise they make is such that no person can write, or indeed do anything else. I wrote Houston by the last packet, which, as the wind has been fair, he will most likely have received.

Let my letters be sent if possible, in General Warde's First Guards' bag, as by that means I shall get them sooner and more securely. You must not be surprised at hearing seldom, as a subaltern has not so many opportunities of writing as a general, and our allowance of baggage is so small, that we are obliged to leave even our writing-desks behind us, which is a monstrous inconvenience, but we must put up with it. I am to carry 100 lbs., including bed, etc., which is more than half.

We have no news of any consequence, and the army is tolerably healthy. With best love to all at home,

    I am, dear mother, your dutiful son,

Saltoun.

The First Battalion, First Guards disembarked at Corunna two days after the date of Saltoun's letter, and the third battalion disembarked on the following day. A writer of the period noted:

> The conduct of the officers and soldiers of the Guards was highly to their credit from the time they disembarked; fewer excesses were committed by those men than many regiments of similar numbers, and their officers preferred sharing with them their quarters, to profiting by the billets offered them. Out of 2,500 men, when they were put in motion, they only left 20 sick at Corunna: other regiments not half their number left twice as many.

Moore meanwhile, despite his forebodings and the realisation that his was an isolated independent command with approaching 300 miles dividing him from Baird, resolved to be of assistance to the conflict with the resources he already had at his disposal. To that end, he decided to hinder the French armies advance into the south of the country by throwing himself on their lines of communication. This diversion was so successful that the French corps *en route* for Valencia, Badajoz, and Saragossa were halted and Napoleon put aside all other considerations so that he could draw upon whatever resources he decided were necessary to crush the British Army in Spain.

In the north of the country Baird's division at last left Corunna. The Brigade of Guards marched to Santiago, arriving in the first days of November. It then marched by wings to Lugo, and after halting two days advanced to Cambanos in the vicinity of Astorga, Leon on the 23rd and 24th of November. Baird then divided his force into two divisions, one of which was placed under Major-General Warde, whereupon the command of the Brigade of First Guards temporarily devolved to Colonel William Anson, one of the acting majors; the flank companies being formed into a battalion under Colonel John Lambert.

Whilst at Astorga, Baird learned that the enemy was in force at Rio Seco, so he halted to concentrate his troops, but then received orders from Sir John Moore that he should, though it was barely a month after he had landed, fall back on Corunna, embark again and sail to Lisbon. The First Guards retired on the last days of November, moving towards Villafranca and Nogales; the six flank companies, under Colonel Lambert, were detached from the main column on the 1st of December to proceed to Cacabolos, and rejoined it at Herrerias.

Little time had elapsed before new orders were received countermanding the retreat, but directing Baird instead to prepare magazines for the army on the road to Corunna; whereupon the division again advanced. The Brigade of Guards arrived at Astorga for the second time on the 14th of December, at Benevente on the 16th, and Mayorga on the frontiers of Leon and Castille on the 20th, where the flank companies were again incorporated with the battalions.

In the meantime, Moore, having marched from Salamanca on the 12th of December by Alargos and Toro, on the 20th December at last effected a junction with Baird's force at Mayorga, a point some ninety or so miles from Salamanca and approaching fifty miles from Astorga. Moore's army, consisting of 23,500

Officer of the First Foot Guards

First Foot Guards, 1807

infantry, 2,000 cavalry, and sixty pieces of artillery, was finally in one place under his command.

Before the union of the armies, Moore had intended, once they were combined, to retire his force on Lisbon, but at this point he changed his mind again (almost certainly influenced by considerations other than the logical or soundly military) and decided that the army could not leave Iberia without striking a blow (preferably useful) which might include a raid on Valladolid or even Burgos, though any operations in the vicinity of the latter city would take his army much farther away from the assistance of British ships at Corunna.

★★★★★★

Moore Disney, now a brigadier-general, had as before mentioned, returned to Sicily at the beginning of 1808 in command of the Messina citadel and garrison until mid-April, when Sir J. Stewart arrived and took command of all the forces in the Mediterranean. Disney was ordered home to take command of a brigade at the end of July. He arrived at Lisbon on the 6th of October, in temporary command of a brigade of the line, consisting of the 2nd, 3rd, 6th, and 50th regiments of foot, with orders to join Sir John Moore's army. By the time his column had reached Castel Branco by the 27th of November, he received the intelligence that the British troops were going to retreat. Moore Disney was then given the command of another brigade (28th, 91st Regiments), forming part of the reserve, under Major-General Paget, so he left Castel Branco, and joined the main army at Toro on the Douro.

★★★★★★

Warde had now resumed the command of the First Guards, and occupied a convent at Majorga. The right of the main army was on the 17th of December at Toro, with Moore Disney, his brigade of the line and the rest of the reserve, in front. Moore Disney continued his march northwards to Grajal on the 21st, two or three miles from Sahagun, which was then occupied by the Brigade of Guards. All of the army by this point had been marching about the country for almost a month.

The kind of opportunity for battle that Moore was hoping for then fortuitously materialised comparatively close by his own position. He had discovered that Marshal Soult was in an isolated position on the Carrion River in command of less than 20,000 men and so he proposed to surprise and defeat him before he could be reinforced. Matters began auspiciously as when the French advanced guard came into view, the 10th and 15th Hussars, under Paget, went forward, and drove the enemy's cavalry off the field. As the French held the bridge over the Carrion, the Guards Brigade, with the rest of Baird's division, were ordered on the night of the 23rd of December to prepare to attack.

Napoleon had already discovered the whereabouts of the British Army and had left Madrid in pursuit of it. Moore, in turn had learned the emperor was on his way at the head of a formidable army of approaching 45,000 men. The moment of crisis had arrived. Fully appreciating that he was not strong enough to take issue with the combined French armies and, with no expectation of assistance from the Spanish, Moore realised that his options had expired and that there was no time to lose. He immediately abandoned his plans for a battle and prepared for a retreat into Gallicia towards Corunna where the army could be evacuated by sea.

We may speculate upon the mood of officers and in the ranks in Moore's army at this juncture. The Spanish, until comparatively recently in league with the French, had failed, for one reason or another, to be remotely effective allies in the prosecution of a war that was principally their own. Indeed, there can be little doubt that the distrust, frustrations and ultimately contempt that the many of the British soldiers in Spain felt towards their Spanish ally began in this period and endured to the end of the entire conflict.

Moore's army had undergone long marches and its sole achievement, which was no stipulated part of its original mission, had been to create a diversion which had been conceived by Moore himself in the absence of any better alternative objective. Though this manoeuvre was undoubtedly of value (and the subject of some focus in retrospective positive consideration of Moore's expedition), it is not difficult to suppose this was considered by the army to be meagre recompense for all its efforts. Indeed, the price to be paid for Moore's military effectiveness was that he became a target for Napoleon's particular attention. When the emperor learned that the British Army had quit Salamanca he remarked, 'Moore is the only general now worthy to contend with me. I shall move against him in person', and so he did at the earliest opportunity.

Baird's force had marched long and hard only to be deprived, on the eve of a redeeming engagement, of a 'cut at the enemy' which would have justified their trials. Now in rough terrain and harsh weather the order had come to escape to save the army. British soldiers, in the main, did not do well with notions of impotence or in retreat in situations where they could not be held under the strict discipline upon which order depended and that augured poorly for what immediately lay ahead which was a gruelling march of some two hundred and more miles.

CHAPTER SEVEN

The Retreat to Corunna, 1809

Mid-winter in northern Spain was now hard upon the British Army. The Guards, with Baird's division, retired on Christmas Day by Valencia de Don Juan, and, preceded by the rest of the infantry, crossed the River Esla the next day, occupying Villa Manian, where they halted for two days to give the main body time to pass at Benevente. When the cavalry of the emperor's vanguard reached the Esla, Lord Paget, who would command the cavalry at Waterloo as the Earl of Uxbridge, turned back with his hussars, and cut to pieces the Chasseurs à Cheval of the Imperial Guard (December 29th), capturing Lefebvre-Desnouettes, their commander, and many of his men. The Guards reached Astorga, some twelve hours' march farther, on the same day, where Hope's and Fraser's divisions had already arrived.

The Brigade of Guards was lodged in the episcopal palace of Astorga. At four the next morning, Baird's division, preceded again by Hope's and Fraser's, was *en route* but the weather deteriorated rapidly and before long stragglers began to drop behind. After a halting progress, it was late in the evening before the column reached Manzanel, a small village surrounded by snow covered mountains but, at ten o'clock that night and before the men could find anything to eat, the retreat recommenced. Early on the New Year's Eve the troops arrived at Bembibre, where wine-cellars were broken into, looted of their contents and discipline in the army began to unravel as drunkenness became widespread. The weather was wild and storm driven, rain and snow had made the roads almost impassable, and numbers of the column increasingly perished by the roadside or were taken prisoners as they fell to exhaustion, inebriation or other reckless conduct.

Napoleon advanced towards Astorga just two days' march behind the rearguard of the British Army and eager to snap at its heels. However, at that moment, Destiny intervened at its most capricious, for the emperor received intelligence from France that the Austrians were about to return to the contest, inspired in measure by events in Spain which demonstrated that, contrary to hitherto widely held conviction, the French were demonstrably not invincible. Incisively aware, as ever of his priorities, the emperor abandoned his personal commitment to the destruction of Moore's army and returned immediately to Paris (where he also had domestic intrigues aplenty to contend with, in addition to the actions of his honestly declared enemies), diverting a large portion of the army from the pursuit to proceed to Madrid, Leon or central Europe.

Soult's command was now charged to trail Moore's increasingly demoralised, exhausted and bedraggled column alone and so bring it to account. Ironically, Moore was now retreating before the very commander he had intended, with some confidence and expectation of success, to defeat on the Carrion.

This turn of events had even farther-reaching consequences, for now Moore was not fated to fight a huge French Army under Napoleon at Corunna. The emperor's commanding presence and massive numerical advantage on that battlefield would certainly have increased the probability of a British defeat, ensuring the evacuation of the bulk of the army would be impossible. The political consequences of such an outcome had the potential to shake British Government resolve and craft future policies. The effect of such an outcome on the governments of the Continental nations needs no elaboration.

However, this also meant Napoleon was not fated, in 1809, to experience (and so profit from) fighting a desperate British Army in a defensive position under the command of an excellent general. He would only discover what that would be like, having in ignorance denied its unique qualities against the advice of those of his officers who knew it from bitter experience, on the afternoon of his downfall in June, 1815. It is on the turn of cards such as these, when converging paths fail to make their conjunction by mere hours, that empires fall and the fortunes of future centuries are dependent. As for the young Alexander Fraser, Lord Saltoun; irrespective of his eventual destination, we may safely speculate that he had more immediate matters and concerns on his mind at this time.

When the French cavalry again made contact on the 3rd of January, the army withdrew through Cacabolos where the rear guard formed at bay and the enemy were soon disabused of any thoughts that their quarry had lost its teeth or the will to bite when pressed. The artillery caused havoc among the advancing French horsemen and skirmishers of both sides were hard at work. It was here that Rifleman Plunket of the 95th made his legendary, long range shots to bring down General Colbert and his *aide*.

At the close of the action the army reformed column of route and trudged through Villafranca, where Moore had calculated that the pursuers would probably no longer follow him. The French pressed him continually however, forcing him on to Alilea, where the army arrived at about one in the morning of the 4th of January. At seven in the morning the troops were again *en route* for Santa Maria upon a steeply climbing road over the mountains which separate Leon from Castille. A thaw brought no relief and the already poor road became a quagmire of mud and filth, clogged with the ghastly, stinking detritus of war in all its forms; broken down carriages, dead horses and mules and the pitiful scattered corpses of men and women, their still shapes captured within a maelstrom of driving rain, sleet, and clawed by an unabating bitter, cold wind. Through it all the starving, fatigued and miserable column, heads down, continued its march.

On the 5th of January the army marched through Santa Maria to a rising ground beyond Constantine, and having failed to break up the bridge behind them, were closely harassed throughout the day by a strong body of French cavalry and *voltigeurs*. The 28th Regiment, under Disney, faced this encroachment and a few cannon shots dissuaded the French from further advances. According to a British witness during the retreat the French *voltigeurs* actually lived up to their literal appellation. These diminutive skirmishers were (theoretically) both able and intended to 'vault' onto the croup of a cavalry horse, the more quickly to be taken into action. Whether leaping was involved or not, they were regularly seen being carried by French cavalry, which was wryly noted in the British ranks since their own green riflemen had to march everywhere, yet nevertheless always gave good account of themselves.

The bullocks drawing the carts with the money-chests could now go no further and so, after something of an altercation as to what should be done with the money, 90,000 dollars were thrown down a precipice. In the evening the troops, having passed Nogales, arrived at Lugo, and took up a position in front of the town. When Marshal Soult's vanguard arrived in front of the British position, he opened fire on its centre, but soon discovered that the red ranks before him constituted more than a rearguard. After making a feint on the right, a column and five guns attacked the British left, but these were repulsed by some companies of the Guards and General Leith's brigade.

On the morning of the 8th the British Army was still in position about a mile in front of Lugo. Moore knew he could not afford to delay his departure any longer. Before quitting Lugo, he issued the following order:

> It is evident that the enemy will not fight this army, notwithstanding the superiority of his numbers, but will endeavour to harass and tease it upon its march. The commander of the forces requests that it may be carefully explained to the soldiers that their safety depends solely upon their keeping to their divisions and marching with their regiments; that those who stop in villages or straggle on the march will inevitably be cut off by the French cavalry, who have hitherto shown little mercy even to the feeble and infirm who have fallen into their hands. The

army has still eleven leagues (about 38 miles) to march, the soldiers must make an exertion to accomplish them; the rearguard cannot stop, and those who fall behind must take their fate.

The enemy army that followed the British was, of course, suffering the same debilitating weather conditions and was at this point barely superior in numbers, so could not afford to be less than prudent in its conduct. This does not imply any parity between the British and French armies at this point, for Soult's advantage was that he could march back into the Spanish interior to continue operations linked by lines of supply and communication in concert with other friendly forces whereas Moore, most decidedly, could not. However, at that moment both protagonists continued to doggedly march westwards, each commander carefully focussed on the actions of the other.

Shortly after nightfall on the evening of the 8th, the British Army quietly withdrew from its position and marching through Lugo, recommenced the retreat to the sea, leaving its bivouac fires burning in the darkness so that the vigilant enemy would not immediately learn it had slipped away. Once again, the weather broke and Paget's division, followed by the brigade of Guards and Baird's division, moved off in a terrible storm.

The first men in the retreat filled the buildings on the roadside to escape the deluge and had to be forced onwards. It was daybreak on the 9th before the Guards arrived at Vaamondas (now Baamonde), a little over twenty miles further on, where the army took up another position. Here the men lay scattered over a bleak and desolate heath with nothing to protect them, or lined ditches to escape the cutting wind and there many perished. Regiments became mixed together and stragglers continually dragged themselves in, though many were never seen by their comrades again. The respite was necessarily a short one and after a few hours' halt, the main body continued its retreat, arriving at Betanzos on the evening of the 9th of January after another punishing night and day. The toll on lives within the army during this period had been particularly heavy.

In the midst of the difficulties of this day's march, the Brigade of Guards preserved some order and discipline; the reserve covered the retreat, and these soldiers, who were in frequent contact with the enemy, nevertheless lost fewer men than succumbed in other regiments. It is, perhaps, understandable that those troops, who belonged to units renowned for especial *esprit de corps*, discipline or physical fitness, fared better in these extreme circumstances. A contemporary writer commented:

> The corps in which there was the least straggling were the artillery (who had ever a special regard for their guns), the Guards, and the reserve (which included the riflemen of the 95th and others). The Guards were the strongest body of men in the army, and consequently suffered least from fatigue; besides, they are strictly disciplined, and their non-commissioned officers are excellent.

On the morning of the 11th, Major-General Disney's brigade of the 28th and 91st Regiments was still forming the rearguard, and so was actively engaged in protecting the rear of the army at the bridge over the river at Betanzos, which they had in vain attempted to blow up behind them. The army continued its march on the 12th, in the knowledge that this was to be their last day on the road and, in the course of the day, it finally reached Corunna.

Sir Robert Arbuthnot later recalled that he was standing near Sir John Moore who was watching the troops coming in to Corunna, when Sir John called his attention to one particular column.

'Arbuthnot,' exclaimed Moore, 'look at that body of men in the distance. They are the Guards, by the way they are marching.'

'It was a fine sight', Sir Robert recalled, 'and one I shall never forget. We watched them and saw them march into Corunna by sections, their drums beating, the drum-major in front flourishing his stick, the sergeant-major at the head, and the drill-sergeants on the flanks keeping the men in step, exactly as if they were on their own drill-ground at home'.

The first and third battalions of the First Guards, with the rest of Baird's and Fraser's divisions, occupied the town itself, while

Hope's division was quartered in the suburbs, and the reserve at El Burgo.

CHAPTER EIGHT

The Battle of Corunna

The British Army that arrived at Corunna was in a parlous condition. An eyewitness recalled:

> The soldiers lay scattered about, wearied and dispirited, ragged in their dress and many of them sickly and broken down by the fatigue of the retreat. Most of their chins had been untouched by a razor for days, perhaps weeks, and their faces blackened by the smoke of their muskets and the charcoal of their cooking fires.

Moore's divisions, approaching 15,000 strong, after two days' rest, moved on the 14th from their quarters in the town and took up their positions for the coming battle on a ridge about two miles from the town. The British position and its objectives were simple. Behind the army, formed in a defensive arc, lay the town and sea. In the harbour would lie the ships of the Royal Navy and the means by which the army might be excricated. The French would attack to prevent that escape and the British would attempt to defeat the French so that it might safely evacuate the majority of the army.

The advantage of motivation demonstrably lay with the British Army which was fighting to save itself, but it fared better than might be initially imagined compared to the French Army, since it had rested, now had the advantage of numbers and had been substantially resupplied. Few lessons are original and Soult was about to be taught one as old as humankind, which is that one should mindful of what one elects to chase for one may ultimately catch up to it.

Baird's and Hope's divisions were formed in line; Baird's on the right, and from the direction of the ridge, obliquely approaching the enemy's position, so that a great battery on the French left enfiladed it. The Guards, under Sir Henry Warde, were in column in support of Baird's right, this being the weak point of the position. Fraser's division was posted a short distance in rear of the Guards, while Paget with the reserve was in rear of the centre.

The long-awaited transports arrived, entered the harbour of Corunna and had begun to load the stores of the army together with the greater part of the artillery. Before the infantry could embark, however, there was a battle to be fought. At about two o'clock on the 16th, the French Army under Soult, advanced in three columns, covered by skirmishers, against the British position; attacked the left column, carried the village of Elvina, and thereafter dividing, one wing attacked Baird directly in front while the other wing attempted to turn his right flank. If this attack had succeeded, the destruction of the British Army would have been inevitable. The 4th Regiment on the right of Baird's line was thrown back on its left, and opened a flank fire on the advancing French column, while Paget's reserve descended into the valley in order to check its further advance.

The 42nd Highlanders and 50th Regiment, forming the right centre of Baird's line, then advanced and stormed the village of Elvina. Baird received a bullet in his arm, which forced him to leave the field, and Sir John Moore, observing that an gap was left in the line, by the advance of the 42nd and 50th regiments, sent orders to the brigade of Guards instructing it to move forward and occupy the village. The first battalion of the First Guards deployed and advanced down the hill to the assistance of the regiments in Elvina with the third battalion forming in support.

As Major Henry Hardinge (later Governor-General of India at the time of the First Anglo-Sikh War and Commander-in-Chief of the British Army during the Crimean War), who had

The First Foot Guards at Corunna

carried the order to the Guards to advance, was reporting to Sir John that the French cavalry had been repulsed, Moore was struck by a cannon shot which carried away his left shoulder and part of his collar bone. Upon his falling, the command of the army devolved to Sir John Hope.

The reserve on the extreme right overthrew the French column, and approached the great artillery battery on the French left. The British left wing also repulsed the attack made upon it. The tide of the battle had turned and the British advanced driving the French force before it. By five o'clock, the enemy was confining itself to a long-distance cannonade as it disengaged and by six o'clock Soult was unequivocally retiring. The opportunity to destroy Moore's army had not been taken when it was at its most exposed and debilitated and so the battle that was fought by the French at Corunna came too late with too few resources to achieve a positive outcome for them on the field.

The mortally wounded Sir John Moore was carried off the field by six soldiers of the First Guards and 42nd Highlanders and brought into Corunna, where he died in the course of the evening. He was interred in the north-east bastion of the citadel, by the side of his friend Brigadier-General Anstruther, formerly of the Third Guards, who had commanded a brigade during the retreat, but who died on the day the army reached Corunna. The funeral service was read by the Rev. Symonds, one of the First Guards chaplains.

The retreat to the ships commenced at ten o'clock at night with the exception of the brigades of Generals Hill and Beresford, which remained as a rearguard to cover the embarkation, and the majority of army, including the Brigade of Guards, boarded their ships during the night. Hill and Beresford's brigades embarked the following day, harassed by French artillery from a battery brought on to a height commanding the harbour.

The muster-rolls of the First Guards revealed that the first battalion had only lost five men and the third battalion eight killed on the day of the battle. However, during the following weeks, the first battalion lost a further eighty-six men and

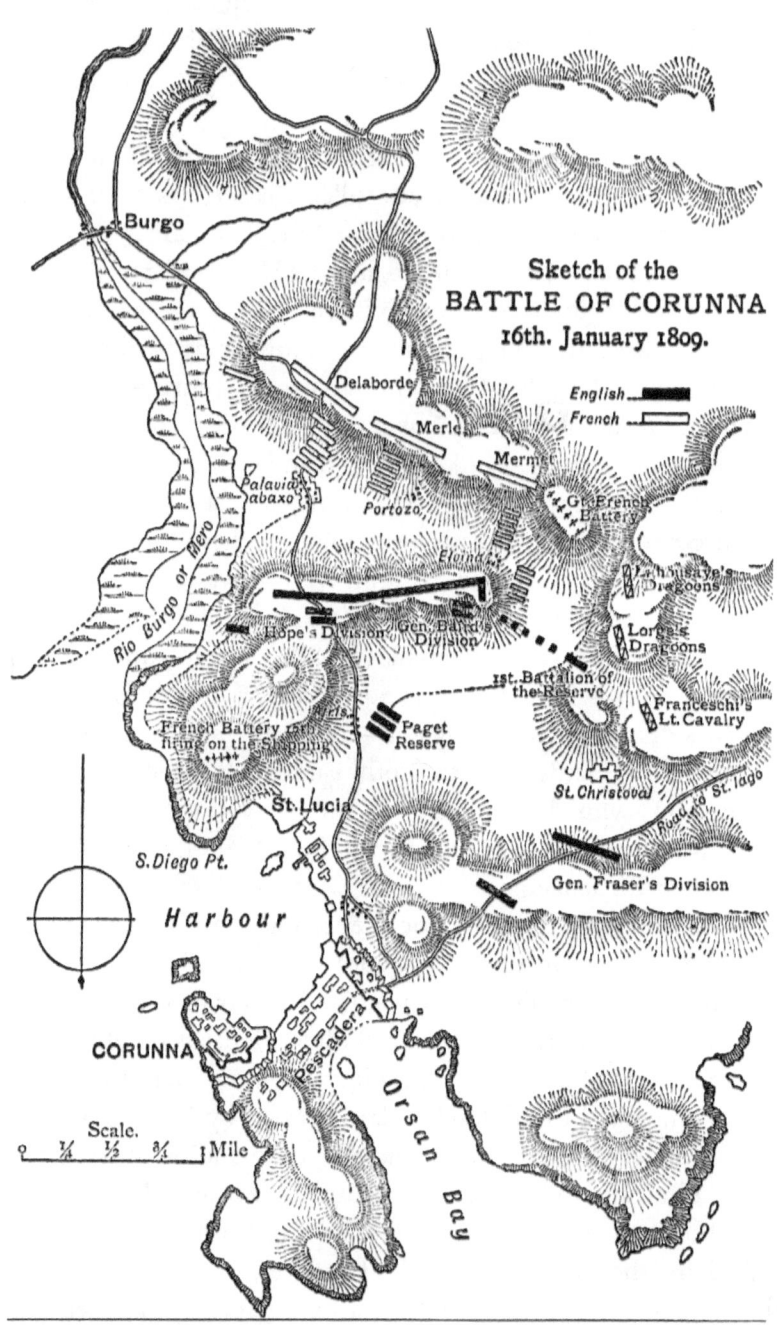

the third battalion fifty-four men who died as a result of their wounds, sickness or fatigue. Sixty-nine men of the first battalion and fifty-six of the third battalion were taken prisoner by the enemy during the retreat. The total loss to the British Army during the campaign, including the advance, the retreat to Corunna, and in the subsequent action, was in the region of 4,000 men,(Oman says 6,000) of whom 800 subsequently found their way to Portugal and where they were formed into battalions of detachments.

Moore's last words were that he hoped his nation would do him justice which suggests that he had a presentiment that it might not do anything of the kind, for a victory at the end of a hard retreat and on the eve of an evacuation would never qualify as unequivocal good news from which credit would be attributed to the commander who had presided over the affair. Military reverses usually require someone to have blundered and blamed so, justified or not, the pointing fingers of accusation were inevitable.

That having been said, Moore came to realise his situation was hopeless, that he would get no assistance from the Spanish and so he could not fulfil the intentions of his mission. He made it clear in his last letter writing that 'as a military man I should have retired from Salamanca'. He possibly should have been on his way before that time or at least soon after his arrival at Salamanca for the 'writing was on the wall' early in his expedition and nothing then occurred which might have encouraged him to believe that his situation would improve.

Notwithstanding his clear appreciation of his harsher realities, Moore, aware that he would be appraised as a 'military man', then concerned himself with the intangibles of honour and the politics of perception and those distractions were his undoing. Considerations only matter before the fact. Thereafter, uncompromising verdicts upon outcomes are delivered by everyone with the inclination to voice an opinion. Since Moore was now dead, he could no longer appeal his case even if, had he lived as unlikely as it would have been, he had been inclined to do so.

Moore admitted that he was disappointed with the conduct of the army during the retreat, but that behaviour was always likely to surface in the British Army of the day on campaign when it broke lose, for whatever reason, from the strict bonds of discipline that held it together. The Duke of Wellington could attest to that fact as readily as could Sir John Moore, for he also had no remedy for widespread disorder among the ranks before the fact and in extreme circumstances could only regain control of disorderly soldiers driven by drink, lust and rapacity with the threat and application of the lash and the gallows.

We may speculate whether Wellesley would have fared better than did Moore in his shoes. Certainly, he would have found himself in the same position as regarded his Spanish allies for little changed in that respect during the time he was commander-in-chief in the peninsula. Both generals were talented and resourceful tacticians who could have depended on the army to perform well under their direction when it came to fighting, for then it was in its element. In fact, had he not fallen at Corunna, Moore would have probably attacked, driving the French into the River Mero which lay at their backs.

However, based on what we know of Wellington, we might believe he would have marched for the ships when he realised it was the only viable solution, irrespective of other considerations, for he repeatedly demonstrated in the peninsula that he was ever the pragmatist, manoeuvring the army (advancing or retreating, with no discarnate luggage attached to either direction) until he arrived at the right place, at the right time, to realise his immediate objectives. Indeed, Wellington not only continued to employ this very methodology to position the army in the last great battle he fought, but also applied the same principle during his subsequent political career, including in circumstances where, in the absence of bloodshed, it was seen to be an unacceptable *volt-face* on matters of policy.

Alternatively, aware of his disadvantages in Spain, Wellesley may not have stuck his neck out quite so far as Moore had done in the first instance, though in either event he would certainly have drawn the emperor's attention upon himself at which time the distance between the British force and Madrid would have become critical to any outcome.

Be that as it may, Sir John Moore's death made a change in the command of the army in the Peninsula certain for good or ill and his place would be, in due course, taken by another general. That man, as it transpired, would be Arthur Wellesley who was shrewd enough to know that the campaign fought against the French revolutionary armies in the Low Countries was 'precisely how not to conduct a campaign' and so able to learn, if that was necessary, the lessons that Moore's campaign taught any commander who might find himself in a similar position.

As the Duke of Wellington, he would ultimately demonstrate he was the right man, possibly, though irrelevantly the better man, for the challenges that lay ahead. In fact, as the First Guards sailed back to England another British Army was making its way towards the Iberian Peninsula and ere long Wellesley would join it as its commander. The regiment had earned its first battle honour in the Peninsular War, 'Corunna', for their battle had been won, if the campaign had not.

CHAPTER NINE

The Return to Portugal, 1809

The homeward bound fleet encountered a storm which scattered the convoy and actually wrecked some vessels, but the transports which carried the First Guards came through it all unscathed, anchoring safely in Portsmouth harbour on the 25th of January. The troops returned to their barracks at Chatham where they received numerous transfers from the second battalion, which was garrisoned in the capital, in the course of the Spring months. The evacuation from Corunna may have been the end of an episode, but the war against Napoleonic France was far from over and so before the end of that summer, the Guards would yet again be sent on foreign service.

Meanwhile, after the British had sailed away from Spain, Soult's command, unimpeded by opposition, returned to Corunna to re-establish the French grip on the region, concentrating in the vicinity of the port for about a month. Having rested, the marshal and his force then struck southwards, marching on the city of Oporto in Portugal, which was stormed in late March.

The British Government had already realised that it would be necessary to dispatch reinforcements to the Peninsula and so at the end of the year 1808, had assembled another expedition under Major-General Sherbrook to join the forces already in place, about 9,000 men, under Cradock. This force comprised the Second Brigade of Guards (Coldstream and 3rd Regiments) under Brigadier Henry Campbell of the First Guards, together with the Irishmen of the 87th and 88th Regiments. This expedition sailed in the middle of January, 1809, and so, of course, ran into the same gales that beset the homeward bound fleet carrying the First Brigade of Guards from Corunna. Adverse weather conditions kept the fleet at Cork in Ireland for a month, arriving eventually in Spain at Cadiz, where the Spanish authorities were as usual obstructive, though in the event orders arrived from England ordering the transports to Portugal.

So, the fleet moved on towards the mouth of the Tagus, landing the Second Brigade of Guards in the vicinity of Lisbon in the middle of March. The remainder of the troops of the line regiments which had served under Sir John Moore were also sent back to Portugal as soon as they had recruited replacements, together with other additional reinforcements sent out from England. In February General Beresford had been sent out to reorganise the Portuguese Army, amply accompanied by numbers of British officers to assist him, with a huge supply of new arms and equipment.

Sir Arthur Wellesley arrived in Lisbon on the 22nd of April, assuming not only military command from Cradock (who had in the interim showed little enterprise, though had at least, provoked no disasters), but supreme authority in the country. Wellesley had over 28,000 British and German troops (some admittedly *en route*) and 15,000-16,000 Portuguese at his disposal. This was yet another comparatively small army with which to oppose the numerically superior French presence in the region, given it was almost certainly going to be required to depend upon its own resources.

Nevertheless, Wellesley had boldly asserted, contrary to Moore's views, that with a British Army of 20,000 or 30,000 men and the control of the native forces, he would hold Portugal against any French Army not exceeding 100,000 men. The British Government elected to take the gamble that he was right. The new general had arrived at an opportune moment for the French invasion had come to a standstill. Marshal Soult would not move without reinforcements from Marshal Ney, and Marshal Victor would not move without reinforcements from Madrid.

Wellesley, appreciating the potentials of this isolating procrastination, saw he could deal a blow at either Soult or Victor, while leaving a detached force to 'contain' the other.

He resolved to deal with Soult first leaving 12,000 men at Abrantes to watch Victor and given success, he then intended to move swiftly to Estremadura to deal with the second French Army. The army crossed the River Douro near Oporto in the face of Soult's army on the 12th of May. Such was the marshal's surprise at this development that he left his dinner on the table in his haste to be away, whereupon it was appreciatively devoured by General Rowland Hill's divisional staff. Hill established himself in the town, while Sherbrook's, division with the Second Brigade of Guards, consisting of the first battalions of the Coldstream and Third regiments, under Campbell, threatened the enemy's rear. Comprehensively wrong footed, Soult was compelled to retreat over the mountains to Braja and Orense, losing his artillery and baggage, and 5,000 men on the way.

Wellesley followed up this blow, as planned, by marching against Marshal Victor and thence on Madrid, joining with the forces under the Spanish general, Cuesta. The army then advanced on the 22nd of July to Talavera, and on the 28th fought a bloody battle in which the French attack was completely defeated, and for which victory Wellesley was created Viscount Wellington. Tellingly, on examining the thin line of redcoats before his attack, Victor had proclaimed, 'If we do not enforce this, we should give up the war'. The British general then turned northwards towards Soult, but finding that the French marshal had 50,000 men at Navalmoral, he prudently retired to Almarez and Merida, in Estremadura, where the army went into cantonments.

Wellington could have had few illusions, based on his initial experiences in Iberia and re-enforced by what he had learned of Sir John Moore's campaign, that he could rely on co-operation or support from the Spanish authorities, generals and armies. The defence of Portugal and the success of the British Army

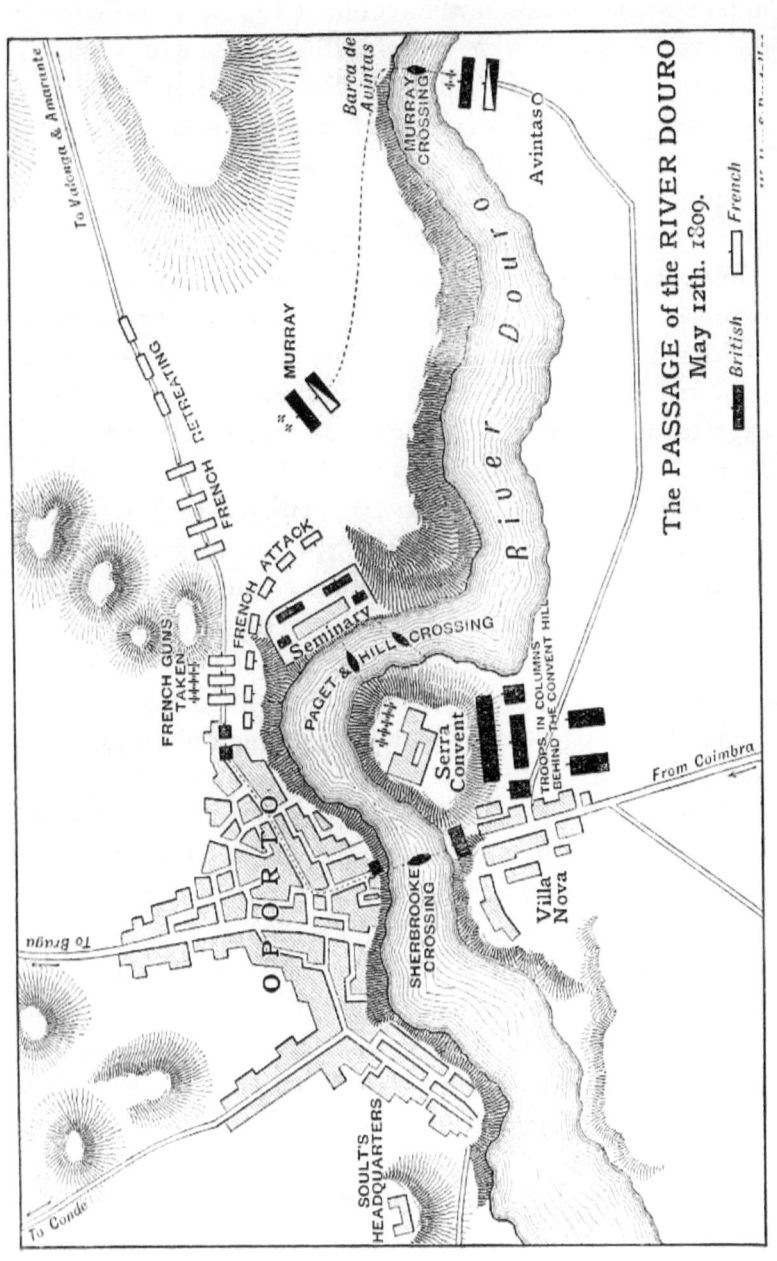

in Spain must, therefore, depend on his own judgement and those resources of any kind over which he had authority, though indirectly the Spanish armies continued to be of assistance by their very existence which required the attention of numbers of the French who might otherwise have been entirely employed against the British. However, it is not the purpose of this narrative to describe the activities of the Spanish armies.

Aware that the time would inevitably come when his army, given its modest size and in the absence of support by Spanish armies, would find itself faced by a French force of superior numbers in the field, Wellington determined that he would not find himself in the same predicament that had so fatally compromised Moore. There would be no retreat to the sea in the expectation of waiting transports and another precipitate evacuation courtesy of the Royal Navy.

A large safe haven on the Iberian Peninsula itself was needed which could accommodate the entire army in addition to a civilian population. All parties would be required to sustain themselves and thus the means to be readily resupplied. That no such initiative was instituted during the period of Moore's campaign cannot be laid to that general's account for that would have required a foresight that nobody at that time had demonstrated they possessed.

The Portuguese capital, Lisbon, sitting upon the tip of a broad peninsula flanked by the ocean and the River Tagus was the ideal location for Wellington's enterprise, for the river is accessible to maritime traffic and leads towards safe anchorages. Accordingly, Wellington directed the construction of the formidable and virtually unassailable defensive works across the landward approaches to the city which became known as the Lines of Torres Vedras and, furthermore, ordered forts to be built so they might defend the wide mouth of the Tagus from enemy incursions from the water.

Behind these lines, not only could the army and populace find safety, but be indefinitely supported by sea whilst an enemy force, deprived of the means to live off the land, would not only remain impotently excluded but, if disinclined to retire, eventually be the architect of its own dissolution.

However, since we are principally following the First Guards and Alexander Fraser, Lord Saltoun we must leave the Peninsular War for the struggle with Napoleon's France was being fought on other fronts in the summer of 1809 and a plan was formulated for an expedition to the the Low Countries. The two battalions of the First Regiment lately returned from Spain were ordered to hold themselves in immediate readiness to join this force and, unfortunately for the third time in this conflict, the guardsmen were on their way to a place where affairs would not go favourably according to plan.

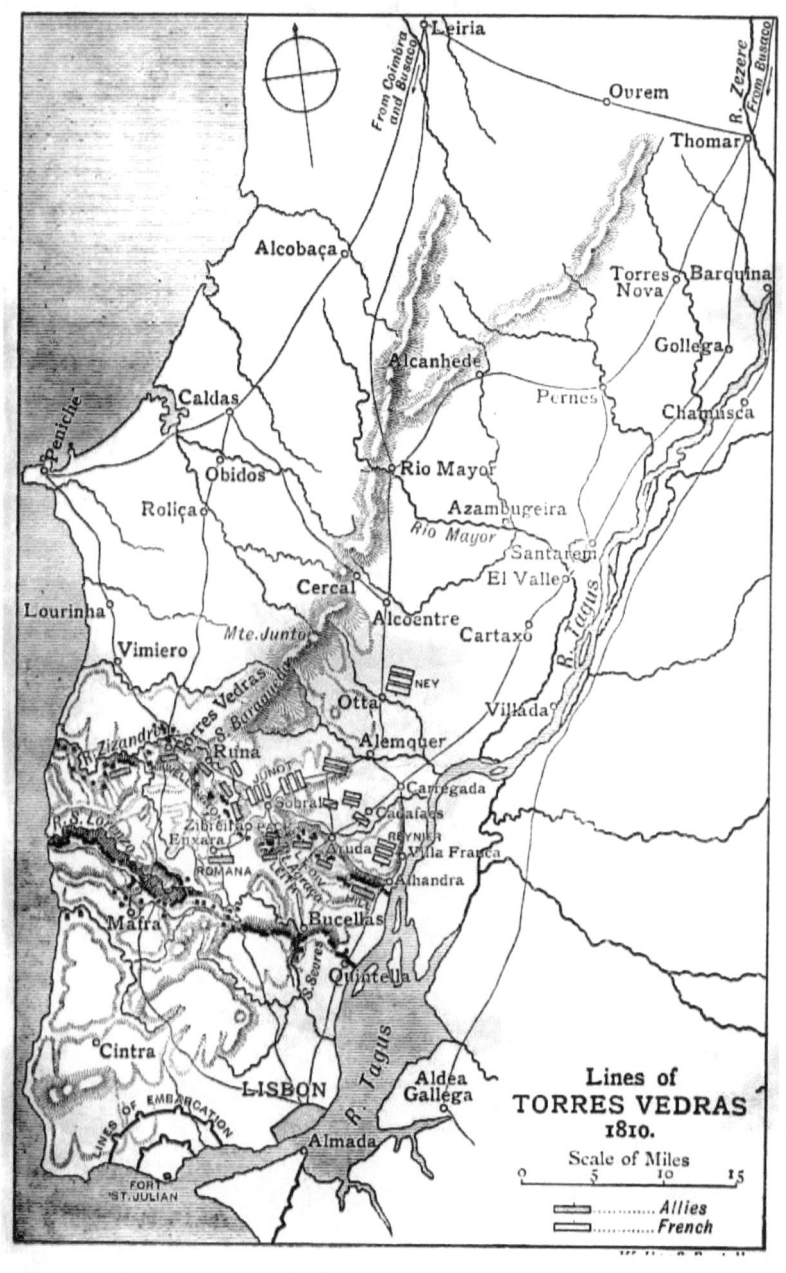

CHAPTER TEN

The Walcheren Expedition, 1809

Whilst the British Government was aware that the imminent danger of a French invasion launched across the English Channel had been averted, it felt a potential threat against the British homeland somewhere from the sea remained. Of particular concern to it was the French concentration at Antwerp in the Low Countries.

The Scheldt waterway gave access to the seaways from that city and provided secure maritime passage, anchorages and shipyards as it flowed between the main land and the oddly shaped peninsula of North and South Beveland with Walcheren on its western extremity. Antwerp, at the farthest eastern reach of the Scheldt (before it becomes a river of usual proportions), provided a secure base for the French Navy, removed from coastal waters and so inaccessible to enemy warships at sea. The city also supported a sizeable military arsenal.

The British view was that this 'pistol at the head of the country', on its left flank should be neutralised, but in any event it was hoped a robust attack launched from the west would also create a diversion which could provide some relief for Austria and others who were opposing Napoleon in central Europe. In retrospect, this initiative had the hallmark of 'someone's bright idea', for the Scheldt is some distance (compared to the width of the English Channel) from England's shore and so enemy ships would be exposed for some time (during which they would be vulnerable) to the attentions of the Royal Navy which dominated the seaways. Simply put, given Napoleon knew he could not cross to England without risk of disaster from Boulogne/Calais, (1805), why would he then attempt a crossing from Antwerp (1809)?

Nevertheless, in late May the British Government determined the time was right for a pre-emptive strike. Antwerp was poorly garrisoned, some of its troops having been withdrawn to reinforce the *Grande Armée* engaged on the Danube. An ambitious plan was conceived to capture or destroy the enemy's ships wherever they could be found between Antwerp and Flushing, destroy the Antwerp, Terneuse and Flushing arsenals and dockyards and reduce Walcheren. Ideally the Scheldt would then be made no longer navigable for ships of war, after which the army was to return to England, leaving a garrison on Walcheren. The fleet was to be commanded by Admiral Sir Richard Strachan and the army would be under Lieutenant-General, the Earl of Chatham.

The First Brigade of Guards, the first and third battalions of the First Regiment, now commanded by Major-General Moore Disney, received orders to embark on the 23rd of July; and the flank companies of the three second battalions, forming the Third Brigade of Guards, were also ordered to join the expedition. The total strength was 109 officers and 3,091 men. The two battalions of First Guards were under the command of Colonel William Anson and Colonel George Cooke respectively, with Lieutenant-Colonel Hon. Philip Cocks and Lieutenant-Colonel Kelly as seconds in command.

The army, 21,000 strong, was organised in four divisions, under Lieutenant-General Sir John Hope, the Earl of Rosslyn (who had assumed command at Corunna after the death of Moore), Lieutenant-General Grosvenor, and the Marquis of Huntly. The size of this expeditionary force is noteworthy, particularly compared to the forces that had been dispatched to Portugal and Spain thus far, though of course, the Low Countries were closer to home than the Iberian Peninsula and the perceived enemy threat one that bore directly on Britain itself.

Lord Chatham proposed the establishment of a base in a strong position from which to launch further operations, on the north side of South Beveland. From that point the enemy's batteries could be taken in the rear, forcing the French fleet, which was off Flushing, to move up the river, for fear of having its line of retreat cut off. This would allow the approach of the British fleet to Flushing. Hope's division, which was the reserve of the army, was selected to be the military component of this operation and was composed of the Brigade of Guards under Disney, the first and second battalions of the 4th and 28th regiments under the Earl of Dalhousie and the 20th, 92nd and Vet. Battalion under Erskine totalling 7,261 effectives. Admiral Sir Richard Keats commanded the transporting of this division, and as it was to precede the rest of the army, it sailed from the Downs on the 28th of July. The Earl of Chatham, with the other divisions, set sail on the 29th and 30th.

The grenadiers and First Battalion, First Guards, and other regiments of Hope's division, were taken some distance up the river in boats and landed without opposition on the morning of the 1st of August, on the north side of South Beveland at a point between Wilmenduye and Cattendyke. The grenadiers of the Guards, and a detachment of the 95th (Rifles) then moved forward towards Cloeting. Strong patrols were pushed towards Goes, whilst leaving three companies of infantry of the 20th Foot at Cattendyke. Goes capitulated, occupied by the 92nd Regiment and the enemy retired towards Batz.

The Guards remained that day at Capelle and Boulingen, and Erskine's brigade at Hexendenkinder and Goes. The Third Battalion of Guards did not land until the following day, the 2nd of August. The division already on shore, again advanced, the Guards towards Vaarden, the 4th Regiment to Hanswardt. The grenadiers of the Guards then pushed on to Kruyningen, there surprising seventy or eighty of the enemy and making them prisoners without loss to themselves.

The Dutch evacuated Vaarden, and subsequently, on the 4th of August, as the British continued their advance, abandoned the town and important fort of Batz, on the low ground opposite to and commanding the entrance of the Scheldt. The Guards then took up a position between Cattendyke and Batz. It came as something of a surprise to Hope that this fort, considering its strength and position, should be so readily given up without resistance since it was manned by some 600 troops.

Nevertheless, passage was now free for the fleet between Walcheren and South Beveland, so Hope stressed the importance of naval support near to the fort. This was not, however, forthcoming and its absence was soon felt, when on the 5th and 8th of August the enemy began to heavily bombard the fort from twenty-five gunboats. Whilst the bombardment was at its most intensive, Grenadier John Skinner, performed an act of extraordinary bravery. Under fire, Skinner un-spiked twelve guns that had been spiked and abandoned by the French in Fort Batz with tools he made himself so that they were able to be turned upon the enemy gunboats.

Eighty guns and a quantity of ordnance stores had fallen into the possession of General Hope's division. On the 9th of August the Earl of Rosslyn's division landed on South Beveland, when, as senior officer, the earl assumed the command. While operations against Fort Batz were taking place, the troops under the immediate command of Lord Chatham had landed, on the 30th of July, at Veere. They came ashore on the north-east shore of the island of Walcheren, without opposition after the fire from the mortar and gunboats had driven the enemy from their defences.

The town of Camour was cannonaded, and soon surrendered, and on the 4th of August Fort Rammekens was taken by General Fraser. The flotilla could now advance, preventing enemy relief from being thrown into Flushing, which was subsequently invested. After a bombardment, which set the town in flames, it also capitulated. The garrison marched out having been granted 'the honours of war' on the 18th of August.

After the fall of Flushing, Lord Chatham, with his headquarters, moved to Goes, in South Beveland, and subsequently to Fort Batz, joining Sir John Hope's division with the Brigade of

WALCHEREN CAMPAIGN, 1809

Guards. About this time the most dangerous enemy the British troops would encounter began to make its appearance, in the form of a debilitating fever, 'occasioned' as contemporary sources referred to it in an all-embracing term of medical ignorance, 'by the fatal miasma arising from the inundations'. It is now widely accepted that what beset the troops was a lethal cocktail of malaria, typhoid, typhus and dysentery which would lay low many more soldiers than bullets and become the defining feature of the expedition.

The first part of the operation having been eventually accomplished, the proposed attack on Antwerp was the next and final objective, but Louis Bonaparte, a younger brother of the emperor and King of Holland since 1806, had in the meantime arrived with reinforcements and Bernadotte had assumed the supreme command of the French troops.

The strength of the enemy in Antwerp was now about 11,000 men; between Antwerp and Bergen-op-Zoom, a further 15,000; and in Bergen-op-Zoom, Breda, and Tholen, and on the left bank of the Scheldt, 11,000 more, making a total of 37,000 men either in or within striking distance of Antwerp. The effective force of the British Army was about 30,000 in total, but if the siege of Antwerp was undertaken, 6,000 of them would be required to remain in Walcheren, and 2,000 more remain in South Beveland. It would also be necessary to mask Bergen-op-Zoom and Breda; 10,000 or 12,000 men would be required to cover the siege, leaving only 10,000 men for the siege itself. Simply put, the practicability of the initial plan of the expedition had demonstrably unravelled.

The admiral, Sir Richard Strachan pronounced that the fleet could not move higher up the Scheldt as long as the two forts of Lillo and Liefkenshoek, situated on opposite sides of the river, half-way between Fort Batz and Antwerp, remained in possession of the enemy. The navy, Strachan conceded, would co-operate with any attack upon them, but taking them would necessarily be a task for the army. He further stressed that time was pressing and supplies in the fleet were running low especially of fresh water, so immediate action, was to take place, if it was required.

It is clear from Lord Saltoun's letter to his mother despatched at this time that he was already aware that the useful service of the army in this operation was over, which rather suggests that there were few, if any, officers in the British force who were unaware of it. He writes, as one might readily expect, of the sickness that plagued the army, but notably that the Guards suffered less from it than other troops and one may speculate this was a consequence of their general fitness and the high standards maintained in all things, including cleanliness, within the regiment. The contents of his missive reveal, once again, that Saltoun was both well informed and astute. However, this letter appears to suggest, since he makes no reference to it, that he was not sick himself at this time or previously. We may readily speculate why, in writing to his mother, that may have been the case. His nephew, the 17th Lord Saltoun, from a perspective of intimate knowledge, in his writings provides more illumination on that subject by informing the reader:

> Lord Saltoun did not escape the terrible Walcheren fever, caused by malaria, that proved fatal to so many, from the effects of which even his iron constitution suffered in no slight degree during future years.

We may assume that the 'Ross' referred to in the last paragraph of this letter was John Ross, a lieutenant-colonel of the Coldstream Guards who had been killed at Talavera in the previous month. He was 65 years old at the time of his death, had seen service dating back to the Seven Years' War and had fought with Butler's Rangers in the Mohawk Valley during the American War of Independence.

South Beveland,
August 26th, 1809

Dear Mother,
Since I last wrote you we have remained in the same situation; the headquarters have been moved from Walcheren to this island, and the other day they came down to Batz, near where we are, and with them I was in hopes they would have brought

our letters, and given us some opportunity of writing home; but not in the least, and we are likely to return without any opportunity of either hearing from or writing to England.

It is now the general opinion that the business is at an end, and we shall shortly retrace our steps, as the enemy have in their hurry and confusion on our first appearance inundated the country between Bergen-op-Zoom and Lillo, as well as that on the left bank of the river, which renders our further progress, if not impossible, at least attended with such difficulties and loss, as would be greater than the taking of Antwerp is worth, and it is therefore concluded that we shall either move to some other part of the enemy's coast or return home; in case of the latter a large force will most probably be sent to Spain, and I should not wonder if the brigade of Guards were amongst the number. The army in general, officers as well as men, have been very sickly; the complaint is an intermittent fever, attended with much giddiness in the head. I never remember, even in the worst of times in Spain, so many sick as we now have in the brigade, and we are much less so than the rest of the army; the worst is that it seems to be a complaint of the country, and they are not likely to get better as long as they remain in it.

There has been a council of war sitting all day, and has not as yet broke up; it will most probably determine what is to become of us. Montague Wynyard of the Coldstreams, who has got his promotion by the death of Ross in Spain, is just going home, and will take this with him. I think we shall soon follow.

    I am, dear mother, your dutiful son,

                                                   Saltoun.

Love to all at home.
27th August 1809.

A memorandum, on the increased strength of the hostile forces compared to the British, was submitted to the generals for their consideration. Its disconcerting contents required little deliberation on their part and they came to the inevitable conclusion that the siege of Antwerp was impracticable, and so that there was no advantage to be gained by the reduction of the Fort of Lillo, or from any other operations in the vicinity. The expedition was at an end and South Beveland was evacuated.

By early September no troops were left in the Scheldt, except a small garrison at Walcheren, under General Don positioned to prevent the enemy's fleet escaping from the river. He then received orders to evacuate the island, and after destroying the basin of the harbour and naval defences, his force embarked for England in mid-December

The First Brigade of Guards had already landed in England at the beginning of September, and moved to their former quarters. In his history of the Grenadier Guards, Hamilton informed his readers:

> They had suffered much from sickness, both officers and men bringing with them the seeds of disease from which many suffered to the latest hour of their lives; none had fallen in action, but many a grave was filled from the 'Walcheren Fever' contracted in this fruitless campaign.
> By a return made out five months later, at the beginning of February, 1810, it appears that, of the ninety-one officers of the First Guards, one died of fever on service, and two on their return, all of the first battalion; and that of the 2,574 non-commissioned officers and men of that regiment, twenty-one died on service, and 208 on their return. In the whole army no less than sixty-seven officers and 4,000 men died of the fever, and at the date of the report in February above 200 officers and 11,000 men were still in hospital.

The Walcheren Expedition was a failure, made the more poignant since nothing like the threat that was the inspiration for it ever materialised (nor was likely to do so) and it, furthermore, achieved nothing which might have been assistance to the Austrian war effort. Most modern military history students would throw up their hands upon reading the mission brief, for it was too complex; over reaching in its objectives and required significant distances to be traversed, given there were points of contention to be reduced along the way, before the ultimate objective was reached, much less won. Unfortunately, most military students can bring to mind similar plans made in more recent times.

The notion that the army could finally quit Walcheren and

return to England leaving behind a garrison that could endure to be influential for the longer term was fanciful. Essentially, the expedition's best chance of success would have been an effective raid in force (in effect a demonstration of intent and capability) which would inflict the maximum damage in the face of least resistance in the minimum amount of time, before promptly withdrawing.

The motivation for the operation was the intelligence that the ultimate objective, Antwerp, was insufficiently defended by the enemy at the time. At no time could it have been assumed that Antwerp would not be strengthened by the enemy (whose presence dominated western continental Europe) as readily as it been depleted of troops and that single consideration ensured 'time' was the principal command consideration for the British operation. Had the operation been more limited in its goals and shorter in the time allocated to its execution, it is probable the incidence of sickness would have been much reduced, though one could not expect that any military planner of the period would have been aware of the likelihood of 'Walcheren Fever' much less have made provision for it before the event.

That accepted, any degree of success depended upon the joint military and naval commanders effectively co-operating in perfect co-ordination without delay and in the absence of the caution that may have been appropriate in a campaign of longer duration. This simple requirement was demonstrably beyond their grasp to conceive or implement, though apparently it was clear to contemporary British commentators, for at the time an epigram began to circulate extensively enough to become well known.

> *The Earl of Chatham, with his sword drawn,*
> *Was waiting for Sir Richard Strachan:*
> *Sir Richard, longing to be at 'em,*
> *Was waiting for the Earl of Chatham!*

In the words of Alexander Fraser, the 17th Lord Saltoun:

> The French and Dutch strained every nerve to assemble a su-

perior force for the protection of Antwerp. Sickness of a most fatal description broke out in the British ranks, and the opinion of the seven lieutenant-generals of the army having been taken towards the end of August, further progress was decided to be impracticable.

Napoleon, as has been explained, left his marshals to prosecute the war in Spain, and found on his return to Paris that Austria was, indeed, about to resume hostilities. The emperor had, of course, lost none of his talent for the waging of war and beat his enemies at Landshut, Eckmühl, and Ebensberg and was, by mid-May, once more in Vienna. He crossed the Danube, but was beaten at Aspern-Essling, though not decisively, so he needed only to withdraw to the island of Lobau in the Danube. In early July of 1809, the French resumed the offensive and fought the Battle of Wagram. This was a bloody affair for both sides, but the Austrians were eventually obliged to retire.

The Austrians called for an armistice, which led to a peace treaty ratified in Vienna in October. The emperor had once again, for a time, prevailed and though the Austrians were temporarily cowed they were not conquered and that outcome in Napoleon's campaigns was becoming a perpetual problem to France. Napoleon's enemies were several, their resources massive and they remained prepared to oppose him. By contrast his allies were few. The allegiances of many of them were more compelled than willing and so begrudging in their affiliation. Others would eventually become disillusioned as they became aware that there was little substance to French promises. The War of the Fifth Coalition was over, but the glimmer of hope ignited in Spain had grown brighter at Aspern-Essling and so it was a certainty that before long hostilities would renew in northern Europe.

As for the Walcheren Expedition, it was unnecessary, ill conceived, poorly executed and would probably have brought few rewards of worth had it been successful. The high loss of life among British troops as a consequence of 'Walcheren Fever' served to transform a blunder into a tragedy.

Evacuation from Walcheren

CHAPTER ELEVEN

The Siege of Cadiz, 1810

The invasion of the southern provinces of Spain had been delayed for a time by Sir John Moore's diversionary tactics in 1808, though the value of those manoeuvres was demonstrably confined only to the period during which they were being carried out. The south of the country was spared again by Wellington's march towards Madrid after the Battle of Talavera but, once again, the subsequent British retreat into Portugal (where the Lines of Torres Vedras were soon to prove themselves an insurance policy more than worth the cost of its premium) cleared a way for the French, which they consolidated by defeating the Spanish Army at Ocaña, thirty miles south east of the capital, on the 16th of November, 1809.

If Seville was to fall, as surely it must since there was no force on the peninsula to oppose it, then the road for the French was open to the valuable harbour at Cadiz on the Atlantic coast. Though the fortress at Cadiz was ostensibly formidable, very few guns were mounted on its ramparts, whilst the garrison consisted only of a few thousand Spanish militia who were undoubtedly not equal to the task of holding the place against a concerted French assault.

Notwithstanding its indisputable vulnerability, the British had always been aware of the importance of preventing the French obtaining possession of the fortress and harbour of Cadiz, and so had sent General Sherbrooke there in the Autumn of 1808 with 4,000 men, and Major-General Mackenzie followed him with a brigade in February, 1809, but neither of these expeditions actually landed to take up the task, being recalled for the more pressing requirements of the defence of Portugal.

The situation was, on the face of it, looking grim for the allies in the Peninsula at this point for nowhere were their fortunes in the ascendant. Napoleon had been diverted from Iberia by the resurgent Austrians, but that matter, as has been explained, was now settled—at least for the time being. The emperor accordingly focussed his attention once again on Spain and Portugal making his intentions unambiguous by massively reinforcing the French presence in the theatre.

In 1810 Napoleon felt he was faced with two options for the direction of his principal offensive efforts in the region. The first was the subjugation of Andalusia and the second was to overwhelm Wellington's army and drive the British out of Portugal once and for all. He decided, probably correctly so far as he was in a position to judge the matter, to prioritise the first option since it represented the line of least resistance. The emperor calculated that the destruction of the British Army could be postponed until 1811, amply demonstrating (for the British Army) the legitimacy of the phrase, 'It is an ill wind that blows nobody any good'. Unfortunately for Napoleon's schemes, a Spanish general in Andalusia was about to display an act of good judgement and timely energetic resolution and the British general who would be required to do nothing, but obligingly await the hour of his own destruction was Wellington.

The French Army in the south of Spain was now under the command of Marshal Soult. Both Cordoba and Seville were predictably captured and Cadiz then appeared to be within his grasp. It seemed probable that the Spanish Army of the south was about to be driven into the sea, for the passes of the Sierra Morena had been forced at three points and the demoralised troops under Areizaga had dispersed or fled eastwards into Murcia. The Duke of Albuquerque meanwhile retreated westwards by forced marches and with 8,000-10,000 men threw himself into Isla de Leon, near Cadiz, in early February, 1810.

Marshal Victor however, was swiftly following the Spaniards, reaching Chiclana, within a few miles of Cadiz, only two days afterwards and on the 10th of February he summoned the town to surrender. That demand was promptly rejected, so the French began an investment, establishing lines which surrounded the bay. Rota, Santa Maria, Puerto Real, and Chiclana were fortified, and entrenched camps established in essential positions, the principal one being at Chiclana, near Barrosa. The First Guards would, in due course, take part in the long defence of Cadiz which lasted from February 1810 until late August 1812, becoming one of the most important sieges of the entire war.

A deep inlet of the sea, the Santa Petri, was the first Spanish line of defence; the second was the Isla de Leon, an irregular triangle, the apex called Torregardo, pointing to the city, the base resting on the Santa Petri, the right on the harbour, the left on the sea. The Isla, which was about seven miles long, and half a mile broad, was marshy, except a ridge four miles in length, on which the town of La Isla stood. A narrow isthmus about five miles long connects Cadiz with the apex, and across this isthmus was a cut called the Cortadura, defended by the unfinished fort of Fernando. Wellington expressed an opinion that, 'If the Isla was lost the town would not, and probably could not, hold out for a week'.

A tongue of land projected from the eastern shore of the harbour, and separated the inner from the outer harbour; this tongue was divided by a canal called the Trocadero and at the extreme point stood the fort of Matagorda, opposite to which, at 1,200 yards' distance, on the isthmus leading to Cadiz, stood a powerful battery called Puntales. From Cadiz to Matagorda was 4,000 yards and from Matagorda the French could completely command the upper or inner harbour, as well as the fort of Fernando. Wellington visited Seville in December, 1809, and had drawn up a memorandum advising the completion of the work on the isthmus about Cortadura, in order to secure the communication between the Isla and the town. He also recommended the construction of another strong work at the Torre d'Ercole (Torregorda).

On receiving information of the French advance upon Cadiz, Wellington despatched Major-General Sir William Stewart with 2,000 men comprised of the 79th, 84th, and 89th regiments to assist in its defence. This brigade arrived on the 11th of February, and was soon joined by a Portuguese regiment 1,300 strong. The British Government also decided to dispatch Lieutenant-General Graham from England with an additional reinforcement of 5,000 men, of which a portion of the Third Brigade of Guards under Major-General Dilkes of the Third Regiment formed a part. The remainder of the Third Brigade was to be left in England.

Early in March six companies of the Second Battalion, First Guards, under Colonel Sebright, and three from each of the second battalions of Coldstream and Third Guards, under Lieutenant-Colonel Onslow, left London for Portsmouth; embarked on board their transports and were landed at the Isla de Leon on the 24th of March, with the rest of the reinforcements under Graham, who immediately assumed the chief command in the Isla, where all the allies were quartered.

Fort Matagorda, which had been dismantled by the Spaniards, was hurriedly reconstructed to provide a serviceable defensive position, but after an obstinate fifty-four days contest, its isolated position revealed that holding it was untenable. At the end of April it was abandoned to the French, who promptly occupied it, but although they held the fort for over two years, were never able to make good use of it. The defenders were able in turn to constantly subject it to their own accurate and well-directed fire. The British force in Cadiz had been raised in July to 8,500 men, but in October, a hard-pressed Wellington sent for some of the regiments, reducing the garrison to 5,000 troops. Before the close of the year, however, it was again reinforced from Gibraltar and Sicily.

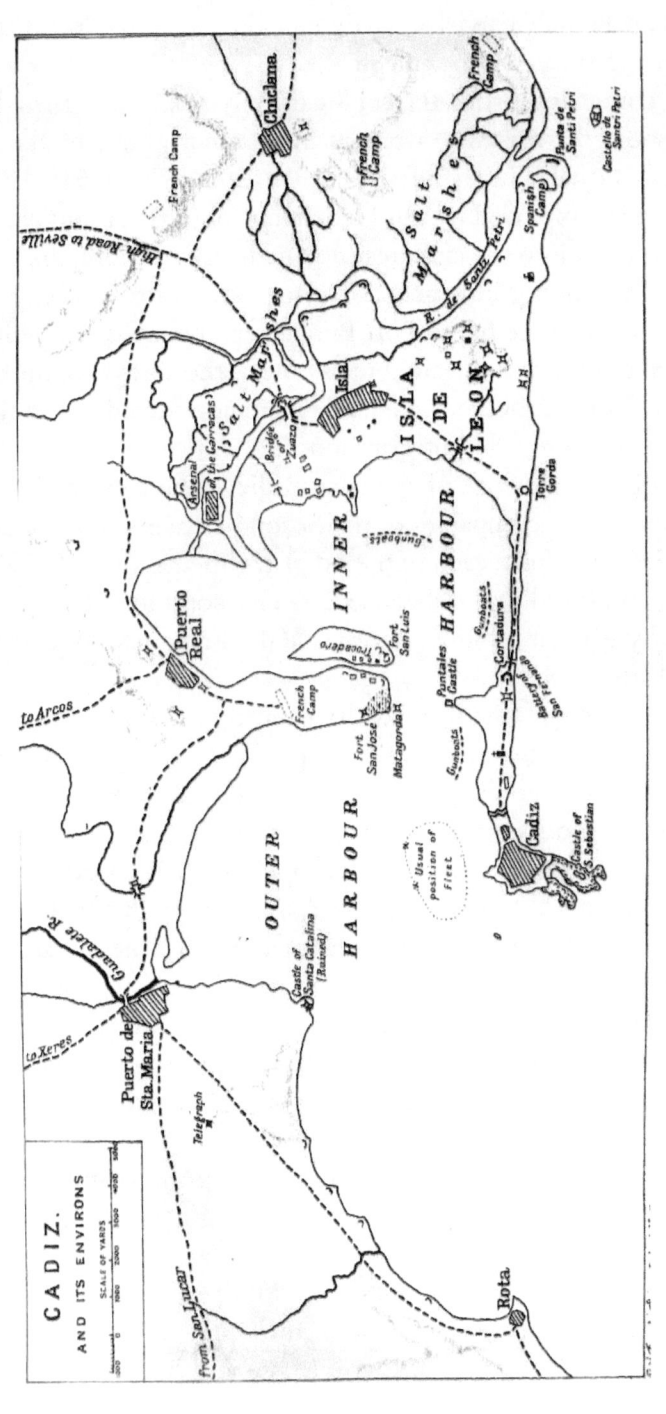

The French tried hard to conclude their assault, including from the water by the imaginative use of 130 gunboats which had come down the River Guadalquivir and had then been transported overland on rollers from Santa Maria to the Trocadero Canal. Huge mortars, which threw shells 5,000 yards, were also employed by the French, but only an occasional shell plummeted into the city, creating much alarm among the population, but doing little actual damage. Soult's first objective was to overpower the fire of Fort Puntales, and establish himself between the Isla and the city, but as long as the allies held the great redoubt of Cortadura, General Graham considered the communication secure from interruption.

This was the state of affairs at Cadiz at the close of 1810, in which the six companies of the Second Battalion, First Guards, besides three from each of the other regiments, all under Dilkes, were employed in the defence. The city continued to be accessible by sea, but on its landward side the French continued their blockade.

The French had opened the campaign of 1810 in June in Iberia by the besieging of the Spanish held walled towns of Ciudad Rodrigo and Almeida on the Portuguese border, both of which soon surrendered, and in September, Masséna, at the head of 60,000 French troops, advanced into Portugal. Wellington responded with a retirement which brought his forces to a strong position on the heights of the Sierra de Busaco. The French marshal engaged him on the 27th of September, but his attack was comprehensively repulsed and his troops driven down the mountain in a battle that, once more, pitted defensive line against attacking column, contributing to the catalogue of Wellington's triumphs fought, 'in the same old way'. Nevertheless, Masséna then succeeded in turning the British left, and Wellington continued his retirement towards his secure base of Lisbon.

On the 10th of October, 55,000 British and Portuguese troops passed into the Lines at Torres Vedras and defied the following French to breach them. Masséna examined every feature in the entire line of defences to discover a potential weak point but, so comprehensive were they, he found none. Weeks of impotent exclusion dragged by and the French position not only failed to improve, but grew progressively worse since the country had been laid waste to ensure the marshal could not benefit from it. His own army's supplies soon began to dwindle and, without the means to replenish them, hunger began its cruel work. Winter was approaching and with it came rain and outbreaks of sickness among the French troops. Accepting the inevitable, Masséna eventually turned away from Wellington's army, secure in its warm billets, and marched his own miserable soldiers into winter quarters in the vicinity of Santarem. The historian, Professor Charles Oman, suggested that from this turning point the fortunes of the French in Iberia were ever in decline and he wrote:

> The offensive power of the French hosts in Spain was spent; and it may be said that the retreat which began at Santarem only ceased at Toulouse.

Meanwhile far to the south, in the first weeks of 1811, the apathy of the Spanish authorities with regard to the siege of Cadiz remained conspicuous and while General Graham praised the exertions of the British engineers and soldiers who toiled to improve and extend the defensive works, he complained that the Spaniards, always in part the architects of many of their own misfortunes, endeavoured to prevent the execution of some of the essential measures required to secure the defence of the city.

CHAPTER TWELVE

The Guards at Barrosa, 1811

In January, 1811 the allied commanders attempted to force the enemy to raise the siege of Cadiz, encouraged by the absence of Soult and his Fifth Corps which had been diverted for the siege of Badajoz. The offensive plan required the creation of a combined force of Spanish and British troops which would embark on ships and land in the vicinity of Tarifa, behind the concentration of the enemy, so it could fall upon the rear and flank of the comparatively modestly sized French Army of the First Corps under Victor in camp at Chiclana.

Meanwhile, a Spanish force in the Isla was to throw a bridge over the San Petri and threaten the French lines in front. The allied force destined for this operation amounted to 14,000 men, of whom about 4,300 were to be British and allied soldiers including a component of Guards. In reality, the Anglo-Spanish Army was probably not quite large enough for the task in hand given an expectation of certain success.

The British contingent consisted of a battalion from Gibraltar made up from the six flank companies of 1/9th, 1/28th, and 2/82nd regiments of Foot, eight companies of the 28th from Tarifa, whilst Cadiz provided the Guards, the 2/67th and 2/87th foot, the flank companies of the 2/47th Foot, six companies of the 95th Rifles and two light companies of the Portuguese 20th regiment. The cavalry element was two squadrons of the excellent 2nd Hussars of the King's German Legion. Artillery support was provided by 10 guns under the command of Major Duncan and totalling about 4,314 men.

The Brigade of Guards, under Dilkes, 1,221 strong, with a detachment of the riflemen of the 95th regiment embarked at Cadiz, sailed to Algeciras, disembarked and marched westwards towards Tarifa on the 28th of February. Command of the British contingent was held by the able Lieutenant-General Thomas Graham who, (given the experiences of the past regarding cooperative efforts in concert with the Spanish Army), uncharacteristically and, as it transpired, unwisely waived claim to overall command of the operation. That responsibility was conceded, probably for the usual intangible political reasons given the disparity of numbers of troops from each allied nation involved, to the Spanish General, Don Manuel de la Peña.

The long column of the army advanced on the 2nd and 3rd of March *via* Casas Viegas and Vegas de la Frontera, and, with the Spanish element in the lead, about noon on the 5th of March reached the heights of Barrosa, which are situated four miles from where the River San Petri joins with the sea. The ridge of Barrosa stretched about a mile and a half from the coast, being bounded on the left by cliffs, on the right by the Forest of Chiclana, and in front by a pine wood. Beyond this there rose a narrow height called Bermeya, which could be reached by moving through the wood or along the beach under the cliffs.

The troops had marched twenty miles all through the night to reach their objective and were exhausted. La Peña, nevertheless, pushed forward sending the Spanish vanguard to the mouth of the San Petri, where it joined forces with the troops on the Isla. General Graham was then directed to follow the vanguard, but could immediately see the error of such a course of action and strongly advised La Peña against it, emphasising that since it was certain the enemy would imminently make an appearance, it was imperative that the British force take action to hold the commanding position of the ridge.

Graham was well aware that the advance of the Allied Army to its present position could not be a surprise to Victor who was, indeed, essentially waiting for the arrival of the Anglo-Spanish column to present him with his best opportunity to deliver a decisive attack. Neither force, likely to be brought to the actual battlefield, possessed an influential numerical superiority, though Victor could draw upon a further 6,000-7,000 men which were dispersed along his entire line. Furthermore, and fortunately for Graham, Victor had considerably over estimated the size of the Allied Army; an error which governed his own manoeuvres. Prudence, therefore, in every decision was essential to avoid a defeat which would inevitably be far more problematic for the Anglo-Spanish Army than for the French.

Graham's judgement, which transpired in every respect to be correct, was however, over ruled by La Peña and so in obedience to his orders Dilkes's brigade of Guards and Wheatley's brigade, marched off to the left in front and over the heights, leaving only the flank companies of the 9th and 82nd Regiments, under Major Brown, together with the baggage, in an untenable position on the hill and facing overwhelming opposition. Almost incomprehensibly, no sooner had Graham entered the wood than La Peña, having sighted and been overawed by a body of French troops on his flank, led off his Spaniards by the sea-road to San Petri leaving the Barrosa ridge unprotected and covered with baggage.

The French in the meantime were intently watching these movements from the Forest of Chiclana, and Marshal Victor, observing the opportunity presented by the separation of the Allied Army, promptly advanced onto the plain with 7,000 or more veteran soldiers and fourteen pieces of artillery. A Spanish guerilla guide informed Graham that the enemy were coming round the wood and were on the plain they had just quitted. The Brigade of Guards, under Dilkes, was immediately faced about. The Second Battalion, First Guards, which was in front, formed line to the right, the men filing into line under a galling fire as they came out of the wood. The three companies of the Third Guards, under Barnard, were formed in support in a second line, while Wheatley's brigade, with whom were the three companies of the Coldstreams, under Colonel Jackson, were told off to cover Duncan's guns, formed on the left.

When General Graham debouched into the plain, he discovered the high ground key of the position had fallen to the French, the Spanish rearguard in full-flight heading towards the sea and no sign at all of La Peña. The situation was demonstrably desperate, for the British force was not only isolated, but barely constituted half the numbers their enemy had the potential to deploy. Graham, whose instincts were always inclined towards the aggressive and, in any event, seeing no alternative open to him but to assume the offensive, rode forward and waving his hat, reportedly cried out to his troops, 'Now, my lads, there they are, spare your powder, but give them steel enough.'

Covered by the fire of Duncan's guns, the little army advanced. Dilkes, with the Guards and part of the 67th Regiment, forming the right wing, marched rapidly against the French General Ruffin's column, bringing up their right shoulders on the march, while Wheatley's brigade advanced against the right of the French under Laval. The Guards had to cross a deep hollow, under a severe fire, before they could close with the enemy. They came up its farther side in loose skirmishing order and, without stopping to reform, rushed up the hill and crashed into the French upon its crest where the fighting became severe and, for a time, the outcome indecisive.

Ruffin fell mortally wounded; Sebright, commanding the Second Battalion, First Guards, also wounded, was carried off the field, at which point Colonel Sambrooke Anson assumed the command of the battalion. Brigadier Dilkes had his horse killed under him, but the Guards and their comrades resolutely drove forwards delivering an 'incessant slaughtering fire,' of musketry from their line and driving the enemy columns before them.

Wheatley's brigade on the left was equally successful; a determined charge of three companies of the Coldstreams and Gough's, Irishmen of the 87th Regiment overthrew Laval's first line, driving the French 8th Regiment, whose eagle was captured by the 87th, upon their second line, whereupon the broken columns of the French began retiring from the field. They made one more attempt to turn, but Duncan's guns forced them to continue their retreat, and the British troops, who had been twenty-four hours without food, were unable from sheer fatigue to pursue them further. During the whole day 'no Spanish soldier fired a shot nor drew a sabre' to assist their outnumbered allies. This short but fierce battle lasted but an hour and a half, and in that time approximately 1,200 British and in excess of 2,000 French combatants were either killed or wounded.

The casualties in the Second Battalion, First Guards were two ensigns, two sergeants, thirty-one rank and file killed. One lieutenant-colonel, three captains, four ensigns, eight sergeants, 169 rank and file wounded; total, 216 casualties. The officers killed were Ensign Commerell and Ensign Eyre, acting *aide-de-camp* to Colonel Wheatley. Of the eight wounded, six were severely wounded namely Lieutenant-Colonel Sebright commanding, whilst Captains Stables and Colquitt were very severely wounded as were Ensigns Sir H. Lambert, Cameron, and Vigors. The detachment of Second Battalion, Coldstreams had three ensigns and fifty-three rank and file killed or wounded; Second Battalion, Third Guards, three officers, ninety-nine rank and file killed or wounded.

Brigadier-General Dilkes, commanding the Guards Brigade, afterwards made his report on the engagement and the following is an extract from it which describes the action from his perspective with the usual formality which disguises the extent of the achievement of the British force in gaining an incredible victory in the face of superior opposition.

> About two hours after the reserve had been ordered to halt in close column on the east side of the heights of Barrosa, on the morning of the 5th of March, I received Lieut.-General Graham's orders to proceed, together with Colonel Wheatley's brigade, towards Santi Petri—this was done, and the column began its march left in front over the height, and descending the other side entered a conifer wood, so thick as to be nearly impracticable for the guns and mounted officers. Having advanced about a mile, N. Reade, a staff-officer, overtook me, seeking General Graham, informing me that the enemy had made his appearance

on the heath or plain we had quitted; the deployment was soon after effected under all disadvantages (the detachment battalion forming a second line to the 2nd battalion of First Guards). At this time an application being made for a party to cover the guns, I sent three companies of the first-mentioned battalion for that service.

The line was advanced obliquely to the right, towards a body of the enemy already occupying the heights we had lately passed over, a heavy fire of artillery and musketry being kept up on both sides; but our line continuing to advance, I may say with distinguished gallantry, that part of the enemy's force immediately opposed to us withdrew towards another corps on his right. Our army still advanced, bringing up their right shoulder, and threatening his left, so that at last he formed that flank *en masse*, continuing his retreat down the hill, and ascending another rising ground, halting occasionally and keeping up a severely destructive fire. When fronted at one time, I perceived him push forward two or three divisions from the *masse* as I conceived, to charge our line, whose well-directed fire still advancing, obliged him to desist. Unfortunately, our men were so completely exhausted by their march, &c. &c., as to be quite unable to return the compliment.

That Graham had fought and won a gem of a battle which demonstrated the mettle of British troops under skilled leadership was beyond dispute. Wellington, who had a refined appreciation for a well-managed engagement, unreservedly declared 'admiration of the principle of the attack, and of the distinguished bravery which won the battle.' That having been said, there was never any point in an expedition from the besieged Cadiz, venturing out with all the risks that entailed, only to return to its lines without achieving its purpose which was to relieve the city by defeating the force which constrained it. That final outcome was the more galling not only because the affair had so closely come to catastrophe, but most especially because with the engagement of about one third of the available Anglo-Spanish force employed for the task it had, nevertheless, come so close to success.

Graham remained for some time on the heights waiting for

BATTLE OF BARROSA

La Peña, however despite all his urgent entreaties the Spanish general refused to send him cavalry reinforcements or even to take up the pursuit of the routed French force. Indignant and disgusted with the conduct of his ally, Graham at last led his own wearied troops to the Isla. La Peña came within the walls two days later and the two generals 'embarked on a campaign of intense wrangling' for all the good, after the fact, that could do. The hard truth was the expedition had the means within its grasp to wreck half the French lines, but had come back a failure having achieved nothing of value but military laurels for Graham and his soldiers. However, once again the British had been given a hard lesson on what they might expect (or not expect) when acting in concert with a Spanish Army in the field, and this fundamentally influenced the decision to take no further offensive action from Cadiz during the following months.

Shortly after the army returned to the Isla, Colonel Wheatley rejoined the Second Battalion, First Guards, and assumed the command, but owing to the severe losses it had sustained during the Barrosa expedition, it was ordered home. The third battalion of the regiment, commanded by Colonel G. Cooke, now completely recruited from the severe losses it sustained in the Corunna campaign and during the Walcheren fiasco, received orders in March to embark for Cadiz to relieve their second battalion comrades. With this battalion, Alexander Fraser, Lord Saltoun would return once more to the Peninsular War.

Six companies of the third battalion accordingly marched from London for Portsmouth on the 2nd of April, and disembarking at Cadiz on the 27th, occupied the St. Helena barracks. Two days afterwards General Graham inspected them on the glacis, at which point several men of the second battalion, who were selected to remain at Cadiz, were incorporated into the third battalion. The embarkation for England of the remainder of the second battalion, was delayed till the 4th of May,

The final four companies of the third battalion left London, embarking at Portsmouth on the 30th of May and, sailing in the middle of June, reached Cadiz on the 23rd. On their ar-

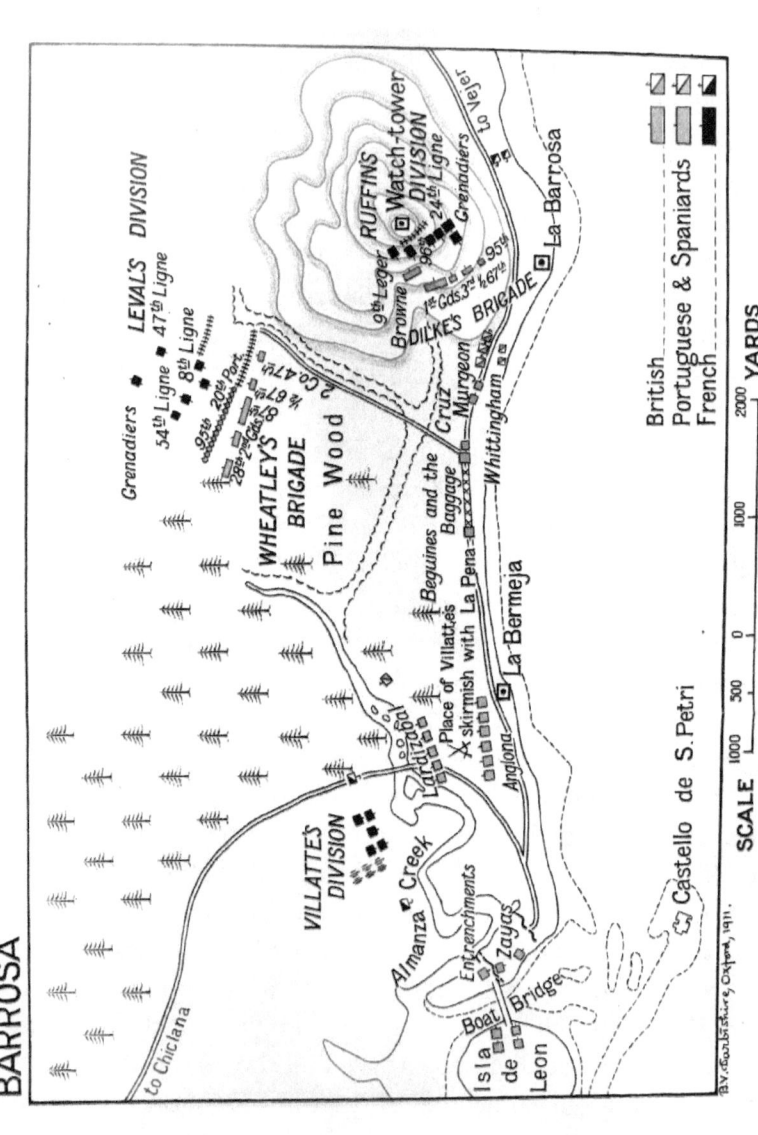

rival Colonel George Cooke, commanding the battalion, was promoted to the rank of Major-General, and placed on the staff, and Colonel J. Lambert took command of the third battalion. At the same time, Major-General Dilkes returned home. During the summer of 1811, Graham, was also removed to the command of a division in the field under Wellington, and was at first succeeded by Major-General Moore Disney, First Guards, but he then returned home in November, and the command at Cadiz eventually devolved upon Major-General George Cooke, First Guards.

Long unresolved sieges tend to become very dull affairs with little to do for the besiegers or the besieged. The duties of the Third Battalion, First Guards at Cadiz underwent very little variation in the course of the year. The construction of a redoubt was entrusted to them, for which purpose they found eighty men daily, while a detachment of seventy-five men, relieved weekly, was stationed at Cantera. The monotony of the siege was occasionally relieved by a bombardment from the French lines, but no attempt was made to storm the entrenchments. The siege of Cadiz became most problematic for the garrison in view of the continual friction that existed between the Britons and the Spaniards enclosed within the walls.

Lord Saltoun, who had arrived in the spring of 1811 with the third battalion, wrote a letter home from Isla de Leon, written 22nd of September 1811, in which he related an instance, from his perspective, of typical jealousy and misconduct on the part of the Spanish authorities.

> You say I do not send you any politics, the fact is there is nothing going on here but the old story; the Spaniards make no efforts themselves and lay all their losses to the fault of the English government and generals.
> Mutual dissatisfaction had been brewing a long time, but did not openly break out till after the Battle of Barrosa, in which, notwithstanding it was clearly proved that the English Army saved the whole of the Spanish Army and the Isla de Leon; notwithstanding that two of their own generals, namely, Sayis and Ladizabal, were so convinced that we had gained a com-

plete victory, that they repeatedly urged La Peña to advance on Chiclana; although General Graham offered to advance on Chiclana if they would support him, which they declined; yet the Spanish government countenanced a false account of the action, which was published by General Lacy, the head of their staff (a runaway rascal who had been turned out of the French service), in which he gives the whole merit of the action to the Spanish Army, denies General Graham's statement, and attributes the failure of the general plan to the ill-judged attack (as he calls it) that the English made.

This produced a correspondence between them, and General Graham obliged him to eat his words. Lacy had been put under arrest after the Battle of Barrosa, but, soon after this statement made its appearance, was reinstated in his rank and command; this of course created an open rupture between our heads of departments and the Spanish Government, which is likely to continue, at least as long as things go on in their present style.

The mass of the people and the army are with us, and if we were to offer them our pay, we might revolutionise the place in three days; but that is not our system. So much do the Spanish Government fear this, that false accounts are circulated, in order that the people may not be acquainted with the extent of their obligations to the British, and to excite, if possible, a jealousy between the two nations. They yesterday ordered away four thousand men, against which our minister remonstrated very strongly. Some of the troops, however, marched yesterday evening. Whether they will embark or not I know not, but if they do, our force will not be sufficient to defend the place, as our works are now become very extensive; but we must do the best we can, and I do not think the French will attack.

The reference to the apparently infamous General Lacy in Saltoun's letter is not without some interest. Luis Roberto de Lacy was the son of an *émigré* Irish soldier who had been in Spanish service. In 1811 he was 36 years old and serving in the Spanish Army in charge of a portion of the Cadiz defences. His career had, indeed, been chequered for he had fought against the French with the Royal Spanish Army, been jailed for duelling and maintaining a feud and dismissed, but then joined the

French Army serving with the Irish Legion.

He then deserted the French as they invaded Spain and rejoined the Spanish Army as a colonel. By 1813 he was Captain General of the Kingdom of Galicia. He opposed the return of King Ferdinand VII as an absolute monarch, after the end of the war in Iberia, following the king's *volte face* on the subject of a Spanish constitution, and in 1817, led one of the several failed coups. He was captured, sentenced to death and in July of that year executed by firing squad on Majorca.

The only other event of importance in this part of the campaign during this period was the defence of Tarifa in December, under Colonel J. B. Skerrett; Colonel Lord Proby, First Guards, being second in command. The successful result of this defence was mainly owing to the persevering skill of General Sir Charles Smith, of the Royal Engineers, which eventually caused the French under Victor to raise the siege of Tarifa, on the 4th of January, 1812. In the same month, an expedition under the command of Colonel J. Lambert, of the First Guards, was sent to Carthagena, though in April, he returned to Cadiz.

CHAPTER THIRTEEN

Operations in the Peninsula, 1811-12

Soult had captured Badajos from the Spaniards on the 10th of March, 1811, and Masséna was driven out of Portugal in the same month, but, upon hearing that Wellington had marched south, he advanced again to relieve Almeida, then besieged by the British. Wellington, however, suddenly returned and met him at Fuentes d'Onoro, which developed into a hard-fought contest in and around the village which, after two days, compelled the French to retire.

In the meantime, Marshal Beresford having invested Badajos on the 8th of May, Soult advanced to its relief, and Beresford encountered him on the 15th of that month on the ridge of Albuera, where one of the bloodiest contests of the war took place. The French were, however, defeated though at enormous cost. Soult now united his army to that of Marmont, who had superseded Masséna, and their superior forces compelled the British to raise the siege of Badajos. The French marshals, however, soon separated again, and during the remainder of the year, Wellington, manoeuvring brilliantly, maintained himself on the frontiers of Portugal. Soult returned to Seville, and General Hill, after surprising Gerard at Arroyo del Molinos, was left undisturbed in Estremadura.

Wellington invested Ciudad Rodrigo in the month of January, 1812, and after twelve days it was taken by storm. The truculent, General Robert Craufurd of the Light Division, so memorable from Moore's retreat to the sea was killed. Among

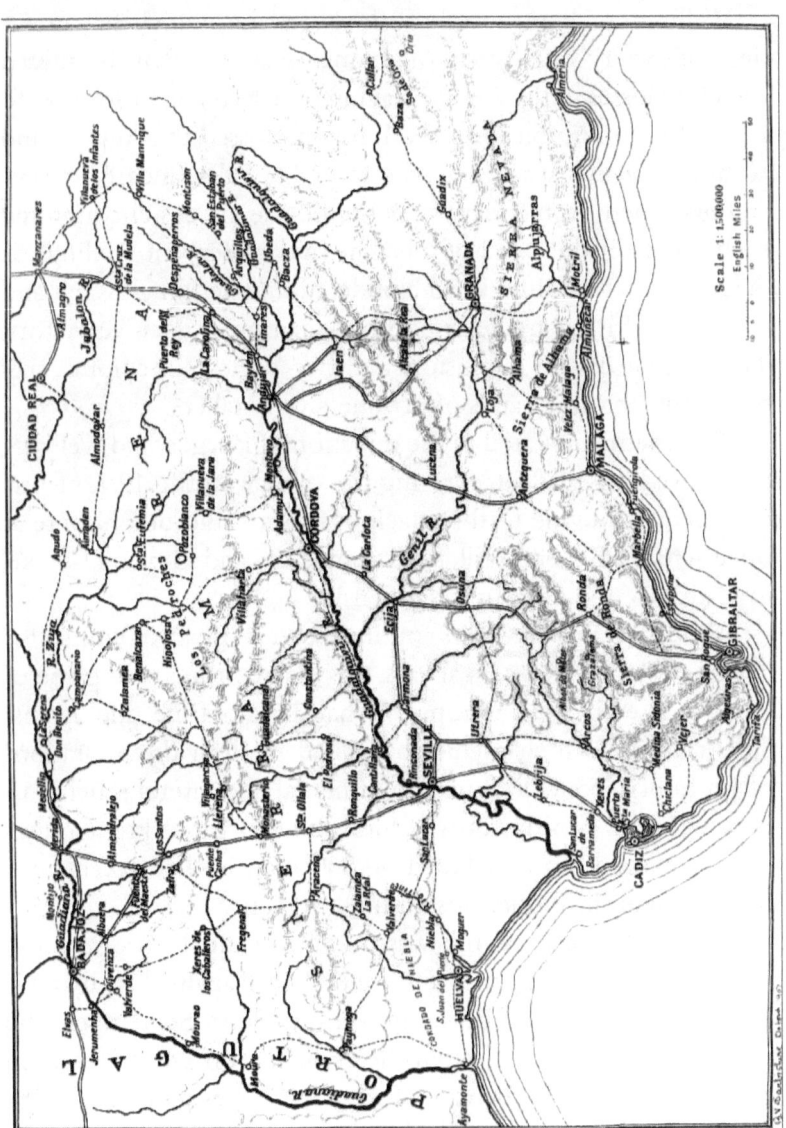

the officers of the Guards, Captain Hon. James Stanhope, of the First Guards, who, as *aide-de-camp* to Lieutenant-General Graham, was present at the siege of Ciudad Rodrigo, was wounded on the 14th of January.

Wellington then moved south to Badajos, which fell after a siege of twenty-one days, though once again the British suffered appalling losses in the assault. Having now two large fortresses to secure his communications, Wellington crossed the Agueda and advanced against Marmont, who retired to Salamanca. After several days spent in manoeuvring, the hostile armies encountered each other on the 22nd of July. The ever-observant Wellington, detecting that Marmont had blundered in extending his left and weakening his centre, fell upon him, gaining a decisive victory. The French fled in confusion, and two eagles, six colours, sixteen guns, and thousands of prisoners were taken.

The enemy retreated in the direction of Burgos, and Wellington moved on Madrid, entering the capital on the 12th of August, before moving to the attack of Burgos, and orders were at once sent to General Hill, in Estremadura, and General Cooke, in Cadiz, to now take up the offensive.

Whilst the war in Spain continued on its positive course for Wellington, Napoleon, as always, was playing the grand game of empires elsewhere in Europe. He had by this time, and against ardent advice which predictably failed to stem the aspirations of his hubris, conceived his monumental and fateful scheme to invade Russia. On the 24th of June, the enormous French host, which tellingly now included 30,000 men he had taken from the campaign in Iberia, crossed the Niemen.

The Battle of Smolensk was fought on the 16th of August, and the Russians doggedly retreated to stand again close by their capital at the Battle of Borodino on the 7th of September. The battle was a stalemate though the casualties on both sides were enormous, which in the case of the French was particularly significant for they were far from home and deep in the heartland of their enemy. The Russians once again retreated passing through Moscow, and, on the 16th of September, Napoleon slept in the

Kremlin palace, occupying a city which patriotic incendiaries forthwith transformed into a funeral pyre. As the emperor contemplated the price and value of his achievement in the heat of those flames, the patient Russian Army, as the winds of Autumn grew progressively more chill, awaited the perennial and familiar arrival of its most formidable ally.

CHAPTER FOURTEEN
The Advance from Cadiz to Seville, 1812

As Wellington was advancing into the heart of Spain, the defence of Cadiz continued. Whilst the city remained indisputably under siege, the denial of its harbour to the French meant that Cadiz was also making a positive contribution to the war effort, since it remained a viable entry point in southern Spain for both men and materiel to move directly into Andalusia. The French were compelled, therefore, to commit resources to the region, remaining on the alert for sudden developments at hand which also prevented them from sending reinforcements to Joseph in Madrid. On the 16th of May, 1812, the town was subjected to a serious bombardment from thirty French gunboats in the Trocadero canal. This bombardment against the town and shipping was repeated on the 4th of July, but attention to the siege for a moment became less of a priority for Soult, by the landing of troops from English vessels farther to the east on the coast of Grenada.

No change, however, took place in the respective positions of the besieged and besiegers at Cadiz until August, when, the bombardment became serious and opposition to British influence within the walls increased from all quarters. However, these matters would, before long, become irrelevant for the victory of Salamanca in July, and the subsequent occupation of Madrid by the British Army, shook French confidence, and made it necessary for Joseph, if he wished to save the throne of his new kingdom, to concentrate his armies of the North and South. Joseph, after retreating into Valencia, sent Soult orders to come with all his forces to the assistance of the Army of the Centre for the recovery of Madrid. Wellington sent orders, at more or less the same time, to General Cooke to make a direct attack upon the French lines round Cadiz.

Prior to these last orders having been received, Colonel Skerrett, who had held Tarifa, had been ordered to embark at Cadiz with 4,000 troops, and land on the coast to the north. Six companies of the Third Battalion, First Guards, under Colonel Peregrine Maitland, who was appointed second in command, formed part of this expedition. The detachment of Guards accordingly marched on the morning of the 9th of August from their old quarters on the Isla de Leon to Cadiz and embarked the same day. On the following morning the expedition sailed for Huelva, on the coast, seventy miles to the north-west, arriving there in the middle of the night of the 11th.

Saltoun was of course, serving with this battalion in Cadiz and so took part in this joint expedition under the Spanish General Cruz Mourgeon and Colonel Skerrett which occurred in conjunction with Wellington's movements in central Spain, and with the eventual intention of joining with Hill's division, which was operating to the south of Wellington's advance upon Madrid. During the day the troops were put into boats, and after thirty-six cramped hours spent in them, the Guards were landed at Huelva on the night of the 13th whilst the rest of the army and its stores were landed on the 14th and 15th. The British element consisted of the Guards, the 87th and the 20th Portuguese Regiments amounting to 800 men. The Spanish force added a further 600 troops.

On the 16th the troops began their march up the country towards Seville, threatening the French lines of communications round Cadiz on their way, and, after halting that night at Trigeras, moved on the following day, to Niebla. Skerrett expected to make contact with the French in Niebla which was supposedly occupied by the enemy, but the place was discovered to be deserted. So, he continued his march on the 18th and 19th through Palma to Manzanilla, where the troops rested until the 24th. From Manzanilla a detachment of the Guards and others were despatched at eleven at night with instructions to attack the enemy known to be at St. Lucar la Major, near Seville (this enemy force was estimated to be about 350 cavalry and 200 infantry) and this assault was carried out successfully, driving in its outposts and pushing the enemy, 'through the streets with precipitation leaving some killed, wounded and prisoners', to quote Skerrett's report, without any loss to the attackers.

Soult by this point had no alternative but to abandon the siege of Cadiz, and on the 25th of August, after destroying the immense works at Chiclana and the Trocadero, as well as many guns, and a vast amount of stores, he retired, moving off in the direction of Seville. The blockade by land, which had lasted upwards of two and a half years, was finally at an end.

Skerrett's corps meanwhile, including the six companies of the Third Battalion, First Guards, under Maitland, preceded by the light company of the Guards, under Colonel Colquitt, with some hussars of the King's German Legion, marched all the night of the 25th from San Lucar, and reached the heights to the north of Seville on the following morning. They came in contact with the advanced posts of the enemy about three miles from Seville, drove them in, and about seven in the morning (Skerrett's report says it was the 27th) moved to the attack of the city. Seville is situated on the south bank of the Guadalquivir, and the allies approached it from the north, through the suburbs of Triana.

The Spanish element was directed to turn these suburbs on the right flank, while the British and Portuguese attacked in front. The British column advanced for more than two miles at the 'double-quick' and were, at the point of the bayonet, just in time to drive the French from the defence of a principal gateway and bridge of Triana as they were attempting to destroy it. As soon as the Spanish column had reached its appointed objective, the British cavalry and artillery advanced at a gallop, followed by the grenadiers of the Guards with the remainder of the infantry bringing up the rear. The bridge was damaged, but not sufficiently so to prevent the grenadiers of the Guards, preceded by the Spanish troops, who led the column, from passing over it. For a moment the attackers were checked by a heavy fire of musketry and grape in the streets, but they renewed the advance driving everything before them. Meanwhile volleys from the flanking columns made the enemy's position on the other side of the river untenable. The enemy's forces, which consisted of eight battalions and two regiments of cavalry, retired hastily and disorganised down the road to Cordoba, leaving behind them 200 prisoners together with all their baggage and valuables.

Colonel Skerrett's despatch stated:

> The conduct of every officer and soldier has been above praise. Where all have behaved well it is difficult to distinguish. I must, however, mention the detachment of the King's German Legion, commanded by Cornet Wiebolt; the artillery, by Captain Roberts; the detachment of the 95th, by Captain Cadoux, and the grenadiers of the First Regiment of Guards, by Captain Thomas. To Colonel Maitland, First Guards (second in command), I am much indebted, from the commencement of this service; and in the attack of Seville his military talents, intrepidity, and zeal were particularly conspicuous. I am also much indebted to Lieutenant-Colonel Colquitt, commanding a detachment of the First Regiment of Guards.

The captain of Rifles, Daniel Cadoux became famous in the annals of the 95th for his intrepid defence of a bridge across the Bidassoa in 1813 known as 'The Combat of Vera', when a company of seventy riflemen under his command held off Clausel's escaping rearguard under General of Division, Vandermaesen. Realising he was vastly outnumbered Cadoux called for support, but this was denied and he was ordered to retire. He ignored this order, fighting on doggedly until attrition wore down his little command. Vandermaesen and Cadoux both lay dead at the close of the action and the officer, by this point a major-general, who failed to support him was the same man who had once sung his praises at Seville. Skerrett was replaced by Colborne and whilst commanding a brigade during the assault on Bergen-op-zoom in 1814 he was killed in action.

Saltoun kept a diary of this period which has survived and his own annotations of his experiences during the month of August 1812, obviously echo the historical record, but carry an immediacy of personal experience:

> *24th.*—Marched with a detachment at eleven at night, and attacked the enemy's outposts at San Lucar le Major, and drove them in with little loss on their side, and none on ours; distance four leagues.
>
> *25th.*—Fell back one league; took post near a river in the rear of San Lucar.
>
> *26th.*—Marched at five in the morning with the hussars to make a reconnaissance; the troops joined us next morning.
>
> *27th.*—Marched with the whole of the force towards Seville, fell in with the enemy at his advanced posts at Castellega, one league from Seville, drove them in, and about seven in the morning advanced to the attack of that place; distance of march four and a half leagues. The British column advanced for more than two miles at double-quick, and were just in time to drive the enemy from the bridge with the bayonet, as they were trying to cut it; at ten we were in complete possession of the place. The French force was eight battalions of infantry and two regiments of cavalry, commanded by Victor; ours consisted of 3500 Spaniards under Cruz Mourgeon, and 1500 British, with three six-pounders, under Colonel Skerrett, and the place was only carried by the rapidity of the British advance, which terrified the enemy.

The remaining four companies of the Third Battalion, First Guards, under Colonel Lambert, left the Isla on the 1st of September marching by a direct route for Seville though halting at Xeres, a few miles from Cadiz, until the 6th, as they waited for the infantry brigade under Lord Proby to join them. On the 7th, after a twenty-seven mile march over level country, but under a punishing burning sun, the command arrived at Utrera,

BATTLE OF SEVILLE

a day's march from Seville, where, on the 11th, the four companies were joined by the six companies of the battalion that had entered Seville on the 27th of the previous month.

These six companies, after halting four days in Seville, marched to nearby Alcala, where they remained till the 7th of September, when they moved for two days to Mayrena, returning on the 9th to Alcala, and on the 11th, after another short march, they joined their other four companies at Utrera. While the Third Battalion, First Guards remained in this town, the riflemen of the 95th and part of the artillery were stationed at Alcala, and the cavalry, the 47th and 87th British, and 20th Portuguese Regiments, and a brigade of guns remained at Headquarters in Seville. Colonel Colquitt, who had been severely wounded at Barrosa, unfortunately died of a fever brought on by fatigue while the battalion was at Utrera.

After a week's halt, the battalion received orders to join Wellington's army in the north of Spain so it moved to Seville on the 19th, and after again halting some days, Skerrett's brigade began its march on the 30th for Truxillo, passing Los Santos, Villafranca, Guarema, and Medellin. On the 11th of October they halted at Mayados, and next day at Truxillo, arriving at Talavera by Almarez on the 18th of October.

CHAPTER FIFTEEN

The Siege of Burgos and the Retreat, 1812

Wellington's talents, in many respects, epitomised the definition of military expertise of his time. Perhaps most importantly, like Marlborough, he was often able to prevail irrespective of the obstacles and difficulties with which he had to contend. These obstacles would include the limitations of his own resources of every kind to the behaviour of his unreliable allies, as well as the unambiguous intentions of his enemies. In the field, when able to manoeuvre, his efforts, supported by his brilliant little army 'that could go anywhere and do anything', were invariably met with qualified success if not, in every case, with an outright victory. It was well that Wellington possessed military genius, for he was invariably outnumbered in the Peninsula which made it essential that he chose his engagements with care, for his lines of communication and supply were long and he could not afford a contest of attrition.

The reduction of walled towns and citadels in this campaign was necessary, but these were perpetually problematic for the British Army. An assault required a concentration of suitable artillery, facilitated by a sizeable train and the skills of engineers, (all of which were in very short supply) and a commitment to the expenditure of seasoned troops that Wellington knew he could ill afford to lose for they were not readily or reliably replaceable.

Ciudad Rodrigo and Badajoz had both been bloody examples of the cost of assaults on formidable defensive works and by mid-September, 1812, the fortifications of Burgos now stood in Wellington's way, for he believed it must be captured before he might safely pursue the French into Alava or Navarre. Furthermore, the decisive outcomes of his most recent successes meant that the French armies had consolidated into two dangerous masses. Soult, Suchet and Joseph had between them in excess of 130,000 men available for deployment. Once again, Wellington had to face the reality that with approximately 60,000 men as his disposal he could not afford to face such overwhelming numbers were they, or even a superior portion of them, sent in his direction.

The siege of Burgos lasted just one month from September 19th to October the 19th and was according to the historian, Professor Charles Oman, 'the most unfortunate operation he (Wellington) ever conducted'. Burgos, though small, was deceptively strong, whereas the materiel and personnel, as Wellington well knew, that could be brought for the attack was insufficient for the task, most especially in a dearth of heavy artillery. The transport needed to bring guns and their ammunition to the front was in particular short supply. Nevertheless, the assault commenced, but though some of the outer works were taken, four attempts to storm the castle failed. To their credit, the French made a determined defence of the place which resulted in time wasted for the British force (which was of necessity stationary), but which was time well spent in reorganisation and concentration elsewhere in preparation for an advance by the enemy.

Accordingly, King Joseph and Soult's forces, marched with 60,000 men on Madrid and towards Hill's inferior detached command, from the direction of Murcia, in the south-east, while simultaneously Souham was marching to relieve Burgos, at the head of a host comprised of the Armies of Portugal and the North. Wellington may well have been persuaded to fight Souham, were it not for the certainty of Hill's destruction by Soult.

The impossibility of that option meant it was imperative that the British Army be reunited at the earliest opportunity.

The retreat from Burgos had commenced on the 22nd of October; on the 24th the army halted behind the confluence of the Carrion and Pisuerga Rivers, and while in this position, the First Battalion, First Guards, under the command of Colonel M. C. Darby Griffith, joined it from England.

★★★★★★

The first battalion had returned home after the Walcheren campaign, in 1809, and on the 7th of September, 1812, it marched to Portsmouth, embarking on the 13th aboard the *Alfred* man-of-war, bound for Corunna, where after an easy passage it disembarked on the 26th of the same month. It had been originally planned, after the raising of the blockade, that the Third Battalion, First Guards should sail to Lisbon, with the other troops that had been employed in the defence of Cadiz. Having arrived it would be brigaded with the first battalion which would arrive, also at Lisbon, from England. However, as described, Wellington subsequently ordered the third battalion to depart Cadiz by land and join the army in the field, and in consequence the first battalion was sent to Corunna as its point of entry into the theatre. The 91st Regiment, 950 strong, was to be temporarily brigaded with it, and placed under Lord Dalhousie, while a draft of 250 men for the several battalions of Guards already in the Peninsula was to accompany the expedition.

Wellington wrote to Lieutenant-Colonel Bourke, on the 21st of September:—

> Sir,
> I wish the First Battalion, First Foot Guards to move through Gallicia, as already arranged; but, instead of turning off from the high road at Villa Franca, as directed when the enemy was in possession of Astorga, and it was supposed they would maintain that position, I wish them now to proceed to Astorga on to Benavente.
> Mr. White must make provision for them till they will arrive at Benavente. At Benavente, or before they will arrive there, a staff officer of this army shall meet them, and they will receive

further orders for their march.

The messenger who takes this has a letter from the quartermaster-general, for the commanding officer of the First Battalion, First Foot Guards, of which I enclose a duplicate, in case there is any mistake about that with which he is charged.

We took by storm on the 19th the outwork of the Castle of Burgos, with some loss.

I have, &c.,

Wellington.

The First Battalion, First Guards having landed at Corunna, marched by wings on the 30th of September, crossing over the battlefield which was painfully familiar to many still in the ranks. It halted at Lugo on the 5th and 6th of October, and was at Astorga on the 16th. The castle there had been destroyed and much of the town levelled with the ground including the chapter-house which lay in ruins. The cathedral had also been severely damaged. On the 19th the column reached Benavente, which had shared much the same kind of destruction. The battalion arrived at Ampadia, on the 23rd of October and on the following morning it was on the march for Palencia, at which time the commanding officer learned that Wellington was retreating from Burgos, and that the enemy was in close pursuit.

✶✶✶✶✶✶

Following the line of the canal to Duenas, the battalion eventually joined the main body of the British Army, where it bivouacked, with the rest of the division of Guards, on the right of the line. No sooner had the first battalion joined the main army, than it came in contact with the French. On the following morning, now part of the First Division, the battalion marched to the left to support the Fifth Division, who were engaging the enemy as it attempted to cross the Pisuerga River.

On the following day, the 26th, the retreat was continued towards Valladolid, the First Division halted at Cabeson. On reaching Valladolid, on the 29th, the news arrived that the French had crossed the river at Tordesillas, whereupon the First Division was sent to oppose them. Wellington had intended to await the arrival of Hill's corps, in a strong position, between Tordesillas and Rueda, but on the 6th of November the army fell back again to San Christoval, seven miles north of Salamanca. The First Division moved to Villares de la Reyna, within three miles of the city.

******

While these events were in progress, Skerrett's little army, including the Third Battalion, First Guards, moved from Talavera de la Reyna on the 19th of October, and marching due east by Toledo, reached Puente Largo near Aranjuez on the 26th, where it fell in with Hill's corps, which, since the Battle of Salamanca, had been occupied in opposing the return of King Joseph and Soult to Madrid. The Guards were removed from Skerrett's command, and attached to the Fourth Division, under Cole, forming part of Hill's corps.

The notes from Saltoun's journal reveal that this junction had barely taken effect before the enemy made its appearance and fighting ensued

> *26th.*—To the park at Aranjuez, four leagues, there had been an alarm during the night, and General Hill had ordered the bridge to be destroyed. Bivouacked. The park very fine; a number of trees planted in avenues, but marshy.
>
> *27th.*—Halt; the enemy made his appearance in front of Aranjuez.
>
> *28th.*—The enemy occupied the town and gardens of the palace, on the opposite side of the Tagus.
>
> *29th.*—Retired at one in the morning over the Jarama River, and took post on the Madrid road, in rear of the Puente Larga, which we were preparing to destroy. In the evening marched to Cien Pozuelos, one league.
>
> *30th.*—The enemy attacked Puente Larga, the mine of which failed, and were repulsed with loss by the 47th regiment.
>
> Joined headquarters as orderly officer.

The historical record of this period corresponds with Saltoun's brief notes. In consequence of the raising of the siege of Burgos, Hill was now, by order of Wellington, making preparations for a retreat from the advanced position he had occupied, and the outposts of the Fourth Division (which was selected as his rear guard) were, on the 27th of October, engaged with Soult's advance on the Jarama. Hill decided, in order to protect his retreat towards Wellington's army, to blow up the bridge across the Tagus at Puente Largo, and the Third Battalion, First Guards was tasked to cover this operation by holding any interference by the enemy in check. The engineering work, as usual owing to a lack of equipment, progressed slowly and on the 29th the third battalion was relieved by Skerrett's brigade, consisting of the 47th and 87th Regiments, and marched to Cien Pozeulos (Ciempozuelos), south of Madrid.

On the 30th the enemy attacked in force, and the attempt to blow up the bridge having failed, the French tried to carry it at the point of the bayonet, but were vigorously repulsed by the 47th Regiment. However, Nature was about to break the impasse in the favour of the French in ways no one could forecast.

Over the next twelve hours, a sudden fall of four feet in the depth the River Tagus made the fords across it once again practicable to effect a crossing without reliance on the bridge and the British position became untenable. The division continued its retreat without delay, marching all night towards Madrid and halting outside the city.

On the 1st of November, General Hill destroyed his stores and blew up the Retiro palace which had been put to use as barracks and an arsenal, and on the same day, the Third Battalion, First Guards, still forming part of Cole's rear guard, marched through Madrid, and halted on the 2nd at Alvara. The French Army entered Madrid as soon as it was evacuated.

Saltoun accompanied Hill's headquarters to Aravaca, and to the Escurial, on the 4th. The battalion crossed the Guadarama mountains, and onwards through the province of Old Castille, and across the Tormes River, to Espinar, Lavajos, and Villa Nueva de Gomez, where on the 5th November Saltoun rejoined his battalion, which retired to the heights of San Christoval, in the vicinity of Salamanca, on the 9th November, just one day after

Wellington with his army had reached them.

Saltoun noted in his journal the astonishing distance he and his men had travelled since coming ashore from the boats at Huelva.

> 9th.—Marched in the afternoon to Salamanca, and were quartered in a convent. The first time we had been under cover, except at Cien Pozuelos, since we left Añover on the 26th October. Distance marched from Huelva 636 miles. Joined Lord Wellington's army, which had retired here from Burgos.
> With Wellington's army the battalion retreated through Ciudad Rodrigo, Gallegos, and past Fuentes d'Onoro, until the 8th of December, when the troops went into cantonments, and the Guards were quartered in Viseu, Mondeo, and Spraida. Had at this place marched from Huelva 800 miles, computing the Spanish league at four English miles.

On the 11th, the third battalion went into cantonments at Aldea Seco, about three miles from Salamanca, having marched 640 miles from Seville, and here the first and third battalions of the First Guards again met and were brigaded together. The Brigade of First Guards, and the Second Brigade, consisting of the first battalions of the Coldstream and Third Regiments, was now formed into a division.

Major-General H. F. Campbell, of the First Guards, who had formerly commanded the Second Brigade, was promoted to a Division, and Colonel Hon. T. Fermor of the Third Regiment, was placed in temporary command of it until Major-General Hon. Ed. Stopford, also of the Third Guards, could take over. Major-General G. Cooke, of the First Guards, had been ordered to remain for a time at Cadiz. Major-General William Wheatley, who had commanded a portion of the Guards at the battle of Barrosa, died at the Escurial on the 1st of September and the command of the First Brigade of Guards, (first and third battalions First Guards) went to Major-General K. A. Howard, of the Coldstreams.

The united British Army now mustered an impressive 64,000 men and seventy pieces of artillery, but it was pursued by the combined three French corps with in excess of 95,000 men with 120 guns. During the whole war the French had never before gathered so large a force upon a single line and it presented an intimidating prospect. Wellington turned at bay momentarily on the night of the 13th to 14th of November. The Brigade of First Guards, and the rest of the First Division, under Sir Edward Paget, took up a position on the Arapiles, near Aldea Tejada, to secure the passage over the Zurgain, but nothing came of it.

Soult, however, pressed on, always turning the allied right, passing three divisions over the Tormes, and threatening the allied communications. Wellington, after destroying his stores and banking on the inability of his pursuers to maintain the chase for much longer, retreated further to Valmuya.

On the 17th the First Division halted at San Munos, on the Huebra, where to the relief of all concerned, the active pursuit of the French ceased from 'a dearth of provisions and the effects of miserable weather'. The French also were, in fact, in a desperate state of exhaustion, and were in no better condition than their quarry. On the 18th the fugitives marched on by very bad roads to San Spiritus. On the 19th they arrived at Ciudad Rodrigo and on the 20th, the First Guards, passed through it, crossing the Agueda. The first battalion was then cantoned at Carpes, and the third battalion, after an arduous march, arrived at Gallegos, near the Portuguese frontier.

This retreat from Salamanca, though it has been given far less retrospective consideration, bore more than passing similarities to Moore's retreat to Corunna, for its demands had been very severe, and the army was utterly exhausted. The weather had now broken as the winter months progressed, the rain fell in torrents and thick mists regularly obscured the way. The column churned the ground into a quagmire so that the troops could hardly move as the roads were transformed to ribbons of mud.

Saltoun wrote in a letter home an anecdote of this period which, with the benefit of retrospection, has an element of humour to it which was probably absent at the time these events occurred and to those who were involved in it.

The British Army on the march in Spain by Thomas Rowlandson

When on a march, I generally carried a large and strong umbrella. It served for a walking-stick, and as I had coated it with oil varnish, it was waterproof, and many a wetting it saved me. Upon one occasion, however, it took revenge for all its previous benefits. We had halted after dark in ploughed land, on the steep slope of a hill, and tired as we all were, it was impossible in the dark to attempt to better our position. The men settled themselves to rest as best they could. It was raining heavily, and blowing hard; but, fortunately, the drift was down the slope of the hill, and I therefore sat down, with the umbrella over my shoulders, to pass the night.

A brother officer sat down between my knees, and another took a similar position between his knees, all three more or less sheltered by the umbrella. After moodily chatting a while we dropped off to sleep, but how long we slept I cannot say, I only know that I was suddenly roused by the most unpleasant hip bath I ever got: the rain water descending the hill side had been dammed up in the furrow, above where we sat, by the edge of the umbrella resting on the ground; some movement of mine, in my sleep, must have raised it, and the water rushed down upon us, drenching me and the one next to me up to the waist, but our friend below did not escape even so well; in his sleep he lay down, and the rush of water took him in the nape of the neck, and went right through him from head to foot. Three such miserable wretches, as we were till morning broke, were never seen.

The soldiers of the rank and file, as usual, fared poorly on the retreat for they were frequently under arms for long periods without rations. So hard pressed were they, that meat, when it was available at all, was eaten half-cooked from the embers of their camp-fires and, at times when no provisions were brought up at all, they were reduced to eating boiled acorns as a substitute for bread.

In the field, British soldiers of the time had demonstrated that they were incapable, in extreme circumstances, of self-control or collective responsibility and for that they cannot be blamed, for the ruling classes (which embraced many officers of the army) had, in the main, little faith in them and believed that the only way to control the lower orders was to hold them strictly in check by the disciplines of fear of punishment.

The British oligarchy, in turn, were fearful of the power of the masses for they had seen mobs of the disaffected running riot at home in recent years. Rebellions of disaffection in Scotland were still considered probable and garrisons were positioned to repress them should they arise, whilst affairs in Ireland were in seemingly perpetual foment. These anxieties became more acute within the age of revolutions which appealed to the oppressed, especially as the fruit of that tree was Napoleon's army. Parliamentary reform demonstrations which occurred in England in 1819 resulted in civilian deaths and reinforced all prejudices including, no doubt, those of the Duke of Wellington.

During hard retreats or costly assaults when the leash of discipline was loosened or irrevocably lost, the 'dangerous and unruly beast' was bound to shake itself free, for the army had no solution to restrain it before the fact. There was, furthermore, no institutional will to countenance systems to foster self-reliance and initiative, nor were measures instituted which would avert dire consequences when order was tested to a potential breaking point. That initiative was needed for most (if not all) the regiments of the army, as was the creation of effectively functioning essential support services. Both would come about much later, but in the meantime those who could readily understand that the way to improve a horse was not to neglect it then beat it ever more severely, could not countenance that the same principle could be applied to a man.

So inevitably, as the conditions of the retreat from Burgos worsened there came a point when discipline broke down and straggling became ever more prevalent. Hundreds of sick and exhausted men were left behind to perish or to fall into the hands of the French, whose inclinations to be merciful were inconsistent. At the point that men concluded they must ensure their own personal survival, all the constraints that bound them were abandoned to the necessities of the moment and so rapacity, marauding, and the usual degradations ensued. Wellington issued severe orders to recover discipline and a memorandum of censure, attributing the rank and file's conduct to the inattention of their officers, though he had been as impotent as had Moore to avert an issue he knew was certain to arise. He never received an epiphany on the matter to the end of his days, for he was no reformer. In fact, these kinds of occurrences only confirmed Wellington's reactionary convictions, though to be fair to him, once the army was in the field *sans* reform the die was cast.

The soldiers of the Third Battalion, First Guards had the advantages of veteran campaigners, having spent an extended period in the field, and were in a fine state of discipline to cope with the hardships that came their way. Since leaving Cadiz, on the 20th of August, the men had been constantly on the march, a distance of 650 miles. The problems arising from a breakdown of order which beset the army did not generally apply to the Guards or to the Light Division. It had been so during Moore's retreat and so it was again on the retreat from Burgos and these exceptions were, as a matter of record, not a surprise to Wellington. One may speculate that these troops, who suffered equally with no preferential treatment, had the greatest sense of their own identities creating an *esprit de corps* and self-worth which positively influenced their behaviour. Perversely, the fine examples of these paragons served as a double-edged sword as regarded addressing or ignoring the fundamental issues that beset the army.

CHAPTER SIXTEEN

The Decline of the Empire of the French, 1812

Despite the ostensibly disappointing end to the campaign, the net results of the year 1812 for the allied cause in the Peninsula for Wellington and his army were most satisfactory. Professor Charles Oman summarised it thus, 'Though the French had reoccupied Madrid and Toledo, they had been compelled to evacuate all of southern Spain. Estremadura, Andalusia and La Mancha had been completely freed from the invaders; and the casualties inflicted upon the imperial armies had exceeded 40,000 men. They were now thrown upon the defensive and had lost confidence in their ultimate success.'

Nor was the situation in Iberia the limit of Napoleon's problems. His vainglorious campaign to invade and humiliate Russia and its monarch had been over reaching in its aspirations and had gone disastrously awry. The emperor, in the early part of October, recognising that he had over played his hand and that he had brought his army very far from friendly territory was trying to induce Emperor Alexander to open negotiations which would lead towards an unchallenged withdrawal, but no reply was given to his proposals. The Russian Army knew that time was on its side and was waiting to fall upon the forlorn French with all its forces, as soon as they should begin to retreat.

As winter approached Napoleon left the Kremlin in Moscow on the 20th of October with 100,000 men and 600 guns. A battle was fought at Milo Jaroslovitz, in which the French remained masters of a ruined town, but still threatened on both flanks, they were forced to continue their retreat. By November the Russian winter set in with its usual vengeance, snow fell to blanket the landscape, winds howled through the forests and temperatures plummeted. The French Army staggered westward, poorly clothed, short of provisions, rarely able to find shelter and all the while the Russians gnawed at the enormous, but ever depleting column like wolves upon the trail of a herd.

The emperor was at Smolensk in early November and, with the Old Guard, quitted it by the middle of the month. He left the remains of his army at Smorgoni early in December, and, travelling night and day, arrived in Paris on the 19th of the month. When the French rearguard left Russian soil on the 14th of December, the army which had marched towards Moscow some 685,000 strong had, according to legend, been reduced to just 22,000 bedraggled survivors Allowing for considerable disparity of opinion on that matter and even discounting the multitude of civilian camp followers who had perished along the way, it was indisputable that the magnificent *Grande Armée* that had marched to the east under its eagles had effectively ceased to exist.

******

After remaining for eight days at Gallegos, close to Ciudad Rodrigo, Wellington's army continued its retreat towards Portugal, and the First Brigade of Guards, marching on the 28th to San Pedro and Val de la Mula, and passing the site of the Battle of Fuentes d'Onoro, eventually crossed the frontier.

Saltoun in a letter to his mother of the 26th December, wrote that the likelihood of his return to England to take his seat in the House of Lords as one of the Representative Peers of Scotland depended upon whether military operations would begin early in the following year or not.

On Sunday, the 29th December, the Third Battalion, First Guards was quartered at Medo, and the first battalion, after crossing the River Coa, reached Castello del Mendo. Thereafter, the two battalions advanced by easy marches to Lamegal, Alverea, Francesco, Aguiar de Beira, through Asamel, Villa Formosa, and Tugal; and finally, on the 8th of December marched into winter cantonments. The first battalion took up residence in Viseu and the third battalion was allocated to Mondao, Spraida de Rondio, and adjacent villages.

Here the brigades, after their recent sufferings and hardships, were able to enjoy a period of rest from their labours. Saltoun had come to the end of six years of soldiering with the First Guards against Napoleon's French Army and on reflection it had not been a period that had involved him in much military success, for he had taken part in two terrible retreats, a disastrous blunder of a campaign in the Low Countries and had been incarcerated behind the walls of besieged Cadiz for months. Whilst his regiment had the battle honour of 'Barrosa' to its credit he had missed the battle, for he was with the third battalion in London. Nevertheless, the tone of his communications was never less than confident, positive and animated. He wrote a letter to his mother during this rest period on the 10th of January, 1813.

Nel Spraida, Portugal.
10th January

My Dear Mother,
I have no news, and very little to write about, but as Tuesday is our post-day for England, I just send you a few lines to say we are all going on well, and as comfortable as we can expect to be. Lord Wellington is daily looked for from Cadiz, and when he arrives, we shall probably take the field, or soon after, as our pressing the enemy here will keep up the spirit in Russia more than anything else, should Napoleon determine to try another campaign in the north. Besides there is no reason why our cavalry should not eat the green forage in Castille, instead of the enemy's, as by this means the harvest in this country will be saved to the people, which otherwise must be consumed when green by our cavalry, should we remain in our present cantonments.

I do not think I shall go to England if I can avoid it. In the first place, I cannot stay with you more than three or four days consistently with my own opinions as a military man; moreover, as I must travel with the greatest expedition, it will cost me between two and three hundred, which I have many other ways of disposing of, although none that would give me so much satisfaction.

Macdonald is here, and begs to be kindly remembered to you. He wishes you would do him a favour, which is to thank Mrs. Montgomery in his name for the music which she sent him. I do not know if you are acquainted with her, but she is the mother of the Miss Montgomerys who dance French country dances.

It is at present a hard frost, and we have turned one of our landlord's windows in the principal *Sala* into an excellent fireplace, to the great annoyance of the landlady; however, when we are gone she may return it into a window, and the *Sala*, which in our opinion is much improved by it, will not then have suffered in hers, and it is easily done, for glass is not a necessary article to a window in this country.

If any friend is coming out to join the regiment, pray send me some snuff; but it is no use sending it to Lisbon, as it is as difficult to get anything from thence to the army on a private account as it would be in England to transport Somerset House all standing to Aberdeen.

    Love to William (*his brother*) and the girls.

    Your dutiful son,

                                   Saltoun.

The First Division of the British Army now consisted of the First Brigade of Guards, under Major-General Howard and the Second Brigade of Guards, under Major-General Hon. E. Stopford. Also included were two other brigades, consisting of the first, second, and fifth battalions of King's German Legion, under Major-General Lowe and first and second King's Light German Legion, under Colonel Halket, all under Lieutenant-General Hon. Sir William Stewart. Captain Carey le Marchant, of the First Guards, (eldest son of John Le Marchant, one of the finest cavalry commanders of his day, who was killed at Salamanca the previous year) was appointed *Aide-de-Camp* to the Lieutenant-General. Carey Le Marchant was seriously wounded at San Sebastian and died at St. Jean de Luz shortly afterwards.

The First Brigade of Guards had not been long in their winter quarters before the reaction from hard work to repose produced widespread sickness, and a low fever broke out amongst the men. Within a few days of their arrival at Carpes and Gallegos, nearly 700 men were declared sick out of a total of 2,541 men, while there were only 176 effective reinforcements available attached to the second battalion in England to make up the shortfall. Shocking though this was, the Guards fared better than the army taken as a whole wherein 18,000 men were sick to 31,000 effective, or about two to three, while one regiment had above 700 sick and 500 effective.

The light companies of the First Guards presented a very great contrast in health to the rest of the army. The light company of the third battalion, which included Saltoun, quartered in advance at Spraida, covering the rest of the army since the 12th of January, had retained its health and at the beginning of February had only eight men on the sick list. Sickness, however, generally persisted throughout the winter months and only partially improved by the warmer weather of approaching Spring so the battalions of Guards were, on the 18th of February, removed to the neighbouring villages in the hope that they might become healthier. The change of scene did nothing to improve the situation, so at last they were ordered to Oporto, about sixty miles away on the coast, in the hopes that the sea air might bring the troops back to health.

On the 8th of February Saltoun once again wrote to his family and within his letter, perhaps inevitably, made reference to his concerns about the sickness which had struck the Brigade of Guards. Interestingly, in the same letter, he passed comment on the criticisms Wellington had made about the conduct of the army during the retreat from Burgos and Salamanca. It is quite apparent that Saltoun was very annoyed at Wellington's high-handed allocation of blame to regimental officers and that Saltoun believed, with some justification perhaps, that responsibility ultimately lay with the person in the position of most authority. It is clear that Saltoun understood that the key to the maintenance of order lay in ensuring that the basic needs of the troops in the logistics of provisions, elementary requirements of subsistence and transportation for the sick and wounded were available and maintained at all times.

> I am very sorry, but not surprised, at a certain letter having crossed the Atlantic; it should never have gone beyond the orderly books of the army, . . . and it is foolish for a general to abuse his army for disorders arising from the want of a proper commissariat, which Frederic the Great says it is his first duty to provide.
>
> It is no excuse for him that there is no wood in a country, but it is a very great one for a soldier pulling down a house to cook his provisions with the materials; and in everything, when one disorder is permitted, another will soon creep in upon the heels of it.
>
> I do not mean to say that the army was not in a very bad state, but every man knows, who has ever seen an army, that such must be the case, if that army be ill supplied with bread; and the saddle should always be put on the right horse.
>
> To say nothing of the hardships of the first part of the retreat, which were tolerably severe, the commissary might, and ought to have been at San Muños with a supply of bread for the army; we should then have had ample means of carrying the wounded and those men who were unable to march from fatigue, and their number would also have been very much lessened by the seasonable arrival of the bread, which would have enabled many to go through the very severe march we had from that place, for an extra half pound of over-driven beef is a very poor substitute for a pound and a half of bread, especially when that is issued for three days running.

Saltoun, in common with many other good officers, resented Wellington's censure. In measure, he felt the understandable sting of personal criticism with regard to the discharging of his duty in circumstances which he felt he could not control and secondly from the feeling that it was unjust to blame the soldiers for the disorder caused, in particular, by the failures of the commissariat. That Saltoun had a reasonable point there can be no doubt, but whether his suggested solution would have actually provided a remedy to all the army's ills under all of these kinds of circumstances remains moot for the societal influences that created the nature of the soldiers of Wellington's army were several and deep rooted.

Nevertheless, Saltoun had every reason to feel affection for and faith in his own guardsmen and this would have fundamentally informed his opinions. One cannot take the contents of the following extract from one of Saltoun's letters home as necessarily typical of the relationships between officers and their men of every regiment in the British Army of the period, but it does speak to the quality of the Guards of all ranks and underlines the veracity of the often quoted Biblical quotation from Galatians, 'Whatever a man soweth, so shall he reap'.

> We had been marching (during the retreat) through difficult country, and on very bad roads, when, upon the halt for the night being ordered, we officers of the light company had the unwelcome intelligence conveyed to us that although the rations for the men had arrived all right, our mule, with all our supplies, had broken down some miles to the rear, and that we were in consequence supper-less.
>
> As we were very hungry this was far from agreeable, and we sat down under a tree in no very cheery humour; but after a while were roused by the approach of the senior private of the company.
>
> He carried a mess tin in each hand, which prevented him from saluting; but his words were very much to the point, 'Gentlemen, the men are very sorry to hear as how your mule has broke down and you ain't got no supper, so, says we, let's each give a little bit of our own, and it's in these here tins, and we hope you'll take it, gentlemen.'
>
> Take it! we were only too glad to get it, and capital it was; but the circumstance showed what care soldiers will take of their officers if they like them, and I especially noticed that the oldest private was the spokesman, and that none of the non-commissioned officers were asked to interfere in what was an affair of kindly feeling, and not of duty.

The brigade broke up from its cantonments on the 26th and 27th of March, and on arrival at Oporto, on the 1st of April, occupied the St. Ovadio Barracks. The sick moved on the 7th by Lamego and Rego on the bank of the Douro, and down to Oporto. The numbers of men in hospital steadily decreased, but the effective strength of the First Brigade of Guards, was still very low, the first battalion having only 355 men, and the third battalion 430 men, fit for duty.

Chapter Seventeen

The Remote Courtship of Lord Saltoun, 1813

Saltoun obtained a leave of absence and returned to England where, however, he remained only a few weeks before sailing on about the 11th of April from Falmouth to rejoin the army in Spain. However, this visit, though short in duration, proved to be one of the most important interludes of his life, as he then made the acquaintance of the lady who would become his future wife, Catharine, one of the three daughters of the late Lord Chancellor, Edward Thurlow, 1st Baron Thurlow, who had died in 1806 never having been married. The peculiar spelling of Catharine is confirmed as correct since it appears on Saltoun's letters to her.

As Saltoun was about to return to the peninsula he wrote a letter to Catharine Thurlow, and of course, in this correspondence quite another tone appears compared to the letters he had written to his family. It appears from the contents of this letter that the developing romance was an event that both Alexander and Catharine accepted was best kept a secret at that time (and for the foreseeable future) from Saltoun's mother, Lady Margery Saltoun, and we may readily speculate, given Saltoun's position and times, why that may have been the case.

His reference to Lady Lansdown(e) in this letter, probably concerned a ball or *soirée* to which he and Catharine Thurlow had both been invited. Their hostess would have been Lady Louisa Lansdowne, who was the wife of Lord Henry Petty

Mary and Catharine Thurlow as children

who had been Chancellor of the Exchequer following Pitt, the younger. The simple fact was that Saltoun heartily disliked society occasions of this kind and often made excuses to avoid attending them.

Falmouth,
Friday night, 10 April 1813.

Dear Miss Thurlow,

Was ever anything in the world, my dear Miss Thurlow, half so provoking?

The mail has just this moment come in with an order to detain the packet till tomorrow, so that after all I might have remained in town another night, and gone to Lady Lansdown's; not that I myself had any wonderful inclination to wait on her Ladyship or the amiable Miss Giffard—for I could have passed the evening much more to my own satisfaction in Grosvenor Street—but you wished me to stay for it, and that is quite a sufficient reason for regretting I did not.

I believe the packet was detained in consequence of a dispatch, which I met between Bagshot and Egham, and which most probably brought some letters that it was necessary to answer immediately. I had a great mind to return when I found out that it was a dispatch from Falmouth; but as it might have been from America or any other place, as likely as from Spain—which I had then no means of ascertaining—I was obliged to proceed, doubting all the way, and now find that I might have returned without risk.

I have just written two long letters to her Ladyship (*his mother*) on business, and after sealing one of them, and just as I was going to send it to the post, I by accident looked at the seal. I had put more wax on than I generally do, and in pressing my own seal some of the wax had risen from the corner, and had taken the impression of your cipher so perfectly, that I thought her Ladyship had seen that seal so often that she must have known it again; at least I should anywhere. I thought it a lucky chance that had made me look at the seal, and with a dab of hot wax blotted it out. It will, however, make me more careful in future. This is a horrible dull place—nothing in the world to be seen except the surrounding country; but that I am well acquainted with, as I was here three weeks once. And moreover, it is horribly ugly. But I am telling a bit of a story, for I see they have got the invisible girl here, and I believe the actual one that we went to see in Leicester Fields. Do you remember that? It was before you left St. James' Square.

When I was here before, there was a play, a tolerable good set, but the waiter—who, by-the-by, is a Methodist, and a rank one—told me that a play-house was Satan's ground, and that the people of this town would not countenance such profane works. I told him they were a parcel of d— fools, but could not convert him for all that.

By this time, I dare say, you will be tired of reading, though in this instance, on my honour, I am not tired of writing, for I *must* think, and so it is easy work to write, even although it is nothing but nonsense, and shall not therefore venture to read it over. Pray tell me how Lady Lansdown's went off, and if my mother was there. If you write me, direct 1st Guards, 1st Division, British Army, Spain.

God bless you, my dear Miss Thurlow, and believe me ever yours,

Saltoun.

Saltoun's letter to Catharine Thurlow, written and posted immediately prior to his sailing for Portugal was followed by another written after his arrival in Lisbon. It is not difficult to appreciate how a young man with romance primarily on his mind would feel the compulsion to write more frequently than had been his habit. The tone and content of this letter is accordingly light-hearted and full of gossip intended to entertain his lady, as one might expect. The A.D.C or *aide-de-camp* referred to in the letter was James Hay, the son of William Hay, 17th Earl of Erroll.

He was an ensign in Saltoun's regiment and in 1813, just 16 years old and had lost his mother in the previous year. In this letter we discover he was acting the *beau* to a young lady at a society ball. He would also attend the Duchess of Richmond's famous ball in Brussels given before the Battle of Waterloo. The duchess's daughter, Georgiana later wrote that, 'he was a dashing, merry youth full of military ardour, delighted at the idea of going into action and all the honours he was to gain'. Tragically, however, he was shot and instantly killed as he rode at Saltoun's side in the battle at Quatre Bras.

Lisbon, Portugal,
1st May 1813.

My dear Miss Thurlow,

I have now, my dear Miss Thurlow, been here ten days, and am as heartily sick of the place as ever I was of anything in my life; it is certainly, take it altogether, the dirtiest town that ever a man got into.

Tomorrow I leave this to proceed to Oporto, where my regiment is now stationed, which place I shall reach on the 10th, and I understand we are likely to march from thence, in order to take the field, about the 12th, when the work for the year will begin.

I have been detained here waiting for some things that were left behind by my servant's negligence, and which came by the last packet. By the same conveyance I was given to understand that the A.D.C., Lord J. Hay, has had the supreme felicity of succeeding me in Mrs. B.'s good graces, and had the honour of starting Miss Di. at the second ball; but I strongly suspect, from the wording of said information, that poor I was again to have been brought forward, which would have been rather too much of a good thing, and too much, they say, is good for nothing. Had I remained, which—not on that account—I now regret I did not, I might, you know, have got tipsy and forgot it, or perhaps, indeed I may say more likely, Grosvenor Street might have seen me instead of Portman Square.

How fond the world is of manoeuvring, while we poor devils have not the credit of even the slightest penetration. Since I have been here, I have gone through the regular forms of the place, dined with all the great people, been to some routs and to one ball—a most Hottentot concern. Fancy a parcel of people, whom God never meant to be active, striving to dance Scotch reels, while the fiddlers were doing their best to play them as like waltzes as the music will admit of. I was obliged to perform in one not to seem fine, and that I thought was quite sufficient. They are certainly the most humdrum set I ever met with; very different from Spain, equally depraved, but do not carry it off so well.

This is opera night here as well as in London. I do not know if you have been there; I, you see, have not, for by this time it must be over in both places; but I have been, if not more usefully, at least more agreeably employed. Since I have been quartered in an excellent house, and as accident would have it, it stands on the Monte de Santa Catherina, so you see my saint does not forget me even in this country.

I mean to go to Oporto by Cintra and Mafra, both which places are well worth seeing, and perhaps I may not again have such a good opportunity of going to them, and from time to time, if you do not prevent me, I shall give you an account of my peregrinations.

It is now very late, though I believe I have left you later; but as I have a long way to ride tomorrow, I must go and get some sleep: so goodnight, my dear Miss Thurlow, and believe me ever yours

S——

By the middle of the month of May, Saltoun had travelled as he had intended to Oporto to rejoin his regiment. As one may readily expect, Saltoun was still taken with his burgeoning romance with Catharine Thurlow and had received a letter from her to which he hastened a reply. The reader will discover the usual reports concerning pleasurable distractions, but the losses among the troops from sickness were demonstrably of concern to Saltoun and he makes reference to them within this letter. He also reported that although the army was taking to the field, the Guards were, for the time being to stay in Oporto.

Oporto, Portugal,
14 May 1813.

My dear Miss Thurlow,

Yours of the 20th April I received the morning after I wrote you. The packet came in during the night, and as I expected I should hear from you I was determined not to leave Lisbon till the letters were given out, and should have answered you sooner, but from the road that we came by not being the one of communication, I was obliged to wait till I came here, which I did yesterday; and as you assure me you will not tire of reading whenever I write, depend upon it there is nothing next to hearing from you that gives me so much pleasure as writing to you.

I was obliged to leave off writing to go and fire a salute in honour of the Prince Regent of Portugal, it being his birthday; but it is of no consequence, as I find this letter cannot go before Tuesday next, which is our post-day for England, and as this is Friday I shall at all events have time enough to finish it.

The general orders for the commencement of the campaign are arrived, and the divisions will march to their separate points in a few days. Lord Wellington has, however, determined not to move *us* for the present, and they say it will be a month before we begin our march.

We are certainly much better, and the men begin to look something like soldiers again, but it is shocking to think that since the month of December last we have buried eight hundred men out of two thousand, that is three hundred more than had died when I left the Brigade to go to England, but I am happy to say we have lost no men during the last three weeks, and those that are still in hospital are in a fair way of recovering; but, however, this is all Greek to you.

This is a fine large town, much cleaner and better in every respect than any place I have yet seen in Portugal, and the people have been very civil to the officers, and have given them a number of balls and other entertainments. We are to have a grand ball tonight, but I have not determined as yet whether I shall go to it or not; and if I am in the same mind after dinner that I am at present, I shall certainly not go to it, for just now I have not the slightest inclination. We have also a theatre where they act Portuguese plays, and I believe sometimes an opera, which last may be tolerable; but as to a play it must be but a very moderate performance, at least cannot have much to amuse an Englishman who does not understand ten words of the language.

And so you were disappointed in not hearing from me on the Monday after I left: I own you had hit the day off cleverly enough, and I had intended my letter to have been in town that morning; but although I knew that the mail-coach left Falmouth at three in the morning, I did not know that the post-office closed at ten at night, which was the reason you did not hear before Tuesday.

My tent and everything that had been left behind came to Lisbon a few days before I received your letter, and I have got them with me, and the only thing I now wish is that I may not be long without an opportunity of using them, for it is very provoking to be kept hanging on in this place when the army moves, as I could have passed the same time so much more to my satisfaction in England. You say it is not fair to trouble me with cross-writing; all I can say is that, as long as the writing is not cross, I do not care how much cross-writing there is: I shall not, however, give you any more of it at present, but leave what is not already crossed in case anything should happen before Tuesday.

Last night I went to the ball, which was really a very good one; two sets of about thirty couple each, and some tolerably pretty women. I find everybody here can speak French, and most of them English.

I have just got my papers from England, but no letters from home. I see your name mentioned as a dancer at the Miss Pritchards' ball in Green Street; was it you or your cousin? The people appear to be quite mad about Cossacks, and the Princess of Wales—certainly the people of England are, without any exception, the greatest fools in the world. I must own, however, I should like to see this Don Cossack myself, for if he is anything near the description of him, he must be a very fine fellow.

By this time, you must be heartily tired of deciphering this scrawl. I long to hear from you, and believe me I remain affectionately yours,

Saltoun.

P.S.—James Macdonald, whom you know, left this yesterday for England.

(This final note refers to the son of Lord Macdonald who was also an officer in the First Guards, killed at the disastrous assault on the French garrison at Bergen-op-Zoom in 1814.)

At the end of May, Major-General Howard, the brigadier, was promoted to the command of the First Division and Major-General John Lambert succeeded him in the command of the First Brigade of Guards. Major-General Disney, third major, continued in command of the Home District.

The main body of the army took the field towards the end of May. At that time the First Brigade of Guards were beginning to recover from the fatal sickness which had ravaged it and the men began again to look like soldiers. Since the month of December, the deaths had been averaging four or five per day. Given these severe losses it was decided to leave the brigade at Oporto some time longer. By the month of July, the First Guards had actually buried, since the beginning of the year, 800 out of 2,500 men.

In Saltoun's letter to Catharine Thurlow, sent in the middle of June he once again focused on the lighter aspects of his time in Portugal, but he also informed Catharine that he knew the time was approaching when the Guards would march to join the main army. In this estimation he was entirely correct, for nine days later on the 24th of June, the regiment received orders to take the field.

Oporto, Portugal,
15th June 1813.

My dear Miss Thurlow,
I did not write you by the last packet, for the post leaves this place on a Tuesday, and last Tuesday was the day before our grand ball which we gave the natives, and as I had been named as one of the committee for conducting the said ball, I had so much to do that I had not time to write.
It went off with great *éclat*, and, thank God, is now over, and what is not the worst part of it, *paid for*. You may guess the crush and trouble in this place—where there are no Mr. Gunters—in getting together the necessary apparatus for giving a hot supper to three hundred and fifty people, and the drill that was required previously to instruct the servants how to put the supper on the tables; but, however, we got them tolerably expert before the day, and it went off very well.
This place is just beginning to be hot, but I believe they never have any heat here equal to what it is to the south of Spain; however, I hope we shall not remain here to try.
We are now as strong as we shall be this year, and daily expect our order to march for the army, which is by this time near Valladolid; we had letters from it the day before yesterday. The 10th Hussars were engaged near Tordesillas, and defeated the 22nd and 23rd French Cavalry, with great loss on the part of the French. Ours was slight; one officer and seventeen men killed,

and Captain Loyd wounded and taken, but left behind on his parole. This is the second time the cavalry have been engaged since the beginning of the campaign, and they have conducted themselves very gallantly on both occasions, which is a good thing, as last campaign they were rather in the background.

The principal lion here now is a man whose name, I believe, is Pearson, and he is a Pat, (*Irishman*) but he calls himself an Italian, and says his name is Personi. He certainly is a wonderful strong man. He walks about with ease to himself with seven men on him, and for his benefit, which takes place this week, he is to carry eleven; but the most singular thing that he does is, he puts a man on a cross, the pole of which is 12 feet long, and balances it on his chin. I confess I have no wish to be the man on the top of it.

I have this moment got a letter from Eleanor, (his sister), by which I find my mother is still at Brompton. She says you are well. I hope to date my next from some place up the country.

Adieu, and believe me yours ever,

S——.

The action that Saltoun referenced in his letter was a cavalry skirmish known as, 'The Battle of Morales de Toro', fought on the 2nd of the month. It took place north of the town of Toro which sits upon the Douro some distance east of Tordesillas. The 10th Hussars were in company with the 15th and 18th Hussars and their opponents were actually the French 16th and 21st Dragoons, under General of Division, Digeon. Though the forces were evenly matched in numbers (about 800 each,) the affair was a running battle in which the French were harassed severely suffering 200 casualties for just 18 British hussar troopers killed. One officer was also killed and two were wounded- one of them taken prisoner, presumably the Captain Lloyd, Saltoun mentioned.

Chapter Eighteen

The Investment of San Sebastian, 1813

Wellington's main army, as previously indicated, took to the field whilst the Guards remained, for a period of time, in Oporto to recuperate from the devastating effects of the sickness which had significantly reduced their numbers.

Wellington initially decided to operate upon the French right, by marching through Tras os Montes in the north of Portugal. An army corps of five divisions, 40,000 strong, under Lieutenant-General Sir Thomas Graham, formed the left wing and crossed the Douro, reaching Braganza on the 22nd, May. Wellington advanced with 30,000 troops on Alba and Salamanca before turning north, uniting the two armies at Carcagales at the close of the month. The Spanish host under Freyre (Freire de Andrade y Armijo) likewise joined this principal force creating an Allied Army on the right bank of the Douro of 90,000 men and 100 guns. On the 4th of June, Wellington ordered its advance towards the frontiers of France.

Joseph Bonaparte was standing at Valladolid with 52,000 men and 100 guns, but could not long hold his positions for Wellington, by continually demonstrating towards his left, compelled him to withdraw. The rapid allied advance put the army at the Carrion on the 7th of June and five days later in sight of Burgos. The castle there was destroyed by the French before they promptly retired, anxious to place the defile of Parnorbo between themselves and the allies, but Sir Thomas Graham acting on the left, and marching by a route previously regarded as impracticable, crossed the Ebro at Frias on the 15th, and getting into the rear of the French right, cut them off from the coast. Wellington had gained a new base of operations on the sea, and the British fleet entered the harbour of Santander. The First Brigade of Guards were ordered to move up to the front at this point.

Sir Thomas Graham drove back Reille's corps, and on the evening of the 20th he halted at Marguia. Wellington gained a decisive victory over Joseph at the Battle of Vittoria on the 21st of June. For the French the defeat was cataclysmic. Professor Oman wrote:

> The defeated host had to retreat by the only route left to them, a rough mountain track to Salvatierra and Pampeluna, unsuited for the passage of an army encumbered with heavy impedimenta. The king had with him not only a vast train of artillery, but a great convoy of Spanish refugees—his partisans from Madrid—and countless carriages and waggons laden with treasure, pictures, state archives, and valuable property of all sorts, the accumulated spoil of six years of conquest. The whole of this heterogeneous mass of vehicles was thrown upon the narrow Pampeluna road, and hopelessly jammed within a few miles of its starting-point.
>
> The defeated army abandoned everything and fled over the hillsides. In actual casualties it had not lost heavily—some 6,000 killed and wounded, and 1,000 prisoners (of the 65,000 total); while the Allies had 5,000 men *hors de combat* (of the 80,000 total). But the French had saved nothing but their persons; the whole equipment of the army of Spain was captured by the victors, 143 guns, 500 caissons, nearly £1,000,000 sterling in the military chest, besides several thousand carriages laden with valuables. Seldom has an army shared such plunder as fell to the Allies that night. Thus, the vanquished French host reached Pampeluna in complete disorder.

Clausel and Foy retreated and, after throwing a garrison into San Sebastian, crossed the Bidassoa into France. Graham invested San Sebastian on the 9th of July, and on the 24th made an attempt to storm it, but the assault failed with heavy losses.

Soult arrived from Germany to take command of the French Army, and reorganised his forces advancing to attempt to turn the British right, relieving Pampeluna. Wellington converted the siege of San Sebastian into a blockade, met the French, and, after a series of combats which lasted from the 25th to the 30th of July, carried the position in front of Sorauren, forcing the enemy to retreat, and on the 2nd of August the French were driven across the frontier into France.

The siege of San Sebastian, following the initial reverse, was renewed, but hostile fire was not opened until the 26th of August. By this time the First Brigade of Guards arrived on the scene of action, and on the 18th of August marched into camp, joining the First Division.

******

Leaving Lieutenant-Colonel Tinling at Oporto in charge of the sick, the First Guards, under the brigade-command of Major-General Lambert, began its march on the 29th of June, passing through Amarante, Villa Beal, Mirandella, Braganza and arriving at Palencia, on the 23rd of July. The men were in good health, marching well and not a single man was left behind.

From Palencia, instead of following the direct road to Burgos, the column took a northerly course, through Saldana to Reynosa and by Medina to Osona. The way was strewn with traces of the retreating French, and after marching over the battlefield of the 21st of June, the regiment passed through Vittoria. On the 10th of August it halted at Zobrano, and on the 11th passed by the Puerto de Francia, which contained a park of all the French artillery pieces, two hundred and ten guns, captured in the recent battle and during the subsequent retreat.

In his next letter to Catharine Thurlow, Saltoun's tone gave the impression he was somewhat 'war-weary' and, if this was the case, it is unsurprising for he had recently completed a long march to arrive at the site of a recently fought major action. The town of Vittoria was full of wounded—some of them Saltoun's personal friends and he also commented that there had been hard fighting in the mountains. It is noteworthy that Saltoun did not appreciate on this occasion (comparatively uncharacteristically given his usually astute and accurate appreciation of developing events) that the French were in irreversible withdrawal, since he appeared to have the expectation that the tide of the war would turn once again following a French counterattack designed to force the allies back into Spain.

Saltoun's report of the death of Cadogan was substantially accurate. The 71st Regiment of Foot was a Scottish Highland regiment that had been reformed as light infantry in 1810. Henry Cadogan fell, aged 34 years, as his regiment stormed the heights above the village of Puebla on the French left during the battle. He was a personal friend of Wellington and had fought a pistol duel on Wimbledon Common with Henry Paget, subsequently the Marquess of Anglesey (commander of cavalry at Waterloo), because Paget had engaged in an adulterous affair with his sister Charlotte, who was at the time married to Wellington's younger brother.

Durada,
13 August 1813.

My Dear Miss Thurlow,

We marched into this place yesterday, which completes our six weeks from Oporto. It is a small village, about two miles from Vittoria, on the Irun road. We halt here today, and tomorrow we proceed to the army, which we are to join on the 18th instant.

I went yesterday to Vittoria. It must have been a very fine town, but at present cuts rather a melancholy figure; not that it has been in any way destroyed, but it is a hospital for wounded, and has at present about 6,000 wounded men and officers in it, many of whom are just now beginning to walk, or rather crawl about; and so many poor maimed devils do not add to the beauty of a place. Several of them are old friends of mine, but all of them, I am happy to say, doing well.

I believe you knew Cadogan (Hon. Henry Cadogan, Lieut.-Colonel 71st Regiment, son of first Earl Cadogan) who was killed in this action. His death was one of the finest things possible. Being perfectly aware that he was mortally wounded, he asked the surgeon how long he could live, and was told about half an hour. He then desired the men who bore him to leave him for a short time. On their return he ordered them to take him to that part of the field where he could best see the British advance, and there died, just as the French line began to give way.

The second, fourth, and seventh divisions have had some very severe work in the Pyrenees, on the 27th, 28th, and 30th of last month, and the enemy were again completely defeated. You will, of course, have seen the details of these actions long before you receive this.

At present we are employed in fortifying the passes. St. Sebastian has not fallen yet, and I believe it to be a very strong place. If it does not fall before the 18th, we shall probably be employed against it. Pampeluna is blockaded, and they say that the garrison are very badly off for provisions, and that they have already begun to eat horse-flesh.

I wish it may be true, for if we can get possession of these two places, we may look to keeping the French out of Spain for this year at least, and next year the Spaniards *ought* to be able to do it of themselves; I say ought, not that I think they will, for they are even more indolent than ever.

By this time all the gay doings in town are pretty near over. I long much to get hold of my letters, as we have not seen a letter or paper from England since the 15th of June, and are quite in the dark as to what is going on in the north of Europe. But, however, in five days more we shall reach our division, and then I hope to have a letter of yours to answer.

    Till then, *adieu*, my dear Miss Thurlow
        Yours ever,

                              Saltoun.

On the 18th of August, the First Guards marched into camp at Oyarzun, two miles from Irun, and joined their comrades of the Second Brigade, in the left wing of the Allied Army under Sir Thomas Graham. Saltoun, of course, very shortly recommenced his correspondence with Catharine Thurlow. Having arrived at their destination, he appears be more business-like and was addressing himself to the soldiering requirements of moment. However, readers may be curious about his enquiry regarding 'the loo and Tabby set'. Loo or Lanterloo is a trick taking card game similar to Nap which was popular among society ladies at the turn of the 19th century in England. Dedicated rooms and tables for playing the game were created and the social circle of ladies who gathered therein were termed, not particularly kindly perhaps, 'tabbies', after a gathering of cats.

Camp before Oyarzun,
23rd August 1813.

My dear Miss Thurlow,

Yours of the 22nd June I only received yesterday, but I have written several times on our march, and mentioned that I did not expect to get any letters until we reached the army. A month is certainly a most unreasonable time for a letter to take from Oporto to England, but this, I trust, will make up for it; for I understand that the *pacquet* is ordered to Santander, which is but a short distance to send by land, and not above three days' sail to Falmouth.

We are quite quiet here at present, and likely so to remain, encamped on the Pyrenees, about three miles from Irun, at which place the bridge over the Bidassoa is destroyed. The French are on the opposite bank, and each party mutually fortifying his position. On our left, about five miles, is the seaport of Passages, so we are well supplied with fish, which is a great luxury, and ought to be also with English articles; but the sutlers have been so often taken in by the rapid movements of the army in this Peninsular War, that they are not inclined to risk any very great speculation.

St. Sebastian is about seven miles from this place, and is besieged by the Fifth Division, under General Oswald. A breach was made some time back, and they attempted to storm, but were repulsed with great loss. Since that time, we have been waiting for heavier guns and ammunition; the batteries are all ready. The guns and ammunition arrived yesterday, and on Thursday the 26th they are again to open against the place. It is of great consequence to take it, but it is very strong, and will cost a great many broken heads.

You wish to know what general we are particularly under; we are in the First Division, which is under General Howard (Lady Charlotte's husband), and the First, Third, and Fifth Divisions form the left corps of the army under General Graham. The Fifth, as I mentioned above, are against St. Sebastian, and we are covering the siege. The Third Division are on our right between this and headquarters.

We shall certainly not advance unless things go wrong in the north of Europe, and I do not think the French are strong enough to try another general action, as the ground in our front is very strong, especially that part which our division would probably have to defend should they attack the positions. By this time all the gaiety is over on your side of the water. I find her Ladyship has gone to the Lodge; I thought she meant at one time to go to Scotland this summer.

I wish you could persuade someone of our regiment to sell out. I am now first for purchase, and dread the tidings of peace more than anything; for then I should not get my promotion before it takes place, which would be a terrible bore, besides the length of time it would throw me back. However, I am not one of those who are apt to despair, and trust now to be home by Christmas as a Lieut. Colonel.

I am going today to see a friend of mine who was wounded the other day in the general action before Pampeluna. I do not know if you are acquainted with him. His name is Campbell, and he is Lady Malpas' eldest brother, a major in the 6th regiment.

Sir D. H. Blair and myself are old hunting friends. A few years back we kept house together for a season. The Vittoria *fête* seems to have been the great lion this year. It must have had a very grand effect; for of all places in London there cannot be a better place for a public sort of thing than Vauxhall; but to be good it ought to have been very full.

How goes on loo and the Tabby set? I dined yesterday with a man whom you must have often met there, Captain R—— of our regiment. He began to talk about Mrs H——, "a little woman with black eyes." I asked him where he had met her. He said he often met her at Mrs. P.'s, and that she was very fond of play, and led her husband a devil of a life. R—— and I happen never to have met at P.'s, and he little thought I could have given him tolerable information on that subject.

You see I take you at your word, and write as often and as long as I have anything to say; and it is accidental whether I have or not, for our life is either a very active or a very dull one, no medium.

I have written this on my knees, and I fear you will have some difficulty to decipher it, for my table, which cannot be very large in camp, is laid for breakfast, and four cups rather crowd it. We are going to have a rare wet day, but I must go and see Campbell for all that, as he is on his way to Bilboa, and I shall miss him if I do not. I hope to see you in less than six months. Till then, my dear, my dear Miss Thurlow, believe me, yours ever.

S——.

On the 28th of August the Guards advanced still nearer to Irun, acting as a covering force to the troops of the Fifth Division, who were carrying on the siege San Sebastian. The camp was well situated, about one mile from Irun, in an ancient wood upon the face of the mountain, from where the River Bidassoa, the French lines, St. Jean de Luz, and Bayonne in the far distance, were visible. The Second Brigade was encamped on the left of the First, whilst the Germans were in position to the left of the Second Brigade. The Bidassoa, from low water to half-tide, was fordable, but the ground in front of the Guards camp was very strongly defended, so there was little likelihood the enemy would attempt an attack from that side of the position.

Major-General Lambert resigned his command on being appointed to a brigade in the Sixth Division. Colonel Peregrine Maitland succeeded to the First Guards Brigade and Lieutenant-Colonel Hon. W. Stuart to the third battalion.

The left wing of the Allied Army, under Sir Thomas Graham, was now composed of the First Division under Major-General Howard; the Fifth Division under Major-General Sir James Leith; Lord Aylmer's brigade and a Spanish Army under Don Manuel Freyre. The Fifth Division, consisting of Major-Generals Hay's and Robinson's brigades, was engaged in carrying on the siege of San Sebastian while the First Division formed the covering force and guarded the line of the Bidassoa from the mountain to the left. Freyre's Spanish corps was posted to the right, on the heights of San Marcial. The order of battle of the First Division was as follows: The First Guards on the right, Hinuber's Germans on their left, then Stopford's Second Brigade of Guards, and the German light infantry on the extreme left.

By the 30th of August the enemy's guns on the ramparts of San Sebastian were silenced, and as the walls had been breached in two places an assault was scheduled for the following morning. It had come to Wellington's notice that some officers of the Fifth Division doubted the practicability of storming the breach, and he felt that such demoralising views would inevitably have filtered down to the ranks creating a potential to turn prophecy into reality. He decided, therefore, to deploy volunteers drawn from some of his most reliable regiments for the task. Four hundred men would be taken from the First Division comprised of 200 men from the Division of Guards and 200 men of the King's German Legion and these would be combined with 350 men drawn from the Fourth and Light divisions to, as Wellington delicately put it, 'show the way to the breach if it should be practicable'.

The storming party of the Guards, consisting of 100 men from each of the First and Second Brigades, under the command of Lieutenant-Colonel R. H. Cooke of the First Guards, marched from their camp at six p.m., with the other detachments from the division, and encamped about two miles from the fortress. They moved off again about two in the morning of the 31st, and occupied the ruined convent of St. Bartolomeo, where they remained until half-past nine.

Sir James Leith, who commanded the assault, would not allow the volunteers to take the lead, placing them instead in support of Robinson's brigade. The troops advancing to the breach were exposed to a heavy fire and it soon became apparent that any concerns previously expressed with regard to the practicability of the breach were founded on nothing other than sound judgement, because it could only be accessed in single file which transformed its entrance into a narrow killing-ground. Nevertheless, the attacks drove forward in succession, and inevitably, acts of courage notwithstanding, all attempts to effect a lodgement foundered and

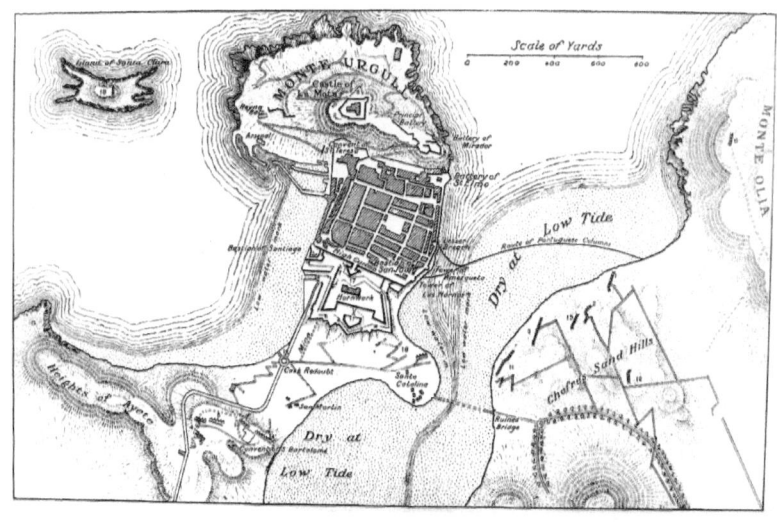

THE STORMING OF SAN SEBASTIAN

the stormers were mowed down in their hundreds.

The waiting volunteers impotently witnessed these events with mounting frustration and questioned 'why they had been brought there if they were not to lead the assault?' Finally, in the absence of any progress the volunteers were finally put to the task and they assaulted the breach ferociously, swarming up the ruins. After an initially promising advance, however, even this desperate attempt foundered and those that reached the crest were struck down leaving none but the dead or wounded remaining on the summit. Other attempts to break through followed, but fared no better than the first.

Graham, by this point realised that simply flinging human flesh at the fortified defenders was unlikely to result in success, so ordered the artillery to open fire over the heads of the assailants to clear the ramparts and as this barrage progressed, quite by chance, one shell upon impact ignited a quantity of gunpowder which the enemy had prepared to explode in *extremis* in the event that the ramparts were over-run. The resulting eruption literally and figuratively 'hoist the enemy by his own petard' and, taking advantage of the ensuing chaos, the British assault force finally burst through the French line to enter the town.

Saltoun did not take part in this assault with the Guards contingent. For that fact, both posterity and Miss Catharine Thurlow may possibly have reason to be thankful for these assaults were not termed, 'The Forlorn Hope', for nothing. Two days following the success at the breaches of San Sebastian, Saltoun once more faithfully put pen to paper in a letter to his 'dear Miss Thurlow'. Of the 207 Guardsmen of all ranks who marched to the assault, Saltoun with little emphasis, reported in his letter that just 50 of them returned to rejoin their comrades. The final section of Saltoun's letter on this occasion is particularly interesting and revealing since it describes an engagement undertaken by the Spanish Army under Freyre and Longa at San Marcial in which it acquitted itself very well despite suffering substantial losses; a phenomenon which is rarely positively reported in contemporary Peninsular War accounts written from British perspectives. Sir Howard Douglas, however, who had close associations with the Spanish soldiers during the war probably came close to the heart of the matter when he wrote, 'I must say they are well deserving to be better led. They possess all the qualities necessary to constitute a good soldier'.

> Camp Irun,
> 2 September 1813.

My dear Miss Thurlow,

We came here two days back in order to support the advance, as the French were making demonstrations on this point with a view of preventing our attack on St. Sebastian; they had not, however, the desired effect, for we carried the place by storm at twelve in the day on the 31st instant. Our loss was very great; they rate it, as well as it can be now got at, to be about fifteen hundred men.

The place was stormed by detachments from the different divisions of the army, and by the fifth division under the command of Sir J. Leith, who is wounded. We sent a detachment of one lieut.-colonel, two captains, four subalterns, and two hundred men, fifty of whom have returned.

Of the officers, Burrard was mortally wounded, and died yesterday. He is son to Sir H. Burrard, the second he has lost in action in the regiment. Ensign Bridgeman slightly wounded, and Chaplin, who belongs to the Coldstream Guards, severely; he is shot in the breast, and his thigh broke so high that they cannot amputate; he is, however, doing as well as possible, but cannot be called by any means out of danger.

On the morning of the storm Soult made a general attack on our line, with an intention to relieve the place. The ground in our front is very strong, and defended by the Spaniards of the Gallician Army, under General Frere. The French attacked one hour before daylight, and carried a small height which they surprised; this enabled them to establish a bridge over the Bidassoa, and at eight in the morning they had passed over about ten thousand men, and made a regular attempt to carry the hill occupied by the Spaniards, without which they could not with safety pass any great force of artillery. The Spaniards defended it with great obstinacy, and about two, when the French had carried the hill, they made a very spirited charge, and with the bayonet drove them fairly to the bottom. Towards evening the French made another attempt, but a very feeble one, and on the Spaniards giving three cheers on being informed of the fall of Sebastian, they retired, and during the night took away the bridge, and have not since troubled us.

I have just come from the field, and from the number of dead lying there I should think the loss on both sides must be about five thousand men, of which number the Spaniards certainly lost the most. The French made an attack more on the right, and were met by the Seventh Division British, and repulsed with great loss. The castle of St. Sebastian still holds out, and will cost some more men; we are at present pounding away at it at a great rate.

I have now given you all the news, and must send this letter to Oyarzun to be in time for the mail if possible. I shall write should anything take place.

Believe me, yours ever,

S——.

The French governor of San Sebastian, as Saltoun had indicated, retired to the citadel, and, on the 9th of September, after a spirited resistance of more than a week, surrendered. The casualties among the officers of the First Guards were one officer, Ensign Burrard, of the first battalion (son of Sir Harry Burrard), mortally wounded, and one officer, Ensign Orlando Bridgeman, wounded. Readers will recall that Burrard was an officer of the Guards and had been present in Portugal in the period leading to the infamous Convention of Cintra.

One of his sons had already been killed in action at Corunna in 1809 acting as an *aide-de-camp* to Moore and it is widely accepted that this second loss broke his heart for he was laid within his own grave in a little over a month. According to Lord Saltoun there were, in round numbers, 150 casualties amongst the 200 Guardsmen at San Sebastian. The total losses of the assault were in the region of 1,500 men though the cost of defeating the French in the town must have been twice that number.

Soult made one more attempt to relieve the fortress on the morning of the assault, by threatening the allied left: but it was easily repulsed. During this attempt the First Division was drawn up in support, in the rear of Irun, but was not engaged. The enemy withdrew over their frontier on the same day. By this point, France was beset on all sides by both land and sea. Napoleon's hubris had led him to monumental ambitions which not only over reached his considerable resources, but led him to squander them. The disastrous retreat from Russia had cost him an enormous army, rewarded him with nothing and laid the foundations for his fall.

Prussia had joined the Russian alliance ready to take the field, and Austria was also covertly preparing to recommence hostilities. Irrespective of the emperor's failures as a strategist on the grand scale he remained a formidable campaign and battlefield commander by comparison with practically every adversary who might come against him. Napoleon, rapidly collected another army of 200,000 men and 350 guns, with which, in May 1813, he fought and brilliantly won the battles of Lutzen and Bautzen in Germany. However, the abiding fact was that the allies would never cease to oppose him until they were done with him and the encouraging news from Spain was a further indication that the First Empire of the French had never been more vulnerable. Austria once again actively rejoined the allied cause, as it was always bound to do, had taken to the field, but was resoundingly beaten at Dresden on the 27th of August, with heavy losses.

Nevertheless, undaunted the allies immediately rallied and, gathering a host 250,000 strong, came to the fray once again to oppose Napoleon at Leipzig and after three days' gruelling combat between the 16th-19th of October, gained a decisive victory, which obliged the French Army to retire across the Rhine. Determined now to follow through with their advantage, the allies doggedly pursued it crossing the north-eastern borders into France in several places. Napoleon had not fought his last battle, nor won his last battlefield victory, but his time was running short and he was now at bay, his enemies were closing in upon him and his nation was tired of war and the perpetual sacrifice of its sons on the altar of his megalomania.

CHAPTER NINETEEN
The Pyrenees—The Bidassoa, 1813

By the end of September, the siege at San Sebastian was over and the British Army had marched away from it leaving the Spanish to garrison and repair their town and its fortifications. Saltoun, in his regular correspondence with Catharine Thurlow, described the scene in the aftermath of the battle perfectly from the perspective of the British regimental officers. Either because he was astute or because the 'telegraph' of the army ensured practically everyone knew what was happening at the time and what would happen next, he demonstrated his typically accurate assessment of current affairs.

Saltoun referred to a forthcoming trip to visit Sir Rowland Hill at Roncesvalles with his friend and brother officer, Edward Stables, who would be killed in action at the Battle of Waterloo.

One aspect of the following letter, however, is particularly interesting since it bears directly on the behaviour of British troops in extreme circumstances. This was a subject upon which Saltoun had decided opinions and, indeed, he had previously written about it in the strongest terms; bridling at Wellington's accusations of a negligent failure in control of the men by their own officers. He reported that after the British troops had entered San Sebastian they had, true to form and past experience, run riot and thoroughly plundered the place, 'in the most barbarous fashion and set fire to it'.

Whilst his condemnation of this sacking of another Spanish town was unequivocal, there was nothing in his comments, on this occasion, to suggest that he did not expect what would happen when the town eventually fell. Furthermore, he raised no suggestions for a systematic preventative measure that might be instituted, as he had by contrast, on the privations of the troops on the retreat from Burgos. In short, he mentioned the fact, but did not make much of it.

That troops were given a period of latitude to despoil a town they had taken by storm after severe losses was a very long established aspect of warfare and, despite their personal opinions on the matter, commanders at this time apparently still accepted it was necessary to tacitly allow (if not condone) and a price to be paid irrespective of whether the place belonged to an ally. The engaged troops likewise expected this 'reward' as their due during this period and retained the inclination to indulge themselves in ghastly full measure. The author has no intention to put a modern moral cast upon these matters, other than to note they significantly speak to the nature of British society and its relationship to the army at the beginning of the 19th century.

Camp Irun, Spain,
26th September 1813.

My dear Miss Thurlow,
I received yesterday, and am most happy to find that our letters on the march have arrived at last; for I began almost to despair about them. You have, I believe, two more still to receive at least. We halted twice between Toro and this place, and I usually wrote on those days, and did not leave you out.
Since my last, which was after the fall of Sebastian, we have been quite quiet in this part of our line—indeed I may say all along the line—and have been employed fortifying the position. You do not seem to like the marching much, and I think working would be still less agreeable to you; not that we officers work, but we are obliged to see that the others do. Since it has begun, this is the first day that it has missed me, and I have generally had the morning party from half-past five till twelve; very pleasant amusement standing on a hill for six hours seeing two hundred men dig, especially in this beautiful climate, where we never have two fine days running. I never in my life was in such a place for rain, and further on the right it is worse.

I wish the *Beau*, as his Lordship the Field-Marshal is called, would cross the Bidassoa and move down into France, as then, at all events, we should not be regularly sluiced night after night in our tents, which is the case here; for no canvas, nor anything else that ever was invented, will stand the rain in these hills, and we have famous fun with the gentlemen amateurs from England with their water-proof coats and *ne plus ultra* pelisses, which they find of very little use here, and they must be content, as we are, to get wet with philosophy, and dry as soon as they can.

Tomorrow I set out on a trip to the right. I mean, if I can, to get as far as Roncesvalles, where Sir R. Hill is stationed, with whom I am acquainted. I mean to see the ground of the late actions, the finest ever fought by the British yet, and on the most extended scale of military operations.

I have a good many friends to call on in the way, which will make it a very pleasant trip. Colonel Stables goes with me, and our leave is for eight days, should the army make no movement, which it probably will not till our redoubts are finished, and they cannot well be complete before ten days more, and then I hope we shall make a start.

Sir James Leith, who was wounded at the storm of Sebastian, is doing very well, and will soon be fit to join his division, which belongs to our column of the army, and, to use the military phrase, is closed up, that is, has encamped in our rear, ready to support us if necessary. They marched from Sebastian the day before yesterday, and that place is now given over to the Spaniards, who have placed a garrison in it, and are to repair the breach. It was a very fine town, but I am sorry to say our troops plundered it in the most barbarous manner, set fire to it (or, as some say, did not put out the fires which caught accidentally). Be that as it may, they have not left a single house standing in it; the Turks could only have done that.

I know Mr. Joliffe, though I am not acquainted with him. Who does not know him, at least his hat, which is tolerably conspicuous! He keeps a pack of hounds, and I have always heard is an excellent good fellow. I must finish this, for the post leaves Oyarzun at three, and now it is past two, and it is more than a league from hence to Oyarzun.

Adieu; and believe me, my dear Miss Thurlow, ever yours,

S——.

The fall of San Sebastian occurred five or six weeks before the pivotal engagement at Leipzig and during the interim, as Saltoun's letter amply illustrates, Wellington remained inactive. His circumstances were, however, about to change fundamentally, for any advance from his present position could not be defined as the expulsion of an invading army from the territory of an ally, but as an invasion of another country by forces under his command. This was not necessarily a straightforward matter under the circumstances, since political consideration as to whether France should actually be invaded was an issue which occupied the sovereigns of the coalition of allies in the northeast and no policy had yet been decided upon it by them.

The military question was should Wellington advance into France before the allies made their own advance given this would create a beneficial diversion which would work in favour of his own operations? The British Government eventually solved his dilemma for him by instructing his own advance to provide the diversion to assist the continental allies, who were, in fact, preparing for the great blow against the French emperor which would become the Battle of Leipzig. Accordingly, Wellington early in October, forced the passage of the River Bidassoa and marched his army, for the first time, onto the soil of Southern France.

The mountains of the Western Pyrenees rose opposite the Anglo-Spanish position, separating the valleys of the Bidassoa and the Nivelle rivers. Wellington's plan was to seize, with his right and centre, the highest point of these mountains—La Rhune (now Larrun), and its dependent ridges, while on his extreme left, he would obtain possession of Fuenterabia. The French position to the north of the Bidassoa was naturally formidable and Soult had further strengthened what nature had provided with additional defensive works.

The French dispositions anticipated that their enemy would attack their centre and left, but the ever-observant Wellington grasped the potential to neutralise Soult's dispositions by passing the army over the mouth of the Bidassoa at low tide. At the crossing point the tide rose sixteen feet, and the sands were half a mile wide. The First Division and the Fifth Division, together with Portuguese troops, which formed the left wing of the Allied Army, were nominated to carry out this part of the attack. This audacious manoeuvre would both surprise and outflank Soult rendering his defence redundant. Bold though this initiative was, it was not without risk, because it would not be long after the troops had crossed that the tide, rising once again, would isolate those on the enemy held shore with no hope of retirement or succour until the next ebb tide, by which time Wellington's intentions would be fatally revealed.

Two brigades of Guards and Brigadier-General Wilson's Portuguese brigade would cross over the Bidassoa, by a ford close by a ruined bridge and also by two fords a short distance down the river. The lowest ford was called the Vado de las Nasas de Abaxo, and was near the point where the *chaussée* from Irun arrived at the banks of the river itself. Some of these battalions were to pass at a ford a short distance above the ruined bridge, and all were to advance upon the fords to coordinate with the time that the Fifth Division from Fuenterabia would move forward. Assembly would begin before dawn, near Irun, and all movements were to be kept concealed until the moment of the simultaneous attack and ford crossing.

A rocket from the steeple of Fuenterabia would signal the advance for the brigades of Guards to coincide with the movement of the Fifth Division. Elements of the cavalry from the 12th Light Dragoons, with the brigade of artillery attached to the First Division, and a brigade of reserve artillery, were to cross the river with these columns. Other guns were to cover the passage from the most available heights of San Marcial, on the reverse slope of which, Alymer's brigade formed the reserve to the First Division.

The first objective of the Guards after crossing was to establish themselves upon the opposite hill known as Montaigne de Louis XIV. and on other high ground, keeping up a communication on their left, if possible, with the Fifth Division. The troops were all to be in position at seven o'clock in the morning, since low water arrived at a quarter past the hour. At three o'clock in the morning of the 7th of October the First Division was under arms and marched off. It passed through Irun, arriving at the rendezvous point on time, unobserved by the enemy, the manoeuvre covered by a violent thunderstorm which fortuitously burst over the French position. The advance began and the fords were approached without an angry shot having been fired as a certain indication that the French had been taken totally by surprise.

Meanwhile, under cover of heavy artillery fire from the heights of San Marcial, the right column of the First Division, comprised of Wilson's Portuguese, supported by the two battalions of First Guards, crossed the river in front of the lower heights of San Marcial, taking the higher right hand fords and advanced towards the enemy. Once upon the opposite bank it drove the French from the village of Andaya and advanced rapidly towards Croix de Bouquet. The left column, Second Brigade of Guards, preceded by the KGL light infantry, crossed the river at the ford, near the broken bridge, and formed on the right of the Fifth Division, covering the building of a pontoon bridge so artillery could also move up.

The eighteen-year-old, Rees Howell Gronow had joined the First Guards as an ensign in February, 1813 and after a few months of mounting guard at St. James' in company with his young, fellow officer friends, Dashwood, Batty, Browne, Lascelles, Hume and Master he joined a detachment of five hundred men bound for Spain. The crossing of the Bidassoa was his first experience of a military campaign and he later made a note of it in his reminiscences.

> Our regiment advanced through difficult country and after a harassing march reached the top of a hill as the grey light of morning began to dawn. We marched in profound silence, but with a pleasurable feeling of excitement amongst all ranks at the thought of meeting the enemy, and perhaps with not an equally agreeable idea that we might be in the next world be-

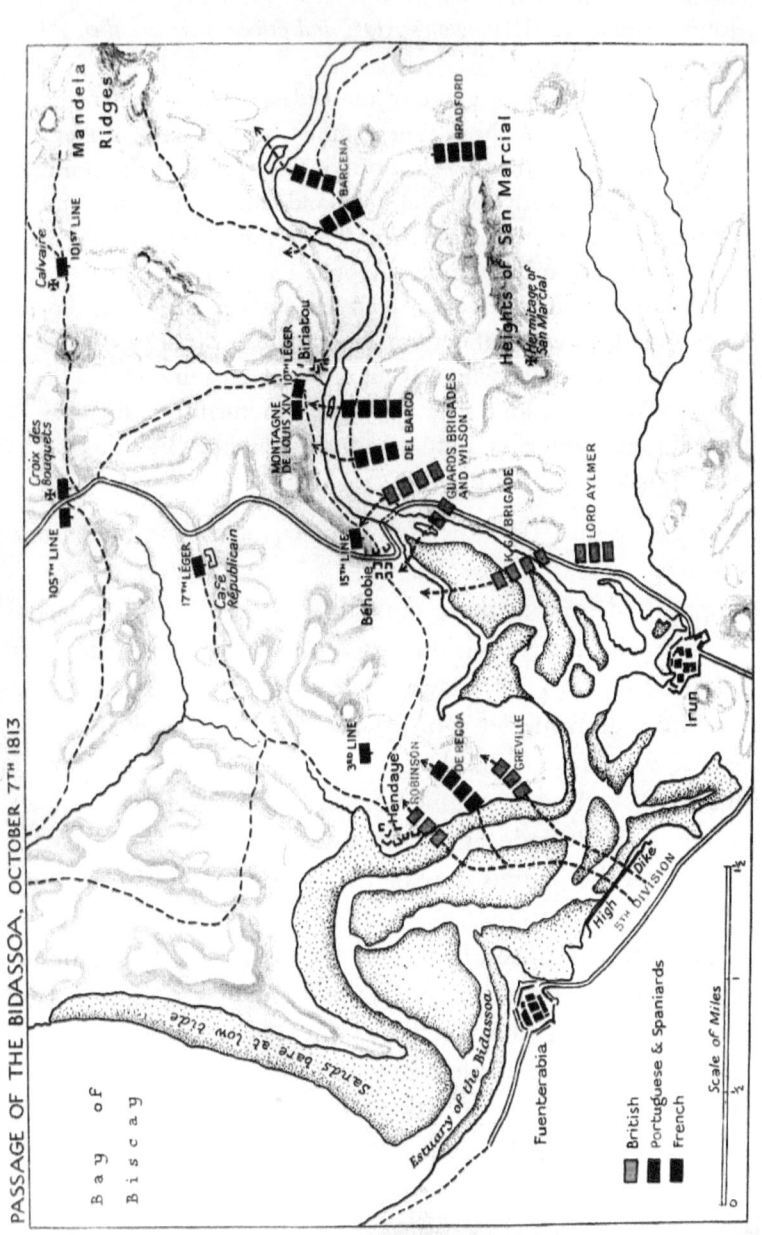

fore the day was over. As we ascended the rugged side of the hill, I saw for the first time, Wellington. He was accompanied by the Spanish general, Alava, Lord Fitzroy Somerset, and Major, John Freemantle *(Wellington's ADC and private secretary, then 23 years old)*.

We commenced the passage of the Bidassoa about five in the morning, and in a short time infantry, cavalry and artillery found themselves on French ground. The stream at the point we forded was nearly four feet deep, and had Soult been aware of what we were about, we should have found the passage of the river a very arduous undertaking.

Three miles above we discovered the French Army and ere long found ourselves under fire. The first man I ever saw killed was a Spanish soldier, who was cut in two by a cannon-ball. The French Army, not long after we began to return their fire, was in full retreat and after a little sharp, but desultory fighting, we took possession of their camp.

Success was, as Gronow reported, virtually immediate and the French forces before Maitland's First Brigade of Guards promptly fled leaving three guns behind them, whilst the left column of the First Division drove the enemy from the Café Républicain and the Montaigne de Louis XIV. The attack swept on to Croix de Bouquet, which was the key of the position and after a severe struggle, the heights there were won. The enemy, outflanked by the left column of the Fifth Division also gave way. The First Brigade of Guards, advanced and encamped for the night on the heights they had won, to the right of the high road leading to Urrugne.

During the advance of the First Guards light infantry, under Saltoun, they passed some French wounded soldiers lying by the road side. To his horror, Saltoun witnessed one of his men walk towards to one of them in particular, and after pausing for a moment, drive his bayonet through him. Saltoun immediately rushed up to the offending guardsman and demanded to know the reason for such barbarous behaviour towards a helpless incapacitated Frenchman.

'It's no Frenchman, sir,' was the indignant reply; 'it's that 'Ev-

The Guards crossing the Bidassoa by Robert Batty

ans' who deserted the night before the Battle of Corunna.' The wounded man was sent to the field hospital for treatment, but died the following day of his wounds. The accusation had been correct. This 'Evans' had, indeed, deserted his regiment nearly five years previously in January, 1809, had taken service with the French at the commencement of the war, and now, towards its close, in 1813, met his death from the hands of his former comrades, by whom he would not have been recognised, had he not, on seeing the uniform of his old regiment, imprudently called out to them for a drink of water.

The fighting had been more severe on the right of the British line, though the French there were also taken by surprise. The Light Division and Giron's Spaniards assaulted the ridge called Bayonette held by Taupin's division, carrying it, in spite of the height of the mountain and strength of the works. Freyre's Spaniards had, in the meantime, assaulted the Mandela heights, and, by advancing on St. Jean de Luz, by Joliment, cut off Taupin's line of retreat. The French had succeeded in repelling the attacks made upon the great Rhune Mountain, but abandoned its defence on the following day.

The army suffered less than a thousand casualties in the affair and the First Guards suffered no loss at all during these operations; the Coldstreams had 2 rank and file killed, and 8 wounded; the Third Guards, 9 rank and file wounded, and 2 missing. The French casualties were over 1,500, but they significantly also lost 14 cannons.

CHAPTER TWENTY

The Nivelle, 1813

Since the British Army was now in complete possession of the formidable position the enemy had occupied the day before, the French begrudgingly retired and took up a new position for the defence of the line of the River Nivelle.

The health of Sir Thomas Graham had been failing for some time so he resigned the command of the left wing the day after the passage of the Bidassoa. In fact, Graham genuinely believed he was (and wished to be) done with soldiering permanently, but before long fate had another military expedition in store for him. He was succeeded by Lieutenant-General Sir John Hope, who had arrived from Ireland on the previous day. This was the Hon. John Hope, ultimately Earl of Hopetoun who had taken command at Corunna after the death of Moore. Other 'John Hope's' had previously served in Spain as divisional commanders, notably at the Battle of Salamanca in 1812, where there had been two of them.

In view of the close proximity of the armies, there was much outpost duty for the light infantry companies of the Guards, and the advanced sentries of the opposing armies often stood at night within thirty yards of each other. Naturally, Saltoun was engaged on picquet duties with his men and at the end of the first week in October he took the opportunity during one such night to write a letter, once again, to Catharine Thurlow. In it he explained his own part in the passing of the Bidassoa and once again he made a comment on the good performance of Spanish troops. In centuries past Spanish regiments enjoyed the highest reputation during the wars in Europe and much concerning their poor performance during the earlier stages of the war in the peninsula bore on the quality of political and military leadership in Spain.

He began his letter with a reference to the 'Song of Roland' which concerns the defeat of the Charlemagne's army under the heroic Roland by the Basque Army in $A.D$ 778. The conflict at Roncesvalles in 1813 occurred when the French under Reille and Clausel advanced with 40,000 men against Lowry Cole's, Fourth Division of 11,000 men which was defending the pass. Cole withdrew in the direction of Pamploma.

Camp Urogne, France,
9th October 1813.

My dear Miss Thurlow,
As we are now proudly fixed in France, and being on picquet within a very few yards of the enemy, and therefore not willing to sleep, I cannot employ myself better than letting you know how we have been going on since I wrote last.
I mentioned that I was going to take a trip to the right of the line with old Stables, which we put in force the next day, and were very much pleased with it. The scenery is of the grandest kind, most particularly the valley of the Alduides and that of Roncesvalles, famous in former days for the fight which we have both heard remarkably well said or sung by poor C. Anguish in these times; not less famous for one of the sharpest affairs that have lately taken place in the Pyrenees; but except at Astley's or Sadlers Wells I much fear it has a bad chance of being again remembered in poetry, unless it should graciously please Walter Scott to give us another part of Don Roderick's Vision, for which he has certainly now sufficient materials.
The Pass of Roncesvalles lies over a very high mountain, the top of which is in our possession; at the bottom of it, on the French side, is the town of St. Jean Pied de Port. This pass forms the right of our line. In the valley, on the Spanish side, stands the convent in which they show you Orlando's club and armour. It is beautifully situated amongst large woods of old beech trees, and open patches of old parkish ground, the arrangement of

which would have made the fortune of any capability gentleman in England—the whole closed, in the grandest manner, by the mountains. From this pass, coming to our left, the next pass is the Alduides, which is very beautiful, but not so grand as Roncesvalles. From that, passing by the Puerto de Viscayret, you reach the Pass of Maya, and so by the Pass of Echallar and that of Vera, to Irun, to which place we returned on the 5th.

On the night of the 6th we got our orders at twelve to attack the next morning, and at three in the morning of the 7th marched to our points, so as to reach them before daylight, that the enemy might not observe our movements, and at a quarter before eight, it being then low-water, forded the Bidassoa in five columns, and advanced against their position, the enemy making but little resistance, being partly surprised; for our plan of attack was so well combined that his position was turned and attacked, hill after hill, nearly at the same moment.

He ought, however, to have defended his position—which is a very strong one—with greater obstinacy. Our loss was small—between 300 and 400 men, I should guess. At twelve we had gained our present position, just above the town of Urogne, which is now the French advance, and before dark were quietly encamped upon it. During the time that this operation was going on, the Light Division debouched by the Pass of Vera and attacked the Hill of Urogne. which is a high mountain on the right of our present line, and carried it in good form.

The poor natives are terribly alarmed, and have all fled; not that they fear us (the English), as they have given us to understand, but they know well the way their troops treated the Spaniards, and they dread the retaliation which they know they deserve from the troops of the Peninsula, whom a year back they looked upon as slaves, called them brigands, and treated worse than dogs, and if they made them prisoners, for it was seldom that they gave quarter to a Spaniard, and the poor devils, from wounds or sickness, could not reach their destination, regularly shot them; and the Spanish soldiers have not forgot it. And although as yet I do not think they would stand hard squeezing, they behave well, mixed as they now are with us, and face their enemy in a better style than I ever thought they could be brought to do.

Everything looks as if we were to make a forward movement,

and I trust my next will be dated from some place further in the heart of France. we can see a long way into the country from our present position, and it appears to be a beautiful and rich country. I shall go on scribbling for ever, but I am sure by this time you must be tired of army speculations, which are but dry ones at any time.

I have just heard that a mail has landed, and I hope to have a letter tomorrow when I am relieved.

You most likely are just now going to bed, so goodnight, and believe me yours ever,

S——.

In a letter home written by Lord Saltoun at the end of October, and also sent from camp above Urogne he describes a very interesting incident that personally concerned him as he served with his men of the light infantry company in close contact with the enemy on outpost duties.

> We have a great deal of duty; our light infantry do the advanced duty and no other. I am on every fourth day; and the posts are so close, our advanced sentries at night standing within thirty yards of each other, that both parties are tolerably alert; indeed the Germans, who take that duty with us, and who have been all their lives on that species of service, say they never saw posts so close, without a ravine or brook, or something of the kind, between them, which is not the case here.
>
> Upon one occasion, when I was in command of the outposts of our brigade, I was going my rounds with a small escort very early in the morning. Our sentries and those of the enemy were at no great distance from one another, and I noticed that one of the French sentries, who was posted on a rising ground affording some view of the country beyond, appeared to be asleep. I determined to surprise him if possible, and obtain a look at what might be the scene of our own operations in a few days. Taking one of the escort with me, and leaving the others to watch, he and I crept, as if deer-stalking, towards the sentry, and managed to reach him without awakening him. He reclined with his back to a tree, against which he had leant his musket, and of this I quickly made myself master; then, while my companion kept guard over the still sleeping sentry, I examined the country

beyond with my glass, and got a good deal of information as to its nature, the disposition of the enemy's troops, etc. etc.

I intended at first to go back without wakening the Frenchman, and to take his musket with me; but reflecting on the severe punishment, perhaps even death, that would await him if discovered by his own officers in that state, and without his arms, and noticing that he was a young soldier, I could not find it in my heart to do so, and we therefore awakened him. His surprise and horror may be more easily imagined than described, and if we had not held him down and stopped his mouth, he would have bolted shouting an alarm.

When he became a little calmer, I said to him, 'My friend, it is far better for you that I have caught you asleep than that one of your own officers should have done so; now, no one will know of it unless you tell, be more careful in future, and keep better watch; I return you your musket, and shall trust to your honour not to fire at us as we retire.'

However, not to depend too much on his honour, I took out the flint, and shook the powder out of the pan before giving it back to him. He seemed very grateful, and thanked me most warmly, and then we rejoined our party.

A few nights after this I was again in command of the outposts, and wishing to visit another post at some distance, I set off on horseback alone. The night was pitch dark, and I lost my way, and got close to the cordon of French sentries, when my horse, crashing through a slight hedge, half scrambled, half fell into a hollow road; and at the same instant came a challenge from the top of the opposite bank, '*Qui v'là?*' and I heard the ring of a firelock brought to the ready.

I sang out, '*Officier de la poste Anglaise*,' and explained that I had lost my way in the dark. The French sentry asked if I was hurt by the fall; and on my replying, 'No,' that I was all right, he most civilly directed me how to get within our lines again; and as we parted said, 'I am happy to be of this service to you; we have all heard of the kindness of one of your officers the other day to a young sentry of ours that he caught asleep.'

I told him that I was the officer in question. 'Ah!' he said, 'that makes me doubly happy, that is the way brave enemies should always treat one another;' and so we parted excellent friends, and I found my way by the directions he had given me.

To this time Pampeluna remained in the hands of the French and Wellington was keenly aware of the potential threat this enemy concentration posed were he to advance before the city was taken. In fact, ultimately no blood was spilled in reducing Pampeluna, because, after a most effective blockade which lasted four months, the French, all but starved into submission, surrendered on the 31st of October, securing the Anglo-Spanish army's position to carry the war into the enemy's territory.

Saltoun's letter to Catharine Thurlow originally dated the 31st of October was written over a period of days and reflects the changing position that occurred during that time because at the letter's outset Saltoun comments, 'as soon as this confounded place, Pampeluna, falls', whereas the latter section, dated November 6th makes it clear that the news of Pampeluna's fall had by that time reached the army. Readers may note Saltoun's romantic closing paragraph of his letter in contrast to what he would write to her a few months afterwards.

Camp Urogne, France,
31st October 1813.

My dear Miss Thurlow,

Yours of the 4th of this month I received a few days ago, enclosing a map most beautifully drawn on silver paper, and I have compared it with the large French map of the Pyrenees, and, considering the scale, it is tolerably correct as far as Maya, but it takes no notice of the valley of the Alduides, nor that of San Carlos, which are leading features in the frontier line between the valley of Bastan and that of Roncesvalles, and are divided from each other by the large mountain of Arola. The situation of the towns on the Spanish side is tolerably well laid down, as well as in most maps; and with respect to the French side I will tell you a little more when we have advanced further up the country, which we shall do as soon as this confounded place, Pampeluna, falls.

Our army is in exactly the same position as when I wrote you last, the left on the sea-coast above Urogne, extending to the right through Zagaramurdi and Urdax to Roncesvalles, which is our right. The right of the French rests on Fort Seres, the centre at Mondarin, and the left at Arosa and St. Jean Pied de

Port. On the Nive River, on their right, they have a second line from Mondarin through St. Pé to St. Jean de Luz, on the small river Nivelles, which is not fordable from St. Pé to the sea except at low tide.

They are doing everything in their power to fortify this position, and all our arrangements are complete for an attack, which will take place as soon as Pampeluna falls, which cannot hold out above a few days longer; indeed we have been in treaty for the place, but the terms that the garrison wanted were, to be sent to France not to serve against Great Britain or her allies for the space of a year and a day. These were, of course, rejected; and after a little more starvation they will surrender at discretion.

November 6th—I was obliged to leave off to go on duty, and as tomorrow is post-day, and I have very little news, I shall tack it on here.

Pampeluna surrendered a few days back; the garrison were 4200 strong, and when they gave in, they had had nothing to eat for three days. Poor devils! how very thin and genteel they must have looked when they came out after four months' low diet. I should not admire the starving much; a siege is bad enough, but a starving bout is ten times worse.

As yet we have made no movement in consequence of the weather, which has been so bad for some days back as to put a stop to all military operations, by rendering the roads impassable for artillery, and the rain has swelled all the small rivulets so much that the troops cannot ford them; besides, what is rain in our part of the line is snow at Maya and Roncesvalles, but yesterday and the day before were fine, and the weather seems again to be settled.

All the arrangements for a start are complete, and we expect our orders to attack hourly. I do not expect we shall have much to do in the first instance, as the position opposite us will be turned by our right, and the enemy must either abandon it, or if he resists stoutly (which, by the by, I do not think they are in a good humour for at present), he must be made prisoner in it, and it is not their game to lose men in that way, for they have not too many to spare now.

I am on the outposts, and we have just had a parley with *Johnny Crapeaux,* (the French officers) who has been sending in money to some of their officers who were wounded and taken when we crossed the frontier. They have no later news from Napoleon than ourselves. No news, they say, is always bad news for them. The officer I spoke to was at Moscow last year; he is very tired of it, and wishes to go into winter quarters. I told him we had no such word in the British service, and that we meant to be in Bayonne shortly, and perhaps Bourdeaux, on which he vociferated, "*Sacre F———,*" and strutted off in grand style.

I am not much inclined to be civil to these rascals, for I hate them most heartily, and they swagger and *cut a big swell* on these occasions, which at present is rather our right than theirs. Some of them, however, are very gentleman-like men, and then are pleasant fellows enough.

Our posts at this part of the line are so close, that the French and our picquets at night are not more than twenty yards from each other, and no obstacle between, which makes desertion very easy, and many of our Germans who have been enlisted from the prisoners of war go off, and a good many of the French come over to us; one came in last night. He says that they are very badly off for bread, but have plenty of meat, and, generally speaking, are very dissatisfied.

You wish to know why I put a little S in the corner of the direction? it is a trick that one gets from writing reports, as it is customary to put your name on the outside, which acts as a pass for the soldier who carries it, in case any post should hesitate to pass him; and when I am afraid that my letter may not be properly directed, I always write my name on the outside, as from its being known at the post-office, they return me the letter without opening it, which is rather an advantage than otherwise.

Before you receive this, you will be thinking of returning to town; I should have no objection to be there with you, in spite of what I told the French officer; and believe me, my dear Miss Thurlow, ever yours,

S———

The French position now before Wellington extended from St. Jean de Luz on the sea coast, on their right, eastwards for about twelve miles, to the hills in front of Souraide and Espelette. The whole enemy defensive line was strengthened by earthworks. The left of the French first line rested on the River Nivelle, extending to the right of the Choupara and Mondarin mountains, while Clausel's corps occupied the heights of Ascain and Arnots, between which were the camp of Sare and several strong redoubts.

Since the passage of the Bidassoa, Wellington noted that Soult had secured his right flank by a triple line of defensive works in front of St. Jean de Luz on the Nivelle. These would have made a frontal assault so costly that, once again, a more imaginative solution was required to affect the British Army's advance. Given this problem was exactly the same kind of situation that had inspired Wellington's plan for passing the Bidassoa, one may have supposed Soult would have foreseen what alternative approach might be instigated by his opposite number. That solution proved to a combination of a feigned attack made by his left wing, now under Hope, while Wellington proposed to force the enemy's left, and threaten the rear of his right, which would compel him to withdraw from St. Jean de Luz, once again abandoning redundant works.

Hope was to operate in three columns. The left column, composed of Halkett's German light infantry, was to act between the heights of Urrugne and the coast, fronting northwards towards Socoa Fort; the centre column, or Fifth Division, and some other troops were to occupy the most advantageous points upon the left bank of the rivulet, which runs between the heights of Urrugne and those of Siboure, and when halted were to face towards Siboure and St. Jean de Luz, while the right column, composed of the two brigades of Guards, were to threaten the front of the French encampment on the right bank of the rivulet of Urrugne, and on the British right of the high road leading from that village to St. Jean de Luz, keeping up at the same time the communication on their right with Freyre's Spaniards, who were to attack Ascain.

The First Division remained under the command of Howard, while the First Brigade of Guards was commanded by Maitland. Heavy rain initially delayed the attack but, in the early morning hours of the 10th of November the weather eventually cleared. During the previous night the army, with approaching 100 guns,

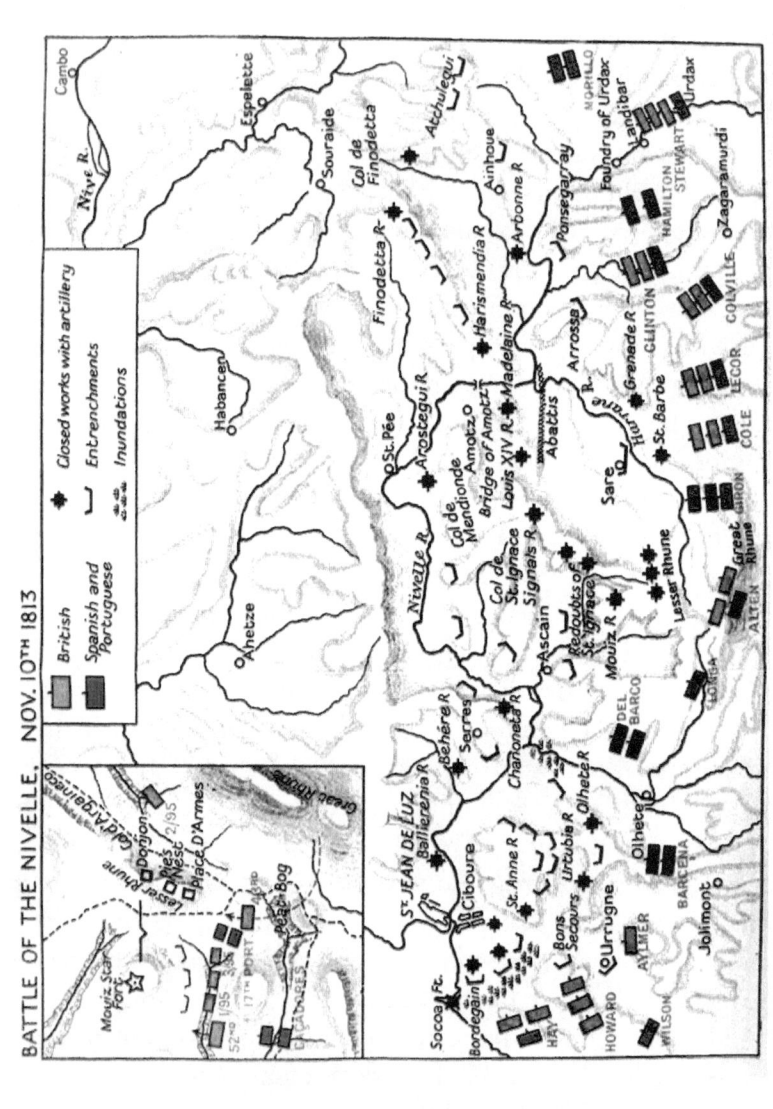

moved quietly and undetected into their positions.

At about three a.m., the First and Fifth Divisions moved down the heights and advanced to the line of outposts, arriving about an hour before dawn. The French picquets of the advanced posts of Reille's and Villatte's divisions, were strongly entrenched, and a large redoubt defended the rising ground in front of Urrugne. At the signal of three guns fired from the Alchabia mountain, the massed allied artillery opened up on the French position, and the army began the attack. On the left, Halkett's German light infantry moved round the hill, whilst the picquets of the First Division, under Lieutenant-Colonel West of the First Guards, made a rapid attack in front, driving the enemy from his advanced position down the hill to the entrenchments,

The brigades to the left of the First Division moved directly upon Urrugne, while Maitland's Brigade of Guards and Hinuber's King's Germans advanced against the heights behind Urrugne, which extend towards Ascain. The First Guards and German light infantry kept up a continued fire, but, as per Wellington's intentions, they received no orders to storm the works before them. Hope, however, had now gained the heights commanding Siboure, so that he was in a position to take advantage of any forward movement the right centre of the enemy might make. He kept up this false attack until nightfall, compelling Reille's and Villatte's Divisions to engage him and so preventing them from sending assistance to Clausel commanding the centre of the French Army.

While the First and Fifth Divisions held their ground on the left, the balance of the army advanced, driving the enemy from their positions and seizing the bridges of Ascain and Arnots over the Nivelle. The French fought stubbornly, but at last retreated, abandoning their entrenched camp of St. Jean de Luz. During the action, Soult arrived with a large body of troops at Serres, and threatened the allied centre, but the position of Hope's wing prevented his aiding Clausel. At the close of the action Hope followed the retreating French across the river.

The brigades of Guards were not significantly engaged in

the main involved and in consequence their losses were trifling, but Captain Charles Allix, First Guards, acting brigade-major of the First Brigade, was severely wounded, and Captain William Miller took his place. Miller would fall, mortally wounded at Quatre Bras.

CHAPTER TWENTY-ONE

The Nive & St. Pierre, 1813

The French Army again withdrew, taking position on the heights of Bidart on the road to Bayonne, where it prepared to defend the passage of the Adour, and on the 11th November the British Army, in turn, moved forward to take it to task. The First Division, after passing over the now abandoned fortified position in front of St. Jean de Luz, sighted the town at midday, descended into the valley, forded the river and advanced to within eight miles of Bayonne. The First Guards' Brigade took post on the right, a mile or so from the high road. The enemy's right rested at Anglet; their centre on the ridge of Beyres, and their left on the entrenched camp of Bayonne, situated near the confluence of the rivers Nive and the Adour.

Bayonne was covered to the south by an entrenched camp created by the genius of fortification, Vauban. Soult's right, in the form of three divisions, under Reille, was concentrated touching the Lower Adour, and supported by a flotilla on the river. A swamp covered his front, and several fortified posts were positioned forward near Anglet, two miles from Bayonne. Clausel's three divisions extended from the entrenched camp to the Nive, covered partly by the swamp, a fortified house, and an inundation near Urdanis; D'Erlon's four divisions extended up the right bank of the Nive; D'Armanac was in front of Ustaritz and Foy, at Cambo.

Wellington, needed to extend his line from his position between the Nivelles and the Nive and took the decision to cross the River Nive, so as to establish himself on the left bank of the Adour. The weather remained too poor to ensure the operation had its best opportunity for success, so the First Brigade of Guards was returned to St. Jean de Luz, and was quartered in the suburb of Siboure.

An officer of the Guards, writing from St. Jean de Luz on the 28th of November, after giving an account of the state of affairs, referred to a rumour he had heard that Napoleon was coming to Bayonne to personally take command of the French armies.

> I am sure that there is not a man in the army, from Lord Wellington himself to the lowest soldier that would not think it the happiest day of his life to be fairly placed in front of the French with Bonaparte at their head. If ever there was a day when British soldiers would be more than themselves, that day would certainly be the one.

Time, marching its inexorable course, was taking that officer towards the day when at last he and all the players of this drama would be together in the fields beyond Waterloo. Whether that day would, indeed, transpire to qualify as, 'the happiest day of his life', remained to be seen. For the present, Wellington intended to pass the Nive with his right wing, and place it on the Adour. Meanwhile, Hope would demonstrate with the left wing of 24,000 men, against the entrenched camp at Bayonne, occupied by Reille and Villatte so as to mask the actual objective of the manoeuvre. Having assessed the position and strength of the enemy in front of Bayonne, Hope was then to reconnoitre the mouth of the Lower Adour, with a view to throwing a bridge across it.

The brigades of Guards paraded in the early hours of the 9th, before an arduous march through wet and overcast weather along the coast road to take up their position. The brigades halted at Barouillet, in front of Bidart. The Fifth Division then crossed the valley between Biarritz and Bidart, with its left resting upon the coast.

At eight o'clock the First Battalion, First Guards advanced, covered by the light infantry and by artillery fire. Shortly after

First Foot Guards in winter dress

the engagement began the enemy stubbornly retired and by one o'clock, the light infantry had driven the enemy through the village of Anglet and down the slopes of the entrenched camp. The First Division had taken the heights on the right of the road near Anglet.

While the attention of the French was focussed on Hope's army, Hill and Beresford were able to pass the Nive near Ustaritz and Cambo. There the enemy fell back without a fight, and so Wellington succeeded in gaining a position for his operations against the French left. At about six o'clock in the evening, he directed Hope's successful troops to return to St. Jean de Luz. The Fifth Division, which formed the rearguard, halted at Bidart, leaving a Portuguese brigade in advance at Anglet. That night the First Brigade of Guards, under Maitland, reached its former quarters at Siboure, the southern suburb of St. Jean de Luz.

Wellington's left was now in a potentially perilous position since it was separated from the rest of his army by the River Nive, and Soult was not slow in appreciating that fact nor in imaginatively seizing the opportunity it presented. He marched from Bayonne on the morning of the 10th of December, at the head of 60,000 men, against Hope's wing. Reille, driving the Portuguese from Anglet, advanced towards Barouillet, while Clausel on his left attacked Arcange, occupied by Kempts' Brigade of the Light Division, which held its ground all day. The sound of heavy firing from the front announced the seriousness of the conflict and in due course, an *aide-de-camp* arrived, warning the Guards and the troops in the rear, that the attack was a dangerous one. The Guards advanced quickly to the scene of action and took their place in the battle line.

However, the difficult terrain had prevented the enemy deploying effectively, the attack had been repulsed, and its renewal was discouraged by the arrival of three divisions near Ustaritz, on the left of the enemy's attack. The First Brigade, however, remained that night in Bidart.

The French again attacked the outposts of the left wing on the 11th, and after passing the flanks, penetrated the first line,

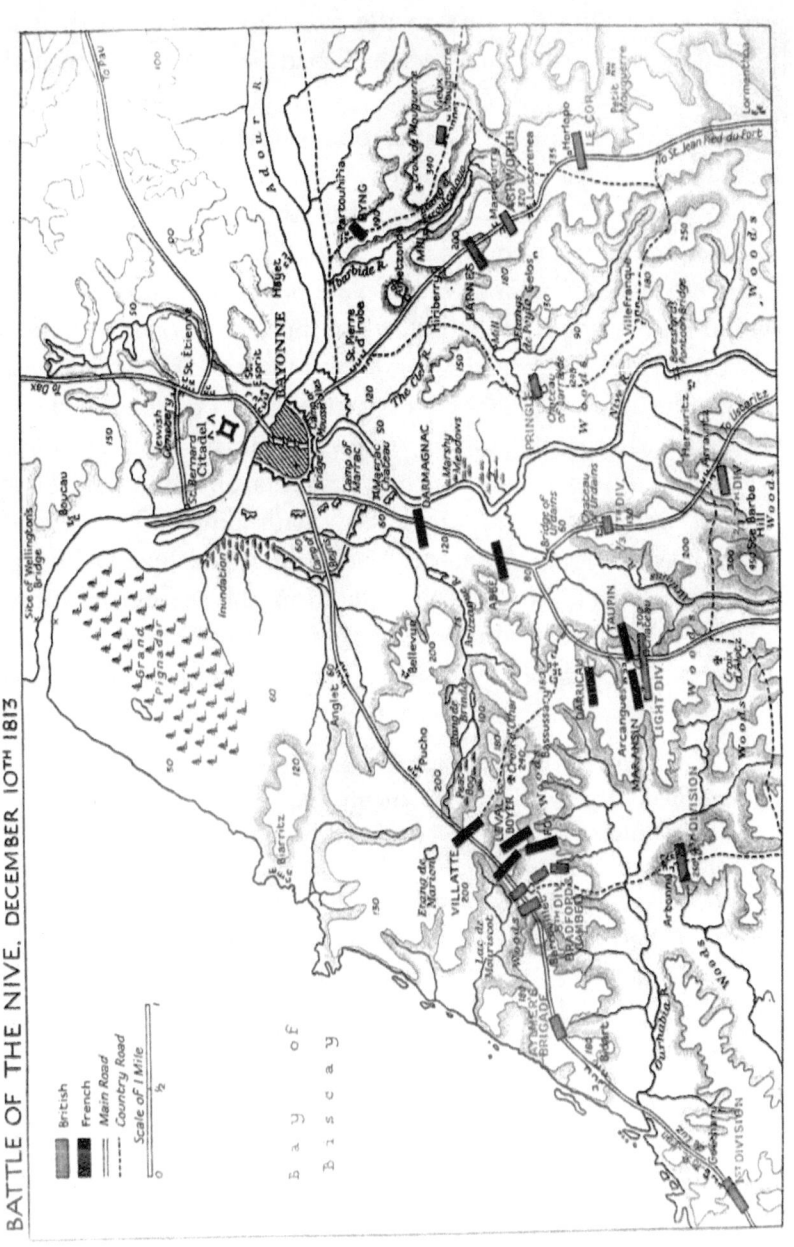

but when Aylmer's brigade arrived, Soult withdrew his troops behind the Etang de Chartreuse, opposite Barouillet. The Guards relieved the Fifth Division in the front line that night, which then formed on the ground which had been recently vacated by the Guards.

The two brigades of Guards took a position in front of Barouillet. The First Brigade, under Maitland, stood near a farmhouse on the brow of a hill, separated by a narrow ravine from the heights which were still held by the French. The picquets of the Third Battalion, First Guards were posted in a thick coppice wood on the slopes of the hill, while those of the first battalion, on the extreme right, commanded by Captain West, were in a large orchard to the right of the farmhouse. The First Battalion, First Guards, under Colonel Askew, was formed on the high ground to the rear, while the third battalion, under Colonel Stuart, was to the left, in rear of the farm, with some artillery. A picquet of the First Guards, under Lord Saltoun, occupied a hut to the left, to watch the road which led from the enemy's position, and to keep up the communication with the Second Brigade, in front of the mayor's house. Rees Gronow, in his recollections, gave a first-hand impression of the fighting:

> The Guards held the mayor's house and the grounds and orchard attached. Large bodies of the enemy's infantry approached, and after desultory fighting succeeded in penetrating our position, when many hand to hand combats ensued. Towards the afternoon we drove the enemy from the ground they disputed with us and then retreated towards Bayonne. Every day there was constant fighting along the whole of the line.

The night of the 11th was overcast and wet, and at day break the French appeared in force with more troops coming up from the rear. About ten o'clock, a strong line of French *tirailleurs* advanced from the west along the brow of the ravine in front of Maitland's, First Brigade of Guards. The artillery opened fire and brisk skirmishing continued throughout the day in front of both brigades causing a loss of about 200 officers and men. Lieutenant-Colonel Coote Martin, commanding the picquets of the First Battalion, First Guards, was shot down in the orchard and almost immediately afterwards Captain Charles Thompson, of the same battalion, was mortally wounded, while leading his men. Captain Streatfield was slightly wounded about the same time, whilst Ensign Lautour also took a severe wound.

Marshal Soult discovered he could make no impression on the allied left, under Sir John Hope. The British position on the left bank of the Nive was secure, with the likelihood that it would be further strengthened. Accordingly, Soult temporarily retired behind his own entrenchments. His next plan was to leave a deceptive cordon of outposts in front of Hope's troops, but to covertly pass 35,000 men quickly through Bayonne during the night, with the intention of attacking Hill's corps the following morning on the right of the Nive. Marshal Beresford, with three divisions, was dispatched early in the morning of the 13th, to Hill's assistance. That general had only 14,000 men under him, but he held his ground at St. Pierre, and repelled every attack, though the struggle at one point became critical, until Wellington arrived with the reinforcements.

The French attacks then became gradually feebler, and at two o'clock Wellington ordered a general advance. The French retreated, fighting hard, and during the night Foy's division retired across the Adour, and were sent to reinforce Reille, opposed to the British left. While the fight was raging at St. Pierre on the 13th, the enemy reinforced their advanced posts in front of the First and Fifth Divisions, and firing was kept up with little intermission till the afternoon. The First Brigade of Guards, the Coldstreams, and Lord Aylmer's Brigade took the brunt of the conflict and Captain Carey le Marchant, of the 1st Guards, *aide-de-camp* to Lieutenant-General Sir William Stewart, was severely wounded.

Saltoun's next letter to Catharine Thurlow begins with a description of the recent fighting which is, the reader will note, very accurate in its appreciation of the action, though in typical style he coolly and dispassionately relates the facts rather than emphasising that the battles around the Nive and at St. Pierre in particular were hard fought. The British regiments, despite the outcome, had been severely tested. Indeed, some writers claim that this fighting represented some of the most brutal of the entire Peninsular War.

Soult had demonstrated a particularly innovative tactical ability on this occasion and Wellington had been, if temporarily, wrong footed. In the end, Wellington's soldiers won the victory for him in the manner which he freely acknowledged they dependably would, even when he had made a mistake. The French marshal was not so fortunate and these operations cost him between six and seven thousand men. To make matters worse Napoleon then ordered Soult to release 10,000 troops to serve on the eastern frontier, leaving him with less than 50,000 men which amounted to a little more than half of those that Wellington had at his disposal.

Soult's weakening position was further exacerbated by the desertion of whole regiments of German troops who served the imperial cause begrudgingly and were quick to abandon it now that it seemed the end of French dominance was at hand. Saltoun reported this detail at the end of his letter to Catharine. The Nassau troops were particularly highly regarded by both the French and the British in Spain. Wellington is on record of expressing his high opinion of them and, in due course, Saltoun would know their worth more intimately, for they would be fighting on the allied side very close to his own post at Hougoumont before a year and a half had elapsed.

> Camp before Bidart,
> 13 December 1813.
>
> You see, my dear Miss Thurlow, we are again under canvas, and have had some sharp work for these four days past; we have had two officers killed, and two wounded. I do not know if you are acquainted with any of them;—Captain Martin and Captain Thompson are killed, and Captain Streatfield and Ensign Latour wounded, the latter severely. We have lost one hundred and fifty men.
>
> Old Soult has been manoeuvring and trying to deceive Lord Wellington, by showing a large force at different points of our

line. On the 9th we advanced and attacked in front of this place, and drove the enemy into his strong ground in front of Bayonne; in the meantime, Sir R. Hill crossed the Nive at Ustaritz, and rested his right flank on the Adour, so as to intercept Soult's supplies, which he received from Pau and Oleron by that river. This obliged Soult to make some decided movement, and on the 10th he attacked us, but was repulsed by the Fifth Division. On the 11th he again attacked us, and got a hill in our front that covered his movements. That night we took the outpost duty, and on the 12th he appeared in force, and manoeuvred under cover of a very sharp affair of *tirailleurs*, but finding us well prepared at all points, he during the night recrossed the Nive, and on the 13th made three desperate attacks on Sir R. Hill, and was defeated and driven into Bayonne with great loss. I do not know what our loss has been on the right, but I understand very small in comparison.

Fortunately, the weather has been fine, and still continues so to be, but very cold in the tents at night; however, anything is better for soldiering than wet, and I dare say it will be some time before we again go into winter quarters, if we do so at all.

I have not had any letters from home for some time, but I understand that my mother has not as yet got her house settled, and moreover is very likely to lose it. I see your cousin the Lord is married by the papers.

The news from the north is very good, and has spread through France; for the day before yesterday three German regiments in the French service—one of Nassau, the others of Baden and Frankfort—came over to us with their officers, arms, and every other necessary; they are marched to Passages to embark for England. This shows that the morale, as Napoleon calls it, is not the same in the French ranks as formerly, and I very much suspect that the material is almost as low.

I have no more news to tell you, so *adieu*, and believe me, my dear Miss Thurlow, yours ever,

S——.

Rees Howell Gronow of the First Guards was present when some of the Germans, who were apparently expected, came over to the British lines. In his reminiscences he wrote:

Shortly before we left St Jean de Luz, we took our turn of outposts in the neighbourhood of Bidart, a large village about ten miles from Bayonne. Early one frosty morning in December, an order came that if we saw the enemy advancing, we were not to fire or give the alarm. About five we perceived about two battalions wearing grenadier caps coming on. They turned out to belong to a Nassau regiment which had occupied the advanced post of the enemy and hearing that Napoleon had met with great reverses in Germany signified us their intention to desert. They were fine looking men and appeared, I thought, rather ashamed of the step they had taken.

The First Brigade of Guards returned to St. Jean de Luz after these actions, and as the final days of 1813 were allowed to pass by without any aggressive demonstrations from the French, the new year began with Wellington establishing a firm foothold for his army upon enemy soil. Portugal and Spain had seen the last of the emperor's machinations, though the legacy of the turmoil he had wrought upon the Iberian Peninsula would mean that years of strife lay ahead.

CHAPTER TWENTY-TWO

The Forcing of the Adour

On the first day of 1814, Saltoun dutifully penned a letter to his, 'dear Miss Thurlow' and he opened his correspondence, as usual, quite charmingly whilst giving the impression that both he and his lady—though apart—were engaged in recreational expeditions in 'the country'. However, when Saltoun more soberly turned his attention to military matters and the consequences of an imminent closing of hostilities, he once again revealed himself to be prescient, for he expressed the opinion that if Napoleon were to be given access to 300,000 released French prisoners of war it would be but a matter of time before he once again employed them as an army in war.

Indeed, Saltoun believed that Napoleon would not, in this conflict, be comprehensively beaten and so a British Army would be certain to fight him again in the future. The accuracy of his forecast in the light of future events requires no emphasis, though given the convoluted course which brought the emperor to his final battlefields in Belgium, it is quite remarkable that it was made a year and a half before the fact. Of course, Saltoun thoughtfully closed his letter, as he began it, with news of a social occasion. The days of peace would indeed soon come, but would be as short lived as winter sun.

St. Jean de Luz,
1 January 1814.

My dear Miss Thurlow,
Since I wrote last, which was after our brush on the 12th, I have

received yours of the 30th November, by which I see you have returned from your expedition to Hampshire, which I hope you found much to your satisfaction, and at all events had better weather than we had here about that time.

Since I wrote you nothing has taken place with us in the fighting line; but for all that we have not been perfectly quiet, for it pleased Soult to cross the Adour in force on the 3rd instant, above the right of our army, and accordingly on the 4th we were all put in motion, and both armies continued manoeuvring until the 8th, when Soult retired across the river and resumed his old position; and today we have followed his example and taken up our old cantonments. At one time on the 7th he had very nearly put his foot into it, and Lord Wellington would have attacked him on the 8th, but he found it out in time and was off during the night. We have fortunately not had a great deal of rain, but it is very cold lying out at this time of the year.

I begin to think the war seems drawing to a close, but I hope we may take the field once more, and put the thing past a doubt by forcing Napoleon to make peace on French ground; for when he receives back the prisoners of war that we and the allies have taken from him, we give him an army of at least 300,000 men, and set him up at once as a formidable enemy, long before the nations wrested from him can reach their place in the scale, as he has taken care to drain them pretty handsomely during the time they were under his dominion; and even Austria will be a long time before she recovers from the great losses she has sustained in this and the last war.

Little England, however, can hold up her head and say, we have beat you at last and will have at you again as soon as you please, for in peace where France gains ten, we gain at least a hundred for the first years of it. I have given you a tolerable dose of my ideas of affairs in general, and shall leave off, but will not finish this till tomorrow, when the post goes, in hopes of having something more to send.

Another mail has arrived from England, but brings no particular news.... We are to have a grand ball here tonight—about two hundred men in fine coats, and certainly not more than ten ladies, including chaperones; not very gay, but it serves to pass the night. *Adieu*, and believe me, my dear Miss Thurlow, ever yours,   S——.

Soult strengthened his position, beyond the rivers Bidouse and Gave d'Oleron. On the 3rd of January, 1814, he attacked the British position on the Joyeuse, and shortly thereafter appeared in front of the left wing of the army. In response to this development, the Guards were despatched from St. Jean de Luz to the outposts of Barouillet, where they relieved the Fifth Division, which then took ground to the right to await the onslaught. No French attack materialised however, so the Guards marched back to St. Jean de Luz, leaving the outposts to Lord Aylmer's brigade. On the 14th of January Aylmer was relieved by the First Guards, who were in turn relieved by the Second Brigade.

The construction of a line of entrenchments for the defence of the ground behind Barouillet along the front of the left wing occupied the following days for the British troops and the drudgery of the chore was impeded, and made the more miserable, by perpetually wet weather that dragged on through the remainder of the month. Furthermore, the left wing of the army was detailed to take part in the investment of Bayonne, which not only removed it from operations under Wellington's immediate command, but prevented its involvement in several more influential actions at Orthez, Garris, Aire, and Tarbes.

Unexceptional as January, 1814 was for the First Guards, there was one ray of sunshine for Saltoun for he realised his ambition for promotion. Accordingly, the light companies of the Brigade of Guards were now placed under the command of Lieutenant-Colonel, Lord Saltoun, who had been promoted to command a company at the end of the year 1813. This promotion would, under normal circumstances, have returned him to England to serve with the home battalion, but this outcome did not suit him. He applied instead to continue on active service as the commander of the light companies, though notably the details of his deliberations before the fact of this decision, for perhaps obvious reasons, had not thus far featured in his correspondence to Catharine Thurlow. He would only reveal his decision when the deed was done. Towards the end of January, he wrote a fairly usual letter combining light hearted news with that of the progress of the army. His post script is worthy of note since this engagement would lead to the disastrous assault on Bergen-op-Zoom

> St. Jean de Luz,
> 30 January 1814.
>
> Yours, my dear Miss Thurlow, of the 4th I received a few days ago.
>
> It had been a most enormous time on its passage, as indeed have all the packets lately; for it is the latest packet we have from England, and now we have two due, and a third will be so in a few days. I cannot conceive the reason of it, as the wind with us has been northerly for some time past, and Admiral Pickmore has arrived in a ship-of-war, and he left Plymouth on the 20th. Some people say that the road to Falmouth is snowed up, and therefore the mail cannot get down; be that as it may, it is very provoking, as I expect to get my promotion every day, and of course, you may suppose, look anxiously for the packet.
>
> I find old Hughes is a very general favourite; he is quite well, and when sober as good a servant as ever, but he has learnt to cure sore backs of horses and mules, which in this army is a very common complaint, and he, James Hughes, having gained the name of a good doctor, is consulted on every occasion, by which means he picks up so many shillings and so many friends, that he gets drunk now past all former example.
>
> You are quite correct as to the country being swampy, but it is not by any means unwholesome, for the army never were known to be so healthy as at the present time; and excepting the regiments just come out from England, we have no sick in the army. It is in the summer, when these swamps are nearly dry, that this sort of country is unhealthy.
>
> I will refer to the little map, but I much fear we are out of the district it particularly notices. Our left is at Bidart, extending to the right by Arcangues and Arauntz, crossing the Nive River in front of Ville Franche, which is in the map, so on to the Adour River by St. Pierre, also in the map, to Petite Moguere on the Adour. We then take the course of the Adour River to Urt, where Sir Stapleton Cotton is stationed with some cavalry and the Third Division of infantry, to watch the movements of General Arispe, who is at St. Jean Pied de Port with two

divisions, and we shall most probably remain in this position for some time, as the immense quantity of rain that has fallen within this week has rendered the roads almost impassable.

I had a letter from my mother the other day; she likes Brighton very much, but I think her house is in very bad hands as far as expedition goes. We must soon have peace; all the French papers talk of it as a certain thing.

Adieu, my dear Miss Thurlow, and believe me ever yours,

Saltoun.

P.S.—We have just heard that our army in Holland has been engaged;—*Viâ* France.

Readers will have noted that in his letter, Saltoun referred to James Hughes, who was his servant and clearly someone that Catharine knew. Hughes was apparently quite a character and something of a reprobate. He served with his master in the Peninsular War and during the Campaign of 1815. In this narrative he will, therefore, appear again.

Saltoun's next letter to Catharine Thurlow, written a week later, is an interesting one. One may imagine its author had deliberated how best to break the news it contained to the two most important women in his life which was that, far from coming home to them as his recent promotion allowed, he was, by his own choice, to remain in the field. Without doubt he knew this was the last place either of them would prefer him to be, particularly as the war appeared to be drawing to a close for there is a particular tragedy in being among the last to die.

Evidently Saltoun came to the conclusion that there was virtually no way the blow could be softened and so he decided to directly inform them of the harsh truth of the matter. He knew well that tears would probably be shed over his letter by Catharine Thurlow and perhaps it is for that reason that for the first time in his correspondence to her he elected to associate his name and hers with the word, 'love'.

This small detail, without doubt, would not have escaped the recipient of this letter since it would have been, from her perspective, its single redeeming feature.

St. Jean de Luz,
6th February 1814.

My dear Miss Thurlow,

You, of course, before this time, know of my promotion, and perhaps are among the number that expect me home; but if so, you will be disappointed, at least for the present, for I have accepted the command of the Light Companies, in which I have always served, and mean to remain with this army till the thing is decided, which must be the case, one way or the other, in a very few months, and then I shall return without the certainty of being sent out again immediately.

This is not any sudden idea of mine; for I had settled in my own mind, when I left England, if I got my promotion not to go home. I never mentioned it to my mother or you, because, although I knew it to be perfectly right in me to do so, I should have had some difficulty in persuading you of that.

Now, however, that it is past altering. I think I could persuade you that it is correct for me not only to serve with a good grace when ordered, but, at the present time especially, to show that I am willing and ready to serve without being compelled to do so; and I have accordingly made an offer of my services to the Commanding Officer of the Brigade, who has been pleased to accept of the same, not but what I would give a great deal for one fortnight in London, if the fog was ever so thick.

Indeed, I look forward to nothing with so much pleasure, and it must soon happen, for things are now come to such a pitch, that we must have a close in a very few months. I have written this in the most horrible hurry possible, for the post is ordered out today an hour sooner on account of the bad roads, so must conclude with hopes of very soon seeing you, notwithstanding my volunteering, and with loves and affections, etc., believe me, my dear Miss Thurlow, ever yours,

S——.

Wellington was aware that Soult imagined his defensive positions beyond the Adour were practically unassailable. Nonetheless, the French marshal knew he must expect an attack somewhere from the British before much time had elapsed. Whilst any such advance would be problematic, it was acknowledged that one of the least tenable places to attempt a crossing of the

Adour, French opposition notwithstanding, would be at the river's mouth below Bayonne. This consideration, persuaded Wellington (as it had Wolfe at Quebec in 1759 concerning the cliffs to the Plain of Abraham) to select that option for his *coup de main*, since it would also certainly be the least well defended. Accordingly, forty ordinary French trading vessels, or *Chasses-Marées*, were gathered for the operation at Socoa, near St. Jean de Luz. Whilst the rumour was spread about that their purpose was to serve the commissariat, they were actually to be employed for the construction of a bridge of boats to span the river.

The first part of this operation was to convey confusing signals to the French marshal by means of feints and demonstrations. During the second week of February, while Hope, with his left wing, showed a bold front towards Bayonne, Hill attacked. On the 16th of February he drove the French advanced posts back to St. Palais, on the Upper Bidouse. Marshal Soult then retreated behind the Gave d'Oleron, with his left resting on Navarreins, leaving a garrison under Thouvenot in Bayonne.

Meanwhile on the 15th of February, the two brigades of Guards, under Maitland and Stopford, advanced to the plateau near Biarritz, and took up a position facing the town with the rest of Hope's troops; the First Brigade, on the right of the road to Bayonne, also occupied the *château* of Pucho. The Fifth Division, on their right, extended from Bussussary to the Nive, while Hinuber's Germans and Stopford's Second Guards Brigade were on the left.

The light companies of the Guards, and the light battalions of the German Legion, were on the advanced posts; the sentries of the First Brigade being posted a short distance from Anglet, which was occupied by the enemy, while Aylmer's brigade with Campbell's Portuguese were in support at Bidart.

It was from this position, with the light companies, which were Saltoun's new command, that he wrote a letter to Catharine Thurlow. The letter reveals that the location of the coming assault was not only a secret, but on this occasion a well-kept one. Predictably, everyone had their own ideas as to where the actual crossing would be made and speculation ran so high that bets were being taken on the subject. Perhaps at this point, having read several of Saltoun's predictions, we should not be surprised that his own conjectures (and perhaps familiarity with the methods of his general) led him to forecast the correct conclusion. This letter, though begun on the 17th of February, was not immediately despatched and contains another section dated the 25th of February which will appear in its proper chronological place.

Heights above Anglet,
February 17, 1814.

My dear Miss Thurlow,

We marched out from St. Jean de Luz on the 15th and occupied these heights, our left resting on the sea in front of Biarritz, and communicating with the Fifth Division on our right in front of Arcangues, who extend to their right as far as the Nive River, and the Sixth Division occupy the ground between the Nive and the Adour. The Light, Second, Third, and Fourth Divisions, with a strong force of cavalry, have moved upon Hasparen and the River Aran, and the French have retired from their position on the Aran, and occupy one on the Bidouse, which they will also retire from.

All this is preparatory to our crossing the Adour, which we shall do in a few days, and probably without being opposed, but at what point nobody at present knows, but most probably at more than one place.

In the meantime everybody has his own particular favourite points, which he will back against any other; or taking the odds against the field—and they vary as they do in the Derby or any other event—my points are the junction of the Gave and the Adour, and at the mouth of the Adour, if possible; but the difficulty at the mouth will be very great, owing to the great width and the force of the tide, which is here very rapid; but should the weather continue as fine as it has been for these six days past, we may pass it anywhere, as the necessity of the high road will be done away with, for the guns will be able to move by the cross-roads, which during the rainy weather were perfectly impassable.

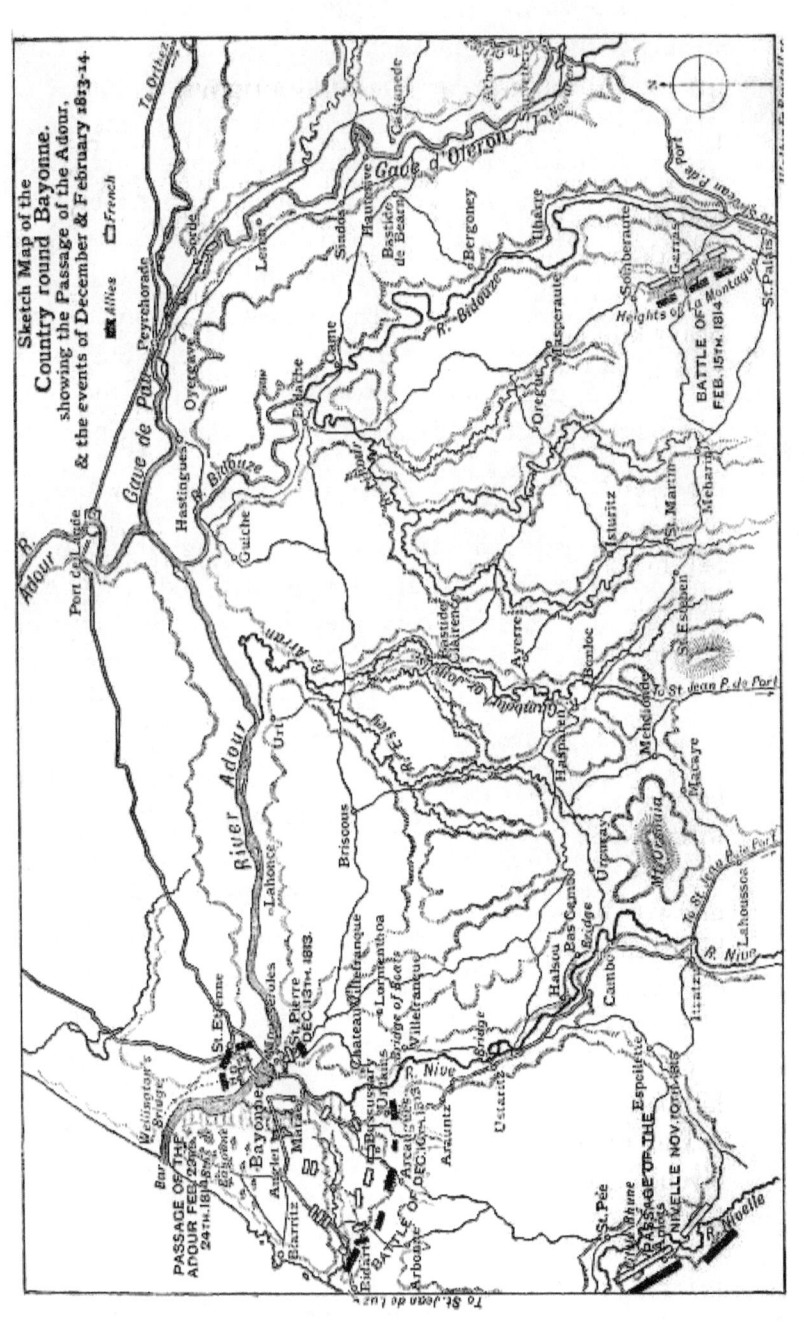

(This letter was concluded on February 25th—see following)

A week later Wellington was ready to put his plan to force the crossing of the Adour into action. At midnight, on the dark night of 22nd of February, Sir John Hope ordered the advance of 28,000 men, including the two brigades of Guards, twenty guns, a rocket troop, and eighteen pontoons. As the force approached Anglet, the First Division, (silently for the enemy sentries were barely a musket shot distant), turned to the left towards the coast. The track the column trod was narrow and muddy, with deep ditches on either side, which perhaps inevitably eventually upset an 18-pounder gun causing frustration and delay. Stopford's and Hinuber's brigades moved towards the mouth of the river with the pontoons, and at daybreak Saltoun's light infantry of the First Guards advanced along the plateau, driving the enemy from Anglet into their camp.

Maitland's brigade followed, advancing through the Bois de Bayonne, dragging the 18-pounders with them, and debouched near to the eastern beacon. Here they formed under cover of the sand hills, close by the marshes, on the western front of the enemy's camp, opposite Boucant. The guns were put in position on the extreme left, near the Adour, fronting the right flank of the enemy's camp. The First Guards, with their guns, were now in a position to prevent the French from hindering the building of the bridge and to suppress enemy fire as troops began to cross over it when it was completed. The enemy's gunboats and a frigate stationed on the river at once opened fire on Maitland's men, but intense return fire from the British gun battery and rocket troop drove the vessels away.

Plans on a grand scale that require precision timing are apt to go awry and so the hope that the *Chasses-Marées* would arrive at the required location at the same time as the column with the pontoons was possibly always overly ambitious. In the event bad weather delayed the arrival of the vessels which necessitated a display of initiative on Hope's part. Aware that his window of opportunity was short, he determined to press ahead with the attack and effect the crossing with the means he already had at hand. Whilst the First Brigade worked hard to engage the enemy's attention, a pontoon raft together with some boats, succeeded in conveying a small force under Stopford, comprising six companies of the Third Guards, two of the Coldstreams, and two of the 60th Rifles, over to the right bank where they were fortunately put ashore unopposed.

The French column, under General Thouvenot, who appreciated that the pivotal moment had arrived, advanced to the attack in the fading light of the day, with drums beating the *pas de charge*. Stopford's men, held their fire until the enemy column was almost upon them and then delivered a barrage of rolling fire to its front, while the rocket troop (giving a notable demonstration of the effectivity of Congreve's invention when well managed) and guns on the sand hills on the southern bank opened a devastating fire upon its left flank. Gronow reported the event in his reminiscences:

> Sir John Hope ordered our artillery and rockets, then for the first time employed, to support our small band (on the opposite shore). Three or four regiments of French infantry were approaching rapidly when a well-directed fire of rockets fell amongst them. The consternation of the Frenchmen was such, when these hissing, serpent-like projectiles descended, that a panic ensued and they retreated.

The enemy was, indeed, comprehensively routed, and on the following morning the 24th, the remainder of the Second Brigade of Guards, the Germans, and Portuguese successfully crossed over the river under the protection of both the beachhead force and the artillery protecting their flank. An imaginative plan implemented by bold and adaptable commanders on the scene had brought the day to a successful conclusion at very little cost.

The delayed flotilla of *Chasses-Marées* eventually appeared in the Adour at midday on the 24th and the construction of the bridge began immediately. The boats were anchored forty feet apart, about three miles below Bayonne, and the enemy once again missed its opportunity and did nothing to prevent or impede the work. The First Brigade of Guards were the last of the First Division to cross over, though since the bridge remained under construction it was compelled to utilise the raft and boats first employed. This proved to be a drawn-out affair since the raft was soon put out of action by the rapid tide and only twelve men could cross at a time in each of the boats. So, it was dark before the last men of the brigade were ferried over, and by that time it became a struggle to prevent the boats from drifting out to sea.

(Saltoun completed his letter to Catharine Thurlow with yet another accurate forecast of developing events)

> *February 25th, before Bayonne*—We crossed the river the day before yesterday in boats, and are now in position round Bayonne, and have cut them off from all communication with their rear. We passed, as I conjectured, at the mouth, and I think our bridge of boats will be completed tomorrow, when the remainder of our cavalry and artillery will pass. It is not as yet known whether we are to besiege the citadel or not, but I begin to think we shall. Lord Wellington has not as yet crossed. I have not time to write a long epistle, as I am in command of the advance posts and wanted every minute. *Adieu*, and believe me ever yours,
>
> Saltoun.

CHAPTER TWENTY-THREE

The Investment of Bayonne, 1814

As Saltoun had predicted, Hope lost no time in investing the citadel which was positioned on a bend on the right bank of the river. The Bayonne citadel is a formidable fortification designed by the redoubtable Vauban, known as 'The Father of the Star Fort', and built during the 1680's for Louis XIV. At seven o'clock on the morning of the 25th of February, the First Division and Bradford's Portuguese advanced in battalion columns of companies. The First Guards on the right, with their right resting on the Adour, halted for a short time at Boucant, while the centre and left brigades moved round, forming to their right, till the extreme left rested on the Adour above the town.

While this was going on to the north of the river, the Fifth Division, which still remained on the south bank, crossed the Nive, and took up a position between the Nive and the Adour. The French garrison was now effectively isolated, though, for the British, surrounding a fortification and causing one to fall remained two entirely different matters.

An attack was also made on the enemy's entrenched camp, to discourage them from interfering with the bridge of boats. Work on the bridge was completed by the morning of the 26th and it remained operational till the end of the war for traffic between the Spanish frontier and Bordeaux. The obligations of his duties had prevented Saltoun from writing a missive of his usual length to Catharine Thurlow and his next short note was clearly hurriedly penned to ensure that it was included in the post

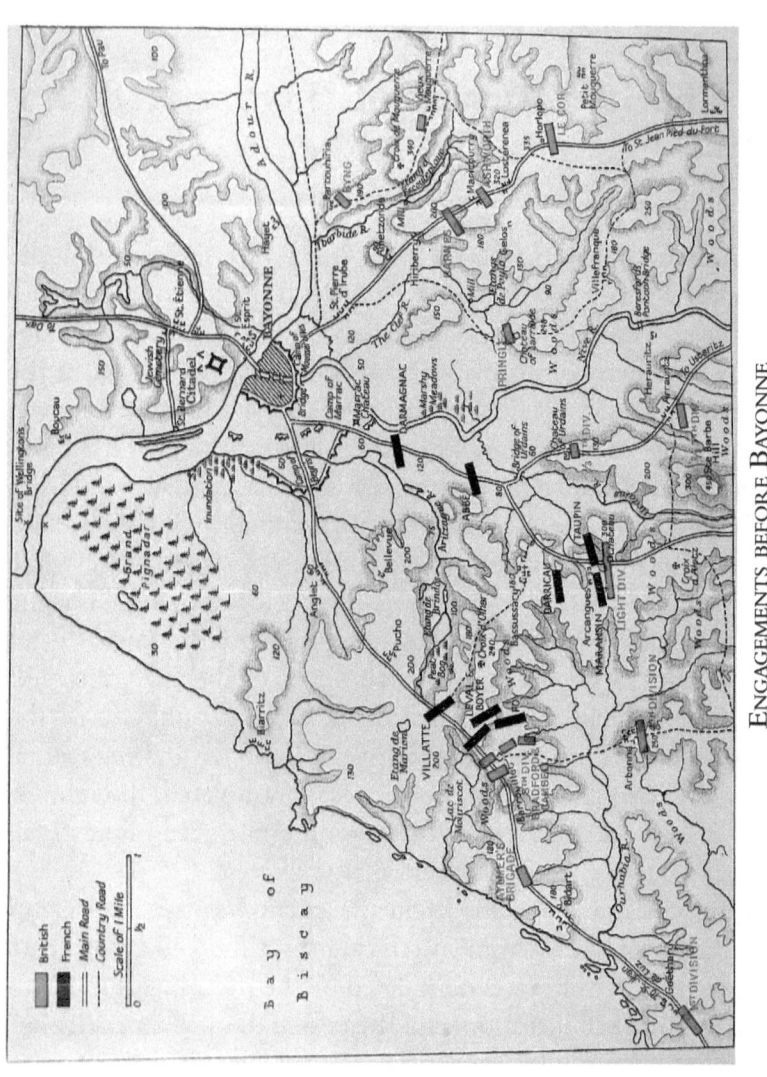

ENGAGEMENTS BEFORE BAYONNE

which was about to depart. Readers of the history of the Peninsular War as it was fought in this period will be familiar with the word 'Gave'. A gave is a river of any size within the Pyrenees region probably derived from the pre-Celtic *'gaba'* meaning a banked river. Since they have their sources in the mountains, they are invariably not navigable, fast flowing and the banks can be problematically very high.

> My Dear Miss Thurlow,
> *26th.*—All quiet here this morning, and the letters will go off in about ten minutes. We yesterday heard from Lord Wellington. He has passed the Gave D'Oleron without opposition, and is to pass the Gave de Pau today. Nothing as yet determined about this column, and I do not suppose it will be for a day or two.
> You will probably see Reeve, who has gone home, at least if he remains any time in town, as he is a great dandy. Her Ladyship *(his mother, Lady Saltoun)* is still at Brighton, and I rather think that the house will go against her whenever the Chancellor takes upon himself to determine it. She must find it a great bore, for in the present state of affairs she cannot look out for another house, for fear this suit should go in her favour.
> By-the-by, I see your cousin has been publishing again in verse, and not much better than the first production. I have not been in bed these four nights, nor shall I be as long as I am in command of this post, as we are rather too close for regularly going to bed. It is now after daylight, and about my time for taking a regular good snooze; so I have tolerable good practice in late hours, and shall be a match for anyone when I return....
>
> Ever yours,
>
>   S——.

Once the bridge was secure, Hope began to contract his lines round the citadel. The enemy had strongly entrenched himself under the protection of guns from the fort in the village of St. Etienne, situated on a ridge, along which ran the roads from Bordeaux and Peyhorrada.

The troops moved forward in three columns, converging on the citadel. The right column, consisting of the two battalions First Guards, advanced in *echelon* of battalions from the left; the third battalion leading, halted for a time on the slope of some high ground, followed by the first battalion. The enemy opened fire, and as soon as the first battalion had crossed the marshy ground in its front, Maitland moved his whole brigade forward together, covered by light infantry, and drove the enemy back into their entrenchments.

The brigade was now within 900 yards of the citadel, the right resting on the Adour, at the Convent of St. Bernard, which, on being occupied by the light companies of the First regiment, was converted into a strong post by Saltoun, who was, of course, in command there. If the French intended to destroy the bridge of boats they would first need to retake the convent which made its security essential. The advance of the left column, consisting of the Second Brigade of Guards, was also successful, but the centre, driving towards St. Etienne, met with more serious opposition, though eventually the French were driven into the citadel, having lost one of their guns.

During March, Hope prepared for an assault on the fortifications, but no heavy artillery arrived to enable him to complete the task. The achievements of Wellington's army were all the more remarkable since it was perennially short of materiel and of artillery in particular. This fact made the most careful planning for engagements essential, but assaults on fortified positions were ever problematic to impossible. No fault can be laid at the feet of the artillerymen themselves, but the Board of Ordnance at home had much to answer for. Meanwhile, at Bayonne the infantry 'dug in'. Every house had to be turned into an entrenched post, which was the more necessary since the accuracy of the French gunners within the fort meant no sentry could expose himself to their view without attracting a potentially fatal shot.

As the populace of Bordeaux and its environs, a little over 100 miles to the north, had by this time declared their support for the Bourbon monarchy, Wellington, on the 8th of March, ordered Beresford to march a force to occupy the city, which he entered on the 12th of March. After remaining there a few days, Beresford left Lord Dalhousie in the city with the Seventh Division, and rejoined Wellington on the 18th.

The early stages of sieges tend to be dull for soldiers and by the middle of March Saltoun's period of intense activity had slowed markedly. Furthermore, his own post was now within St. Bernard's Convent which although substantially in ruins, nevertheless still offered a dry place to work, write and sleep. So, his relaxed letter to Catharine Thurlow is longer than its immediate predecessors and typically well informed.

St. Bernard's Convent,
March 13th, 1814.

I wrote you last week, my dear Miss Thurlow, from Beaucotte (Boucant), a small village in the rear of this place, and the day after we advanced and drove the enemy's posts into Bayonne and the citadel, and since that time we have been perfectly quiet on our part, and have the place closely invested, waiting for orders to besiege it, which have not as yet arrived from Lord Wellington, nor is it certain whether we are to besiege or not. I have the command of this post, which forms the right of the line on this side the river, and is close in with the citadel and dockyard, our advanced posts being about six hundred yards from them; it is on the high road from Bayonne to Beaucotte and the mouth of the Adour.

My mansion has a fine name, but is not very remarkable for accommodation. It was formerly a convent, and was *abimé* during the revolution, and the ladies turned adrift. Since that period, it has been made use of as a glass-house, but for want of trade they went to rack, and since we have taken possession the enemy have destroyed by shot and shell the small part of the house that was habitable, except the kitchen, in which I am now writing, which it will puzzle them to throw anything into; indeed for some days past they have left off firing at us, finding, I suppose, that they did us no harm.

I have no news of any sort or kind to tell you, as before you receive this you will have seen the account of Lord Wellington's victory over Soult, since which time he has been in cantonments in front of Mont Maman, and perfectly quiet. He was wounded slightly in the hip, and has been confined a few days in consequence. Soult has since the action received a reinforce-

BAYONNE FROM THE SANDHILLS

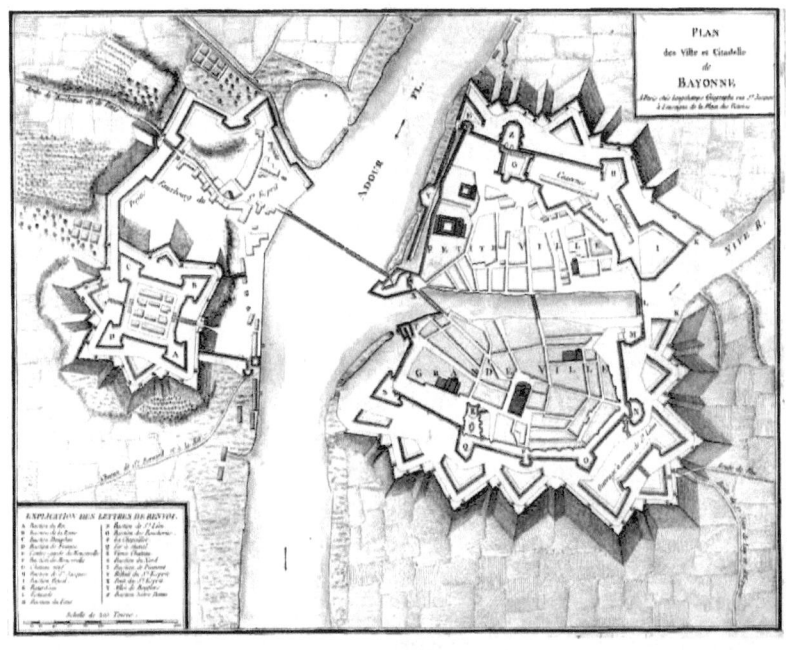

ment of nine thousand men from Suchet's army, which has retired from Catalonia, and we therefore expect soon to hear of another action if Soult should think himself strong enough to attack. In the meantime, all the reports that we get through France are of a pacific nature; indeed, they go so far as to say that the line of demarcation to be observed by the armies during the armistice is now being settled, but I rather think that this statement is premature.

The French people are heartily sick of the war, and if they could have peace, do not care whether Napoleon or a Bourbon is their king. They all seem to look towards the latter, as they say they never can have a permanent peace as long as Napoleon lives, but they are too much afraid of him to rise, as in case of failure they know he would revenge himself most properly; and as there is nothing left in the country but old men, they like to look twice before they leap. Let what will happen it cannot be long before I see you in No. 10, so for the present *adios*, my dear Miss Thurlow, and believe me ever yours,

Saltoun.

Very little of note occurred at Bayonne though it remained a dangerous place to be for the unwary. Those without the walls kept their heads down whenever possible and those within the walls did much the same. Opposing armies in close proximity to each other resort to sniping, though usually, if their situation continues, jointly prudently prefer to be provocative as little as possible. Time ultimately, of course, was on the side of the British for 30,000 men were waiting to take Bayonne whilst Soult had withdrawn his army, in effect leaving the garrison to its fate.

Saltoun remained ensconced behind the walls of his abandoned convent outpost. Although we do not have Catharine Thurlow's letters to Saltoun, it is clear from his reply to her in the following letter that (as expected) the news that he had decided to stay in the field and had not discussed his decision was not sitting well with her and she had, furthermore, made her feelings known to him. Saltoun's letter appears to contain elements of one side of a spat between two people who had acknowledged that they were now a 'couple'. Here we see Saltoun quite on the defensive, giving a reasonable account of himself (if in a deliberately over-complicated way given his situation was exactly what he had wanted), though it would be interesting to know Catharine's reaction to his rather patronising, 'my dear girl'.

St. Bernard's, before Bayonne,
20 March 1814.

Your letter of the 1st instant I received yesterday, and as this is our post-day I do not like putting off answering it till next week, so have got up very early this morning, or rather have not lain down again, for I am obliged now to turn out every morning before daylight, in order to see as soon as day breaks if the bold Frenchman has made any alteration in his lines or not, and to report accordingly.

You seem to think that I meant to have remained in this country had I got my promotion under any circumstances, and therefore of course think it odd I did not tell you so when I was in England last year; but, my dear girl, that event depended so much upon a contingency, that, although I thought it might happen, I certainly did not think it very likely, which I will explain to you as shortly as I can.

When I was in England I knew very well that some sort of arrangement was in contemplation by which the Guards would get promotion, either by taking our generals off the strength of the regiments as captains and giving their companies to the senior officers, letting them receive the pay and giving us the rank, or by removing them entirely from the regiment and giving them a specific pay equivalent to what they now receive.

Either of these things taking place would have made a number of us captains at the same time, and as most of them would have gone to England, there would have been a sufficient number in London to have done the duty without me; but by far the most probable thing at time was, that I, from being first for purchase, should got my promotion by purchase, before any arrangement of this kind could be settled, in which case I should have been the only officer promoted at the time, and must have gone home in my turn to do the duty in London, and have gone to Holland, or come out here again in the regular course of things. Now there could be no use in mentioning a thing which might never take place, and indeed which never has, at least not yet, and was not at all likely to happen in my case; but the circumstance of the augmentation taking place, which never came into anybody's head, put me exactly in the same situation as had the first happened, by promoting Reeve and Thomas at the same time as myself, and enabling me to remain, which I am glad to find you approve of, and I hope will be satisfied as to the explanation. What a lot of paper it has taken up, but I could not do it in fewer words. If I have many more military points to discuss, I shall make an officer of you by the time you thoroughly understand the different forms of speech.

Everything remains in the same state as when I wrote you last week, and as yet nobody can guess whether we are to besiege the place or not. Our casualties are very trifling. One of my men got cut in two the other day on sentry by a cannon-shot, and his comrade made the following epitaph on him:—

On sentry I fell a sacrifice
In cold blood to French cowardice;
Close to my head a cannon-ball you see,
Resembling that which was the death of me.

Not so bad for a private soldier. It is a most cowardly thing the way they fire at the sentries, as we have orders at present not to return fire on any account, and the rascals come up within pistol-shot of our sentries, at the same time that they are practising their recruits in firing at them from the works; but when our guns come up, by God we will make them look sharp enough after themselves.

Bordeaux has declared for the Bourbon, and we expect the whole of this part of the country to follow the example; so Boney must look sharp. I shall see you sooner than you seem to expect in your letter, and till then must content myself with writing.

Adieu, my dear Miss Thurlow, and believe me ever yours,

Saltoun.

As it transpired, the French did not have it all their own way when it came to sniping at sentries as Rees Gronow recalled in his reminiscences. One day when he was on outpost duty, he heard several shots coming from the same location within the French position. His captain, Grant, as the senior officer on duty arrived upon the scene to enquire why it was the enemy pickets were firing and he instructed Gronow to make his way to the front to discover what was happening. The following is recounted in Gronow's own words:

> Having arrived at the ravine which separated us from the French, I stumbled upon an advanced sentry, a German, who was coolly smoking his pipe. I asked whether the shots that had been heard came from his neighbourhood upon which he replied in broken English,"*Yes, zir, that feelow you see yonder has fired nine times at mine target,* (meaning his body) *but has missed. I hopes you, capitaine, will let me have one shot at him*". The distance between the French picket and ours could not have been less than four hundred yards; so, without giving myself time to think I said: "Yes, you can have one shot at him". He levelled his musket (which, most notably, was a Brown Bess), fired and killed his man, whereupon, a sergeant and two or three soldiers who had seen him fall, ran down to the front and removed the body.

CHAPTER TWENTY-FOUR

Napoleon's War in the North, 1814

The War of the Sixth Coalition had been waged for less than a year, though it had seen several fierce battles including Lutzen, Bautzen, Dresden and Leipzig. This last confrontation, known as 'The Battle of the Nations' (19th October, 1813) was the largest battle fought in Europe before the First World War and had claimed approaching 130,000 casualties. That war was now, however, coming to an end and it would be the last of the great Napoleonic wars.

Following the reverse at Leipzig and the retreat of the French Army into France in 1813, Napoleon, to replenish his depleted ranks, withdrew large numbers of his troops which had been stationed in Holland and the Low Countries. The Dutch, seizing the opportunity to throw off the French yoke, rose in revolt in mid-November. The British Government undertook to support the Dutch and an expedition of 8,000 men, under Sir Thomas Graham of Barrosa fame, was despatched to assist in driving the remainder of the French forces out of their country.

The Second Battalion, First Guards, under the command of Colonel, Lord Proby, together with the second battalions of the other two Regiments of Guards with several other regiments were nominated to take part in this venture. Proby was subsequently given command of the brigade, so battalion command devolved to Lieutenant-Colonel George Clifton. The drafts selected from the Coldstreams and Third Guards were commanded respectively by Lieutenant-Colonel Adams and Lieutenant-Colonel William Rooke. The Guards Brigade sailed from Greenwich on the 24th of November, arriving at Scheveling on the 6th of December, where the troops landed and marched to The Hague. The Prince of Orange returned to his homeland to rejoin his people at this time.

Graham, in cooperation with the Prussians, engaged in an unsuccessful investment of Antwerp which held the largest concentration of French forces in the region and followed this reverse with a disastrous assault on the fortified town of Bergen-op-Zoom (March 8th-9th, 1814) which was occupied by a garrison of between 5,000-6,000 French troops. The assaulting force of four columns, under Major-General George Cooke, consisted of about 4,000 men, of which approximately 1,000 were selected from the Brigade of Guards. The attack, which took place at night, quickly lost coordination and momentum. The French, who knew their ground intimately, opposed it by contrast with a determined resistance. The total loss of the British troops was 300 killed and 1,800 prisoners, about half the troops engaged, many of whom were wounded. The French lost about 460 men in killed and wounded.

Among the officers of the First Guards, Colonel Hon. James Macdonald was killed. Lieutenant-Colonel G. Clifton and Captain John Bulteel were mortally wounded and Captains James Lindsay, J. L. Duckenfield, and H. B. Trelawny, and Ensign Edward Pardoe, were all severely wounded. Major-General G. Cooke, Lieutenant-Colonel L. G. Jones, Ensigns R. Master, and J. O. Honyman, and Surgeon Curtis were all taken prisoners.

An agreement for an exchange of prisoners was made (which included Major-General Cooke) except for the wounded, who remained in charge of British surgeons in the fortress. This agreement was conditional that they should return to England as soon as the navigation of the Scheldt should become practicable. However, wider events in the war now rapidly progressed making these terms irrelevant and the Guards before long became part of the garrison of Antwerp.

Wellington's own war inside the borders of Portugal and

Spain was also now over and he was pushing a stubbornly retreating foe deeper into France. Though the 'Spanish Ulcer' had been a particularly influential component of the greater conflict that wore Napoleon down, the emperor was, in the end, personally compelled to fight a desperate campaign in the north east on the plains of Champagne as the Northern powers closed in on Paris for the *coup de grace*.

Military historians are unanimous in their assessment of Napoleon, that as a battlefield commander during this period, he displayed his incomparable genius for war. In this he had ample motivation, for his enemies were marching on to the soil of France in overwhelming numbers and his own forces were seriously depleted, since he had spent the human coin of his nation profligately. In the winter campaign of 1814, he engaged his enemies in detail and beat them repeatedly against the odds upon the field, but this had now become a war of attrition and no amount of tactical skill or personal courage on behalf of his often-raw troops could ultimately prevail. His ruin on the greater stage was inevitable.

The emperor left Paris on the 27th of January, 1814 and fought a successful though hard action against Prussians and Russians on the 29th at Brienne. The French were then beaten in a snowstorm at La Rothiére on February the 1st by a combined army of Austrians, Prussians, Russians and the armies of the German states he had once counted among his allies. On the 21st, at Arcis sur Aube, 55,000 men of the French Army withstood the shock of 100,000 allied soldiers, and retired in good order behind the Aube. As a final recourse Napoleon marched to the north, in hope of reinforcing his depleted army from his frontier garrisons, though this necessitated leaving the way to Paris clear to the enemy.

On the 9th of March the headquarters of Prince Blücher was at Laon. Notwithstanding his best efforts, Napoleon was unable stem the advancing tide and he was gradually forced to retire. The combined armies of Russia, Austria, and Prussia, under the command of their respective sovereigns, continued their inexorable advance with a force of 250,000 men, arriving before the French capital city, which had been entrusted to Joseph Bonaparte to defend, on the 29th of March. Given the hopelessness of Joseph's position and his meagre talents, it is difficult to imagine what his brother might have expected of him.

On the 30th of the month the allies entered Paris, after a brief struggle in the suburbs of St. Denis, Montmartre, Romainville, and Belleville. The Emperors of Russia and Austria and the King of Prussia entered on the following day, proclaiming they would no longer treat with Napoleon. A provisional government was established pending the return of Louis XVIII and on the 3rd of April the senate decreed the deposition of the emperor.

Napoleon, upon hearing the news, retired to Fontainebleau, and, after several fruitless attempts at negotiation, from an impotent position on his part, abdicated the throne of France on the 6th of April, bringing an end to the First Empire of the French.

Naturally, the formal moment that signatures were put to paper to ratify the fact could not be immediately connected to the actual cessation of hostilities. So, the conflict in the South of France continued unabated for the period between the emperor's abdication and the receipt of official confirmation that peace had finally been declared in the theatre of war.

Wellington, having beaten the enemy at Tarbes, had advanced and arrived on the left bank of the Garonne above Toulouse on the 27th of March to discover Soult well entrenched in a good position outside the walls. The allies stormed the fortified heights on the 10th of April, and drove the French into the town. The following day Soult abandoned Toulouse, and Wellington entered it a day later. On the same afternoon messengers arrived announcing the emperor's abdication together with a formal instruction to the French commanders to cease all further hostilities. The tragic struggle for Toulouse cost approaching 8,000 needless casualties and over half of them were among the allied troops.

At Bayonne, on a very much smaller stage, Saltoun remained crouched behind the walls of his ruined convent outpost, for the soldiers of the French Army within Bayonne were still intent to put an end to any red-coated soldier who was careless enough to present himself as a target. Lady Margery and Catharine Thurlow in England remained anxious that they would lose Saltoun to one of the final shots of the war and, as it transpired, they were fully justified in those kinds of misgivings for there would be many British soldiers of all ranks needlessly laid low in the days to come at Bayonne and among them the Guards would suffer severely.

Chapter Twenty-Five
The Sortie from Bayonne, 1814

Hope learned that Paris had fallen to the allies on the 7th of April, but since this intelligence had come to him unofficially, he was prevented from sending a formal communication regarding it to his opposite number inside Bayonne. He did, however, convey the news to the French *via* the outposts, presumably in the humane expectation that this would in measure de-escalate hostilities until the appropriate documentation could eventually arrive. The French commander, Thouvenot, was not however, of the same mind. He may have believed that this development might be no more than a ploy to persuade him to surrender, given he had only the word of the enemy upon which to base his opinion. To be fair to him, there had been a number of occasions, during the late wars, when subterfuge rather than an assault costly in lives had been employed to bring about the surrender of a fortified position—not least by the French themselves.

So, another week of the *status quo* passed by until, at one o'clock on the morning of the 14th of April, a deserter from the citadel came over with vital information. He informed General Hay, whose Fifth Division brigade had moved to the right bank, and who was, at the time, in charge of the outposts, that an enemy sortie was intended. This was an incredible development given no-one could have had any doubts that the war was in effect over and lost to France, which seems to suggest that zealots were influencing events behind the walls. In any event, given their circumstances, an attack by the French, *sans honneur*, could have had no beneficial objective for them. Hay at once sent the man to General Hinuber, who put his German brigade under arms, forwarded the news to Sir John Hope, and ordered his own brigade to form at Boucant (near to Saltoun's position), in the event that the forecast attack actually materialised. In view of what ensued one may speculate that less than complete credence (or at the least, severe under estimation as to the scale of the sally) was given to the authenticity of the deserter's report.

Two hours later, at about three o'clock in the morning, a strong force of about 3,000 French troops, under cover of fire from the guns on the ramparts, burst forth, and struck the picquets of the left and centre of the allied force who belonged to Major-General Hay's brigade and the Second Brigade of Guards. The outpost soldiers were killed, fighting in the onslaught with the bayonet. The picquets of the First Guards covered the right of the line. As ill fortune would have it, the night was particularly dark, making it almost impossible to distinguish friend from foe and the situation quickly became chaotic.

On the left, the rush of the attack was so swift that the enemy quickly carried the church and village of St Etienne, with the exception of one house which was held by a detachment of the 38th Regiment under Captain Foster. The Staffordshires within the building hung on desperately until the King's Germans, together with Hay's brigade, came to their rescue and drove the French back to their own entrenchments. Andrew Hay was killed in the counterattack while giving the order that the church should to be defended to the last extremity.

In the centre the enemy also succeeded in driving the picquets of the Second Brigade back, so that the left rear of the First Brigade became exposed to the enemy's attacks. Major-General Stopford was wounded, so the command of the Second Guards Brigade devolved upon Colonel Guise. Maitland's Brigade of the First Guards on the British right suffered less since the attack in its sector had not been so vigorous. The picquets fell back upon their supports, and Lieutenant-Colonel Hon. H. Townshend, First Guards was severely wounded and taken prisoner.

The enemy began to destroy the allied entrenchments, so Major-General Howard gave directions to Maitland to move forward with his brigade of First Guards to the support, and cooperate in retaking the ground between the right and St. Etienne. Maitland formed his brigade on the hill above the convent, in readiness to take the enemy in the flank, if it attempted to push on in the direction of Boucant, and to reach the bridge. When he discovered that the attack was entirely directed against the lines opposite the citadel and that the enemy had penetrated to the left rear of his picquets, he advanced with the Third Battalion, First Guards, against the French who were in possession of the hollow road and field.

The night remained so dark that figures were invisible and positions could only be discerned by the flashes of firing muskets. The battalion was ordered to lie down, and, orders sent to Lieutenant-Colonel Woodford to make a simultaneous attack with the Coldstreams. The signal was given to charge and the two battalions sprang to their feet, ran forward with the loud shouts and hurrahs that distinguished the British infantry and after a brisk close quarter fight with the bayonet dislodged the enemy from the hill, and reoccupied all the posts which had fallen.

The French troops did not long stand to contest the issue and, fearing they might be cut off from safe haven, retreated. As morning dawned a destructive fire was opened upon their retiring concentrations as they crossed the glacis, and they were eventually forced to seek refuge in the citadel, having lost nearly 900 men.

Lieut.-General Sir John Hope was taken prisoner, when moving up with the reserve, so command devolved to Major-General Howard, commanding the Division of Guards. Hope had been riding towards St. Etienne with his staff when he collided with French troops and took two wounds—the second time by an English bullet. His horse was shot several times and fell, trapping Hope's leg beneath it. Three of his staff officers dismounted to extricate him, but were also captured.

The casualties amongst the allies were nearly as great as those of the enemy, amounting to 150 killed, 457 wounded, and 236 missing; but the losses of the First Guards Brigade were small in proportion to those of the other brigades, being three officers wounded, three men killed, thirty-seven wounded, and fifteen missing. There were no casualties amongst the officers of the First Battalion, First Guards. The three in the third battalion were, Lieutenant-Colonel Hon. H. Townshend, severely wounded, and taken prisoner; Lieutenant and Captain J. P. Percival, and Walter Vane, were both also severely wounded. There were, altogether, sixteen casualties amongst all the Guards officers, and 490 amongst their men and no less than nine officers of the Guards subsequently died of their wounds.

Within two days of the action at Bayonne, Saltoun wrote a letter to Catharine Thurlow and in it he announced that the war was, indeed, at last over. The sortie at Bayonne had been its last engagement and, of course, he reported it to her at length including the casualty list. Saltoun's disparaging reference to Napoleon's behaviour at the last as being comparable to Whitelock is principally worthy of note, because many modern readers might not understand its relevance. The grounds for Lieutenant-General John Whitelock's notoriety with the British Army and public came from his bungling of a comparatively minor operation in 1807, when he commanded a military expedition to Buenos Aires in South America, which was then part of the Spanish Empire.

The enterprise failed with heavy losses among his troops, leading to an ignominious surrender which resulted in a guilty verdict at his court marshal and his dismissal from the service. Saltoun's weighing of the reputation of Napoleon against that of Whitelock (given the latter has all but disappeared into obscurity, other than for military historians) may, with the benefit of hindsight, appear peculiar, but of course he was writing these lines with the enthusiasm of the first flush of victory and from the perspective of his own moment in time and circumstances.

More relevantly Saltoun had made the error of evaluating

Napoleon by his own standards of behaviour and integrity. In his time he was very far from being alone in fostering this kind of perspective and, in measure, a chivalric philosophy on the part of the victorious sovereigns would lead to the defeated Napoleon being placed at considerable liberty within his own virtual fiefdom on Elba, for they imagined, against all the evidence of their own experience of him, that he would finally subscribe to their own rules of conduct.

In this they were fatally mistaken, for he was an irredeemable unscrupulous chancer. The emperor knew very well that notions of honour held a pre-eminent place in his world. He understood well the importance and influence of awards and titles, but cynically (or pragmatically, dependent on one's perspective) placed absolutely no value in them or what they might represent, other than as tools of manipulation to be employed upon the gullible to achieve his own objectives.

Saltoun's verdict on Hope's capture at Bayonne is also worthy of notice. He rightly disapproved of a senior officer coming to grief through his own fault by doing what he should not do in a place where he had no business to be, though this was far from the first time (or the last time) in wartime for that kind of ill-advised risk taking.

St. Bernard's,
16 April 1814.

Yours of the 29th of March, my dear Miss Thurlow, I received yesterday, and am happy to say that my predictions about the war are not, only likely to be fulfilled, but are already come to pass, sooner, I must confess, than I thought they would; for I certainly thought old Boney would have made a harder fight of it. He has made a most miserable finish, and given up all claim to the name of a great man. One can hardly conceive it possible that a man who has held the rank he has done in Europe, could hesitate an instant between death and a despicable existence, and in spite of all his talents, and all his victories, we must write him down in the same page with Whitelock. But to return to ourselves.

Since I wrote last, we have had a very sharp affair, and one that has fallen very severely on the Guards. The enemy made a most desperate sortie on the morning of the 14th, about three o'clock, and were not driven in without very great loss on our side. They got through the picquet line near the Bordeaux road, and the night was so dark that it was impossible to tell friends from foes.

Sir John Hope very imprudently rode to the front during the dark, met with a party of the French, whom he mistook for Germans, and in endeavouring to get away his horse was shot, and he was wounded twice and taken prisoner. He was endeavouring to rally a picquet that had given way, which would have been a very proper place for a lieut.-colonel, but was a very improper one for a commander-in-chief.

General Hay was killed, General Stopford wounded; poor Sir Henry Sulivan *(who was an absentee member of Parliament for Lincoln)* and Captain Crofton killed; Captain White and Shifner dead of their wounds; Colonel Collier, Captains Burroughs and Woburn very severely wounded and in all about sixteen officers of the Guards and Colonel Townshend taken prisoners, and I believe wounded, but am not certain. What makes this loss the more provoking is, that we had learnt of the abdication of Bonaparte the day before the sortie took place. We expect that a suspension of hostilities will take place today or tomorrow, as we have sent in the confirmation of the news to the governor of the place, and it will not be his interest to make war against the Bourbons any longer.

I did not know till I received your letter that my mother had taken a house, but I had heard that she was looking out for one, as the Grosvenor Street house was not likely to be settled in a hurry. *Adieu.* I shall not be long now before I see you.

    Ever yours,

                                Saltoun.

The official news of the abdication of the emperor did not reach the Allied Army camp for another two days, on the 18th of April, whereupon it was communicated to Thouvenot, the governor of the Bayonne fortress. Wellington and Marshal Soult, agreed on the suspension of hostilities, and at midday on the 20th, the allies in front of Bayonne, hoisted the Bourbon standard, saluting it with twenty-one guns. The French garrison of Bayonne hoisted their tricolour, and responded by firing two shells. On the 27th an *aide-de-camp* from Soult arrived with the official intelligence of the suspension of hostilities and that an armistice had been signed. The following day the white flag of capitulation flew above the fortress.

Saltoun's next letter to Catharine Thurlow seems to imply that soon after hostilities had officially ceased he had departed from Bayonne and taken the first opportunity for recreational travel, though it is also possible he had been ordered on detached duty whilst at the same time intending to enjoy all the liberties that would have afforded him. Within the week he had already visited Toulouse and had arrived in Bordeaux *en route* for Paris. The tone of this letter is decidedly good humoured as one may expect, for he had survived the war and had, on the previous day, celebrated his 29th birthday.

Although he informed Catharine that he was about to attend a ball for the Duke D'Angoulême he was at pains to suggest that there would not be many beautiful ladies in attendance, though how convinced Catharine Thurlow would have been by that claim we may imagine. The *fêted* duke was a French royalist who had been living in exile in England, the elder son of the Count of Artois, who was the youngest brother of Louis XVI. In his future he too would be king of France—for approximately twenty minutes! It is worthy of note that Saltoun was unimpressed with the newly empowered Bourbon French; a view, which if it was justified, augured poorly for France's immediate future. Yet again Saltoun's judgement on current affairs transpired to be only too tragically astute.

More interesting perhaps, in this missive, is Saltoun's allusion to the possibility of his being sent to America. This is a reference to the 'War of 1812' which embroiled the United States, Canada and Britain. War had been declared by the United States in 1812 motivated by a number of factors which it could categorise as the usual hostile interference of the British in its affairs. Veteran regiments which had fought in the Peninsular War were, indeed, being sent to contest the war in America at this time. The final engagement in this war (and the one most abidingly significant to the United States of America) was fought at New Orleans, January 8th, 1815, and was another example of pointless loss of life, for it occurred two weeks after the signing of the Peace of Ghent in Europe and the news that the war was over did not reach the combatants in time to avert the battle.

The Americans under Jackson inflicted a decisive defeat on the British who had carelessly assaulted a strongly defended earthwork over open ground. The attack, reminiscent to those which would occur a century later in Flanders, cost the life of the Duke of Wellington's brother-in-law, Edward Pakenham, who was in command. This war, fought far away from Europe across the Atlantic Ocean, would significantly influence who would and would not be standing on the high ground facing Napoleon beyond Waterloo in Belgium come the fateful day.

Bordeaux,
23 May, 1814

I wrote you, my dear Miss Thurlow, before I left Bayonne, but I should not be surprised if you receive this letter first, as from the packet being changed from Sebastian to this place, I much fear our letters have not been sent as they ought to have been, which is rather a melancholy thing for the friends of our poor fellows who were wounded in the sortie, as no less than nine have died of their wounds, and their friends will hear of their death before they have the least idea of their danger.

We have had a most delightful trip from Toulouse to this place, by way of Montauban and Ajen, (Agen) along the course of the Garonne, through the most beautiful country. We passed through the whole of Soult's army, which was cantoned on that side of the Garonne. The behaviour of the troops, although perfectly respectful towards us as officers, clearly showed that they were not by any means well satisfied with the new order of things, and that they considered the thing as forced upon them. However, I know enough of soldiers to be perfectly convinced that, if the present government can find means to pay them their arrears, they will be as faithful an army to Louis as ever they were to Napoleon, and the king should strain every nerve to gain that point; however, I never did, nor do I now expect much exertion from a Prince of the House of Bourbon.

This is one of the finest towns I ever saw in my life, fine wide streets, with avenues of trees, a number of public walks, etc. The Duke D'Angoulême is here; we have just been at his levee. The natives give him a grand ball tonight, to which we are invited, so we shall have an opportunity of seeing all the beauty of the place, which, if I am to judge from the specimens I have hitherto seen, is certainly not great.

Tomorrow we set out for Paris, by way of Tours, etc.; we shall arrive there in about ten days, as we mean to make several digressions to see the country. Our stay at Paris will be very short, so you may expect me soon after you receive this. I shall write from Paris, and if you write, direct—Post-office, Paris. None of the Guards are as yet ordered for America, but if they do order us, it shall not prevent me coming home and seeing you before I go. I am perfectly determined on that head, so *adieu* till I arrive in Grosvenor Street.

Ever yours,

Saltoun.

The brigades of Guards remained in camp for about six weeks in the vicinity of the citadel of Bayonne. Peace was signed at Paris on the 30th of May; the official account of its signature reached Bayonne on the 9th of June; three days after which, on the 12th, salutes were fired by the governor at daybreak, at midday, and at sunset, in celebration of the event. Orders were at the same time received for the First Brigade of Guards to march to Bordeaux, where they were to embark for England. The camp was broken upon the 16th of June, and the brigade, marching through the country of the Landes, arrived at Bellevue on the 21st. On the following day they entered Bordeaux.

Here the brigade remained for a month until the 23rd of July, when the first and third battalions, were embarked in large boats which transported them down the river to the mouth of the Gironde, where the frigates, *H.M.S. Tigre*, *H.M.S Belle Poule*, and *H.M.S Freya*, were ready to receive them. These ships sailed on the 26th and 27th of July, reaching Portsmouth at the beginning of August. The two battalions of First Guards then marched to London, arriving on the 9th and 10th of August, 1814 respectively.

CHAPTER TWENTY-SIX

A Brief Interlude

Lord Saltoun resigned his temporary command and travelled, as he had intended, from Bordeaux to Tours, and thereafter onwards to briefly visit Paris. Within a few weeks he had reached England, where he was, of course, welcomed by his friends and family; most particularly by his much-relieved mother, for few emotions can compare to those experienced by a parent who embraces a child come home safe from a war.

Saltoun lost little time in making his proposal of marriage to Catharine Thurlow which was, we may reasonably assume, readily accepted. The recently concluded wars with France had been waged for over 20 years with little respite and had resulted in the restoration of a Bourbon monarchy, which had every reason to have peaceful inclinations and sentiments of gratitude towards its sovereign neighbours. So despite the forebodings Saltoun had expressed in his correspondence regarding the possible return of Napoleon after the end of the recently concluded conflict, we may speculate that, given the 'imp was safely stoppered in his bottle', the engaged couple had confidence to expect there would be many unhindered halcyon days ahead for them.

Propriety required, in any event, that an engagement of a respectable length of time would be observed, which would allow preparations for the forthcoming nuptials to be made. Perhaps that is why Saltoun, given his long absence from his estates and business affairs, before long took leave of his *fiancée*, and in the late summer of 1814, travelled north to Scotland and the family home at Philorth.

We may readily discern the change in the couple's relationship from their correspondence, for now the more formal, 'My dear Miss Thurlow,' with which his numerous letters had hitherto begun, had been transformed to, 'My dear Catharine'. Little comment is required with regard to Saltoun's delightfully giddy letter to Catharine written in August, 1814, for it is demonstrably one penned by a young man smitten by his lady love.

Fraserburgh.
August 1814,

My Dear Catharine—

I shall not see you again for these three months; it is a devil of a time. I did not meet anybody this morning, being rather too late for the watchmen, but the Jubilee Jacks were returning in great numbers, and, as they call it, smoked my trousers.

I did not tell you last night where to direct to me, but in case you should ever wish to write to me in *propria persona*, my direction is—Philorth, Fraserburgh. However, as now I am reduced to my old resource, and have no greater pleasure than writing to you, I shall frequently do so, and will give you such directions about writing as you may require, although I do not see the least occasion for it, nor any reason why you and I should not correspond if we feel inclined. My head was in such whirl that for once in my life I dreamt, and could recollect most of it. It was all about you and the Park, and I was just going to kiss you, when my brute of a servant roared out ten o'clock, and I awoke not a little disappointed to find it was not reality. By-the-by my old maid of a landlady was in the Park, knew me but not you, and has laughed at me today, when I wished her goodbye, about the care I took of my little woman, as she was pleased to call you. Goodbye, my dearest girl, for I could go on writing nonsense till the paper could hold no more, and believe me ever yours,

S——.

During the winter of 1814-5 the ambassadors of the victorious European states debated at the Congress of Vienna in an attempt to unravel the effects of the Revolutionary and Napoleonic wars and lay the foundations for an abiding equanimity on the continent. Meanwhile, Europe remained in a state of armed peace. Belgium remained occupied by the Dutch and the Belgians themselves together with a body of British troops, under Sir Henry Clinton, including the three second battalions of Guards, under Major-General G. Cooke, (late of the First Regiment) together with some Hanoverians.

In the Springtime of 1815 on the 6th of March, Lord Saltoun was married to his Miss Thurlow, and she accordingly became, Catharine, Lady Saltoun. The couple then travelled to pass the honeymoon at Worthing House, which they had hired for the purpose. The property was situated in the coastal town of Worthing, ten miles from Brighton, at the foot of the South Downs in West Sussex which at that time was described as a 'small watering-place', where they 'hoped to remain undisturbed for some time'. The author, Jane Austin, who was a contemporary of the Saltouns, knew Worthing well and visited it on several occasions. Indeed, her unfinished novel, 'Sanditon' is believed to be based upon the town. After the wedding Catharine received a warm and welcome congratulatory letter from her mother-in-law, the now, Dowager-Lady Saltoun.

March 13th, 1815.

My dear Lady Saltoun—
We all wish you and our dear Saltoun all happiness. I shall rejoice to embrace you both, and I hope you and he may enjoy many years of felicity, at least if the best that mortals can enjoy may be termed felicity. I do not like to allow a post to pass without writing to your Ladyship, and having not above two minutes and a half to write in, must be my excuse for this hurried scrawl. The girls join in love with your affectionate mother,
M. Saltoun.

This charming note of support and affection from Margery Saltoun could not fail to have been well received by Catharine. It may be that the acknowledgement that life was not expected to be all 'felicity' was based on some of the bitter experiences of her years, though admittedly something of a dampener given the occasion. In this instance, unfortunately, the sentiment could not have been more appropriate.

On the evening of the 26th of February, 1815 the exiled emperor, Napoleon, had reached a fateful step from the small western Mediterranean island of Elba, where he had resided in open incarceration since the end of May, 1814. He placed his foot on to the deck of the waiting felucca, *Caroline* which then transported him to the brig, *Inconstant,* bound for Golfe-Juan in the South of France. By the first day of March, (about a week before the Saltoun wedding), Napoleon was once again standing upon French soil. He advanced northwards in triumph, passing by Grenoble, Lyons, Mâçon, Chalons, and Auxerre, cheered by the peasantry, his ranks constantly expanding as he was joined by soldiers who greeted his return as a second coming. The Duke of Wellington was at the time at Vienna, where he had gone to replace Lord Castlereagh as one of the representatives in Congress of the eight European sovereigns. On the 13th of March, the Congress declared Napoleon an outlaw and that it would be prepared to assist France to restore order.

By March 20th, a week after the Dowager-Lady Saltoun's note to Catharine was written, Napoleon had reached Fontainebleau, where he heard that the king had abandoned Paris and fled to Belgium seeking the protection of the alliance. On the same evening the emperor was reinstalled in the palace of the Tuileries in the heart of Paris without a shot having been fired to oppose him and was re-establishing his former grip on power. Having landed in France with 600-700 soldiers at his back, he once again commanded the immense armies of France, led in many instances by his own chosen men; the generals and marshals who had once brought Europe to its knees at his behest. Alexander and Catharine had been enjoying their honeymoon time together for just two weeks.

Napoleon's reappearance on the stage of history and Louis XVIII's rapid decampment from Paris was by this time common knowledge. The European powers had fundamentally misjudged and under estimated the former emperor of the French when they had ensconced him upon the island of Elba. For Napoleon, a life of imprisonment (irrespective of how cosseted it may have been) was no life worth the living and an opportunity to regain his former position, at any peril, was worth the game of chance by comparison. The odds were inevitably heavily against him, for his enemies had consistently demonstrated, when he was an emperor, that irrespective of the defeats they suffered at his hand upon the battlefield, they were resolved to be eventually done with him and would employ all the vast resources at their disposal to accomplish the task. That they would come to terms with him, as a renegade, was beyond countenance for they knew he would be politicking simply to buy time. If he was allowed enough of that precious commodity, war would follow inevitably so, without delay, they prepared for war themselves. All that having been said, given what they assuredly knew of him, they had been tardy to imprison him in a cage without a lock because—*bien sur*—he had departed from it, given the opportunity, as if driven by compulsion.

In the First Guards, promotions within the regiment had transferred Lord Saltoun back to the third battalion. On the 1st of April, 1815 the first battalion was ordered to join the second battalion in which was already in garrison in Belgium. Since one battalion of the Guards would certainly be withheld for home service, it appeared that there would be little chance of Saltoun being called to active service. This apparent reprieve endured for no longer than a single day. The order of the 1st April was countermanded on the 2nd of the month; the third battalion was nominated to be sent abroad instead of the first battalion.

All hopes of a peaceful beginning to married life for the Saltouns were in that moment dashed. The honeymoon was cut short and Lord Saltoun was called upon to bid farewell to his bride and rejoin his regiment. Chance (aided by the influence of higher authorities with agendas of their own) had diverted Saltoun's immediate future from the gentle pursuits of the domestic drawing-room to the perils of the military campaign. Little imagination is required to understand how this development impacted upon Catharine and his mother. The Dowager-Lady

Saltoun had returned to Scotland and from there she wrote to Catharine having received the dreaded news from her son that he was returning to action. This letter speaks for itself with a poignant clarity undiminished by the passing of time.

Philorth,
9th April 1815.

My dear Lady Saltoun,

I have just received Saltoun's most distressing letter. Alas! it seems my evil destiny never to be for any time free from some very heavy pressure—some cause either of deep regret, or some object of constant anxiety. I have enjoyed more ease of mind for the last ten months than I had known for years, but the term is over; I have now only to join my prayers with yours that the Almighty may be gracious and protect him. For you do I feel most truly; it is a severe trial for you, and not the less so as—except in the loss of your kind father—you have not as yet felt the iron hand of affliction. God grant you never may, and that this trial may be happy in its issue and short in its duration: all will depend on the promptitude with which the combined powers set their immense force in active operations.

I am very much vexed that I have so long delayed being in town, but my letters from some who ought to know, and one from Saltoun two days since, satisfied me entirely as to any immediate orders for service. I am unhappy at not having seen him; do, my dear Catharine, tell me if he is quite well, and how you are yourself. You have no friends more anxious for you than the girls and I, and it will be a great comfort to us if by our society we can add to yours, particularly during Saltoun's absence. If you should not feel disposed to write directly, make William (*his brother*) write. I need not, I am sure, recommend him to your sisterly protection; you will, I know, be a real sister to him without any solicitation. I hope soon to see you; a very few days will make me fix my day for setting out; I wait some letters. I began to write on half a sheet, which pray excuse; and with the united love of Margaret and Eleanor, believe me, your affectionate mother,

M. Saltoun.

P.S.—It strikes me as just possible you may be going with Saltoun, if so, I double my entreaties that you will write to us very often.

CHAPTER TWENTY-SEVEN

The Gathering Storm

Upon their return to England from the south-west of France, the First and Third Battalions, First Guards were fortified by an injection of recruits from the home-based companies. The four companies of the second battalion were ordered to join the headquarters of their battalion in the Low Countries at Brussels, the Guards having moved from Antwerp in July, under command of Colonel H. Askew.

The Duke of Wellington was in Flanders making an inspection of the Flemish fortresses and all the troops in the Low Countries, British as well as foreign, were under the command of the inexperienced Prince of Orange, who was at this time just 23 years old. He had never fought a battle, though he held the rank of full general in the British Army having risen by convention through all the ranks of seniority from lieutenant-colonel since he was 19 years old. Had the prince been blessed to exist in a period undisturbed by conflict, none of this disparity between authority and responsibility, in a practical sense, would have mattered very much. Two officers of the First Guards, Captain Hon. A. de Ros and Viscount Bury, were appointed among his *aides-de-camp*.

The command of the Brigade of Guards came, in January, 1815, to Major-General P. Maitland, since General Cooke, had been appointed to command the entire garrison, though Maitland had also commanded the garrison in his absence. In February, Maitland left Brussels on leave, handing over the brigade to

Lieutenant-Colonel Macdonell, of the Coldstream Guards. The role that this officer would play in the coming conflict would, for a time, be the difference between victory and defeat and we shall hear more of him in due course.

Before Napoleon had arrived in Paris, the allies began assembling their forces on a very long line which ran on the left near Basle, on the Upper Rhine, and the right, of which the British element formed a part, near the frontier of Belgium with France, towards Ath and Oudenarde.

In the middle of March, the Second Battalion, First Guards in Brussels was ordered to march to Enghien, thirty miles south-west of the Belgian capital. At five in the morning of the 25th of March the two battalions of the First and Third Guards assembled on the Grande Place, opposite the Hotel de Ville, and began their march to Hal, followed by the Coldstreams. The Prince of Orange, perhaps giving notice of what level of judgement might be henceforth expected from him, had conceived the notion to pre-emptively besiege the northern French city of Lille, so the Guards received orders to pass through Enghien to Ath, which they reached on the 26th, strengthening the extreme right of the allied line, and being in a position to resist any French attack from the direction of Valenciennes.

By the close of March, 1815, before the Duke of Wellington took command of the king's forces on the continent, the British troops in Belgium amounted to 7,300 cavalry and 18,000 infantry together with 14,000 Hanoverians. The three battalions of Guards still formed at this period only one brigade, making part of the First Division strength being:—First Regiment, 974; Coldstreams, 765; Third regiment, 883 men. A light division was also formed, consisting of Sir Henry Clinton's Brigade, Adams's 52nd and 95th Regiments, and a brigade of the King's German Legion,

The Guards were held ready at Ath, to move forward on Lille at the shortest notice, having always one day's provisions ready cooked with them, but Napoleon was already steadily moving his forces into position and so the project of besieging Lille, (predictably given the source of its conception, never a very good idea), was abandoned before it had the opportunity to develop into a disaster. The brigade returned, on the 4th of April, to Enghien.

Meanwhile, the British Government resolved to increase the number of the king's troops in the Low Countries. Many regiments already in England were armed for this service, and those returning from America were, on their arrival, at once sent on to Belgium. Of the Guards, the third battalion of the First Regiment, under Colonel Hon. William Stuart, was eventually selected to join the second battalion abroad, being ordered, on the 2nd of April, to prepare for immediate service, and after several orders and counter orders, it marched from the Birdcage Walk, at six a.m. on Wednesday, the 5th of April, to Deptford.

From Deptford the third battalion marched to Ramsgate, arriving there on the 9th of April. This appears to have been a well-coordinated operation with none of the delay that often interrupted the sea-borne transportation of troops, for the battalion set sail for the continent on the very day it had arrived at the coast. It is quite clear from the brevity of Saltoun's note to his wife that the business of embarkation was fully occupying his time.

Ramsgate,
9th April 1815.

My dear Catharine,
We are this moment arrived and are to embark immediately, and I hope sail this evening, as this is not the most delightful place to remain in. The wind is not very fair, but we hope to get to Ostend by the morning. God bless you!
    Yours affectionately,

S——.

An unfair wind notwithstanding, the Guards reached Ostend safely on the following day. On the 11th the troops were loaded onto barges and moved upon the canal to Bruges, and then onward, still utilising the canals of the Low Countries, to Ghent finally reaching the village of Marcq, very near to Enghien, on the 14th of April. Saltoun's letter to Catharine confirmed his safe arrival on the continent. Readers will note the reappearance of Hughes, who will join his master at a later date.

Ostend,
11th April 1815.

My Dear Catharine,

We arrived here yesterday after a tolerable passage, and everything looks like the bustle of preparation, but except when one's thoughts wander a little across the water, I have been so used to the sort of life that it comes quite natural to me, as skinning does to the eels. Today we proceed to Bruges, and tomorrow to Ghent. Our Brigade are at present at Enghien, a small place between Ath and Hal, where I suppose they will remain for some time, at least till every arrangement is made with respect to this army, which now will not take much longer, as the Duke of Wellington has arrived at Brussels, and is very expeditious in these matters.

This is a tolerable town, but has the appearance of much poverty, in consequence of its having suffered much during the late war by the stagnation of commerce. The garrison is at present composed of Hanoverian troops, who are clothed in red, but are distinguished from the British by their officers wearing yellow sashes. The British troops, as soon as they land, receive their ammunition, and immediately proceed by the canal to Bruges and Ghent, from which latter place they march to their different cantonments. According to our present plan we shall reach Enghien on the 14th, from which place I shall again write to you, as indeed I mean to do every opportunity that occurs.

When Hughes *(his servant)* comes out let him bring with him a pair of saddle-bags as I have none, and also tell William *(his brother, the Hon. William Fraser)* to get a horse at about 40 guineas, and send it out by Hughes, as they are very dear and bad in this country; the horse is not to be too tall, and by applying to Torrens he will put him into a way of getting a passage for him. He must have a saddle and bridle. We are just setting out, so God bless you, my dear girl, and believe me, ever your affectionate husband,

Saltoun.

The regimental history reports that several officers joined the third battalion at Marcq, a few days later, *viz.*, Lieutenant-Colonel J. H. Stanhope, on the 20th; Colonel Hon. William Stuart,

Lieutenant-Colonel J. Reeve, Captain J. Gunthorpe, Brigade-Major, and Captain Boldero, on the 23rd; Captains Ellison and H. Powell, Surgeon Watson, and Ensign Butler, on the 24th; and notably Lord Saltoun on the 26th of April.

It is quite peculiar that in his letter of the 11th of April Saltoun wrote that he expected to be in Enghien on the 14th and for the battalion this arrival date certainly proved to be the case. There seems to a discrepancy between Saltoun's correspondence and the regimental history which implies that from the 11th to 26th-he was somewhere unspecified for two weeks though he had, as he revealed, been in Brussels for a period in the interim. That confusion is exacerbated by the date of his next letter to Catharine dated the 22nd which establishes him in Hoves since this is also a small village in the immediate vicinity of Enghien (*N.B* this should not to be confused with the municipality of Hove near Antwerp, though Hoves is the modern name of the location of the Guards encampment and in Saltoun's time it was, indeed, called Hove. Accordingly, it is termed Hoves in this book). Reeve, his brother officer, did not—according to the regimental history—arrive until the day after Saltoun sent this letter home, though Saltoun expected him on the 24th.

These details notwithstanding, this is another poignant letter from a soldier at war to his new bride. It was not uncommon in this period that wives travelled on campaign with their husbands which is why the Dowager-Lady Saltoun had raised the issue in her correspondence to Catharine. From Saltoun's response in his letter it seems clear that Catharine had, indeed, expressed the wish to join him on campaign.

Hoves,
22nd April 1815.

My dear dearest Catharine,
I did not expect to have seen Hughes and your letter by him quite so soon, or rather, I did expect that Reeve would have arrived before; but he found, I suppose, something so agreeable in Ghent as to induce him to remain there, and I have not as yet got your letter by him; but I know that tomorrow he will be at Brussels, and of course the next day here, so that before

the post can come I am certain of having another letter from my dearest Catharine, which, quiet and idle as we now are, is an event in any man's life, but in mine, considering whence and from whom it comes, a very great one, or at least one which I consider in that point, as it is one that gives me the greatest pleasure.

You wish to know where we are, what we are doing, and what we are likely to do. At present we are perfectly quiet in this village, and are likely so to remain till the army is closed up, and I do not think we shall be ready to act till about the 10th of May or thereabouts. But, however, mine is mere conjecture; yet I hope by that time—and I rather expect it—that we shall be in such form as to be able to take the field with every prospect of success.

Since I wrote you, I have been to Brussels to see the place. It is a fine town, and if we were certain of holding this situation for any time, I should be the first to propose your joining me; but as we must be war soldiers now, believe me, my dear love, it is both for your comfort and mine that you should remain in England. I wish to God I was there with you, but a man must follow his line, and I have taken war for my profession. I was always ready to meet my duty—this time I have forced myself so to do; and although my heart and soul are now with you, I have no doubt they will come back the first time the French eagles want them. ... Believe me, my dear love, I long to kiss you, and so kiss the paper you will read.

Saltoun.

The Duke of Wellington assumed the command, from the Prince of Orange, of the King's British and Hanoverian forces on the Continent on the 11th of April. Major-Generals George Cooke and Peregrine Maitland were originally, on the 15th of April, named to command the two brigades into which the four battalions were to be divided. However, Cooke was put in command of the whole of the First Division of the army composed of the above two brigades of Guards, under the following authority, of the 16th of April, from the Duke of York, Lieutenant-Colonel Rooke being appointed his Assistant Adjutant-General.

Major-General Sir H. Torrens to F.-M. the Duke of Wellington

My Lord Duke—I have it in command from the Commander-in-Chief to convey to your Grace His Royal Highness's wish that the division of Guards now in Flanders should be commanded as follows, *viz.*:

Major-General Cooke

First Regiment 2nd and 3rd Battalions, Major.-Gen. Peregrine Maitland.

Coldstreams, 2nd Battn.; 3rd regt., 2nd battn., Major-Gen. Sir John Byng.

I have etc.,

H. Torrens.

Major Gunthorpe, Adjutant First Guards, and Captain Stodhart, Third Guards, were appointed Brigade Majors of the two brigades respectively, and the former continued to act in that capacity during the whole subsequent campaign. Lieutenant-Colonel Sir Henry Bradford, of the Second Battalion First Guards, was, on the 23rd of March, appointed Assistant Quartermaster-General, and subsequently, on the 5th of May, was attached as such to the First Division.

With the view to consolidating and amalgamating the two armies of Great Britain and Hanover with those of Holland and Belgium, the infantry and artillery of all these countries were divided into two great army corps. The first, composed of the 1st and 3rd Divisions of Dutch-Hanoverians, and of the 2nd and 3rd Divisions of the Dutch-Belgic Army, was put under the orders of the Prince of Orange; and the second, composed of the 2nd Divisions of the British and Hanoverians, and of the 1st Division of the Dutch-Belgic Army, was put under Lord Hill, who was also appointed second in command. Thus, the British Guards were again placed under the directions of the Prince of Orange. They would become part of the Allied Army of near to 70,000 men which would assemble to fight at Waterloo.

The great wheels of politics and war may have been inexorably grinding into motion in Europe in the late Spring of 1815, but for ordinary British regimental soldiers the time honoured routine of waiting until someone higher up the chain of command told them where to go and what to do remained the order of the day. So, the Guards occupied their time as usefully as possible around Marq, Hoves and Enghien. Though they could not, of course, have known it, the farmlands which would become the most famous battlefields in the history of warfare and put many of them in their graves, lay at peace just 20 miles (a two hours and some minutes trot) due east of their camps.

Saltoun had much time at his disposal and wrote to his wife often from the camp at Hoves throughout the remainder of April, May and the first days of June. In fact, his correspondence would be despatched from Hoves until days before the great battle was joined. It is unsurprising that the tone of Saltoun's letter of the 27th reflected the frame of mind of a very recently married young man and for the first time we read that he speaks to her intimately as, 'dear Kate'. The letter concerns domestic matters including the arrival of Saltoun's recently arrived manservant, Hughes, and the care and training Catharine's horses. A royal audience appeared to be notably in the offing.

It is worth noting that Saltoun, 'hopes to burn Paris', which suggests that despite his rank he, perhaps understandably given his military career, was having difficulties with the politics of separating the person of Napoleon from the restored French state and the Bourbon monarch who, despite having fled from his capital city, would have preferred not to have it returned to him in ashes.

Hoves,
27th April 1815.

I wrote you, my dear love, on Sunday last, but, however, I am never tired of writing to you, which is the only reason I can produce for writing now, for it is half-past four in the morning, and I think you know me well enough to believe that I certainly should not get up at this hour to write if I could sleep without writing; but the fact is, that I had a great many letters to write by this mail, and I put yours off till this morning, knowing I should get up to write to you, and also perfectly well knowing I should not get up to write to any other soul alive, I might, it is true, let this mail pass by without writing to anyone, but having written to others, I could not resist the pleasure of writing to you, and it is only to you, dear Kate, that I have any pleasure in writing.

Reeve has come, and brought me your letter, papers, etc., and I have written to William about the horses; for Hughes tells me that the "Larker" is likely to throw out curbs, to which all young horses are liable, and they may and must be taken off. In the meantime, they will prevent him from working for a short time, I have therefore told William to get you another horse to match, so that in case of accidents you will always have two to work, and you may as well quicken him about it, as he is, like me, apt to be lazy about any and everything that he has to do. I have had a long letter from my mother, in which she mentions her wish to go with us to the drawing-room, etc. etc. I am a bad hand at etiquette, so you will find out whether you should pay your respects to Her Majesty during my absence, or wait till we go together. . . .

We are perfectly quiet, and I think are likely so to remain till the 10th or 15th of the next month. The troops are closing up, and everything getting ready for war, but I hope to burn Paris, and be with you yet before August is over.

Give my best thanks to P—— for her good wishes when you see her. As to the music, take care of it, for L—— has brought out one part of the duets and left the other, so they are useless till we meet again, I have found plenty in this country, God bless you, my dear love, and believe me, ever your affectionate

Saltoun.

In his next letter to Catharine, Saltoun re-emphasised what he had previously confessed, that he was uncomfortable attending formal occasions and so would have absented himself from the Duke of Wellington's ball even had he been invited to attend it. His excuse that eighteen miles was an onerous distance to travel for such an occasion is somewhat discredited by the revelation that he was in the process of planning a sixty-mile excursion over bad roads for his own amusement!

At this time Saltoun, somewhat uncharacteristically given his previous accurate assessments, appeared to be of the mistaken opinion that the forthcoming campaign would begin with another invasion of France, possibly pre-emptive, by the combined allied armies who would take the initiative once they had fully gathered together. That potential had, inevitably, also occurred to the former emperor of France, who was no more inclined to be supine than his opposite number had been in the Iberian Peninsula.

Deserters were a not uncommon feature on campaign, so it is imprudent to assume that Saltoun's personal experience of their quantity at this time was abnormal. This kind of observation in his letter to Catharine—that the enemy were preferring to surrender—may, indeed, have been written as a note of encouragement to allay her perpetual anxieties regarding his safety. That having been said, whilst Napoleon's entourage had been greeted enthusiastically by civilians as he progressed towards the French capital, there is some difference in cheering a grand procession of a celebrity and readily coming to terms with the consequences of his arrival. The return of the Bourbon royalty had its supporters, particularly in western France, but had also not been universally popular among the population at large, though neither was the prospect of the return of a dependably warmongering Napoleon.

France had been quite literally bled dry of its fathers, brothers and sons during the long wars and it now seemed certain the next generation would be also sacrificed on the altar of blood, for the nation knew the emperor's ambition knew no bounds. However, for very many soldiers in his army (particularly the rank and file and junior officers), Napoleon remained a venerated figure, for within him lay embodied all their status, pride and influence. It sat poorly with these men that they had suffered slights and had been reduced to poverty by the return of the Bourbons and those considerations gave the French Army of 1815 an enthusiasm for a fight motivated by all the symbols, causes and glories of its own history.

Of course, there were also veterans in the ranks who knew the horrors that lay ahead, had believed war was behind them and had no more fight left in them. Young and inexperienced conscripts were justifiably simply fearful. Some men wearing

French uniform were not native Frenchmen and had always been reluctant confederates with stronger allegiances to their motherlands. Some men felt certain they were destined to be recklessly sacrificed in a lost cause, for this conflict was not to be fought between legitimate nation states, but by an outlaw who had already abdicated his throne, undertaking to leave politics and conflict behind forever.

Many senior detractors, who were in a position to make their own choices, did not rally to their former master's call though they had once been among his most ardent supporters and had benefited significantly from their associations with him. Some of these men had taken new oaths they were not prepared to break. Several of them had the wisdom or guile to know Napoleon would not prevail and so distanced themselves from him before the fact. Nevertheless, the expectation that a sufficient number of soldiers would desert his ranks to paralyse Napoleon's ability to wage war was, alas, fanciful. There remained many thousands of French soldiers eager to march under the eagles at their master's command and it would take another bloodletting on a grand scale before most of the war exhausted population of France would have what they really desired, which was simply peace at any price, brought about by whomsoever.

Saltoun also made reference in his letter to the fortunes of Joachim Murat. Until this time, Murat had led a charmed life for there are few men that have risen from virtual pot-boy in his father's inn to become a commander and master of cavalry, marshal, duke, husband of a princess, brother-in-law to an emperor and finally, if tenuously, a king. Notwithstanding that Murat owed all of his good fortune to Napoleon, he likewise was not prepared to join him in his desperate roll of the dice of fortune. Furthermore, he knew by this time that the allied powers were not prepared to allow him to retain all the advantages and position he had gained as an accomplice of his former master.

He was, however, reckless (or daring, for his personal courage was indisputable) enough to attempt to consolidate his own position as King of Naples, though he had neither the talent nor support for the task. Unless the news Saltoun had heard concerning Murat was accurately forecast rumour, it is probable that Saltoun's letter dated the 30th April was not sent until sometime later, because Murat's Neapolitan Army was defeated by the Austrians at the Battle of Tolentino on the 2-3 of May, 1815. After this defeat the fugitive Murat, temporarily delayed his tragic fate six months afterwards, by fleeing to Corsica disguised as a Danish sailor.

Hoves,
30th April 1815.

My dear Catharine,

I have just received your letter of the 24th, and as tomorrow is our post-day, I lose no time in thanking you for it, not that I have much or indeed any news to give you, for everything, as far as we are concerned, remains just the same as when I wrote last, and will probably continue so to do for some time yet, till the army is properly closed up.

Some gay proceedings went on last week at Brussels. The new Knights serving with this army were to be installed, and the Duke gave a ball on the occasion. He sent eight tickets to each battalion, but by our division of four to the captains, and four to the subalterns, it did not come down to me; and if it had, I should not have gone, but passed it to anyone who wished going eighteen miles for that purpose. I am told that it was a very good ball, and the supper magnificent.

I have a plan for going to Antwerp and Bergen-op-Zoom, which, if I can get leave, I mean to put in execution this week. The distance is about sixty miles, but the road very bad from Antwerp to Bergen. I propose setting out on Tuesday, and returning on Sunday next. Grose and Miller are of the party, and after this trip I shall have seen enough of *les Pays Bas* to be able to form a very good idea of the rest of them, for I trust when we move from this we shall go direct into France, and, if the thing is not settled before, bring the war to a speedy conclusion. Bonaparte is trying all the means he can devise to stir up the spirit of the people by proclamations, etc., but I am inclined to think that these inflammatory publications have been so often tried upon the French people that they have lost their effect. The desertion of the troops to us continues, and the deserters say that numbers of the men are inclined to us, and will come over the first opportunity. If that is the case it is impossible that Napoleon can keep the field. The war has begun in Italy, and at first Murat had some success, but he has since been defeated; but the papers lie so in their different accounts, that it is impossible at first to know what has really taken place, and probably neither party has as yet done anything of importance.

It was rather unlucky about Hughes and the horse, but it can't be helped and was my fault for not thinking of it sooner. Should William have got one, you may send it out by Colonel Thomas, if he has not set off, or any officer of the *Regiment* that may be coming. Should he not have got one on the receipt of this, write me word by return of post, and I will provide myself here. I did not much envy you your dinner at P——'s, particularly the Loo part of the proceeding; however, we cannot always have everything our own way, or I should not be out here at present, but much more agreeably employed communicating with word of mouth instead of pen, which last way, however, when one has no other, has much more satisfaction in it than we are at first willing to allow. . . . .

I have nothing more to say to my dear Catharine at present. . . The sergeant has just come for the letters, so I must conclude, and believe me, my dear Kate, ever yours affectionately,

Saltoun.

CHAPTER TWENTY-EIGHT

Saltoun's Letters from Belgium, May, 1815

Whilst it was in camp at Enghien, on the 1st of May, the Guards division was reviewed by the Duke of Wellington. Saltoun does not appear to have been present for the occasion, for he made no mention of it in his letters to Catharine. Major-General Sir John Byng took over the command of the Second Brigade of Guards on the 3rd of May, and on 4th, the Prince of Orange assumed command of the First Corps of the British, Hanoverian, Dutch, and Belgian troops, fixing his headquarters at Braine-le-Comte. Colonel Stables was, on the 14th of May, during the absence of Colonel Stuart, in temporary command of the Third Battalion, First Guards.

Saltoun was, on the 15th, put in command of part of the light infantry of the Guards and his letter of the 7th May revealed that he went through with his planned excursion into Holland since he reports his return to Enghien to find Catharine's letters waiting for him. He then went on to describe the sights of his expedition at some length, followed by a confirmation that the European allied armies were continuing to coalesce.

Most interesting is Saltoun's comparatively unsympathetic and uncooperative response to Catharine regarding her acquaintance with the anonymous young gentleman, Mr. M., who undoubtedly had an interesting story of his own to tell. Since Lady Saltoun knew Mr. M. he must have been a well-placed young man connected to her social circle. Evidently, notwithstanding his position in society he had quite recently enlisted in the Coldstream Guards as a private soldier and it is intriguing to imagine why such a rash decision might have been made. Perhaps, since the long war had ended Mr M. saw Napoleon's return as his single opportunity for adventure and if this was the case, his situation though notable, was by no means unique in the British Army for accounts of gentleman volunteers and 'rankers' are well known.

Mr. M. would discover he had struck a hard bargain in the disciplined ranks of the Guards before he would ever stand on a battlefield. The terrible conflicts ahead might prove, furthermore, to be the experiences that would be among his last. In any event, someone was evidently seeking to improve Mr M.'s prospects by exploiting their connections in the army. Saltoun, aware that his intercession would become a burdensome liability, wanted nothing to do with him.

The 'great news' in the letter that Marshals Ney and Mortier had been arrested is curious. Michel Ney had given his allegiance to the restored Bourbon monarch and, upon his former master's landing in France, had kissed Louis' fingers, promising to bring Napoleon to Paris, not simply a prisoner, but *'in an iron cage'*. Such a grand eloquent gesture of royalist loyalty left Ney no subsequent room for compromise as he led his command south to confront the usurper. So, when he forthwith went over to Napoleon on the 15th of March, upon meeting him at Auxerre, Ney committed an act of such blatant treachery that his fate would be sealed should his master's gambit fail.

By the time of Saltoun's letter he had been a member of the emperor's entourage for six or seven weeks. Ney, 'the bravest of the brave', fought desperately at Waterloo in the heart of the combat, including in the final attack of the Imperial Guard to the right of the Allied line, so he would have been within yards of Saltoun's own position on the battlefield. Against the odds (and possibly his own intentions) Ney survived the battle, but was executed, shot to death for his treason by a firing squad against a wall in the Luxembourg Gardens in Paris on the 7th of December, 1815.

Mortier was given command of the Imperial Guard during the 1815 campaign, but was struck down by incapacitating sciatica which, (perhaps fortuitously) rendered him *hors de combat* for the great battle. Though his involvement with Napoleon's schemes initially disgraced him, Edouard Mortier eventually returned into favour at the French court. He was accompanying the French monarch, Louis-Philippe to a review in Paris in 1835, when he was shot and killed (though he was not the principal target) by the *Machine Infernale*, a multi-barrelled musket devised by the assassin, Fieschi. The king, by extraordinary good fortune, given the weapon fired at him was designed to be as inclusive in its reaping as possible, was only slightly wounded. Fieschi and his confederates were captured by the authorities and guillotined.

Hoves,
7th May 1815.

I returned here, my dearest Catharine, yesterday, and found your letters of the 27th and 1st May, but the one you sent by Davis I have not as yet received. He is in the country, and we expect him to join tonight or tomorrow.

I set out, as I proposed in my last, for our trip. We reached Antwerp the first day, passing through Malines, the place we call Mechlin, a fine town, and the country very rich and well cultivated, but a great sameness in the whole of it.

Antwerp is a most beautiful city, and very well worth going to see. It has a tolerable gallery of pictures; and one picture in a private house, called the Chapeau de Paille (it is a lady in a straw hat), is very beautiful. Besides the Church of St. Jaques, which is a fine building, the Cathedral of Notre Dame is worthy of notice; but these people spoil all their churches by whitewashing them in the inside, which destroys all the effect which would be produced by the gloom of the grey stone of which they are built. In Notre Dame there is a very high tower of six hundred and twenty-two steps, from the top of which you have a most magnificent view of the surrounding country, and can see a considerable way on the seaside; but that view only had the effect of making me rather melancholy,—not that I have the least occasion to see the sea to make me think of England, for I do that, or rather think of you, without intermission. In the Church of St. Jaques there is a model of the Mount Calvary at Jerusalem, a curious thing, and the statues as large as life.

Seeing Antwerp took up one day, and the next we went to Bergen-op-Zoom, and saw that fortress, interesting to any military man, and particularly so to us after what took place there last year. We returned the same night to Antwerp, and the next day to Brussels. It had been our intention to return through Dendermonde and Alost, but on that road, they have no post-horses, and our time of leave was too short to make that detour with one set from Brussels. We rode over here yesterday.

Everything remains here the same as when I wrote last, except that the troops which are to form our army are closing, and every day more of them reach their destination. The report of the day is that the first division of the Prussians will reach the Rhine on the 15th; if so, we may look to having them in line about the 25th. They say that sixteen battalions of Hanoverians are to enter Brussels in the course of this week, previous to their being sent to the different divisions, which are to be composed of British and Hanoverians mixed, as we were in the Peninsula with the Portuguese.

I am very glad William has got me the horse, and I wrote you in my last how to send him out, and if he is not gone before you receive this, send a saddle and bridle with him, but if he is gone it is of no consequence, as I can get them here.

... The men Hamilton brought out were a draft to complete the battalion of the Coldstreams here, and on their arrival were distributed to all the companies here, and I must first find out what company Mr. M—— (*a young gentleman who had enlisted in the Coldstream Guards*) has got into before I can tell who are his officers; but that would be of no use, as I can do nothing for him even were he in my own regiment, for the only way he can get on is by his own good conduct, and the best thing to do is to get some of his friends to write to him to advise him to conduct himself well, and to offer to come forward as a corporal. He will be put upon the list, and in the event of his being able to write a good hand, and conducting himself well, he will be brought forward as one, and then it entirely depends upon his own steadiness whether he is made a sergeant, or broke.

8th.—I did not close this letter yesterday, in hopes of having something more to say, and we have very great news, but it will be no news to you, as you will have heard it before you get this. Ney and Mortier are arrested, and twenty general officers have sent in their resignations to Bonaparte. We have for some time known that party has been running very strong, but I certainly expected Ney would have been faithful to Bonaparte. Any disagreement, however, amongst them is good news for us.

I have not had any letter from her Ladyship or any of them. I suppose she is in a fuss about houses, which, by the by, my dear love, will be your case, unless something lucky turns up; for getting a house, which one would suppose at first sight an easy thing in London, is the most difficult thing in the world. By this time, my dear Catharine, you must be tired reading, though I am not of writing to you, so I shall close proceedings till next post-day, and believe me, my dear love, ever your affectionate

Saltoun.

Saltoun's letter from the middle of May reports that his new horse had arrived, delivered by his brother's servant. Very little was happening in the Guards' camp and therefore, not uncommonly in correspondence between two people who must write to each other, but have little to write about, some of the content tends to be about very little of consequence. Unsurprisingly, Saltoun had no illusions about the limited abilities and judgement of his commander, The Prince of Orange, and commented that Wellington would always keep him on a short leash to moderate the damage he may do. That task would transpire to be virtually impossible once battle had been joined and tragic consequences would inevitably ensue.

Saltoun reported his visit to General Rowland Hill, who had been Wellington's most trusted lieutenant in the Peninsula and the only general who was trusted to effectively manage an independent command by his master. At Waterloo he would command II Corps and would lead Adam's brigade against the Imperial Guard in the closing stages of the battle, though he had his horse shot from beneath him and for some time was lost in the *mêlée*, believed killed. Saltoun's recently acquired horse was pre-

Privates of the First Regiment of Foot Guards on Service

viously owned by James Hay of his own regiment, whose death at Quatre Bras Saltoun would witness at the closest of quarters.

The disruptions caused by the Saxon troops was reported by Saltoun with a degree of accuracy. These troops, stationed near Liege, had indeed mutinied, refusing to carry out orders. Blücher and his Prussians were disinclined to tolerate this kind of behaviour especially from German troops and on May 6th several Saxons (among them some who had imprudently cried out, '*Vive L'Empereur!*') had been executed by firing squad. These, it may be claimed with some irony, were the first angry shots of the campaign of 1815.

The Saxons continued to be rebellious and were eventually considered to be so unreliable that it would be dangerous to send them into action under Blücher or Wellington. Saltoun apparently considered their loss to the army to be trifling, though his estimate of their number is conservative. Later academic sources put the contingent at closer to a potentially influential 14,000 men. Saltoun yet again reaffirmed his belief that hostilities would be initiated by the allies and that nothing would occur until the Russians and Austrians arrived.

Hoves,
14th May 1815.

My dear Love,

William's servant arrived here last Friday with the horse, which is a very nice one, just the right height, and takes very kindly to the troops. He also brought me your letter of the 4th, and yesterday I received yours of the 8th with the papers. You are so good, my dear Kate, in writing so often, that as I can't find words to express how much pleasure I have in hearing from you, I shall follow your plan, and write to you whenever I can find any opportunity.

You want to know whether I have received your letters that you sent *per* post, and the difference it makes between sending them that way or by Barnard. I can't tell if all you sent *per* post have arrived, but I should think so, for I have received eight, namely, the 11th, 14th, 24th, 27th, 28th April, 1st, 4th, 8th May. Now as to the difference of time. The letters which are sent by

Barnard go in the Duke of Wellington's bag, which as soon as it lands is sent off express to headquarters, so that at present, being no great distance from headquarters, I get your letters that way a day sooner than by post; but should headquarters move any great distance from our division, and they were not at the place appointed for the post-office, then they would have to go to headquarters in the first instance, and would be then sent to me. As, for instance, when we were at Bayonne, headquarters were at Toulouse, and the post-office was at St. Jean de Luz, the letters that came through Barnard went to Toulouse, and then were returned to Bayonne, and those that came by post were left with the division at Bayonne in their way through; but you had as well for the present send them through Barnard, for we are not very likely to be very distant from headquarters, as we have got H.S.H the Prince of Orange to command our column, and I do not think the Duke will let that young gentleman far out of his sight; and if we should be sent to a distance, I can always send you word how to send them; for, thank God, my dear love, the communication here is not quite so long coming as it was in Spain.

I received all the Scotch letters safe, and answered them last Sunday. I think I mentioned it in my letter to you. I went last Wednesday to Grammont to pay a visit to Lord Hill, and meant to have written you a letter from thence on Thursday last, but I found that their post had gone out on the Wednesday before I got there, as their bag goes round by Ath, and therefore sets out the day before ours, and takes our bag on the way from Ath to Brussels, so I was, much against my inclination, obliged to wait till today before I could write to you....

I was certain that the "Larker" would, sooner or later, have thrown out curbs; however, the cure of them is perfectly simple, and not a very long job. I hope by this time you have got another horse. Indeed, I now wish I had left my big horse in England, as he is an excellent match, and I find from his old master, Lord Hay, who is *aide-de-camp* to Maitland, that he goes very well in harness. I did not try him at Worthing, for the coachman said that he had heard in the yard that he would not go in harness. He is an excellent horse, and begins to be less afraid of soldiers, but not by any means tractable as yet, but he stands fire very fairly. We go out three times a week to practise ball at a mark which is excellent training for the nags....

The 10th is past, and the 15th near at hand, but as yet we have no symptoms of a move. They say that the Prussians will be all ready in a day or two, but as yet no Russians have arrived, nor are the Austrians up, and I do not expect that anything will be done by us till after the 25th. Boney is still at Paris, and they say that he is afraid to quit it. That may be the case, but I rather imagine that he does not mean to act offensively against us, and as he knows that we are not likely to move till we are all up, he will not, most probably, join his army till he receives information of that being nearly the case. The lies that are about, some of which have found their way into the papers, are similar to all stories which circulate, no one knows how, in the rear of an army.

The story of the skirmish between the Prussians and the French is perfectly false; not a shot has as yet been fired on either side. I see also in the *Courier* letters about wounded soldiers passing through Brussels. Waggons with sick have passed on their way to Ghent, which is always the case when an army is preparing to take the field. These sick they choose to call wounded, and therefore there must have been some fighting. The only thing that has really taken place has not yet got into the papers. It is this:—the Saxons were not very much to be trusted, and they wished to draft them into the Prussian regiments; I mean those troops that came from that part of Saxony which was given over to Prussia.

They objected to this, and did something which was very like mutiny, and they were accordingly disarmed and sent to the rear, to the amount of about 10,000 men. I am glad of it, as the rascals might have gone over to Boney in an action, in the same way as they did at Leipsic to the Allies. 10,000 men more or less is of no consequence to us, but it is of great consequence that we should all be of the same determination.

We have had most charming weather for some time, and it seems likely to continue. I mean in the course of the week to ride over to Ath, and from thence to Tournay, which is a fine town worth seeing. I meant to have gone tomorrow, but Stables is going to Antwerp, and I am therefore tied by the leg till he returns, as I am next in command at this place. I shall finish this tomorrow morning. Goodnight, my dear love.

I contrived to dream of you last night, but it does not always happen; I wish I had some receipt for it. I am just undressed, and recollect that tomorrow I am to see the Second Battalion Light Infantry, who are put under my orders, at five, so that I must at least get up at four, as they are a good mile from this place; and as our letters must be given in at eight to the adjutant-general's office, I think it more prudent to close tonight.

William's man will be sent off on Tuesday. I would have sent him tomorrow, but I cannot get a route from the quartermaster-general sooner. Hughes has been ill of a fever, but has got better. Goodnight again, my dearest love. You will laugh at our hours—it is just eleven—but as we get up much sooner than you and I are in the habit of doing when left to ourselves, perforce we must go to bed sooner.

I shall see you yet before September if things go on well; and believe me, my dear love, your affectionate

Saltoun.

Whilst Saltoun may have been correct to imagine his letters to his new wife were of little consequence from his own perspective, the modern reader will find within them a plethora of small details which illuminate the life of a British regiment in the field during the Napoleonic period.

The regimental games of cricket are not notable as early examples of its practice since the game had been played with varying degrees of popularity since the sixteenth century. Cricket virtually ceased to be played in the middle of 18th century during the Seven Years War, but saw a resurgence in the 'Hambledon Era' which began in the 1760s. The Hambledon team were regarded as the finest in England having 'raised cricket from a sport to an art'.

However, the game declined again in the Napoleonic age when major matches disappeared due to a lack of investment and quality players. The turning point came in 1815 as soldiers in Belgium began to play cricket as described by Saltoun. In fact, a game was played in Brussels in the Bois de la Cambre park on the eve of the Battle of Waterloo. The location became known as La Pelouse de Anglais (The Englishman's Lawn).

Hoves,
18th May 1815.

My dear Catharine,

I send you a few lines, not that I have any news or anything particular to write about, but, as you say you like receiving letters, and I certainly have great satisfaction in writing to you, I therefore have no great merit in pleasing myself.

We are going on in exactly the same way as when I last wrote. The Duke of Wellington has been for some days back riding a good deal, and we used to say in Spain that whenever the *Beau*, meaning the Duke, took to riding, it was time to look out. However, I believe this time he is only looking at his troops, which have been much increased lately by several battalions of Hanoverian *landwehr*, who are tolerably good-looking men in general, but, of course, from their having been raised by conscription since the breaking out of this business, are a good deal in want of drill and other necessary training. The spirit which the French call *morale* is very good in them, and they are pleased at acting with the British, whom they consider as countrymen. John Bull, however, does not by any means admit them to that honourable distinction, but calls them "rid Jarmins," (*red Germans*) from their being dressed in red.

At present Enghien is quite gay. Some of our officers are good cricket players, and at present a match is going on from A to G—that is, men whose names begin with any letter from A to G inclusive—against the rest of the alphabet, including the Duke of Richmond.

The Duchess and ladies are also here on a visit to Maitland. I must get Lord March to introduce me to her Grace, as she and the Duchess of Bedford are the only Gordons that I am not well acquainted with. The A to G beat the others hollow yesterday, and they are to try it again today.

The desertion from the French Army still continues, but in a very diminished ratio. Two officers came over yesterday, who report that the wish to come over is the same as it was, but that Napoleon's officers have taken so many precautions to prevent it, such as only putting men they can rely on, on advanced duty, and putting all the corps they suspect into towns, that it is very difficult for the men to get away.

I have nothing further to write about, and by this time, my dear girl, you must be tired of reading this nonsense, so I shall close, and write again on Monday.

Believe me, my dear love, your affectionate

Saltoun.

Saltoun's letter written just three days following his last predictably had very little of fresh substance within it. The waiting continued. The allied armies were slowly gathering and time was yet again taken to review the troops. The mention of the Brunswick contingent is, however, worth comment. The Brunswick Ducal Corps was raised by Frederick-William, Duke of Brunswick-Wolfenbüttel in 1809. Comprised of motivated volunteers, its members were not simply soldiers, but vehement opponents of Napoleon's subjugation and occupation of their German homelands and this defined their valour earning them a notable battlefield reputation.

Many of the troops were dressed almost entirely in black uniforms and to the British therefore became known as the 'Black Brunswickers'. Both infantry and cavalry wore the '*Totenkopf*', the skull and crossed bones badge which had a long tradition in German armies and endured to the Second World War. This may have been in recognition of the duke's father who was killed at Jena-Auerstedt in 1806, but it also certainly gruesomely underscored the corps collective animosity towards their French enemies. The Brunswick Corps in the 1815 campaign originally consisted of about 5,400 troops—a mixed force of infantry, cavalry and artillery. They fought at Quatre Bras (where the duke was killed whilst reforming his men at the cross-roads) and at Waterloo. When the Guards were sent down to defend Hougoumont, it was the Brunswickers, who were part of Wellington's reserve under his personal command, who were brought forward to take their place in the line.

Hoves,
21st May 1815.

You were quite right, my dear Catharine, in supposing that I should be in expectation of a letter from you by the last post, as I received the papers by the one before, which I believe I told you in my last. . . .

The little horse goes on very well, and I think he would make a very nice lady's horse, as he has an excellent light mouth, and very good paces, and is, besides, a very safe goer, although his feet are rather small, and have been neglected; but with the help of Mr. Hughes, who has got well again, we shall be able to get them round. I am very glad to hear that the "Larker" is going on so well. It would have been a curb if it had not been taken in time. . . .

Everything here remains exactly the same as when I last wrote, and no idea as yet got about of when we are to move. I have not as yet been able to make out my Tournay trip, and have now put it off till after Wednesday next, as on that day the Duke of Wellington reviews the whole of the heavy cavalry near Ninove, about twelve miles from this, and I mean to go and see them, as it will be a very fine sight. Tomorrow he reviews the Brunswick contingent at Brussels, but we are to have a practice march, and therefore I cannot go to that show.

Old Boney has certainly not left Paris as yet, and some think that he is afraid of leaving it; but I suppose he is waiting for the grand farce of the Champ de Mai, which he will influence by his presence and that of his Guards. It is perfectly certain that party is running very high in France, and if the States-General were left to themselves, they might choose to unemperor the gentleman, which would not by any means suit his purpose. It is also worthy of remark that he is now trying exactly the same means to raise the spirit of the people that he did previous to the last invasion of his empire. The attempt failed then and we have every reason to believe that it will not be attended this time with any better success.

I am going on with the book of drawing, but with very limited improvement; however, it helps to pass away an idle hour, and besides, it always brings you to mind—not that it is necessary for anything to do that. I made a sketch of the Parade today, and if I succeed in getting it up like the place, I will send you one on a smaller scale.

I am obliged to finish this, my dear love, tonight, for we are to be ready formed at Enghien tomorrow morning at six, and as it is about a mile from this, we must get up betimes.

So, goodnight, my dearest Catharine, and believe me, ever your affectionate

Saltoun.

The Saltoun letters are so full of interesting period detail that a book could be written simply by commenting upon them. In his letter of the 23rd of May we learn that Hughes, his servant, has an over partiality for gin—the alcoholic curse of the age—and so his back pay must be sent to his spouse to prevent him from drinking it away. We may only envy Saltoun the spectacle of the massed British cavalry of the period dressed in parade uniform at their finest.

Saltoun's appreciation of current affairs in the enemy camp was, of course, subject to much speculation, some of which is inevitably inaccurate as is to be expected from an age when communication was limited and slow to travel. Catharine was apparently reading the novel, *Guy Mannering* which was published in 1815 by an anonymous author who was, in fact, Sir Walter Scott.

Hoves,
23rd May 1815.

In the first place, my dear love, I hope you were not disappointed in your expectation of getting a letter from me at the time you expected, and before this you have received my letter by William's servant, as I have heard from Ostend of his having sailed. In that letter you will receive £20 of Hughes (his back pay) to be sent to his wife, which, taking into due consideration his partiality for gin, is not very much against him.

I should like much to be of your party to the Caledonian benefit. It will be a fine thing to see the best actors in Europe, I may say, perform together; but I can only now hope that you may be well amused with it, and I am certain I shall derive as much pleasure from your being amused as I should from seeing it myself, you not being of the party.

My sights at present are of a different description, and I had a very fine one today near Ninove, where Lord Uxbridge reviewed thirteen squadrons of heavy cavalry. They were in very fine order, and worth the ride—about fifteen miles out and in. On Monday next the whole of the cavalry, light and heavy, are to be seen by the Duke and Blücher, somewhere near Grammont. I shall certainly go, unless anything turns up to prevent it, which is not likely at present, as nothing yet looks like an immediate move. However, we are all ready, and so situated that six hours would put the whole machine in motion.

In spite of your doubts about Ney, the thing is perfectly certain that he is in surveillance, and dispossessed, for the present at least, of his command; and it is also certain that he was not in the plot, and that he did his best to prevent his army from going over to Napoleon, but finding he could not prevent them from so doing, Went over with them, and in consequence Boney has some doubts of his fidelity, and very properly does not employ him. As to Murat, the story of the day is that he is in Paris, and it is believed, but not by me. That he may be on his way there is very likely, for he has lost another general action of three days' fighting, at which I am not surprised, having myself seen the Neapolitan troops, six of whom are not worth one Frenchman, and therefore, by our mode of calculating, not worth half of one of England's sons.

The Bourbon cause is certainly very popular in great part of France, but they are so much under the thumb of the army that they cannot speak out. The fact is this, that they do not care a straw whom they have, so that they have peace and no conscription. They are perfectly tired of war, and they know the Bourbon will give them peace; but they are, if I may use the term, so *abiné*, that they will not turn out and fight for what they and all Europe (military men excepted) wish for....

You cannot expect to hear so often now from Mrs. Cunninghame, (Lady Saltoun's sister), because if they go to any of the Mediterranean islands, their letters, in the present state of France, must either come across Spain to Corunna—a very long operation, according to their mode of carrying the post—or they must be sent to Gibraltar, and come home in the packet. I long to hear what sort of a turnout you had at Lady Fraser's. Her son in the Seventh is here *aide-de-camp* to Lord Uxbridge. She herself is a very agreeable woman, and the old gentleman very well, if you will listen to his stories, but they are confounded long ones.

Today we have another grand cricket-match—all those who are members of the Marylebone Club to play against the rest of the Guards. I am not much of a cricketer, and do not play, but for want of something to do have taken much lately to quoits, at which we have some famous hands. It is rather hot work, and therefore very destructive to a certain beverage called white beer.

No house, nor any chance of one! you will have plenty of bother before you get one. It is the most provoking thing in the world that, in London, where they have so many, it should be so difficult to suit one's self. I have not sent you, my dear Kate, much news in this letter; but when we are in this inactive state, we can have no news. However, the sooner we get on the move the sooner I shall get home again.

I am sure you will like *Guy Mannering*; it is very well written.

I shall write again, my dear love, on Sunday, and believe me, dear Catharine, your affectionate

Saltoun.

Brussels in 1815 was recognised as one of the most vibrant cities in western Europe and the British aristocracy thronged to it. That a grand battle was in the offing only added a *frisson* of excitement to the occasion and several civilians intended to view the event as a spectacle though others, understandably, became more nervous the more likely it became that the battle would be fought nearby to the Belgian capital and that Brussels would be Napoleon's next objective in the event of his victory. Balls were regular events as Saltoun's letter reveals. More reviews and *fêtes* followed and the campaign in Belgium began to take on the appearance of a military jamboree, though clearly, by his own admission, Saltoun was becoming bored with the inaction.

Napoleon orchestrated a grand ceremony, the *Champ-de-Mai* on the *Champ-de-Mars* before the École Militaire in Paris on the 1st of June. In his letter Saltoun describes the day as 'last Saturday', once again suggesting his letters were written over a period of days beyond their date. Saltoun's assessment of the occasion, irrespective of his prejudices, was not so far from accurate. Speeches were made from an altar-stage elevated in the centre of the field. Oaths of loyalty were solemnly made by both Napoleon and civil leaders in the presence of senior churchmen.

Ostensibly the purpose of the occasion was to reassure the people of France, by means of the creation of liberating initiatives, that a reformed, less authoritarian and enlightened Napoleon had returned to rule them under a new constitution.

Perhaps someone may have believed him, but, the *Champ-de-Mai* principally served, in the manner of dictators before and since his time, to focus attention on to the person of the emperor in the most emphatic way. Despite the pomp of their presentation, these proclamations concerned matters of very little substance which would have almost certainly, in the event of Napoleon's military success, have been reduced to even less relevance to the people of France. In fact, it later came to light that Napoleon was intending to abolish the House of Representatives as soon as it was safely practicable. Suspicious constitutionalists in the government were determined that there would be no return to the old regime, but the emperor's annoyance with them was palpable and we may imagine how he would have ultimately resolved that kind of impediment to his machinations. Domestic politics were at this point, however, the least of his problems.

For Londoners and their city, meanwhile, the laying of Southwark Bridge across the River Thames was a more significant, practical and solidly notable event in the Spring of 1815, though it would not be open for public traffic (for a toll of one penny) until 1819. This bridge, which was replaced in 1921, was the work of the engineer, John Rennie (the elder) who, among his many notable projects, was responsible for the building of several London bridges and was a pioneer in the use of structural cast-iron. In its day the Southwark bridge was a herald for the approaching industrial age and held the record for the length of a span of cast-ironwork at 240 feet.

In Belgium it was clear from his letters that Saltoun (probably in common with his brother officers) still fully expected that the coming campaign would not be long in its commencement and that when the moment came it would be instigated by the allied armies and not by the French emperor.

Hoves,
28th May 1815.

My dear Catharine,

I yesterday received yours of the 22nd, with the papers to that date, and the whole history of the horse, and from the difference of these two professional men, F—— and D——, in their opinions, it is not very easy to decide what is best to be done. I never was over fond of making an imaginary evil a real one, and therefore see no good reason for voting a horse a lame one which is not so. The fact is just this, if you now treat the horse as if he had curbs you must lay him up for a month at least, and when he gets the curbs, he will only have to be laid up for a month then. I should therefore work the horse as long as he remains sound, at the same time using this *terrifying stuff*, which I conceive to be nothing more or less than lemon's essence, which creates what is technically termed a sweat, that is, produces a slight blister on the part affected, without taking the hair off, and will keep the curbs back for a long time, and may perhaps take them off altogether. Hughes, who is the best farrier I ever saw, says, the horse in his opinion will certainly have curbs, but not for these six months at least. They may be kept back for a long time, and advises working the horse till he does get lame.

Since I wrote we have been and are to be for a day or two very gay. The Duke of Wellington gave a grand ball and supper last Friday at Brussels, to which, as I received a special invite, I thought it my duty to proceed. By far the greater part of the ladies were English, the Richmonds, Alvanley, but not Warrender, Lady Hawarden, Sidney Smith and daughters. Lady John Campbell, etc. etc. The supper was very good, and the whole thing went off remarkably well.

Tomorrow we are to have the whole of the Cavalry and Horse Artillery reviewed near Grammont by the Duke and Blücher, about 5000 men; it will be a very fine sight. On Tuesday races and a *fête* given by the Hussars at the same place; and on Wednesday the Guards play the rest of the army at cricket at Enghien. Of course, a cold collation must be produced upon the occasion. I am no hand at cricket, and therefore do not play, but I attend at these places, and make very severe play at the cold beef and champagne about two o'clock.

We are all anxiously expecting Tuesday's news from Paris, as that will bring us the account of what took place last Friday at the *Champ de Mai*,—not that I expect anything particular will have occurred, for old Boney with his troops will be able to overawe the mob; but I should not be surprised if he went through the farce of resigning his Emperorship, of course being re-elected; but it won't do, for he is so well known that the people who are now against him—and there is certainly a very strong party against him in France—are not to be duped by any of these manoeuvres. They may be kept in awe by the presence of his troops, who are certainly well-affected towards him, but as soon as he is obliged to concentrate his army, the Bourbon party will rise in all the places from which he is compelled to withdraw his troops in order to oppose our army; indeed we have reports, which are believed, that very serious disturbances have already broken out in La Vendée, and other places.

I do not see any immediate signs of a move, but I do not think anything will be settled in France till we do move, and time is getting on, and, with the old gentleman, the troops are also getting nearer the different points of the alignment *(Blücher and the Prussians presumably. JHL)*, and I make no doubt, as soon as everything is ready, we shall lose no time in entering the French territory. As soon as any proclamation to the French people comes out, or any order about the strict observation of discipline makes its appearance, I shall take it for a sign that we are likely soon to start. The French have been beforehand with us, and have been forging a proclamation of the Duke of Wellington in the *Moniteur*, in hopes of raising the spirit of the people; but the fact is, that the Duke has not as yet issued anything of the kind, and will not, I should think, until the army are all ready to enter the French territory; and when he does, it will be a very different one from the proclamation given in the French papers. . . .

I hope you were much amused with the operation of laying the Southwark Bridge, although from what I know of you I am apt to suspect that you would require something very *recherche* to make up for being in the Strand at half-past ten. I should be apt to consider it much too early an hour myself were I in London. I wish, my dear love, I was there, for I begin to be deadly tired of this cantonment, although it is probably a much better one than any I shall have after we march; but they say we soldiers always like a change of quarters, and the sameness of a country village is very tiresome, especially when one knows that we must move before we can get back to where I wish to be. We have been six weeks now in this place, and I really believe if we were once on the move that ten more would see me in London. My thoughts are there pretty constantly, and when the time does come, I shall not let the grass grow under my feet in the journey.

In the meantime, my dearest love, believe me, your affectionate
Saltoun.

On the 30th of May the whole First Division marched into cantonments so as to be ready to be reviewed on the following day by the Prince of Orange, at Bruyère de Corteau, near the high road leading from Soignies to Mons. This exercise was considered by some Guards officers to be 'unnecessarily harassing for the men,' which was to describe the matter diplomatically. The troops were marched out in the middle of the night (two in the morning) in poor weather and before their return to their camps they had trudged over forty exhausting miles.

The regimental historian speculated that *'If the order was issued with the view to proving how quickly the duke would be enabled to concentrate his army on any given point, that might be suddenly attacked by the enemy, there was sufficient justification for the fatigue the men were called upon to undergo'*.

The introduction by that chronicler of the possible requirements of the Duke of Wellington into the affair is an interesting justification, since it attempts to imbue an element of common military sense into an initiative that transparently possessed very little of it. That consideration alone would suggest that the duke, the epitome of pragmatism, had little to do with the matter. It is hard to imagine that Wellington had many uncertainties in his mind concerning the resolution or stamina of his experienced infantry, since he had quite recently concluded an arduous long campaign with many of them from the First Division and knew with certainty that they would perform to his satisfaction if called upon by him to do so. Conversely, this unnecessarily taxing march simply to bring the troops to a review for the inspection of the Prince of Orange bore every hallmark of being ill-conceived by the inexperience and arrogance of the Prince of Orange.

After the inspection, Major-General Cooke was called upon by his superior to *'express to the division the prince's entire approval.'* Lord Saltoun, of course, was entirely in agreement with him. In his letter to Catharine he reported that the prince had declared, *'he had been many years with the British Army (and) he had never seen so perfect a body of men'*. If there was any irony in Saltoun's observation he cloaked it prudently, for he knew that the prince had not so 'many years' experience of anything at all. Nevertheless, there is a suppressed tone to Saltoun's comments concerning 'His Royal Highness' suggesting his writing was deliberately restrained which is difficult to ignore. Saltoun lived in a time when patronage and influence was held by some who had it within their power to turn even a lord into a social pariah upon a whim and so it was essential to be circumspect even within private correspondence. In fact, the day would not be long in coming when Saltoun—face to face with the prince—would be required to employ extreme restraint.

Saltoun's feelings about the Duke of Wellington had been ambivalent for some time. Everyone knew the duke was the man to deliver a victory, but that did mean his soldiers liked him very much (particularly in comparison to General Roland Hill-affectionately nicknamed 'Daddy' by his men) and to be fair to him, he made little effort to ensure they would. Wellington was frequently high handed and unjust in his pronouncements concerning his soldiers—perhaps especially so in regard to regimental or corps officers.

His shoddy treatment of the officers of artillery before and after the Waterloo campaign is almost incredible for example. Saltoun had found ample reason to take exception to Wellington's views and judgements in the Peninsula and it is apparent little had changed in that respect by the time of the campaign of 1815.

Hoves,
31st May 1815.

I have just received, my dearest Kate, yours of the 25th, and, as far as post-days go, am at this moment (and that is some comfort at this distance) situated exactly as you were when you wrote yours, having just returned from a grand review by our Royal Commander, the Prince of Orange, at a place about fifteen miles from this, and as tomorrow is our post-day, and that early, I like to write before I go to bed.

Our performance was perhaps not more lively than yours: however it was very good, and those spectators who were good judges have complimented us most highly, as well as the prince, who was pleased to say that, although he had been many years with the British Army, he never before had seen so perfect a body of men. We are very good, as good as we could wish or expect. This brings me to your having heard that the Duke was not well satisfied with his infantry.

He never had so good before, for the Hanoverians are much better than the Portuguese, and John Bull has not, I should think, altered much in a year, or I may almost say half-a-year; for you know as well as myself, that I was not much above that time in England. The fact is, that the Duke was displeased at the number of staff appointments from the Horse Guards, as he thought that patronage lay with him, and this displeasure has been shifted upon us poor foot-wabblers, who have made him a Duke in three kingdoms, and are good enough to make him an Emperor; but as making him that would clash with our ideas of limited monarchy and freedom of election, he stands but a bad chance of being made one.

Never believe any humbugging stories of that sort until we are well beaten and afraid to meet our enemy, which, beaten or not beaten, will never be the case as long as the present race of England's sons exists. These stories are always set about either for some political purpose or by that species of animal—for man he does not deserve the name of—who, having no *esprit* himself, takes it for granted that nobody else has. You, left to your own judgement, don't respect this character; and I am sure I need not tell you what I think of him.

You want to know whether I have any good reason for expecting to be in England before September. It stands thus: our game must very soon be made up, and then it must be played off, and then we shall either dethrone him in two months, or make peace with him as ruler in France; but my idea of the matter is that the ball is at our foot, and we have only got to kick it through.

I have been running on about military subjects, and have thought you were a soldier, forgetting, my dear love, that agreeable nonsense is the only thing that a gentleman should write, but I have the unfortunate knack of not always being able to get at it. In my last I told you about reviews, races, and cricket that were to take place, but, however, His Royal Highness, as he is now called, of Orange and Nassau or Belgium, put a stop to our part of it, by ordering us to be at Le Grand Bruyere, about fifteen miles from this, which place we left, as I told you at the beginning, about twelve today, and are just returned,—a very hard day on the men as they were fourteen hours under arms. The review on Monday, however, I saw, and it was the finest sight I ever witnessed. There were 6,400 British sabres, and the horses in such beautiful condition, that it was the finest sight possible, and I have no doubt there were plenty of spies to give a due report of them to Napoleon. The races took place, and were, I understand, very good, but the cricket was perforce put off, and the weather has been so wet, that no match could have taken place; it is therefore put off *sine die*, but they will probably play it at the end of the week,

I shall now, my dearest love, wish you goodnight ... and believe me, your affectionate

Saltoun.

CHAPTER TWENTY-NINE

The Affairs of Early June, 1815

Whilst the Prince of Orange may have been marching his soldiers about as it amused him, Napoleon was diligently forming his strategy, for he knew the huge allied armies of Europe, aware of their advantages, were inexorably, if sedately, approaching to overthrow him again. The enemy might break through at any point along his eastern frontier, for he had not a mile of neutral border—not even with Switzerland which had declared for the alliance—that might relieve him of concern. His situation was, furthermore, especially perilous for he stood alone, as destitute of allies as he had been in 1814, which meant everything would depend upon his own genius for the waging of war.

Though surrounded by his enemies, the emperor reasoned that he probably had little to fear from the Portuguese and Spanish for after years of debilitating conflict, they had problems of their own to resolve. The Austrians also had far to come and the Russians had not even reached their own frontier. His best opportunity lay in delivering harsh military object lessons to the allied cause, whilst he was in a position to do so, in hope of cowing those who had yet to join the fight.

This meant decisively defeating the only two armies which were close at hand—the Prussians and the Anglo-Dutch in Belgium. It then required Russia and Austria, having assembled for war, to be dissuaded from fighting and would require Britain and Prussia to be so consummately beaten that they, unlikely as that might be, would fight no more. Weighed against the improbability of such fragile prospects, it may seem that Napoleon's adventure was doomed from the outset, but these were the cards fate had dealt him and he would play them to the end of the game.

When Napoleon had escaped from Elba, there was a only small British force remaining in Belgium; regiments which had served under Graham in Holland at Antwerp and Bergen-op-Zoom in 1814, together with two or three Hanoverian brigades. Upon this foundation the British proposed to construct an army of 100,000 men. Since Wellington had arrived in theatre in early April, he had incrementally received further corps from the home establishment as they became equipped for service. The larger part of the old experienced Peninsular Army that had served in the war against the Americans was still beyond the Atlantic, so few battalions of the veterans of Spain could join Wellington at his time of greatest need of them. That he would have ideally wished to have them under his hand there can be little doubt, though how influential their absence may have been to Napoleon (who had no reason to particularly regard British troops) is questionable.

He had, as has been noted earlier, never fought a British Army, having only the experience of one running away from him on the road to Corunna (together with his experiences at Toulon over twenty years previously) upon which to base an opinion of 'John Bull's' worth on the battlefield. The councils of his subordinates like Soult and Reille on the subject did not impress him since, in his hubris, he considered the defeats they had suffered to be their own responsibilities, rather than attributable to any prowess on the part of those who had bested them. By the middle of June, the emperor's spies would have told him the British force had reached 30,000 men. In addition, a quantity of Hanoverian *Landwehr* had marched up to the Meuse and the Scheldt.

From Napoleon's perspective the construction of the remainder of Wellingtons army was even more encouraging, for he understood the value of experienced, motivated troops imbued with *esprit de corps* well enough. There was no doubting the quality of the contingents of Brunswick and Nassau. The Brunswickers, inspired by genuine animosity, might fight as zealots and the Nassauers had been a seasoned and proven component to his own army in Spain before they had changed sides. Paul Thiebault had gone so far as to describe them as the best troops he had served with in Spain. These were, however, very small armies whose sovereigns were mindful of their own agendas, not least concerning Prussia, which had been influential in persuading them to place their commands temporarily at the disposal of Great Britain. Wellington, considering the Germans under the best light, could not assume he might manage or depend upon them as though they had been raised in English shires.

However, if the British field-marshal could not reassure himself that an army comprised of British and German troops was the same as commanding an entirely national army, when it came to the rest of the troops under his command the situation was decidedly worse and those particulars would not, presumably, have passed Napoleon's notice.

The government of the new kingdom which had been created for the Prince of Orange to rule had been surprised by the return of Napoleon at a moment when its own army was still under formation. Given that the First Empire of the French had so recently fallen and its emperor was safely incarcerated leaving the Continent at peace, everyone involved in that enterprise could have been forgiven for believing that the new army would not, in the foreseeable future, actually be required to fight a war. Furthermore, this baptism of fire, for which it was unprepared from top to bottom in every respect, would be a trial of arms against the most formidable captain and army of the age. At the beginning of March, 1815 the entire regular force comprised just 10,000 men. Within three months another 20,000 more men had been brought to the colours, but these were for the most part raw militia

In an army that was always a 'curate's egg', the Dutch-Belgian troops were indisputably the weakest element. Practically all its old soldiers had served as conscripts under Napoleon and the rest were untrained recruits, so the veterans told the young soldiers what manner of men marched under the eagles, what they had done in the past and what they were capable of doing in the future. For some the old memories brought affection, pride and some stirrings of nostalgic loyalty and for others the prospect was terrifying. In a country of Belgium's small size and location, some would inevitably lean towards France and most of the Flemings and Walloons disliked their enforced union with Holland.

Despite the fact that the officers of the Netherlands Army were loyal, none of this was likely to create an army that could be depended upon and Wellington had no illusions and few prejudices on the matter. Nothing would convince him that the Dutch-Belgians would be guaranteed to fight the French and he attempted to quickly import 10,000 Portuguese troops who had served him well in the peninsula to substitute for them, but with no success.

British, Germans, and Dutch included, Wellington had 105,000 men under him in June; but of these, 20,000 were detached to form the garrisons of Antwerp, Ostend, and other Belgian fortresses. Marginally to his benefit, Wellington understood how to successfully deploy an army that required 'stiffening' with British troops, for his entire career had been spent fighting battles where that had been the case, including in India where his victory at Assaye had been won under the most trying circumstances.

The other army at hand was that of the Prussians under General Kleist. It was quartered partly in the newly-formed Rhine Province, which the Congress of Vienna had given to Prussia's Frederick William III and partly in eastern Belgium, about Namur and Luxembourg. In March 1815 it numbered only 30,000 effectives, but the Berlin Government smartly sent three more army-corps in April and May to join it, and given the command to the grizzled old Field-Marshal Blücher who, despite his 72 years, had been fiercely fighting Frenchmen since the Revolution. His recent notable success had been his contribution to the

Battle of Leipzig in 1813 in concert with the Russians and the Austrians and his animosity towards Napoleon, his army and all his works was vehement and unbridled. However, the French Army did not generally respect the Prussian Army and believed, on the basis of past experience, that on a level playing field—man for man—it would always have its measure.

Early in June, Blücher had 117,000 men; something over half of them of them were line troops, the remainder *Landwehr* battalions. The weak part of this army consisted in the newly-raised regiments from Westphalia, Berg, and the Rhineland, who, like some of the Dutch-Belgians under Wellington, had formerly served Napoleon as conscripts. Nevertheless, a preponderance of the old Prussian regiments ensured that Blücher had more of a German Army under his command than Wellington had a British one under his.

Charles Oman speculated that Napoleon acted, *'reasoning correctly from the characters of the two generals opposed to him, if he waited much longer, they would attack him'*. The emperor's reliable information from Belgian sympathisers, however, was that *'their mobilisation was not yet complete, and that both were awaiting reinforcements'*. Notwithstanding that Wellington and Blücher had the broader responsibilities of general officers required to report, take instructions and cooperate within an alliance which would inform their movements, if Oman was correct in his evaluation then Napoleon may possibly have expected the impetuous Blücher to attack him.

The sober Wellington, however, was dependably one for finding his ideal ground and then requiring the enemy to take it from him or putting himself in a position where he could exploit any error his opponent might make. The fact was that neither commander was under real pressure to initiate hostilities, for time and numbers were on the side of the alliance. That alliance, growing in resources, gave every appearance of waiting until it was fully prepared before it began to advance its armies. Once that was eventually in motion, attrition would do its work. That is certainly what Saltoun believed, based on the evidence of his correspondence. Furthermore, since he never disclosed the opinion of a detractor, it was also presumably a view that almost everyone he knew in heart of that army shared.

The necessity for taking pre-emptive action, therefore, lay entirely upon the shoulders of the emperor for time was not his friend and, in the outcome, only he had everything to gain or lose as the consequence of a single enterprise. As he examined his opponents for their weaknesses, he could see that the enemy was widely scattered; the line of their advanced posts covering the whole frontier over 200 miles from the Scheldt to the Moselle. The Prussian cantonments extended from Liege to Charleroi and those of the Anglo-Dutch from Mons to Ghent. This was clearly a holding line, not one conceived as a precursor for an advance. It would probably take three days for either army to mass on the common centre—the line: Mons-Charleroi. If the British right or the Prussian left were the point selected for attack it would take at least six days to concentrate them.

In these facts lay the simple key to the emperor's plan of campaign. Firstly, he must concentrate his total force in secrecy to deny the enemy time to institute manoeuvres. Secondly, he must act quickly, so he was upon them before they knew he was approaching. Finally, he must resource his assault with every available soldier he could gather and thrust them like a spear into the junction-point of the two hostile armies so he could defeat each army separately. To meet them united would be almost certainly fatal, for they outnumbered his own available force at a ratio of almost two to one. The situation was far from ideal, but there could be no strategy open to Napoleon that was not a high risk one and this was his only option that had any potential to lead to success in the longer term.

It has been well noted that the word 'if', though one of the shortest words in the dictionary, is one of the most dangerous for upon it everything may be gained or lost. If the British and Prussians were crushed, Napoleon could (if his victory was not Pyrrhic) rush to the Rhine to meet the Austrians and if needs must assail them before the Russians began to arrive. If he could demonstrate that the Emperor of France, at the head of his unconquerable army, had returned in all their terrible glory then sober heads in Austria and Russia might be persuaded to treat. Alternatively, if he could hold on until September, his new levies would give him 400,000 more men and with such a force anything might be possible. If Wellington's defeat was crushing, the fall of the British Government might follow and whilst Prussia would be irreconcilable, it might be subjugated in time.

All that taken into account, Napoleon was quite incredibly ignoring the fact that coalitions of enemy nations had fought France in six wars over more than two decades. Despite suffering many reverses they had never given up their resistance and one might imagine, that during his deliberations upon Elba concerning the probable outcome of his gambit, it would have occurred to him that they would not abandon that conviction at a time when he was at his most vulnerable and least legitimate. But before any of this might come to pass, his retention of the throne of France firstly depended upon on the chance of gaining three precious days.

The total force which the emperor could march into Belgium was about 125,000 men. It was 10,000 men weaker than he would have preferred, for, at the last moment, he had been forced to dispatch two divisions with a brigade of the Imperial Guard to the Vendée, which had broken out in pro-royalist open insurrection on May 15th. The Vendeans were beaten and their general, La Rochejaquelein, was killed at the combat of St. Gilles, near Nantes, on June 4th, but it was impossible to recall the divisions employed for the task in time to take part in the advance into Belgium and the emperor could ill afford to be without them.

Despite the imperative of offensive action, it remained prudent to attend to the defence of the eastern and southern frontiers of France and for this task Napoleon employed small forces of the line regiments supported by masses of the National Guard. These units were for the Alps under Suchet, for the eastern Pyrenees under Decaen, for the western Pyrenees under Clausel, for the Var under Brune and for the Jura under Lecourbe. In these divisions the National Guards formed half, or more than half, of the total force under arms. All these six armies together numbered only 75,000 men combined. Of the rest of the emperor's available troops, about 130,000, mostly National Guards, had been thrown into the fortresses of the east and north.

Only Jean Rapp, who was sent to command the Army of the Rhine, had a corps of 20,000 regulars supported by a few of the new levies. It was practically certain that Rapp would fight the armies coming from the east at some point and must be capable, at least, of holding them. In fact, Rapp, in due course, engaged coalition forces at the Battle of La Suffel near Strasbourg and beat them. It was the last battle of the Hundred Days and a French victory. Unfortunately, it would be a victory unsung, for by that time Waterloo had been fought and lost ten days previously.

The whole force which the emperor had collected under his own hand to take into battle was composed of veterans of the regular army—practically all he had of his very best.

Chapter Thirty

The Drums Begin to Beat

As Saltoun sat down to pen his letter of June 4th to Catharine, the insurrection of the Vendeans was being crushed by Napoleon's forces in the west of France. Many of the people of the Vendée, situated south of the River Loire, had opposed the French Revolution from the outset and had risen in armed opposition to the new order in 1793. By the time that counter revolution had been suppressed at least 170,000 Vendeans from both sides of the dispute lay dead together with 30,000 soldiers of the new republic, though some estimates of the slain are considerably higher, for the war bore all the brutality of civil discord and atrocities were committed.

Outbreaks of violence against the national regime in the region continued spasmodically throughout the following years, though incidences accelerated from 1813 when it became clear the empire was bound to fall. The motivations of the royalist Vendeans have been the subject of much debate, but the return of Napoleon coming after the victory which brought about the restoration of the Bourbons was, from their perspective, a potion too bitter to swallow and they rose once again. The nations of the alliance naturally encouraged the 1815 rebellion since it was fought in common cause, but isolated and left to their own devices the Vendeans had little chance of success.

The first part of Saltoun's letter shows that he was comparatively *au fait* with developing events at this time though it is also clear that he was reporting information that had come his way through the rumour mill and so was totally unreliable. Joachim Murat, King of Naples, (if only by his own estimation), contrary to reports remained free and at large, for example. As Saltoun had admitted, the Duke of Wellington was notorious for keeping his own council behind an impassive countenance and so everything and nothing could be happening without almost anyone being the wiser one way or the other. Meanwhile, the Guards remained in their cantonments and the entertainments in Brussels society continued

Hoves,
4th June 1815.

My dearest Catharine,

I yesterday received both your letters of the 27th and 29th, and I fully agree with you, my dear love, that the quick communication by letter is the greatest comfort I can have; indeed, it is even as quick as between London and Philorth; but when we begin to move it will cease to be quite so expeditious, both on account of the distance, and also the post-days of the army, perhaps, confined to once a week instead of twice; but I hope not as yet. However, we have no reason to expect an immediate move, although time is drawing on.

Some preparatory arrangements are making, such as putting the men's great-coats into store, as from their weight they encumber the men in long marches; ours went in yesterday. Also, the order has come out for serving out tents to the army, but the day on which they are to be delivered is not yet named.

Our news from Italy is excellent, and goes so far as to state that Murat is taken prisoner. This last comes from the Duke of Wellington, who believes it. One thing however is certain, that his army is entirely destroyed, and that is of more consequence to the Allies than anything that may happen to him personally. Boney, *on dit*, has put off the *Champs de Mai*, as he called it, *sine die*, and everything looks like his being in a scrape. He has been obliged to weaken his army in our front, in order to quell insurrections in the south, and we are led to believe that the north will rise as soon as our army passes the frontier. People begin to speculate about the day we are to march; some say the 10th, others the 14th, but the only thing certain is, that nobody except the Duke of Wellington knows anything about the matter, and he is a very close gentleman on these subjects, and seldom gives much notice....

I wrote you a long letter the last post-day about the "Larker." The reason I did not send the other horse home is that I cannot do without two riding horses, as what with marches, etc., one has enough to do, and I want the other to ride about the country: or in case anything should happen to the little horse, I want the other, as I must perforce be mounted. The big horse is getting into very good condition, for he wanted grass, and the clover in this country is the finest I ever saw, and makes all the horses as fat as pigs. He is a very handsome horse, now that he is filled out, and a good match for the curricle horses; and it is correct, you know, that the horses behind the curricle should match those in it.

I have no more news, except that Sir Charles Stewart, who is now ambassador at this Court, gave yesterday a grand ball at Brussels, preparatory to leaving that place for The Hague, to which place the King of Holland, as he is now styled, goes in the course of the week, which also looks like our going the other way; for if we move by our left—which is the most likely line of operations, in order that we may not be hampered by the fortresses—we shall leave Brussels open on this side, and of course liable to any incursion which the garrisons of Lisle or Dunkirk may chance to make on it—and it would not do for the king to be taken by one of these parties—besides being a considerable inducement to them to make the attempt; not but what we shall have some troops on this side, but their number will be small, as we shall, I suspect, take as many men with us as we possibly can. Our force of British and Hanoverians is estimated at 61,000 men, exclusive of the Dutch and Brunswick contingent, who are also under the Duke of Wellington....

I have been all day employed picking out light infantry men from the battalion companies, as some of my men are getting worn out and too old for our work, which at times requires a considerable deal more exertion than is expected from those in the battalion.... *(He had command of the light companies of the 1st Brigade of Guards.)*

I was obliged to leave off, having some friends to dine, amongst whom was Hepburn, and dinner being ready; and I must, my

dear love, finish this tonight, as we are to be out at six for a brigade practice; and as I have an odd fancy of never putting off anything that I ought to do, I may have some excuse in doing what I wish to do, and if I do not finish your letter tonight, perhaps we may not come back time enough for the post, and then, dear Kate, I should be in the worst rage a man can be in—one with myself. So, you can't abuse me for writing at night with so good a reason as I have above given, for I should not have slept if I had not done it, and having so done, hope not only to sleep but also to dream of you, my dearest love, which, sleeping or waking, is the greatest pleasure of your affectionate
Saltoun.

We may speculate that an intelligent officer like Saltoun, by the 11th of June, with connections within the army and in society, holding a high regimental rank within an elite corps, though not a staff officer, was as well placed as anyone to appreciate current affairs. However, by comparing his correspondence with what we now know as the facts, we may correlate those events about which he knew nothing with some certainty. So, it is apparent that information he was passing on to Catharine in the first portion of his letter of the 11th remained, as it had been in the past, entirely founded on speculation or misinformation for Napoleon on the 10th of June was nowhere near to Maubeuge, just 20 miles south of Mons. Saltoun knew the details of the Allied Army's own dispositions and with his typical insight understood the inherent dangers of their wide dispersal. Those considerations notwithstanding, in his letter he tellingly wrote, concerning the emperor, *'I have not the least idea that he can be mad enough to attack'*. Demonstrably, he felt no reason to revise his opinion that the campaign would only commence with an invasion of France by the massed armies of the alliance.

As usual Saltoun reported on the lively Brussels social scene and tantalisingly mentioned that the Duchess of Richmond had invited him to a ball which was to be held the following Thursday, which would be the 15th of the month. Saltoun's mention of Sir Lowry Cole is worthy of note since he had appeared in the earliest part of Saltoun's career in Sicily and found distinction at the Battle of Maida and later throughout the war in Spain. He did not, however, serve at Waterloo.

Hoves,
11th June 1815.

This morning, my dear Catharine, I received yours of the 5th, enclosing the Sunday paper; and you judged quite right with respect to Mr. Hutchinson's parcel, for I have not as yet heard of his being in the country. He is, I believe, to be *aide-de-camp* to Sir Lowry Cole, who is expected here to command a division. Pat. Hutchinson of our regiment, his brother, is very ill, and has been obliged to go to Brussels to take the hot-baths there.

Napoleon has at last made a start, and arrived yesterday at Maubeuge, which you will see by the map is on the French frontier, opposite to Mons, and he is concentrating his force near that place.

Our army at present occupies Mons on the left, extending from thence to Ath, Lessines, and Grammont, on the right, for the front line, and the second line is Braine, Soignies, Enghien, and Ninove, with troops also in Hal and Brussels. The right of the Prussians comes to Nivelles, and they are on the line of the Sambre from Charleroi to Namur. Our line, you will see by the map, is very extended, and, of course, if Boney collects any great force at Maubeuge, we must of necessity come nearer together. I have not the least idea that he can be mad enough to attack; but, of course, if we were not to take the necessary steps to prevent him, he might have an opportunity of gaining some advantage over us.

I do not expect that we shall have to move, as we are very near our proper part of the line, but some of the other troops that are distant will, of course, be more concentrated if he, Boney, assembles any large force. They say he has about 70,000 and that the Army of Metz is on its march to join him, about 30,000 strong. We are about 60,000, and the Prussians about 130,000; at the same time, I do not think we shall attack him till the whole of the allies come up, and we shall then invade with about 500,000 men.

We are going on in the same way with cricket matches, races, and so forth. The Duchess of Richmond and ladies are over on a visit to Maitland, and I have been accordingly introduced to her, and she has invited me to a ball, which she gives on Thursday next at Brussels; but I have not by any means made up my mind to go, and it will depend very much how I feel inclined for an eighteen-mile ride when the day comes off.

You wish to know what the ladies at Brussels will do when we begin to act. It will depend very much upon what line we move on; and if we go by the left, most of them will, I believe, go to Spa or Antwerp, and so into Holland; but as long as we remain in our present position they are perfectly safe, as they would have time to get away even were we to retire, which is an event that I do not think likely to take place, except we go back a little for the purpose of getting a better position, but, at all events, I do not think we should give up Brussels without an action.

Saltoun was forced to pause his letter to Catharine that he had dated the 11th of June by the obligatory duty of attending a church service with his battalion. His letter continued, dated June 12th, not with news or rumours of Napoleon and war, but of glittering balls, cricket matches and not unusually, the recurring subject of curbs (an equine condition of the leg) suffered by his wife's horse, Larker. Meanwhile, from the French capital, Napoleon took the first steps of his audacious campaign to keep his throne and started out for the front. The five army corps which were to form the bulk of his army were quietly drawn in from their scattered cantonments, extending from Valenciennes to Thionville, without alerting or alarming his enemy just as he had intended. As it transpired the commanders of the two allied armies in Belgium, despite their elevated positions and intelligence sources, were no better informed than Saltoun as to what was actually taking place, for only the vaguest rumours of the emperor's intentions had at this point reached Wellington and Blücher.

In fact, to confirm the situation by a matter of record, on June 13th, Wellington wrote to Sir Thomas Graham:

> We have reports of Buonaparte joining the army and attacking us. But I judge from his speech to his Legislature that his departure (from Paris) is not likely to be immediate, and I think we are now too strong for him here.

As the duke was writing these lines, the emperor's carriage was furiously driving forward from Laon to Avesnes and that night its imperial passenger slept within ten miles of the Belgian frontier. Blücher was likewise no better informed than Wellington, for he was in the very act of drawing out his own plans for the Prussian advance into France, when the emperor completely wrenched the initiative from the hands of the allies and his army burst into Belgium.

Saltoun resumed his letter to his wife:

June 12th—I was obliged to leave off writing in order to go to church with the battalion, which goes to Enghien for that purpose, where the rest of the troops are formed in square in the Duke D'Arenberg's park, to hear, in general a bad sermon from a Mr. S——, who is staff-parson to our division. I was in hopes to have picked up some news there, but yesterday, for a wonder, had not even a shave, as we call a report, and the only thing was they had a little betting about the cricket match to be played today between the Duke of Richmond and the ten best players, against Maitland and the twenty next best. I am included in the latter number, and we are to begin this morning at eleven o'clock.

I see by the *Morning Post*, which is taken by Clements, that Mrs. B—— has been giving more grand balls, etc., and that the lovely Miss B—— danced with Lord P——, and I think that, and two or three bad puns, is the only thing in the paper. . . .

I am glad the "Larker" still remains sound. I should not be much surprised if the curb goes away altogether; however, Hughes says that he certainly will have curbs some time or another, but that is of no consequence, as they are easily cured. Both my horses here are doing very well, and getting quite fat—indeed, everything gets fat in this country, and I do not think I have got any thinner myself; but I do not know how we shall get on when we march, for it always is the case that we have some scrambling, and the greater the number, of course the greater the scramble, and all put together we shall have certainly not less than 200,000 horses.

I can fancy an English farmer seeing them grazing in his finest wheat fields and paying nothing—what a rage he would be in. I have often thought a little war would do our farmers a great deal of good.

I have written this in bed this morning, for it is now time to get up to go to parade, from whence this must go to Enghien to the post-office.

So, God bless you, my dear love, and believe me ever your affectionate

Saltoun.

Napoleon's plan was unfolding perfectly from his perspective. On June 14th the whole French force was concentrated on a front of not more than thirty-five miles, pinpointed where the French frontier projected most deeply into Belgium. Saltoun, once again, dutifully wrote to his wife reporting the news that Napoleon had not yet departed from Paris and that the previously enthusiastically reported sighting of the emperor at Maubeuge had, indeed, been entirely mistaken. Furthermore, he told her that the Vendean rising was progressing well, quite unaware that it had already been extinguished ten days previously. Interestingly, in this letter Saltoun touches upon the practice of 'chequering' British regiments among foreign troops to provide support on the field, which continued throughout the Victorian period and beyond. He closed in the familiar manner with news of cricket matches and the usual discussion on the subject of horse husbandry.

The Duchess of Richmond's ball in Brussels has passed into the popular chronicle of the Waterloo campaign, but despite his invitation to attend, Saltoun, who had no taste for those kinds of occasions, had predictably decided not to go. So he missed, probably without regret, the glittering occasion that the historian, Elizabeth Longford cited as 'the most famous ball in history'.

He concluded his letter to his young wife, which but for providence may have been the last one he would write to her, as he had often done with an affectionate 'goodnight'. He little realised the long waiting had come to an end and, before he would write again to his dear love, he would take his part in what were possibly the most famous conflicts in the history of warfare.

Hoves,
14th June 1815.

I yesterday, my dear love, received yours of the 8th, together with the newspapers, but, as yet, have heard nothing of Mr. Hutchinson's despatches; not that that in the least surprises me, for I am used to that sort of thing, and know that when a man first lands in a country he has to fit himself out for service before he thinks about anything else, and when he begins to think about parcels he is some time before he finds out where the owners are, and still longer before he can send them, or at least till he thinks he can send them with safety; but I make no doubt he will find his way to Brussels, and from that place he will find his way to dine with me, according to his practice in the Peninsula.

Our Royal Chief, whom you inquired about, is the very man who was to have married our princess. The father is now King of the Netherlands, which makes his son a R.H., whereas before he was only Serene Highness.

In my last I wrote you a long account of Boney's arrival, and of our positions and so forth; but the truth is, that, as yet, Napoleon has not left Paris, and our mistake arose from the imperial salute having been fired at Maubeuge, in consequence of some person having passed through that place, invested with full powers to inspect that and the other fortresses.

Our news from France is good, in as far as party runs very high at Paris, and the risings in La Vendée and other parts of the south begin to take a more organised and respectable appearance. As yet we have no immediate idea of a move, indeed some preparatory things are necessary, such as the means of transport for the spare ammunition, and the tents, which have not as yet arrived here, and, excepting in a case of necessity, we should not certainly move before we get the necessary means for transporting these things with us.

And so, my dear Kate, you thought I was vexed at your story about our infantry: we are by far too well aware of our own strength to do anything but laugh at what the news mongers in England choose to say of us; and if I wrote rather strongly it was only to give you the same idea of our perfection that I have. I can assure you I do not think small beer of them, and the Duke of Wellington and old Boney, you may depend upon it, are very much of the same opinion; not that the British are all together, as probably they suppose in England, but they are divided among the separate divisions in the proportion, in some divisions, of one brigade of British to two of Hanoverians, and in other divisions two brigades of British to one of Hanoverians, the same as we were chequered with the Portuguese in Spain.

In our mode of speech, we call it making very fair grog, holding ourselves, with regard to them, as brandy is to water, but by the mixture making that water a very palatable concern. Our division is as yet an exception to this rule, as we have no Hanoverians with us, and are composed of Guards only, with two brigades of artillery. You like to know all about the army, but I suspect this is not quite so plain as the other.

Our grand cricket-match did not take place, for the day turned out to be a very rainy one, so it stands over till next Saturday, when the Duke of Richmond is to come over for the purpose. I do not feel the least inclination to go to her Grace's ball tomorrow, and shall therefore not do so.

I hope you have bought Blakemore's mare, but if you have not, pray do so. Your having a fancy for her is quite sufficient reason for me, and I hope to see you as much yourself on horseback as you used to be, some of these days; but time draws on, and we have as yet done nothing, and it will take us some time after we start before we can finish the job; however, I have not as yet given up September, but I begin to suspect that August will be far gone before we finish the business.

I have no scandal or news to tell you, and must therefore, my dear, dear love, wish you goodnight, and believe me, my dearest Catharine, your affectionate

Saltoun.

The emperor's campaign had begun well for him and he had won his three-day advantage over the Allies. His own 125,000 troops were already massed for the next stroke, while his enemies remained strung out on a front of at least a hundred miles and more. At dawn on the morning of June 15th, the French Army crossed the frontier and threw itself upon the first outposts of its enemy. The first blow, struck the furthest right of the Prussian Army at Charleroi, was just short of Wellington's extreme left at Mons. On the first day of fighting, only Ziethen's Prussian corps was engaged; caught before it could concentrate, overwhelmed by superior numbers, and rolled back to the north and east having been mauled.

The British and French outposts came into contact late in the afternoon of the 15th, when the cavalry at the head of the emperor's left columns struck the pickets of the Nassau brigade under Prince Bernard of Saxe-Weimar at Frasnes, and drove them back to Quatre Bras, where the prince, to his credit, though true to the spirit of his command, turned to fight. Ney, who was in command of the part the French Army that opposed it reported the fact to the emperor, and encamped opposite Quatre Bras, waiting for his infantry under Reille to come up. Unknown to both Napoleon and Ney, there were only 4,000 men in front of them and the Nassauers could expect no assistance from Wellington until the morrow.

That night Wellington remained at Brussels attending the Duchess of Richmond's famous ball and if his nerve temporarily failed him then, as usual, no one was ever aware of it, though he knew by then that he had been 'humbugged' and had dangerously underrated Napoleon's resolution and ability. In the meantime, he was in the unenviable position of knowing that when dawn broke, he would have no troops on the Brussels-Charleroi road with the exception of one Dutch and one Nassau brigade, at Quatre Bras and Nivelles.

That night the emperor had the satisfaction of knowing he held Charleroi and the bridges of the River Sambre and that the Prussians had retreated beyond Fleurus. Blücher, ordered his whole dispersed army on the march westward and by midday on the 16th, Ziethen was joined by Pirch's and Thielmann's corps giving him 90,000 men under his hand. Bülow's corps was still a day's march distant, but Blücher decided to offer battle without it and took a position on the hill-sides behind Ligny and St. Amand, some seven and a half miles south-east of Quatre Bras. Napoleon, for his part, decided that Ney's *corps d'armée* would deal with Wellington's army, whilst he would personally attend to the dispatching of Blücher's Prussians.

CHAPTER THIRTY-ONE

The Battles of Ligny & Quatre Bras

The Duke of Wellington had not received details of the enemy's initial movements as readily as he would have wished. It was true that Ziethen had promptly sent him news of the attacks on his outposts, but thereafter the Prussian general, presumably preoccupied by the fighting, then neglected to keep British headquarters abreast of developments in French activity. It was not until about four in the afternoon that Wellington received the definitive intelligence which revealed that the French attack in the direction of Charleroi was being made by such a substantial force that it must be part of a general advance.

The duke forthwith ordered all his divisions to be ready to march at a moment's notice, though he remained uncertain, denied reports from his own cavalry screen, if the assault against the Prussians was the only threat or whether a second enemy column was also advancing on the high-road to Brussels *via* Mons. In fact, Wellington held the view that the Mons road was the better option for the enemy, so he would not concentrate on his extreme left until it was confirmed that his left-centre was secure. By the time he finally considered he had an accurate understanding of developing events it was late in the evening, so he directed his scattered divisions to concentrate on Nivelles, Braine-le-Comte and Hal.

The Guards had their first intimation that a French advance had begun when a dragoon messenger bearing the news arrived at Enghein at about 2 p.m. on the 15th. The Second Battalion,

First Guards was quartered in the town, the right wing of the Third Battalion at Marcq, the left wing at the village of Hoves. At eight o'clock in the evening, the right wing of the Third Battalion was directed to join the left wing at Hoves, and remain with it till further orders.

That morning the duke had given directions for the First Division to assemble at Ath, but as events developed that order was superseded and he issued another order (at ten o'clock) directing the First Division to move from Enghien to Braine-le-Comte. This order reached Enghien at half-past one in the morning of the 16th. The drums immediately beat to arms, and at two o'clock the Guards, who had assembled at Hoves, were ready to move off. At four o'clock in the pre-dawn they began their march, the First Brigade leading, preceded by its light companies under Saltoun, and they reached Braine-le-Comte at nine in the morning, having been joined on the march by the Second Brigade under Byng.

The First Division halted for a few hours while General Cooke, who was in command, made a reconnaissance to the south. He returned at midday having decided to continue the division's march towards Nivelles, ten miles farther on. The heat of the day was by this time excessive and the men were suffering from the weight of their packs but, nevertheless, the division arrived at three o'clock within half-a-mile of Nivelles. There it halted to rest, but the men had no sooner piled arms and begun to boil their kettles, than an *aide-de-camp* arrived with an order to immediately advance.

The sound of firing soon became heavy and apparently very close, suggesting that enemy troops were entering Nivelles from its other side, so the Guards moved off at the double, down the hill, to engage them. The town was traversed without opposition, however, allowing the troops to move on onwards towards Hautain le Val. There they were compelled to stand aside to allow some artillery to pass to the front, whilst wounded British soldiers streamed by in the other direction on their way to the rear.

One of them, an officer of the 44th Regiment with a foot

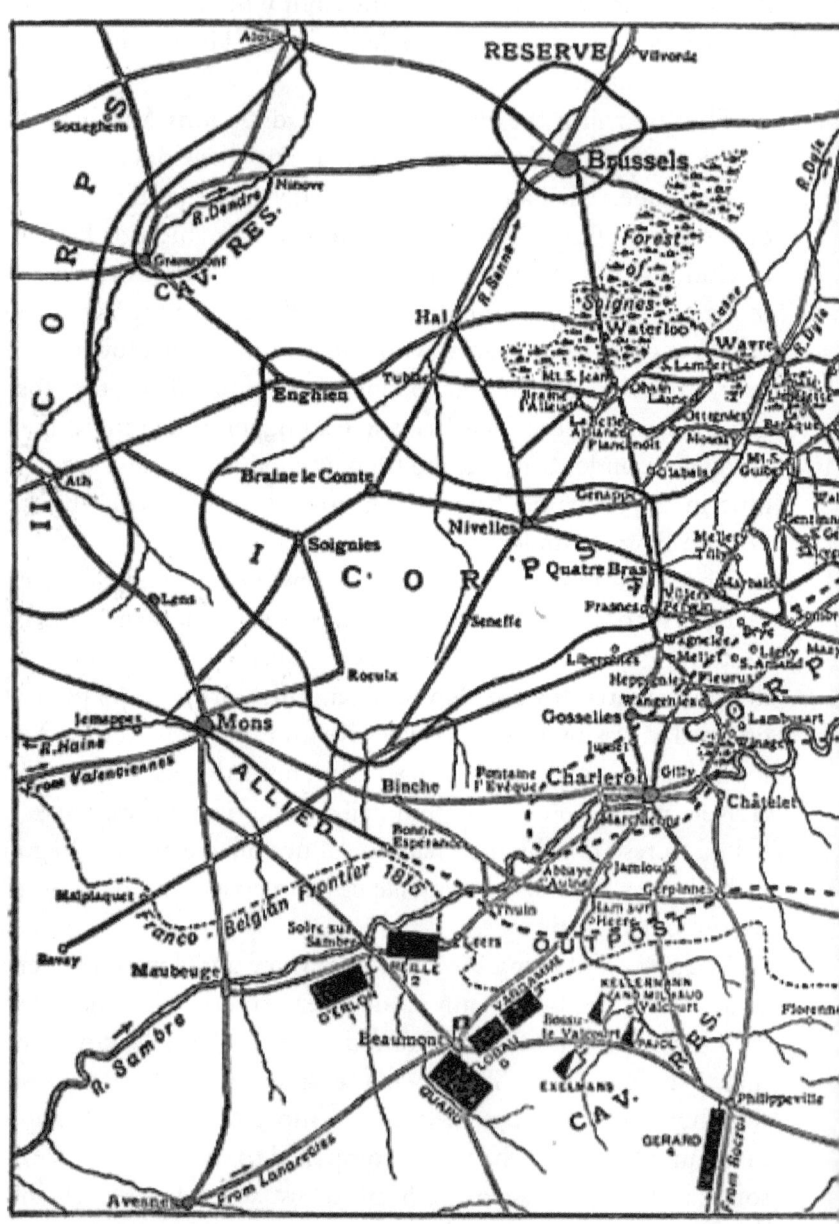

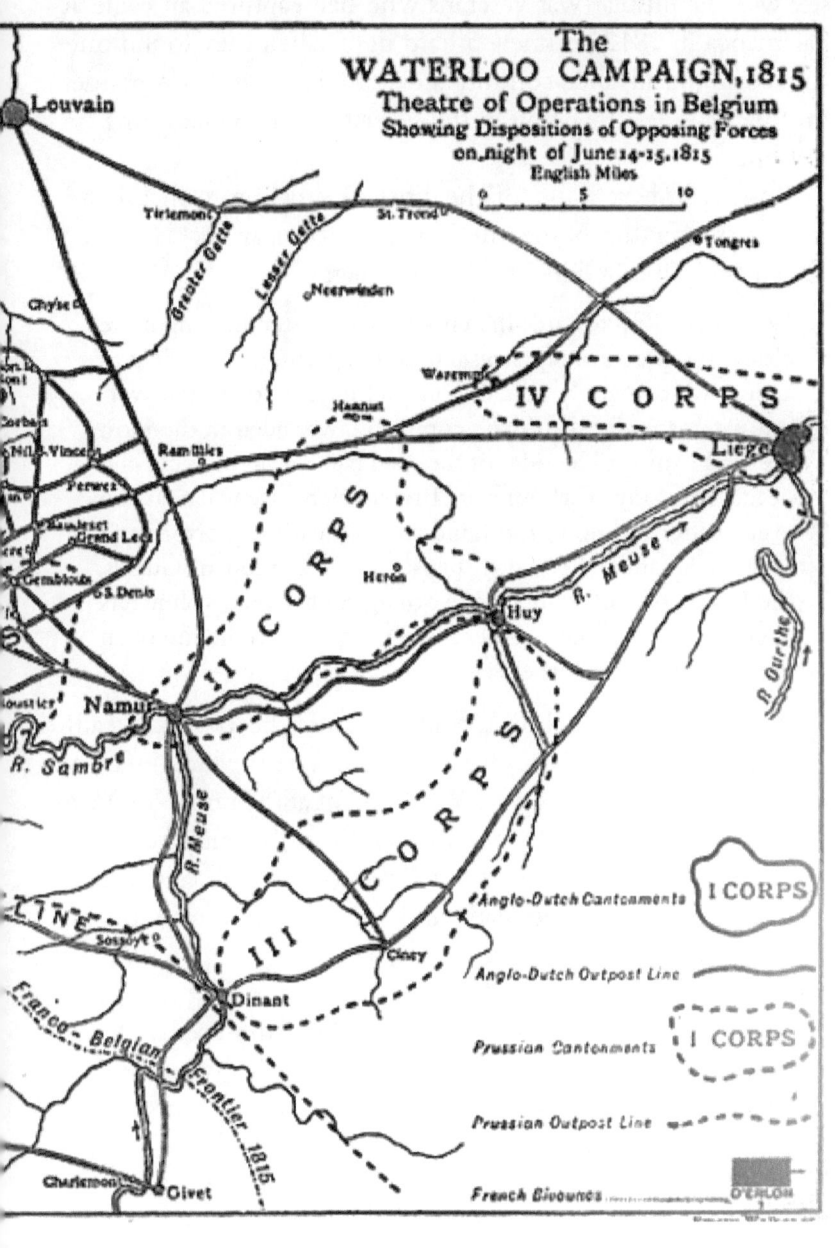

wound, urged them to move forward quickly, as 'things', he said, 'are going on badly for us'. The second battalion of the East Essex were Peninsular War veterans who had captured an eagle at Salamanca in 1812, so knew a hard fight when they found one. Indeed, as the advance continued ever more wounded were met on the roadside, indicating of the severity of the work going on in front.

Ensign Robert Batty of the First Guards wrote in a letter from just over the border into France at Bavay six days later, which was published in Booth's miscellany:

> We marched up towards the enemy, at each step hearing more clearly the fire of musquetry; and as we approached the field of action, we constantly met wagons full of men, of all the various nations under the duke's command, wounded in the most dreadful manner. The sides of the road had a heap of dying and dead, very many of whom were British: such a scene demanded every better feeling of the mind to cope with its horrors; and too much cannot be said in praise of the division of Guards, the largest part of whom were young soldiers and volunteers from the militia, who had never been exposed to the fire of an enemy or witnessed its effects.

At about five o'clock in the afternoon of the 16th, the leading companies of the First Guards, which were the light infantry under Saltoun, arrived at a critical moment at the north-western extremity of a wood called the Bois de Bossu, recently occupied by the French, which was about three-quarters of a mile long and 300 yards broad (see plan), and which lay to their right on the south side of the *chaussée*, near Quatre Bras.

★★★★★★

As morning dawned on the 16th of June, the French Army was in an excellent position. By noon Blücher, had yet to gather three quarters of his army at Ligny and it was many hours before Wellington could bring just a third of his own army to Quatre Bras. The emperor directed Ney to drive away everything that lay in front of him at Quatre Bras, and thereafter fall upon the flank of the Prussian force at Ligny. This was possibly Napoleon's first critical error of the campaign, because not only were there increasing numbers of the enemy coming onto the field as the day progressed, but they proved harder to defeat than he had envisaged.

At Quatre Bras, Ney imprudently delayed opening his attack, waiting until all of the infantry of Reille's corps arrived so, since the emperor was waiting for him to facilitate his own plan, very little occurred on either battlefield until noon had passed. Wellington rode to meet Blücher, and assured him that he would assist him at Ligny if he was able, but as the day progressed, Ney's efforts ensured that offer could not be fulfilled, for the British divisions, as they successively reached Quatre Bras, became fully engaged.

By mid-afternoon the emperor, who had not appreciated he was actually outnumbered at Ligny, had massed in front of the Prussians and initiated an obstinate struggle. Though the Prussians suffered most heavily, Ligny did not develop into the battle the emperor wanted or required. He expected Ney to appear, as instructed, behind the Prussian right wing to close the business at least cost in men and time, but no fresh French troops arrived for Ney had found himself embroiled in a bitter grapple with Wellington at Quatre Bras and was unable to spare a man to facilitate his masters turning movement.

His tactic foiled, the emperor was predictably unsympathetic to Ney's problems and sent orders directly to d'Erlon, the commander of the First Corps, which formed Ney's reserve, to march towards Ligny, to fulfil Ney's task for him. General d'Erlon obeyed his master, but arrived on the field in the wrong position, joining the emperor's left, rather than coming round the Prussian right. Napoleon was temporarily perplexed by the appearance of this development, but having appreciated they were his own troops, ordered an all-out assault on Blücher's line. However, d'Erlon had now received furious appeals from Ney, to return and save him from being overwhelmed by Wellington's growing numbers. If d'Erlon had elected to remain on the emperor's battlefield, the opportunity lay before him to deliver the decisive blow against the Prussian right as Napoleon demanded (which had the potential to cripple them as regarded their further involvement in the campaign), but instead he withdrew his corps and started for Quatre Bras.

Napoleon had then to fight his own battle unsupported and finally secured a victory as evening drew on by dashing the might of the Imperial Guard against the Prussian centre. At the last, Blücher imprudently charged with one of his cavalry brigades, was thrown from his horse, and narrowly escaped being taken prisoner. Almost insensible, he was dragged away to safety by his *aides*. His army had used up its reserves and with nothing more to give, fell back two miles behind its original position. Blücher had lost more than 20,000 men, but Napoleon had also suffered heavily with about 11,000 casualties he could ill afford.

The emperor had gained his initial time advantage, but squandered some of it in delays and his first gambit had gone awry. After such an auspicious beginning, this was not a very satisfactory second act and matters had not progressed according to plan at Quatre Bras either. Perhaps this disappointing day brought on the dark depressed humour which appeared to increasingly envelop the emperor. He knew he needed swift and comparatively straightforward victories based on manoeuvres as never before, but Ligny, entirely against his intentions and laden with consequences, had become reduced to a costly pummelling contest that lacked an unambiguously definitive outcome.

★★★★★★

At two o'clock in the afternoon of the 16th of June, Ney delivered his attack on Wellington's advance-guard under the Prince of Orange at Quatre Bras, as he intended, with the whole of Reille's corps. Predictably, the fragile allied line crumpled under the weight of the blow but, at the critical moment, Picton's Fifth Division, the first of the Brussels reserves to reach the front, arrived on the field, followed quickly by the Duke of Brunswick and his corps. At about the same period, the Duke of Wellington rode up and immediately deployed his troops which were principally infantry since he had little in the way of artillery

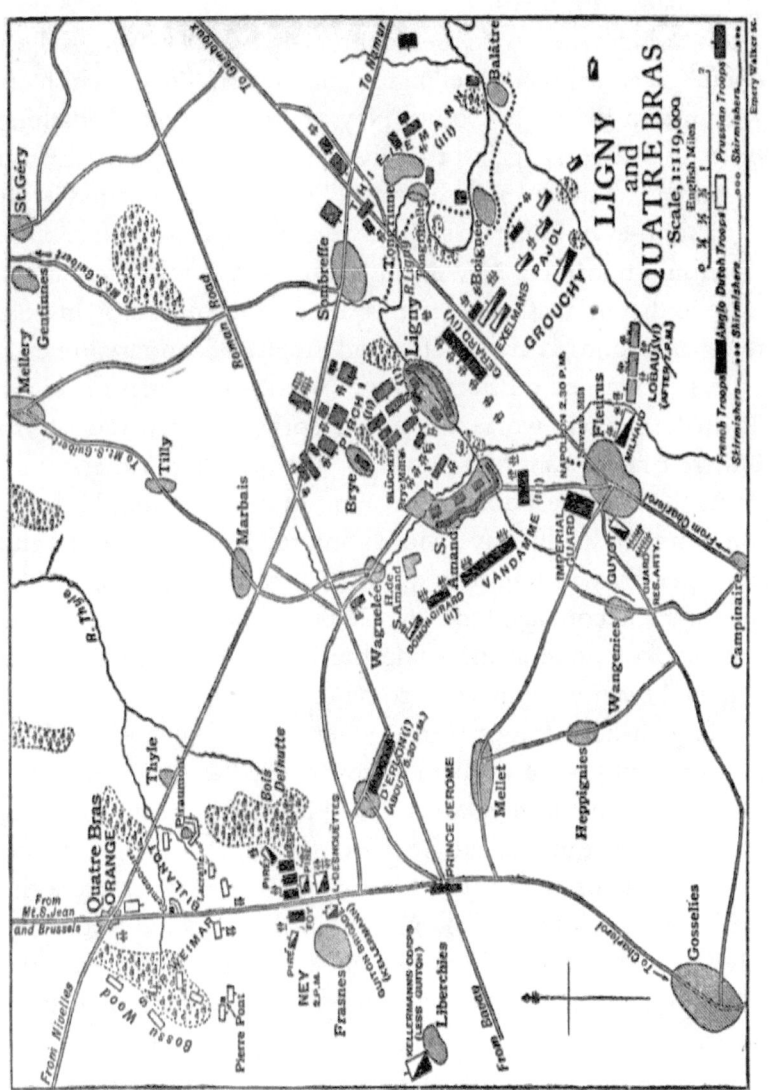

and few cavalry. The French attack drove forward and a fierce struggle ensued during which the Duke of Brunswick was shot and fatally wounded. As the initial French attack was beaten off, the retiring troops carried Ney's hopes of an easy victory at the cross-roads with them.

Both sides began to be reinforced. Ney received Kellermann's *cuirassiers* while Wellington gathered in Alten's British division from Braine-le-Comte. Ney resumed the attack, dashing his cavalry fiercely against the allied centre causing some British regiments to suffer most severely. The cavalry penetrated as far as the houses of Quatre Bras, but were finally driven off and the allied line reformed. Ney, at this point (as has been explained), learned that his master had requisitioned d'Erlon's corps, his sole reserve. Anxious to avoid defeat and in spite of contrary imperial orders he recalled d'Erlon, ruining Napoleon's tactics for Ligny. To make matters worse, the errant corps returned too late to Quatre Bras to assist him in turning the tide there either.

As the late afternoon was turning to early evening, Wellington assumed the offensive. More reinforcements had arrived and his superiority in numbers was now significant; he had 32,000 men in hand compared to Ney's 22,000. Among the newcomers was Cooke's division including the British Guards which had marched twenty-six miles to come to the front.

French light troops were dangerously occupying the Bois de Bossu, and some of them almost cleared the space between the wood and the high road. The Prince of Orange, realising the urgency of immediate intercession galloped along the road to intercept the first of the advancing Guards which were the light companies under Saltoun. The prince ordered Saltoun to advance into the wood to the right of the road, and drive the enemy out of it and although no reporter, perhaps predictably, enters into much detail on the subject, we have the impression that the prince was in an excited state of mind. The newly arrived Saltoun quite simply could not see any of the enemy with which he was to contend at that moment and asked the prince to clarify their position. The prince bridled, presumably electing to view this query as hesitation founded in a lack of resolution and snapped, 'Sir, if you don't like to undertake it, I'll find someone.'

This insult, in this period, suggestive of an accusation of cowardice, spoken for all to hear to an aristocratic British officer had all the potentials to escalate out of control and that it was spoken by a royal personage made the matter incomparably worse, for there could ultimately be no satisfactory outcome for Saltoun. His position in that moment was more precarious than the perils of the battlefield and so it was fortunate that he possessed the presence of mind to simply, calmly repeat his question. Upon receiving the intelligence, he required, Saltoun, without delay, formed his skirmish line, and led his men into the trees. The third battalion appears to have veered to the right of the wooded area. Ensign Robert Batty later, of the third battalion within a letter, recalled:

> The moment we caught a glimpse of them we halted, formed, and having loaded and fixed bayonets, advanced; the French immediately retiring; and the very last man who attempted to re-enter the wood was killed by our grenadiers.

A small stream ran north and south, through the centre of this wood, and at its eastern extremity, furthest from where the Guards approached, was a hollow way, which would provide protection for any troops occupying it. As the light companies disappeared into the wood, the leading battalion companies of the Second Battalion, under Colonel Askew, came up. The prince ordered these troops to forthwith enter the wood, two companies at a time, and, as Hamilton wrote, 'though wearied with a fifteen hours' march, the men received the order with a cheer, and, with fixed bayonets, pushed forward after their comrades'.

Some men were, in fact, were so exhausted that they sank to the ground, unable to go on, but the issue at this point seems to have been that these newcomers did not know that they were following, 'after their comrades'. Once in the wood, the leading battalion companies had nothing to guide them but the sound of firing. The enemy appeared to be driven back; 'the loud sharp rattle of musketry, which was heard gradually but steadily advancing'. A Guards officer who was present later noted that the growth of trees were so thick that they impeded progress and that the enemy made full use of them firing from the cover of every trunk and bush. The French skirmishers attempted to take advantage of the rivulet, which crossed the wood, to form up, but their stand was short lived, for the Guards forced their way across, charging as best they could with a shout and driving everything before them.

Hamilton, the regimental historian noted that, 'during this manoeuvre, the light companies sustained some additional loss from the hasty and hurried manner in which the battalion companies were ordered forward by the Prince of Orange, to support Saltoun, for, upon entering the wood, and hearing a heavy fire in their front, these imagined it was the enemy, and commenced firing'. Simply put, if this report is to be given credence, the battalion companies, since they had no information to the contrary, believed that they had only the enemy before them and discharged their weapons into the backs of, at least, some of their own light company comrades. Hamilton on this occasion felt confident enough to put the responsibility for this blunder where it properly lay. Saltoun's subaltern, 'Charley' Ellis, was sent back to explain what was happening, but it was difficult to stop the punishing fire till the Guards were clear of the trees and could properly identify their targets.

As the Guards broke through into the open, they saw the 33rd Regiment lying sheltered, behind a low hedge, about 150 yards to their left rear, while on their right was the deep ravine or hollow way before mentioned. Interestingly, the Duke of Wellington had served as a young officer in the 33rd. It had served in the 4th Anglo-Mysore War in India under him and in 1853, in the light of these connections including Quatre Bras and Waterloo, the 33rd assumed the title of The Duke of Wellington's regiment.

On open ground the Guards became exposed to the direct fire of the enemy's artillery, reserve infantry and the predations of its cavalry. The undergrowth within the wood had caused the line to lose cohesion and the infantry could make no response to such an intensity of fire. There was no other option, but to retreat into the cover of the trees. The Guards withdrew to the stream in the wood, which was initially considered to be out of range; but some men were, nevertheless, killed or maimed there by French artillery fire. Some casualties were caused by the crowns of the trees, having been cut by the enemy artillery, crashing down onto the soldiers below.

The Third Battalion, First Guards, under Colonel Stuart, had come up and were ordered to form line outside, and to the left, of the wood so their passage towards the enemy was somewhat easier and thus faster. Companies had become mixed as they advanced through the thicket, but formed up in succession to the right as they came into the open, whereupon men of other regiments, who had been engaged before the First Division arrived, fell in to fight by its side. The right of the line now rested on the trees, while the left extended through the fields of standing corn, towards the *chaussée*, leading from Brussels to Charleroi. One report noted the third battalion forming square.

Maitland urged the First Guards onwards and though the enemy drew back; each attack was eventually checked and the contest became a stalemate. The Guards could not break the enemy's line, but poured a steady withering fire into the French, as they attempted to deploy; while the French cavalry perpetually milled about, seeking an opportunity to charge. Askew and Stuart, the battalion commanding officers were both eventually wounded and put *hors de combat* so were succeeded by colonels, Edward Stables and Francis D'Oyly.

When the brigade had emerged from the wood to form line, a battalion of Brunswickers followed it into the open, and was forming up on the Guards' left, when French cavalry came suddenly down upon the left flank of the second battalion, forcing it back towards the wood. As the horsemen were hard upon them, it could not form square, so the men ran for the protection of the hollow way. Once secure, the line reformed and de-

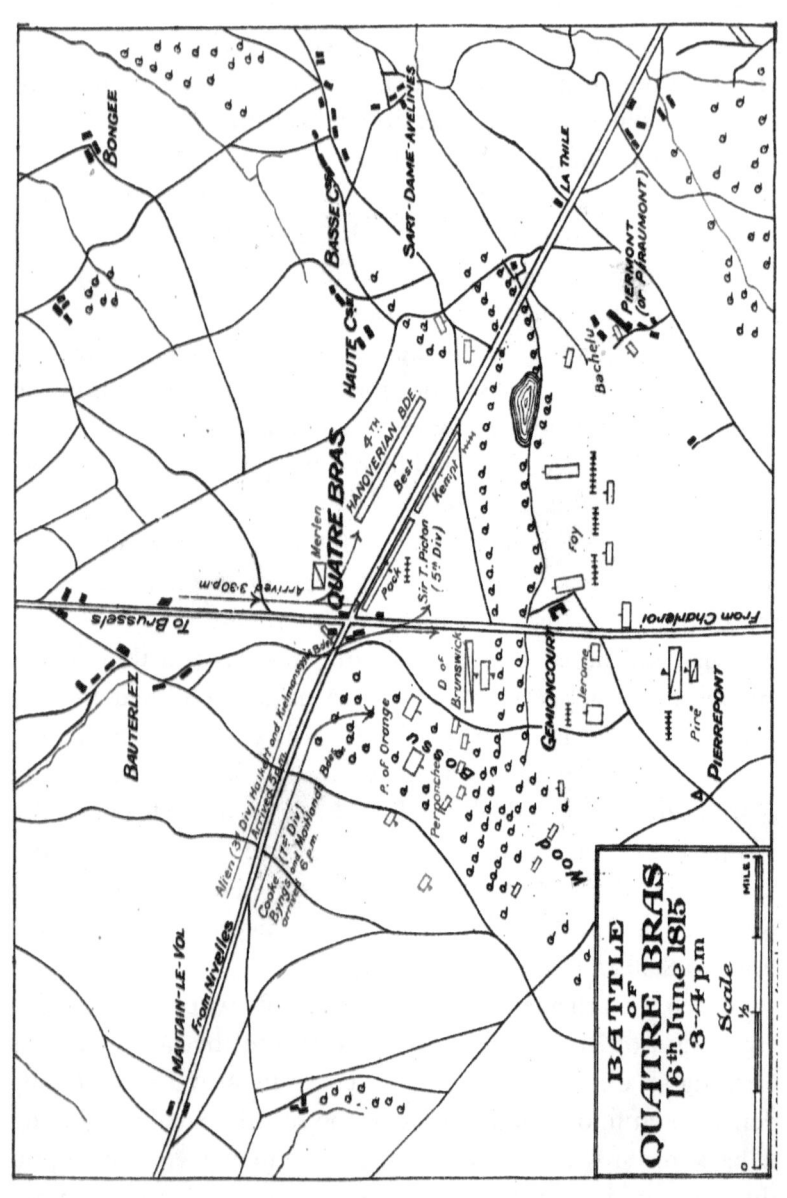

livered a destructive fire emptying saddles in quantity.

It was during the cavalry attack that James Lord Hay, (eldest son of the Earl of Erroll), an ensign of the First Guards and *aide-de-camp* to General Maitland, was killed. He was temporarily acting as adjutant to Saltoun who, noting that his young friend was mounted on a well-bred horse, advised him not delay in going down a narrow path leading into the wood before the French cavalry came close, in case his charger, which was of a type inclined to be skittish, refused when it found itself in an awkward place.

Hay replied there was no fear of that, because the horse, 'was such a perfect hunter'. The two officers stayed together until the time came for them both to go down the path, whereupon Hay's horse, as forecast, refused, reared, and attempted to turn about.

A man's body, at that instant, fell across the neck of Saltoun's horse and rolled off to the ground. He could not immediately identify who it was and called out, 'Who's that?' Whereupon one of his men nearby answered, 'It's Lord Hay; but I shot the man that shot him.' The momentary delay had enabled a French cavalry skirmisher to accurately fire at Hay killing him instantly. He was only eighteen years old, so that he had been promptly avenged was of cold comfort. Meanwhile, the Brunswickers, who had managed to form square, opened fire upon the passing cavalry increasing the rate of its destruction. Prisoners were taken and several riderless horses were gathered as fresh chargers for the Guards field officers.

The firing continued for as long as daylight lasted, but as the evening came on Maitland led the third battalion forward beyond the outskirts of the wood and threw out a line of picquets in his front for the night. Each army reluctantly drew apart like exhausted equally matched pugilists. Colonel Stables brought the second battalion out of action and moved his men to the *chaussée*, at the end of the wood, where they could briefly rest.

Later Maitland wrote a report of the action addressed to the Duke of York:—

It was at Quatre Bras that the (First) Brigade came in contact with the enemy. Here they arrived very opportunely after a march of twenty-six miles. At that moment the French with two battalions had occupied a wood, which extends from the road leading from Nivelles to Quatre Bras, about a mile and a half to the right. Had the enemy maintained himself here, he would have cut off the communication between Lord Hill and the corps of the Prince of Orange. The brigade formed across the wood, advanced (with bayonets fixed and cheering), and drove the enemy entirely from the post. He, however, continued to harass us, and to make frequent attempts to regain the wood, with a reserve of three battalions on the right of the wood, which is long but not broad, and with two pieces of artillery at the extremity. He also pushed on a corps on our left which attempted to cut us off from the high road, but all his efforts were rendered vain by the spirited resistance of the brigade. I caused the brigade to advance frequently against the last-mentioned corps of the enemy, and as frequently drove them back.

The French fought fiercely, but when darkness brought the battle to an end they had been compelled to return to their original positions. To say that Wellington owed everything to his infantry at Quatre Bras was more than an understatement, for he had very little of artillery or cavalry to match those of the enemy and yet still did not suffer a devastating defeat. The Guards were able bring their wounded out of the wood. Ney had retired on the road to Frasne, three miles to the rear. Losses were equally distributed, for each contestant had suffered about 4,200 or 4,300 casualties, so neither side could claim a qualified battlefield success, though the French held none of the ground they had taken at its conclusion.

The losses of the two battalions, First Guards, at Quatre Bras were very severe. In the Second Battalion there were 3 officers, 1 sergeant, 22 rank and file killed; 4 officers, 6 sergeants, 250 rank and file wounded. In the Third Battalion 3 officers, 2 sergeants, 1 drummer, 17 rank and file killed; 4 officers, 9 sergeants, 1 drummer, and 225 rank and file wounded. Total casualties, 6 officers killed, 8 wounded; 43 men killed, 491 wounded: in all 548 casualties. The Allied Army suffered 4,700 casualities and Ney's command suffered 4,300 casualties at Quatre Bras.

Robert Batty wrote in a letter he sent from Gommignies on June the 22nd:—

> We succeeded in finding the bodies of our four officers, Captains Grose and Brown, Ensigns Lord Hay and Barrington who were killed; and had the melancholy satisfaction of paying the last tribute of respect to their remains. They were buried near the wood and one of our officers read the service over them. Never did I witness a scene more imposing. Those breasts which had a few hours back boldly encountered the greatest perils, did not now disdain to be subdued by pity and affection.

The four officers were buried the following morning under a large tree on the right of the wood nearest towards Nivelles.

> (Readers should note that much of the material that the present author has drawn from Hamilton's regimental history concerning this period appears to have as its own source within a journal kept by Captain H. W Powell of the First Guards who was present. Substantial entries of the journal appeared in the 'Waterloo Letters', collated by William Siborne's son, Herbert, which were published in book form in 1891.)

Tactically, Quatre Bras was a severe check to Ney, but, in the short term, the action had served Napoleon's purpose fairly well, since it had prevented Wellington from supporting Blücher. Ligny would have had another outcome if Wellington had been able to defeat the initial corps before him early in the day and had then marched for St. Amand. The reason why he failed to do so was his inability to fully concentrate; he had to fight Ney with the Brussels reserves almost unaided in consequence of his position of reaction. Professor Oman suggested that had Wellington's troops from Ghent, Oudenarde, and Ath had started for the front twelve hours earlier, Ney would have been thrown back.

However, whilst the contingent from Ath may, under those circumstances, have just arrived to be of use, the much longer distances from Oudenarde and Ghent would have severely tried the infantry making their effectiveness questionable, had they

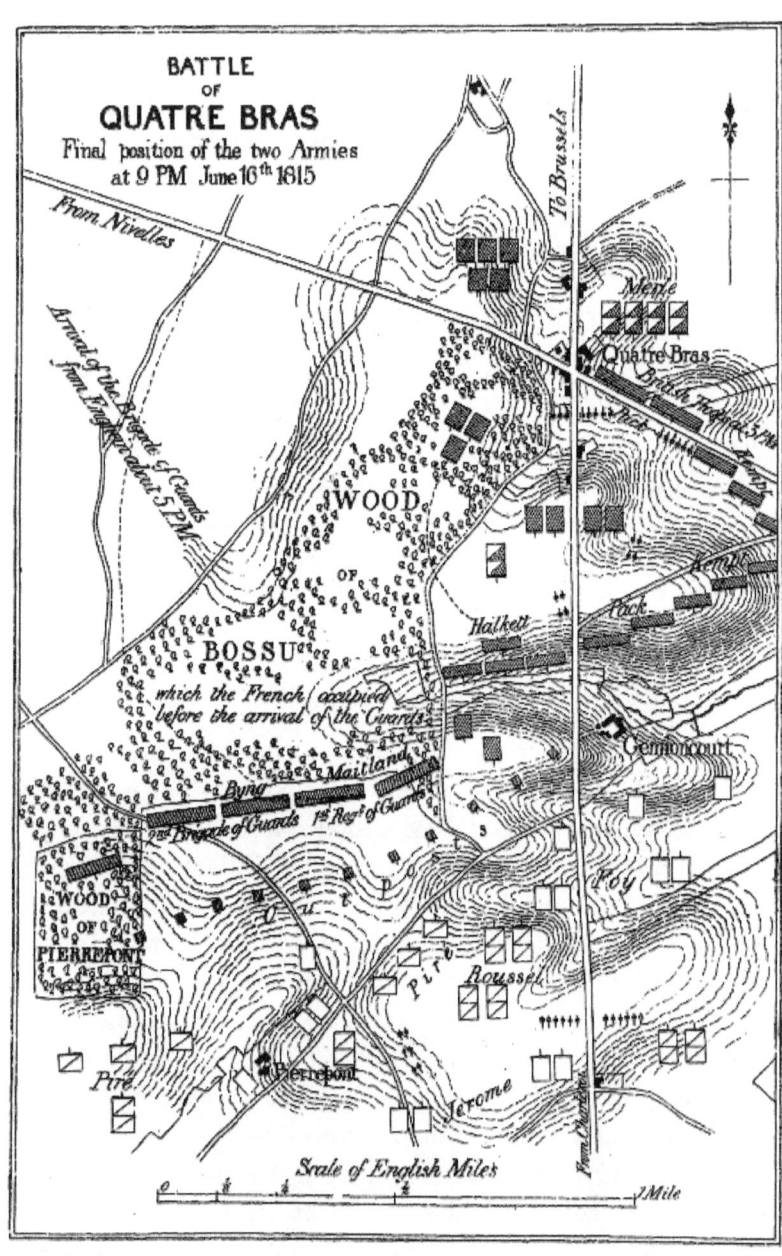

managed to arrive in good time at Quatre Bras. As noted, many of the troops that did arrive on the field were already on the point of collapse from their exertions. So, on that account, Napoleon must be credited with making his initial move brilliantly, quite simply, wrong-footing his opposite numbers.

During the night, the belated allied divisions poured in till nearly the whole army was concentrated on the morning of the 17th, though it was now too late. The news of the events at Ligny had arrived and Wellington knew that the emperor would certainly unite with Ney before the day was out. It is difficult to see the guiding hand of any commander in the outcome of the events of the 16th and each one would have, henceforth, to make the best of what might follow. For Napoleon, who was walking the razor's edge, that situation might have been at least acceptable in any practically any campaign of his career—excepting this one.

CHAPTER THIRTY-TWO

Belgium, June 17th, 1815

If the Battle of Ligny can be assessed in isolation of its context, then Napoleon had won a victory. However, it was not a decisive one, for his enemy was neither destroyed nor pursued in confusion. At dawn on the 17th the defeated Prussian Army had, in fact, quietly gathered itself together and retired unmolested northwards in the direction of Wavre.

That morning Napoleon, who was unaware of the particulars of Blücher's withdrawal or the condition of his army, was slow to move. He was fatigued by recent events and uncharacteristically lethargic, wasting the morning in talking politics, touring his late battlefield and reviewing his troops. Around noon he directed Grouchy to take charge of the corps of Vandamme and Gérard and half the reserve cavalry—some 33,000 men and to follow the Prussians who, he believed (and hoped), would probably fall back eastwards towards their base at Liege. Grouchy was cautioned to keep in touch with them at all costs, whilst Napoleon would join forces with Ney, though neither column got away until mid-afternoon.

Much time was lost in fruitlessly seeking Blücher on the road to Namur, though by nightfall Grouchy knew that some Prussians, at least, must be moving on Wavre. However, he was still uncertain of their numbers and whether their main body was marching in the direction of Liege. The consequences of the difference between these destinations could not have been more acute, for if the Prussian main body was moving to the eastward it meant that a beaten Blücher was abandoning the contest, whereas his movement to the northward meant he was almost certainly moving to join Wellington and his army. Tardy work by the French cavalry patrols had failed to find the Prussians in good time and heavy rain, falling throughout the afternoon and evening, delayed the progress of Grouchy's infantry which did not reach Gembloux until nightfall. They had covered less than ten miles during the day, whereas the Prussians had covered twenty, and were now securely concentrated at Wavre, where they were at last joined and reinforced by Bülow's fresh corps.

******

After Quatre Bras, Wellington was fully aware that he must draw back and seek a junction with Blücher before he offered battle again. Early in the morning he sent word to the Prussian headquarters that he would stand on the position of Mont St. Jean before the Forest of Soignes, if he could rely on support from one of the Prussian Army-corps and in expectation of agreement he would maintain an open line of communication on his left. The duke began to withdraw from Quatre Bras at 10 a.m. moving the entire army towards Brussels over a bridge spanning the River Dyle at Genappes, and to cover this operation he initially left a substantial rearguard on the higher ground above Quatre Bras, to give the impression that his army remained in position facing the enemy. The two light companies of the Second Brigade of Guards were ordered to mask the retreat on the right, and did not leave the ground till past two o'clock,

Napoleon eventually arrived at Quatre Bras and had completed his dispositions to renew the attack, when he discovered he was only facing a cavalry rearguard, which then also retired. The British infantry had been marching steadily and were, by this time, well on their way and out of reach. The French cavalry set off in pursuit of them and there was a fierce cavalry action at Genappes, in which some of the British light cavalry fared poorly, until the Life Guards intervened and charging down, resolved the business. The British and Allied Army then began to take up its positions for the battle which would become known as Waterloo.

It was nearly seven o'clock in the evening of the 17th before the foremost French soldier reached the front of the allied position of Mont St. Jean. A reconnaissance in driving rain showed the emperor that his enemy was standing ready to receive him. Viewing Wellington's position with satisfaction, Napoleon told his staff, 'Now I have these English', whereupon General Foy, who knew his subject from personal experience in Spain, was heard to remark, 'Sire the English infantry in a duel are the devil', but his master was not listening. The emperor called his army to his side, but its column was so long that many of the infantry regiments did not reach the front till after midnight, and one division only appeared on the following morning. The Frenchmen were soaked through, exhausted and hungry and in this condition those who were in a position to do so made their night bivouacs in the mud.

★★★★★★

The Guards left their position at Quatre Bras just after eleven o'clock in the morning of the 17th, and moved along the *chaussée* leading to Brussels. The day was excessively hot, with the sky full of promises of the coming storm. The road was crowded, but movement was steady with few stoppages, except at Genappes, caused by the funnelling effect of the bridge over the Dyle. 'I will not invite you to accompany us on our march,' wrote Ensign Robert Batty, 'which was only marked by fatigue, dust, heat and thirst. Having halted for a short time, we were greeted by one of the hardest showers of rain I remember which lasted nearly half an hour—then it ceased'.

After marching about eight miles the First Division moved off the high road to its left along a cart track that brought it behind the *château* and farm of Hougoumont. Here the division appeared to have halted, but when the men were preparing their bivouac for the night, orders came to move to the right and take up a position on the next rise along the south-west side of the *chaussée* leading from Nivelles to Mont St. Jean. No sooner had the battalions moved to their new position than the expected storm burst upon them and continued throughout the night.

About six o'clock in the evening, the four light companies of the Guards division were ordered to take possession of the buildings and grounds of Hougoumont;—the two light companies of the First Guards (second and third battalions), under Saltoun and Robert Ellison, occupied the orchard and wood, while the two of the Second Brigade namely Second Battalion, Coldstreams under Wyndham and Second Battalion, Third Guards under Dashwood (under Lieutenant-Colonel James MacDonnell, who had overall command of the position), occupied the buildings and garden, but excepting the orchard.

According to Mackinnon, the Coldstream historian, the light companies of the Second Brigade initially took possession of the orchard for a short time, after which they were placed in the wood, but then the two light companies of the First Brigade under Saltoun occupied the orchard. Batty remained on the ridge in the position looking down on Hougoumont. 'Around seven o'clock in the evening.' he wrote in a letter, 'the French cannonaded Hougoumont and our position for near an hour and a half.'

The night and the following morning were spent by the light companies in making the place as strong as they could with the tools and materials at their disposal, barricading the gates and transforming the buildings and walls into defensive positions by knocking through loopholes and erecting platforms.

During the first part of the night the French had advanced close to the picquets in the wood and orchard. Robert Ellison, was picquet officer for the night and he later wrote to Siborne that, 'during the whole of the night we were occupied in making our position as strong as our means would allow. The French brought their advanced posts close to ours, but gave us no molestation.' The wood was an open grove without undergrowth, and easy to move through so the advanced files of the Guards picquets could maintain their cohesion. He was reinforced, according to Mackinnon, by three companies of Hanoverian *Jägers* and these men joined the advance picquet under Captain

The march from Quatre Bras

Evelyn and Ensign Standen of the Third Guards. Gronow later wrote of Ellison in his reminiscences and the following incident is worthy of note because, once again, it demonstrates the special relationship the guardsmen maintained with their officers as described by Saltoun in his account of the war in Spain.

> He was one of our best officers. After joining the brigade at Cadiz, he was present in every action in the Peninsula and was with the light companies at Hougoumont. He greatly distinguished himself there and on one occasion, when he was forced to retreat from the orchard to the *château*, he would have been bayoneted by the French, had not the men, with whom he was a great favourite, charged back and saved his life.

★★★★★★★

There has been some speculation on the states of mind of the three principal commanders during the dark hours of the 17th and early 18th of June, 1815. Wellington had disposed his army in a defensive line upon and along a low-lying ridge. This was good ground, for the French columns would eventually be compelled to labour to its crest and that task would be made the more problematic because the torrential rains had turned the fields below, which were inclined to hold water in any event, to cloying mud. Nor, indeed, was the position at Mont St. Jean new to the duke.

He had recognised its value in the past during examinations of the terrain (and had written to Lord Bathhurst on the subject almost a year previously) and noted the protection of the forest on his right and the availability of farm buildings in front of this line. These could be transformed into outworks which would be required to be taken by an enemy attack on the line and which could unleash flanking fire upon any troops that attempted to by-pass them. Of these bastions Hougoumont was the largest and sat significantly on the right extremity of his line—perfectly positioned in every way to secure that flank from a turning manoeuvre.

All of this taken into account, despite the fact that he had carried out his retreat in good order, Wellington was, nevertheless, fully aware that he was about to be assailed by a formidable host led by a master of war who could possibly defeat him. Now everything depended on the Prussians, for he had only taken up his present position on the understanding that he would be supported by one of their army corps and that proposal had not yet been accepted. If they refused him then he would have to retire again, sacrificing Brussels just eleven miles in his rear, and he could readily imagine the panic and uproar which would then ensue both on the continent and across the Channel. How much anxiety Wellington may have felt during his hours of waiting for an answer and how much inherent faith he had in Blücher to be equal to the task before them we can never reliably know.

The first hour of the 18th had arrived before Wellington received news from the Prussians. Any concerns he may have had about Blücher's intentions were, though he had no way of knowing it, academic because the marshal had been *hors de combat* as a result of the contusions he had suffered in his fall at Ligny. Wellington may have been more concerned had he known that the sceptical, cautious, and potentially uncooperative Gneisenau, Blücher's chief of the staff, had been in command during the interim. However, during the night, Blücher, ever the indomitable old warrior, recovered sufficiently to retrieve the reins of control.

Understandably partisan given their history with Napoleon, Gneisenau and his peers had expressed concerns about the perils of a flank march in close proximity to the enemy and the abandoning a safe line of retreat on Maestricht, but theirs were not the deciding voices. Blücher was made of more resolute stuff and his position remained characteristically straightforward, unambiguous and unfaltering. He had come to wage war to put a final end to Napoleon in battle. To reject the opportunity to launch a massive assault on the French right flank would, therefore, be unconscionable.

So, when he received the duke's proposal, he accepted it without hesitation. Blücher wrote to his ally that he proposed to dispatch a single corps, which would be Bülow's, as requested, to join him at daybreak and thereafter, without stint, send on Pi-

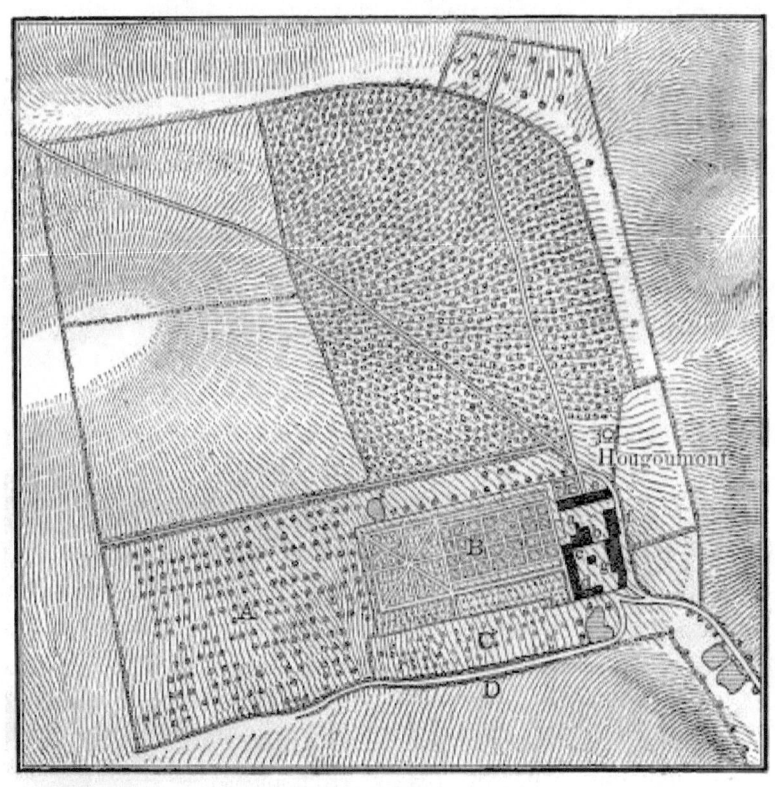

THE PLAN FACES TO THE SOUTH.
A, Great Orchard; *B*, Garden; *C*, Small Orchard; *D*, Hollow Way; *a*, Chapel; *b*, House; *c*, Farmer's House; *d*, Cowhouse and Stabling; *e*, Gardener's House, Stables, &c.; *f*, Barn; *g*, Great Barn; *h*, Small Garden; *j*, Haystack.

PLAN OF HOUGOUMONT AND SURROUNDING AREA

rch's corps. Two further corps would follow if not prevented. He knew Grouchy's location and considered it prudent to detach Thielmann's and Ziethen's corps to hinder him. His plan did not proceed according to his timescale by some degree which had its consequences in loss of life, but Blücher's decision and personal commitment ultimately decided the outcome of the campaign.

Napoleon's thoughts at this time are, perhaps, more difficult to gauge. At the peak of his powers he was renowned for his consideration of every eventuality, but in the years that led to his fall he increasingly considered reality through a skewed glass of his own making which took into account only those factors which aligned with his desires. Indeed, irrationality conceived the invasion of Russia which was the beginning of the end for him. The emperor became brooding and introspective in Belgium and it would be tempting to speculate that his was a dark night of soul searching which embraced a presentiment of coming disaster.

That having been said, had he not defeated an enemy that he had every expectation, based on his experience of them, of beating? It has been suggested it would have been barely conceivable to him that Wellington and Blücher—representing separate nations—would continue to keep faith with each other for future action following the less than encouraging outcomes for them of the opening engagements, since both of them had been forced to retreat. Each commander would surely look to his own interests, for experience had taught Napoleon he could not expect any more from his own marshals.

Ney had not fared as well he might have done against the British, though that battle had been fought more or less to a draw irrespective of his absence. The emperor astutely had no regard for the military worth of the Dutch-Belgians and nothing, from his own perspective, had occurred to make him particularly concerned about the prowess of red-coated soldiers of any nationality. The indisputable melange of his opponents presented him with greater opportunities than a parity in numbers might otherwise suggest.

Of his own renown and abilities Napoleon thought highly

to the point of delusion and he was equally certain of the capabilities of his motivated veterans, for together had they not won great victories and marched across Europe to forge an empire? He had no personal experience of Wellington as an opponent and may have brought Moore's retreat to Corunna to mind in consideration of the British Army. However, in reality all of that was in the past and in 1815 neither Wellington or Blücher was in awe of the emperor or his army.

Wellington had been defeating French Armies, in the 'same old way'—line against column—with an unparalleled record of success, though his battles had been fought in a single theatre of the wars of the Napoleonic Age, which certainly would have influenced the emperor's opinion of him. It was inconceivable that the Emperor Napoleon would have countenanced Wellington to be his equal among great commanders of men in great engagements and that was a fatal error of judgment in consideration of an unknown adversary.

Military history abounds with examples of armies that had surrendered their position of strength upon elevated ground and, having come down to contest the outcome with their initially disadvantaged adversaries, paid the price for it. However, those armies were not commanded by the Duke of Wellington and he would not behave out of character on this day of all days. In essence, the coming battle would be fought by one army proven to be at its most effective in the attack against an army, the backbone of which had proved itself formidable in defence, upon ground well configured for that purpose.

Options were fundamentally limited for both commanders in that respect. Unless Napoleon's legendary genius could bring something new to his attack—for attack he must—essential considerations of time and endurance notwithstanding—the British Field-Marshal knew very well how to deal with him for he had fought and won battles on positions much like the one he now occupied on several occasions. Simply put, Wellington would nail his army to the ridge, hold his ground in defiance and wait for Blücher to arrive.

CHAPTER THIRTY-THREE

The Battle of Waterloo—Morning

On the morning of Sunday, June 18th, 1815, Wellington's army was arrayed on the crest of the gentle slope of Mont St. Jean, some hundred and twenty feet above the level of the valley which divided it from the French lines. Across it ran the two high-roads of Nivelles-Brussels and Charleroi-Brussels.

Before the right of the British line lay Hougoumont, while in front of the centre, on the Charleroi high-road, stood the smaller farm of La Haye Sainte. On the extreme left stood two other farms, Papelotte and La Haye. All were occupied by the Allied Army: Hougoumont by a brigade of the British Guards; La Haye Sainte by the German Legion; the other two by Bernard of Saxe-Weimar's Nassau brigade. Most advantageously, behind the fighting line was a broad plateau which fell slightly away from the higher ground. Upon this area reserves could be kept invisible from the sight of the enemy and, indeed, could be brought forward unseen till the crest was actually reached.

The numbers of men engaged at Waterloo can differ dependent upon whose report one reads, so the present author can make no claims about the absolute accuracy of those following other than to note that they give the reader something of an understanding of the scale of this struggle which would be fought out on a comparatively small field. Wellington had in the region of 67,000 men on the ground. Of these, 24,000 were British; 5,800 King's German Legion; 11,000 were Hanoverians. The Brunswick corps, reduced to 5,500 men by its losses at Quatre

HOUGOUMONT, 1815: VIEW FROM THE NORTH-EAST

Bras; two Nassau brigades (Kruse and Saxe-Weimar) over 6,000 strong and finally, 14,000 Dutch-Belgians.

Opposite Mont St. Jean, Napoleon had arrayed in the region of 74,000 troops, on each side of the farm of La Belle Alliance and the high-road from Charleroi to Brussels. He had received news from Grouchy concerning the whereabouts of the Prussians, but none of his messages thus far had contained a hint that the majority of them were moving on Mont St. Jean. Some authorities put the French numbers lower, though there can be no doubt that they could claim a marked superiority in artillery.

The Guards battalions were posted on the rising ground above Hougoumont. The Third Battalion, First Guards was on the extreme left, on the crest of the ridge, in quarter-distance column of companies, at deploying distance from the right of Halkett's, Fifth Brigade. The Second Battalion, First Guards in the same formation, was to the right rear of the third battalion, on the reverse slope under the crest of the hill. The Second Brigade, Second Battalion, Coldstream and Second Battalion, Third Guards, under Byng, stood on the crest of the ridge between the right of the First Brigade and the Nivelles road, commanding Hougoumont, so forming a reserve support for the troops stationed there.

The principal house or *château* of Hougoumont was a substantial square brick building. Adjoining its north-east angle was the farmer's house, the east end of which abutted on a large garden. In the angle between this house and the *château* was a narrow tower, which housed a staircase to the main building. At the south-east corner of the *château* stood a small chapel.

To the north, nearest to the British held ridge, was a large farmyard, bounded on the west by a large barn and a shed, and on the east by cow-sheds and stabling which adjoined the garden. There was more stabling along the north side, and a gateway. Near the centre of the yard there was a well which featured a dovecot.

On the south, facing the French side of the *château*, was the courtyard, the boundaries of which were made by a barn, the

Hougoumont, 1815: View from the North-West

gardener's house, stables, offices and the garden wall. The courtyard connected to the farmyard, *via* a doorway in the wall between the *château* and the great barn. There was also a carriage way leading from the one court into the other. A gateway, passing through the gardener's house, led from the courtyard to the south. From this gate a narrow road ran across the open space between the buildings and the wood into the fields. A path from this road from the corner of the small garden also went through the wood towards the south-east angle of the enclosure's boundary and onwards towards La Belle Alliance.

The approach to Hougoumont from the Nivelles road was lined by established elm trees. This track led to the gate of the farmyard facing the British line and travelled along the west side of the complex so that it also served the south gate. On the east side of the buildings was a large formal garden in the Flemish style. It was contained on the south and east by a high brick wall, and on the north side by a hedge. Connected to the east side of the garden was the large orchard, and along the north side was the smaller orchard enclosed within high and compact hedges, partially lined by a ditch on the inner side and bounded by a hedge and hollow way.

A continuance of the large orchard's southern hedge formed the boundary of the wood facing the south garden wall, and in the narrow space between these two boundaries was a row of apple trees, which, together with the hedge, served to conceal the garden wall from the view of an enemy, approaching through the wood. There was a small garden in front of the gardener's house, formed by the continuation of the south garden wall until it met another wall coming from the south gateway. There were two enclosures on the west side, of which one served as a kitchen garden.

The wood was about 350 yards long and about 280 yards wide at its widest point. It was bounded on the west by another orchard; and on the east by two large enclosures, of which the one nearest the large orchard was a grass field fenced with hedges, and lined by a ditch on the inner side.

Hougoumont, 1815: View from the South-East

Saltoun probably believed that the light companies of the First Brigade of Guards under his command would remain posted in the orchard and wood of Hougoumont and its defence would be his responsibility throughout the coming action. However, in the early morning, a staff officer arrived guiding a battalion of Nassauers (600 men of the First Battalion of the 2nd Regiment of Nassau), one company of Hanoverian field riflemen, and about one hundred soldiers from the Field Battalion Lüneburg of Kielmansegge's *Jäger* Brigade.

He handed Saltoun an order instructing him to surrender the charge of the orchard to the Nassau officer commanding the contingent, Major Büssen, and to lead his own men to rejoin his brigade. Accordingly, Saltoun took the officer over the orchard, briefed him on the plans and preparations taken for its defence and, his duties discharged, gathered his men and left the area of the *château* as ordered. Readers will note that within accounts there has been variance on the time of these events and, indeed, whether Saltoun left the vicinity of the *château* at all.

The following paragraph is extracted from Mackinnon's history of the Coldstream Guards and is possibly puzzling since the author's presence during the events described would suggest his version is reliable. Readers will have noted that according to Mackinnon, Saltoun had been reinforced with Hanoverians the previous evening and he had been so certain that these troops were present on picquet duty at the time that he was able to name officers who accompanied them. In the following passage he states that Saltoun was relieved at 10 a.m., which is at variance with Saltoun's account which suggests the time was earlier.

Certainly, this later time, though perfectly possible, would have required all of the events described elsewhere to be condensed into a short period of time. He has also positioned some of the Nassau troops within the *château*. Finally, he reports that Saltoun joined the Second Brigade 'on the position'. The present author has no new information on this matter, but assumes 'the position' to be the army's position on the ridge, though Saltoun and his men of the First Guards indisputably belonged to

HOUGOUMONT, 1815: VIEW FROM THE SOUTH-WEST

the First Brigade so it would have been peculiar had they joined Byng's command.

> At ten o'clock the light companies of the Guards were relieved by a battalion of eight hundred Nassau light troops: part of this corps was stationed in the lofts, buildings, yards; and out-offices; the remainder, with the Hanoverian *Yagers*, were distributed in the orchard and wood. Lord Saltoun then joined the second brigade on the position. Lieutenant-Colonel Macdonell with his companies moved to the right of the *château*.

The present author has elected, for the purpose of this narrative, to subscribe to earlier times, because they comfortably allow for the full narrative according to First Guards records and Saltoun's own account.

Saltoun was marching towards the First Guards' Brigade on the ridge, when about halfway there, he met the Duke of Wellington accompanied by Lord Fitzroy Somerset riding out of the early grey of the morning towards them. Somerset was himself a First Guard and Wellington's military secretary. Later in the day he would lose his right arm. Bringing his horse to a halt, the duke called out, 'Hallo, who are you and where are you going?' Presumably the call came from a little distance in the lower light, since the duke must surely have been personally aware of Lord Saltoun. Saltoun halted his men, ordered arms, then directed them to lie down, as was his custom until they should receive new directions.

As he did so, Saltoun distinctly heard the duke remark, 'That don't look like running away, Fitzroy'. Clearly a false rumour of the desertion of bodies of the troops had been drawn to the duke's attention and it was that which had motivated him to ride out at that early hour to ascertain the truth of the matter. Joining Wellington, Saltoun, explained that he was acting upon the orders he had recently received.

Once Wellington was in the part of the line occupied by the Guards it is difficult to imagine he would have believed mass desertion was a probability, particularly so early in the day. In any event, the duke was clearly surprised by this intelligence, and said, 'Well, I was not aware of such an order; but, however, don't join the brigade yet; remain quiet here where you are until further orders from me,' and then he rode away.

Some accounts add that Wellington then commented to Somerset, 'That was one of my old Peninsular officers. See how he had his men lie down'. There is no mention of this comment in Saltoun's account, though it is the case that this order would have identified Saltoun as a former experienced member of 'the Old Peninsular Army'. In any event, Somerset and Saltoun had served in the Peninsular War in several of the same engagements, were both notable aristocrats and regimental brother officers, which altogether would suggest that such an explanation would have been unnecessary. Wellington, incidentally, was well known for taking exception to orders issued without his knowledge or, indeed, without his initiation so someone, somewhere, may have heard more from him about this incident.

******

The foregoing anecdote is interesting because it is fully reported in Saltoun's papers and includes an encounter with Wellington wherein he and Saltoun were in conversation. So, for this reason, as far as authenticity can be assessed, it seems reliable. It seems implausible that a person of Lord Saltoun's standing would record such an incident if it was a fabrication. The regimental historian of the Grenadier Guards, though it is possible that he has taken Saltoun as his source, endorses this version of events which necessarily means that shortly before the commencement of the main attack on the left-centre Saltoun came down the slope again to go into action in the wood beyond Hougoumont.

Some accounts do not mention this occurrence, whilst others give the impression that Saltoun remained in the vicinity of the *château*. Daniel Mackinnon (who was present), in his history of the Coldstream Guards states, with exasperating ambiguity, that Saltoun, 'returned to the position' after being relieved, though he employed the same phrase regarding another matter verifiable as meaning the principal position of the army on the ridge. This narrative continues on the basis of that assumption.

✶✶✶✶✶✶

Once again, despite the fact that time marched against him, Napoleon was in no hurry to begin his battle, though whether he had much choice in the matter remains questionable. He had given his weary army a long rest after daybreak, delaying the initiation of action in the hope that the sodden ground might dry out to enable his artillery to move about more freely. Wellington's army, with no intentions to move, simply waited for the emperor's overture and for the Prussians to make an appearance. It was late morning before the French Army was deployed, when it transpired the crux of the emperor's plan amounted to smashing into the British centre with a massive frontal attack.

Under cover of the fire of a long row of artillery batteries comprising some eighty guns, he proposed to launch d'Erlon's men at the left-centre of the enemy line in four great *phalanxes* containing eight battalions, ranged one behind another. This was, undoubtedly, an unwieldy blunt instrument, though a well-proven one, for in the past Continental troops had broken up in panic at the approach of such a monstrous formation.

The French Army, glittering in colours and burnished metals, was a magnificent spectacle to behold, and every man within it was visible from the British position. The emperor, by contrast, could discern little of Wellington's arrangements. Only the four farms on the slope, and above them a line of infantry and guns along the crest were visible to him. Of the reserves, whatever and where ever they might be, he could see nothing. Napoleon had never massed such large numbers on so short a front and the entire French line was less than four miles long.

When Marshal Soult learned the emperor's intention to simply deploy the infantry as giant fists and punch them through the British line by force of impact he was alarmed, urging extreme caution, for he had repeatedly witnessed French attacking columns thrown back by the British line in Spain. General Reille agreed with him, confirming that, in his opinion, British infantry posted in a good defensive position would repel any frontal attack and appealed for flanking manoeuvres. Napoleon would have none of it and, responding furiously with an outburst that defined his fatal state of mind, snapped, 'You were beaten by Wellington, and so you think he is a great general. But I tell you that Wellington is a bad general and the English are bad troops; they will merely be a breakfast for us!' It was as though the Napoleon of Austerlitz, a decade before, was another man and the Fates had woven the destiny of the emperor to this moment and nothing could prevent the realisation of the final act of his career.

Meanwhile, Saltoun and his men waited in their position of limbo until mid-morning. Eventually, an *aide-de-camp* rode up and told him that he was, in fact, to follow his former orders to rejoin his brigade. According to the regimental history, on reaching the ridge he gave up his temporary command and returned with his company in rear of his third battalion.

******

Napoleon was about to order d'Erlon to begin his attack, when he received disheartening news. In the distance, some six miles away on his right flank, masses of troops could be seen gradually coming into sight. The emperor had received Grouchy's morning dispatch informing him that Blücher had after all massed at Wavre so this was, beyond doubt, a portion of the Prussian Army. Shortly thereafter, a captured Prussian hussar confirmed that Bülow's corps was definitely marching to join Wellington. This pivotal moment caused the emperor to pause for momentary reflection. Napoleon's best-case scenario (if Blücher was proposing to join Wellington) was that it would take him two days to do so.

That hope had now evaporated and his choices were starker than ever. If the Allied and Prussian armies combined quickly and he fought them he would be defeated and if he retreated to avoid this battle then his cause was still ultimately lost whether by consequence of their combined action or under the might of all the armies of the alliance when they eventually coalesced. Bülow, by contrast, commanded a single corps, was still far away and Grouchy, apparently, was in pursuit of him. Of Blücher's entire army there was as yet no sign and so the battle might be won before the Prussians could intervene. Slim though it was, this was the emperor's single chance and only hope, so d'Erlon would attack.

CHAPTER THIRTY-FOUR

The Struggle for Hougoumont

At about 11.30 a.m. the French Army, at last, began its offensive. A Guards officer reported, 'About half past eleven the bands of several French regiments were distinctly heard and soon after the French artillery opened fire. The rapid beating of the *pas de charge*, which I had often heard in Spain—and which few men, however brave they may be, can listen to without a somewhat unpleasant sensation—announced the enemy's columns were approaching. On our side a profound silence prevailed, whilst the French, on the contrary, raised loud shouts and we heard the cry of '*Vive l'Empereur*' from one end of their line to the other.'

On the French left flank, a division of Reille's infantry under Napoleon's brother, Prince Jerome, preceded by a cloud of skirmishers, pressed in upon Hougoumont as though in indisputable acknowledgment that this was the key to opening the allied position, while the guns of the French artillery opened fire along the whole line. Some cavalry were sent against the other end (French right) of the allied line, though these were seen off by volleys from the Nassau troops stationed there.

However, these manoeuvres were distractions, for the emperor had decided to make demonstrations against the allied flanks to persuade Wellington to divert troops from his centre where the decisive blow would in reality fall. That ambition was in vain, for there was no likelihood that the duke would be shaken from his course. Shortly before the action began Wellington had, in fact, visited Hougoumont and as he rode off his parting injunction to the Guards was that the position was to be unequivocally defended by the garrison to the last extremity.

As the French masses advancing towards the *château* came into sight, three British batteries opened a devastating fire upon them causing to the columns to swerve to their left. The French responded with their own field and horse artillery. An advancing French brigade under Bauduin suffered heavy losses and plunged down into the hollow beneath the southern border of the wood.

On the British position Rees Howell Gronow witnessed the opening attack. Gronow was serving with the first battalion which remained in England on home service, so under normal circumstances would not have been present at Waterloo, but he had managed to contrive a place for himself on Picton's staff as a supernumerary *aide-de-camp* to be employed in the event of the death or incapacitation of the general's *aides*, Tyler and Chambers, who were both Guards officers. Picton had humorously quipped that Gronow might get his chance, since Tyler would be likely to be killed. In the event, Picton was killed early in the battle and Captain Newton Chambers, of the third battalion, fell by his side moments afterwards. Gronow in his reminiscences later wrote:

> I could distinctly see, at the commencement of the battle, the Young Guard *(it was not the Imperial Guard in reality, though this detracts nothing from the impressions of an eyewitness)* advance to attack Hougoumont, when a tremendous fire of artillery was opened upon them, which had the appearance of creating some confusion and disorder in their ranks. On they went, however, and in a moment got into the orchard. Then such a fire opened on both sides and such smoke ensued that, like Homers heroes, they were hidden by a cloud, and I could see no more. I had besides, plenty to occupy my own attention immediately afterwards.

Robert Batty, of the First Guards had come out to the Peninsular War in the same detachment as Gronow, He was a talented artist and wrote two books based on his service, 'With the left wing of the Allied Army in the Western Pyrenees and the South of France, 1813-1814,' and 'An Historical Sketch of the Campaign of 1815'. Unfortunately, he elected to take the part of an historian in the writing of both books (Hamilton certainly drew upon his Peninsular War work for his regimental history), thus denying his readers the benefit of the impressions and detail of his unique personal experiences, though we have some of his correspondence. Nevertheless, his evocative description of the opening moments of the attack on Hougoumont, taken from his history, contain the simple, but unmistakable elements of authenticity and the reader can readily, in the imagination, hear the swell of the escalating engagement. He wrote:

> The *tirailleurs* of Prince Jerome's division became engaged with the light troops posted in the skirts of the wood of Hougoumont and along the whole front of the enclosure. At first straggling shots announced the commencement of the action; the intervals of shots quickly lessened, till at length the firing increased to an incessant roll of musketry. The columns of Jerome's division approached the wood to support the light troops and the English artillery commenced firing upon them from the heights.

Jerome and Bauduin led some of the French into the wood and engaged the Nassauers and Hanoverians who were holding its boundary and there the contest became fierce. The French were repelled, driven back into the open and Bauduin was killed, but his men promptly counterattacked only to be driven out again. Eventually weight of numbers tipped the scales as more French skirmishers came up establishing a foothold among the trees. Though the Nassauers and Hanoverians fought stubbornly they could not hold and were forced back—fighting from tree to tree—until they were pressed back into the orchard where the First Guards under Saltoun had been stationed during the night.

The French pursued them rapidly, but were checked at the wall of the garden, which had been pierced by two tiers of loopholes and held by the Coldstream Guards. As the French came into range they were struck down by murderous volleys as they assaulted the wall and attempted to scale it. Bull's, R.H.A. howitzer battery now began to throw shells with precision into the wood, over the heads of the allied troops, causing havoc among the press of enemy troops there. The Guards at this point swiftly counterattacked, rallying the Hanoverians and Nassauers and driving the French back on their supports with heavy losses.

The assault on Hougoumont had quickly become too vehement considering its purpose was intended as a feint. There is a chasm of perspective between the intentions of a general officer and the experience of his soldiers at the sharp end of the action. At what point can an assaulting soldier understand that enough has been done, as he throws himself at a fiercely defended fortified position? How can he grasp that his efforts should be no more than the position's tactical value warrant? If Napoleon's design to breach the enemy centre was successful, Hougoumont would, in any event, become instantly irrelevant, so in reality Jerome needed only to occupy the wood, vigorously threaten the garrison of the *château* and form a barrier to oppose an allied advance in that quarter.

Restraint and clearly communicated control of his battalions were, therefore, Jerome's principal responsibilities. Instead, he foolishly became annoyed that his initial assaults had been frustrated and, driven by his inflated ego, he threw greater resources into actually taking the position, ordering Soye's brigade to attack in the wood yet again, and the remains of Bauduin's brigade to storm the buildings from the west.

The French rushed forward driving the Nassauers before them, but a group of the Coldstream and Third Guards, light company troops, taking shelter behind a lane and a haystack below the south-western corner of the *château* intervened and resisted desperately. The haystack caught fire and, to avoid being cut off, this party ran to the gateway in the northern front of the buildings. Passing through it into the courtyard they began to barricade the gate with whatever came first to hand. A French subaltern, (Sub-Lieutenant Legros of the 1st Light) took a pioneer's axe and broke down the bars. He rushed into the courtyard followed by a few of his men, but, after a brief desperate struggle, all of them were all killed. Four officers (among them, MacDonnell) and a sergeant of the Coldstream famously succeed in shouldering the gate closed.

As more French infantrymen ran round the north side of the buildings, others to the westward, crawled unseen through the crop of tall rye and opened fire upon Smith's artillery battery, forcing it to retire. Four companies of the Coldstream Guards under Colonel Woodford, drove off the skirmishers then attacked the flank of the 1st Light catching them between two fires for they were also exposed to volleys from the walls. The French gave way immediately.

In the Guards position on the ridge, a shout had called out, 'The Nassauers are driven out of the orchard. Light infantry to the front!' Saltoun was reinstated to the command of the two light companies of the First Guards battalions, and led them down the slope towards the *château* to join the battle. The Nassauers were retiring, though eyewitnesses report in good order. As French reinforcements continued to arrive, some of Soye's men, were emerging from the wood and into the orchard. Saltoun and his light companies threw themselves into the effort to impede them, though as they re-occupied the wood, they found nearly all the preparations they had previously made for defending it destroyed, and they had to trust to sheer hard fighting, often hand to hand, to maintain their ground.

By this time Napoleon's dispositions for his main attack were nearly complete, but Jerome persisted in imagining that his private battle was more meaningful than the greater contest. He had already severely depleted most of the seven battalions of Bauduin's brigade together with a regiment of Soye's brigade. He then fuelled the onslaught by throwing in Gauthier's brigade of Foy's division, sending skirmishers to creep along the eastern hedge to turn the enclosures, while the troops in the wood advanced again towards a gap in the fence which separated the wood from the orchard.

Nassau troops at Hougoumont

The Guards of both brigades had resisted stubbornly, but overwhelming numbers forced them to return to their original positions; the First Guards light companies to the orchard, the Second Brigade companies principally to the *château* itself.

The French skirmishers continued to rapidly advance through the wood towards the buildings and garden. A hedge forming the northern boundary of the wood appeared to them to form the enclosure of the garden beyond, and they rushed confidently forward *au pas de charge* only to discover the loopholed garden wall stood thirty yards behind the hedge and running parallel to it, behind which stood the waiting Coldstreams and Third Guards, who immediately delivered an intense deadly musketry fire upon them, stopping the surge in its tracks and laying low its foremost ranks. As the French discovered they could not succeed in storming Hougoumont by any direct attack, they sheltered in the hedge and trees maintaining a desultory fire against the well-protected garrison.

As fresh French battalions pushed forward, the British artillery resumed its fire upon them with devastating effect, causing confusion in their ranks. The garrison and First Guards light companies took advantage of the situation by launching a counterattack from the flanks. They soon regained possession of a large portion of the wood, though then the British artillery ceased firing as the guardsmen advanced which enabled the French to recover, reinforce and advance again forcing the British back once more; the Second Brigade to the flanks of the *château*, the First Brigade to the left of the garden wall.

The Coldstream and Third Guards companies consolidated within the buildings whilst the First Guards under Saltoun retired to the hedge on their left of the garden wall. The French in the wood whose attack against the garden wall had faltered came round its left flank through the orchard, but Saltoun was ready for them and as they appeared through the gap from the wood into the orchard, he launched a deadly headlong charge upon the head of the column, driving the survivors back into the wood.

Once again, the enemy's light troops attempted to turn the left flank of the grounds of Hougomont, advancing along the eastern hedge of the farm enclosures; while a simultaneous attack was made through the wood, and the orchard occupied by Lord Saltoun. He had already lost many of his men, and was once again compelled to retire to the shelter of the hollow way in the rear face of the enclosure, where he waited to be reinforced before he could advance. Robert Ellison later wrote to Siborne concerning the fighting in the afternoon:

> I was sent at one time of the day (I believe about two o'clock) from the orchard with some light troops to drive the French *tirailleurs* back, who had become very annoying to the farm, and were gradually gaining ground, particularly on the right flank of our position. We drove them quite out of the wood upon three French columns which were posted at the bottom of the hill, ready to move up and renew their attack upon the farmhouse, two of these columns just beginning to move, the third unpiling arms and falling in to support. We, of course, were driven back immediately.

Wellington, watching from the ridge position, directed Byng to send down reinforcements from his Second Brigade. Two companies of the Third Guards soon advanced along the eastern enclosure to the attack, whereupon Saltoun resumed the offensive, cleared the orchard of the enemy, and reoccupied its front hedge. His position was repeatedly attacked, but in the end the French were always repulsed though the outcome of these struggles often hung upon a hair.

In one of these attacks, when he had been driven from the front hedge of the orchard to the hollow way in rear of it, the enemy occupied the hedge with infantry and brought up a gun which Saltoun attempted, but failed, to seize. However, he regained possession of the hedge and there firmly established what remained of his command. Mackinnon's version of this activity, which includes the presence of troops from other regiments, follows:

> A detachment from the Third Guards, and the grenadiers of

Closing the gate at Hougoumont

The Guards fighting outside Hougoumont

that corps, with fifty Hanoverian riflemen under Lord Saltoun, bravely charged a howitzer, but did not succeed. This, however, had the effect of stopping anything further on that side, and the enemy contented themselves with firing from behind a ditch which ran nearly parallel to the hedge and ditch in front of the orchard.

CHAPTER THIRTY-FIVE

The Battle of Waterloo—Afternoon

At about 1.30 p.m., Napoleon's main attack ground into motion as four vast columns of French foot-soldiers made their way ponderously across the muddy fields towards the centre of the British line and began to climb the opposite slope. One brigade diverged to storm the farmhouse of La Haye Sainte; the rest struck, as planned, against Wellington's left-centre. Predictably, as they came into range, they were swept by a wave of hot musket fire, but though men fell in numbers, the columns pressed inexorably onward. Encouragingly, the first troops they closed with were from Bylandt's Dutch-Belgian brigade, who fled before them.

They then came up to Picton's two brigades, now reduced to almost half their strength by their losses at Quatre Bras. The British infantry, by contrast, remained steady and delivered a series of unwavering musketry volleys at close-quarters. A searing exchange of fire immediately erupted, but though the French out-numbered their immediate enemy by five to one, their phalanx formation meant they could bring no more muskets to bear than the infantry line standing before them.

As both sides blazed away at each other, through the smoke two brigades of British heavy cavalry (Somerset's Horse Guards and Life Guards, and Ponsonby's Union Brigade) burst from the allied rear in a charge which crashed into the thick of the unprepared French columns who were focused on grappling with Picton's infantry. The effect was cataclysmic as the cumbrous masses were shattered by a wall of galloping horses and their sword wielding riders. The French infantry battalions were thrown down the slope and pursued with the loss of thousands killed, wounded or made prisoner.

The British cavalrymen, not untypically driven out of control by the exhilaration of their headlong career, failed to check, and cutting down fugitives as they rode, plunged into the French lines on the other side of the valley. There the French cavalry fell upon them mercilessly and, their mounts blown, they could not make good their escape and hundreds of them were lost. Ponsonby, the commander of the Union Brigade of cavalry, was killed at this time, as was Picton with his infantry, who foul-mouthed and difficult as he had been, was one of Wellington's most competent generals in Iberia.

Though still in the distance, Bülow's Prussians were now advancing slowly towards the French right flank. Lobau's 6th corps and two brigades of reserve cavalry had been necessarily detached to the east to intercept them reducing the number available to attack Wellington by 10,000 men. Furthermore, Napoleon had received a new dispatch from Grouchy, which alarmingly revealed that his force at 11 a.m. was still far from Wavre and that he was unaware that Bülow had marched to join Wellington.

******

About two o'clock, after Byng had reinforced Hougomont with two companies of the Third Guards under Home, from the Second Brigade, he realised that the persistent efforts of the enemy upon the orchard were seriously depleting its defenders so he ordered Colonel Hepburn to take the remainder of his Second Battalion, Third Guards down the slope as a further reinforcement. When Hepburn reached the hollow way, he found it occupied by the few survivors of the two light companies of the First Guards under Saltoun, who had scarcely an effective man with whom to continue the defence.

Saltoun had been fighting for nearly four hours in the wood and orchard and his own subaltern, Charles Ellis was now wounded. His command at this point, despite its best efforts, was a spent force so he handed over his task to his friend, Hepburn,(who reported the occurrence in the Siborne letters, though other reports have the relieving officer as Mercer) and at three o'clock, rejoined his own Third Battalion on the ridge. A brother officer, Rees Howell Gronow was on the ridge and later recalled his return to the regimental position:—

> About four o'clock, Saltoun and Charley Ellis, who commanded the light companies of the battalions of Guards, joined us with the wreck of those detachments, after their gallant defence of Hougoumont. I remember well General Maitland saying to Saltoun, 'Your defence saved the army; nothing could be more gallant. Every man of you deserves a promotion'. Saltoun replied that it was 'touch and go—a matter of life and death—for all within the walls had sworn they would never surrender'. James Gunthorpe, the adjutant added, 'Our officers were determined never to yield and the men were resolved to stand by them to the last'. (*Readers will note that various sources have spread Saltoun's relief over nearly two hours.*)

The battalion of Coldstreams, under Colonel Alexander Woodford (with the exception of two companies left on the ridge in charge of the Colours), was also subsequently sent forward to assist in the defence of Hougoumont.

★★★★★★

At 3.30 p.m. the emperor directed Ney to resume the attack. The least ravaged regiments of d'Erlon's corps marched against the farm of La Haye Sainte with intent to secure it though they made little immediate progress, whilst a fresh brigade of Reille's corps was sent to further reinforce the frustrated assailants of Hougoumont. Attacks on the *château* were renewed, but they proved no more successful than their previous attempts. Concentrated artillery fire was then thrown upon buildings including a barrage of shells which set them ablaze incinerating their wounded occupants.

The French eventually sacrificed some eight thousand troops to carry a position which was not intended to be taken and yet when the day ended its burning ruins were still in the possession of its defenders. In later years, Jerome apparently insisted that his brother latterly gave him instructions to actually take Hougoumont which, given every other initiative had failed, may have been the case although, conversely, this unverifiable claim serves as a convenient justification for his otherwise insupportable actions.

Marshal Ney then conceived the idea of a great and desperate cavalry charge delivered against the front of the British line between La Haye Sainte and Hougoumont, intended to split Wellington's line asunder. At about 4p.m. Ney ordered Milhaud's two divisions of metal-breasted *cuirassiers* to the charge supported by the light cavalry of the Imperial Guard, forming a mass of 5,000 veteran horsemen rolling across the valley and up the slope. The method of defence employed by infantry in these circumstances was tried and tested, for under no circumstances must a line of foot soldiers dispute with cavalry.

The fifteen British and Hanoverian battalions comprising Wellington's right-centre formed themselves into human squares, bristling with walls of bayonets and prepared themselves for the coming shock. The allied gunners, for their part, waited until the optimal moment then opened fire, blowing advancing French cavalry squadrons to pieces, before abandoning their guns and dashing for the protection of the squares.

Wellington then ordered his own cavalry reserves to advance and drove the enemy horsemen off. The French cavalry assaults were, however, relentless and they came on again and again, whilst in the intervals the French artillery hurled roundshot into the exposed blocks of men with deadly effect, causing havoc for which there was no remedy. The squares were also harassed by the fire of *tirailleurs*, who crept up close to them and could not be driven off. In fact, the Prince of Orange in a final display of his martial acumen, ordered one battalion of the German Legion to deploy, whereupon it was forthwith annihilated by the *cuirassiers*. The prince was wounded shortly afterwards and, perhaps fortuitously, obliged to quit the field.

The cavalry charges had, notwithstanding their grandeur, failed to break a single British square and Milhauds corps was now in disarray, so Ney in desperation threw in the remainder of the reserve cavalry. These were Kellermann's two divisions of *cuirassiers* and the heavy squadrons of the Imperial Guard, some 5,000 men and horses strong, which then also fell upon the crippled squares. Milhaud's scattered brigades reformed and supported the new attack. The scene then became a confused *mêlée* as the French horsemen swirled around the dwindling squares, desperately trying to break into them, but perpetually failing to do so despite acts of prodigious gallantry.

★★★★★★

Upon seeing that the French cavalry were making preparations to attack, the Guards had formed squares on their respective leading companies, the Second Battalion, First Guards in rear of the line of the third battalion, and the latter in advance of the general line. After the cavalry fragmented against the squares, they would retire 100 or 150 yards, and charge again, only to be thwarted once more by musketry fire, whilst those who ventured imprudently close fell victims to bayonet thrusts or the spontoon's of the sergeants. Sometimes the horsemen would halt at a distance and send forward a few skirmishers to fire off their weapons, but the Guards would give no reply to these deadly annoyances, reserving the full effect of their ammunition for the charge which would certainly follow.

The Guards, in fact, were among the most susceptible to the onslaught of the enemy cavalry and the continuous cannonade of their artillery which accompanied it. The Third Battalion, First Guards, and the 30th and 73rd Regiments, were posted in advance of the narrow road which ran along the crest of the duke's position and their exposed post made them prominent marks for everything the enemy could bring to bear upon them.

Rees Howell Gronow of the First Guards later wrote of his experience within the square graphically, revealing the horror and tragedy of the Napoleonic battlefield. Readers will note this extract has been slightly edited to remove information in-

Attack on Hougoumont from the French perspective

cluded in the principal narrative and is comprised of elements of several anecdotes on this subject to avoid repetition. Of the officers named in his account, neither Stables or Adair survived the wounds they received in the battle. Adair's leg was mangled by a cannon ball and he died following the amputation.

> At about four o'clock the enemy's artillery in front of us stopped firing, and we saw large masses of cavalry advance: not a man present, who survived, could have forgotten in after life the awful grandeur of that charge. You perceived at a distance what appeared to be an overwhelming long moving line, which, ever advancing, glittered like a stormy wave of the sea when it catches the sunlight. On came the mounted host until they got near enough, whilst the very earth seemed to vibrate beneath their thundering tramp. One might have supposed that nothing could resist the shock of this terrible moving mass. In an incredibly short period, they were within twenty yards of us. The word of command, 'Prepare to receive cavalry', had been given, every man in the front ranks knelt, and a wall of bristling steel held together by steady hands presented itself to the infuriated *cuirassiers*.
> Our squares before long presented a shocking sight. We were nearly suffocated by the smoke and smell from burnt cartridges. It was impossible to move a yard without treading upon a wounded comrade, or upon the bodies of the dead, and the loud groans of the wounded and dying were most appalling. Within the square was, in fact, a perfect hospital, being full of dead and dying and mutilated soldiers.
> The cavalry charges were in appearance very formidable, but in reality, a great relief, as the artillery could no longer fire upon us. During the terrible fire of their artillery we were lying down when a shell fell between Goodwin Colquitt and another officer. In an instant Colquitt jumped up, caught up the shell as if it been a cricket ball and flung it over the heads of the officers and men saving many brave fellows. I never shall forget the strange noise our bullets made against the breastplates of the *cuirassiers*. I can only compare it to the noise of a violent hailstorm beating upon panes of glass.
> Our artillery did great execution, but our musketry did not at first appear to kill many men, though it brought down a large

number of horses and created indescribable confusion. The horses in spite of all the efforts of their riders, came to a standstill, shaking and covered with foam about twenty yards distant from our squares, resisting all attempts to force them to charge the line of serried steel. Two enemy officers forced their way into a gap in the square caused by artillery: one was killed by Stables and the other by Adair with a single stroke of his sword. In the midst of our terrible fire the enemy officers were seen as though on parade, keeping order in the ranks and encouraging their men. These, unable to renew the charge but unwilling to retreat, brandished their swords with loud cries of *'Vive l'Empereur'* and allowed themselves to be mowed down by hundreds rather than yield.

★★★★★★

The pressure of such concerted enemy effort, whilst not as immediately effective as it was debilitating, was taking its toll. Wellington had used up all his cavalry with the exception of those on the far left and brought forward all his infantry reserve excepting a single Dutch-Belgian division which was so demoralised as to be considered dangerous to put into the line. The essential question, at this point, was, 'For how much longer could this punishment be endured?' In the later afternoon the duke had entered a Guards square by one of its angles accompanied by one *aide-de-camp,* the rest of his staff having been killed or wounded. Gronow recalled that Wellington, 'appeared perfectly composed, but very thoughtful and pale'. As the cavalry assaults continued he sat on his charger, unmoved. Gronow heard him ask Colonel Stanhope the time, whereupon Stanhope took out his watch and replied that it was twenty minutes past four. Wellington was then heard to say, 'The battle is mine; and if the Prussians arrive soon, there will be an end to the war'.

★★★★★★

At about the time the French cavalry first swept over the ridge, the Prussians of Bülow's corps at last reached the Wood of Paris (Bois de Paris), just two miles from Napoleon's right flank, and began to exchange shots with the French *vedettes.* Their late arrival, despite various exonerating theories, was caused by

Blücher's obstructive staff, led by Gneisenau, who had been reluctant to commit to the contest until it was evident that Wellington was inextricably locked in a life or death struggle. Old Blücher remained true to his character and exhorted greater effort, insistent that the Prussian Army must not fail Wellington. The emperor had told Lobau to contain Bülow's troops, which he managed for some time about the village of Planchenoit, though he had no hope of defeating the Prussians for, 30,000 strong, they had him at a disadvantage of three to one.

Inevitably Planchenoit was lost so, the emperor sent the four regiments of the Young Guard to retake it. By six o'clock Bülow's last reserves had been used up, so his contribution was demonstrably not the key to victory that had been hoped for. However, he had succeeded in compelling the emperor to divert some 14,000 men of his reserves to engage him who could not now be deployed against Wellington and far more importantly Ziethen's and Pirch's corps, thanks to Blücher, were now also appearing on the battlefield and pressing into the French right flank. The Prussians had arrived, quite literally, with a vengeance.

******

Three unsuccessful attacks had been made on the farm of La Haye Sainte, defended by Baring's, King's German Legion, but a fourth attack, made in the later afternoon, finally took the position. The exhausted and depleted garrison was out of ammunition and had practically nothing left to throw at the French but insults, so Baring abandoned the farm and led the survivors of his command back to the lines on the crest. The farmhouse's position was a prize worth winning, but there were few resources left to maximise on its potentials and time was inexorably marching on against the emperor's favour. Nevertheless, the enemy began to construct an attack on the allied centre. The emperor, given all he had gambled and committed, was right to attack, but his cardinal error was that he did not send his Imperial Guard to the front *en masse*, the moment La Haye Sainte fell.

French skirmishers assembled under the shelter of some low ground west of the farmhouse, but when they emerged, they began to pour fire into the left flank of the Third Battalion, First Guards, and the Second Battalion, 95th Rifles. This assault became so serious that Maitland realised, notwithstanding the Guards were organised for defence, it must be neutralised. He was within the third battalion square when the crisis arose so directly ordered its commander, Lieutenant-Colonel D'Oyly, to undertake the task.

This was not a straightforward instruction to obey as the battalion was in formed in square, prepared to repel the repeated attacks of the enemy's cavalry, who were still close by at the foot of the slope, ready to destroy any infantry formation that carelessly compromised itself. It would have been fatal to form line in the usual manner so the discipline, precision and the steadiness of the Guards became paramount. The flank faces of the square were thrown back in sections, and in that formation the third battalion advanced, prepared to instantly reform square again should danger threaten.

This initiative was noted by the enemy artillery which, as the battalion was halted to fire, mowed bloody channels through the faces of the ranks whilst the French cavalry hovered ready to exploit an opportunity should one arise. The guardsmen, nonetheless, steadily maintained their fire whilst closing up the gaps made in their lines. The enemy's infantry were compelled to retire, but the artillery fire upon the Guards became too deadly to endure so Maitland ordered the battalion to retire about forty yards up the hill, which it achieved without interference from the cavalry.

Major-General George Cooke quit the field with a wound that cost him his left arm. Lieutenant-Colonel Richard Henry Cooke, of the Second Battalion, First Guards was also wounded. An anonymous Guards officer in a letter published in John Booth's miscellany published in 1817, wrote:

> Unfortunately for us, during the cannonade the shot and shells which passed over the artillery fell into our squares, and I assure you I was never in a more awful situation. Col. Cooke, who commanded the battalion, was struck with a grape shot as he

sat on the ground next to me. The enemy now made an attack with infantry and cavalry on the left in hopes of carrying the *chaussée* to Brussels, but the artillery guns cut them to pieces every time they advanced.

Another anonymous Guards officer wrote in a letter published in the same book:

> Colonel Cooke was struck by a cannon-shot on the shoulder (that passed) about a foot above my head: but I believe his case is not hopeless. Those who were at Vittoria, Albuera and Leipsic say their fire was not to be mentioned or the carnage to be compared to that of Waterloo.

About the same time the two commanding officers of battalions, D'Oyly and Stables were both struck down, so the command of the Third Battalion, First Guards, devolved upon Saltoun. The two colonels were carried off the field, and Stables injury proved mortal and he died the following morning.

Chapter Thirty-Six

The Battle of Waterloo—Evening

As the evening drew in the battle remained unresolved. The emperor, out of time and options, decided to deliver his last desperate blow, and to throw the Imperial Guard into the thick of the battle. Napoleon preceded this attack with concentrated fire by the artillery upon the allied position lying between the landmarks of Hougoumont and La Haye Sainte. Along this part of the ridge ran a cart road, on one side of which was a ditch and bank which afforded cover to the First Brigade of Guards which, without this protection, risked annihilation under the intensity of the barrage.

The French assaulting column was composed of six battalions of the Middle Guard in hollow squares, whilst two battalions of the Old Guard followed some distance behind, to act as supports. The remaining five battalions were still held back in reserve. The attack was not delivered directly up the high-road leading towards La Haye Sainte, but half a mile further west and nearer to Hougoumont. The leading square, that furthest to the east, came up the slope opposite Halkett's brigade; the others were making for the ground held by Maitland's Brigade of Guards. The moment that they began to ascend the heights, all came under a heavy artillery fire, for Wellington's gunners, though often driven from their pieces by the cavalry charges, had returned and were still holding their positions.

Wellington was close to the two battalions of the First Guards, which initially were in squares, when he instructed Maitland to form them into line four deep to provide maximum fire to the front. The formation into line, instead of being made by deployment, was effected by simply wheeling up to the front, the four deep flank faces forming the extremities of each battalion, so that the grenadier companies were in the centre, so the men could more readily form square again if cavalry approached. Maitland covered this change of formation with a line of skirmishers under Swinburn, who only rejoined his battalion a few moments before the enemy was upon them. The new formation was barely completed, and the men ordered to lie down again, when, at a quarter past seven, the French cannonade ceased. As the smoke gradually cleared away, the Imperial Guard could be seen advancing up the slope with loud encouraging cries of '*Vive l'Empereur!*'

As these veterans began to ascend the incline, they became exposed to the concentrated British artillery fire of the right wing of the allies, which mauled them severely. Still they came on, preceded by a cloud of skirmishers; but these were soon driven back upon their main body by a fire of canister, grape, and shrapnel shells, delivered at a distance of less than 100 yards. These formations met no human enemy to obstruct their progress until they arrived within from twenty to thirty yards of the position. Then the shock was short and decisive. The right-hand *échelon* that first reached the crest, engaged in a close and murderous musketry fight with Halkett's brigade. Another fire was poured in upon the right flank of the advancing column by the 33rd and 69th British regiments, which had been promptly pushed forward by Halkett on the left of the Guards. The French column staggered, then recoiled.

The central force then came up against Maitland's Guards and the British battery beside them. When French were seen looming through the smoke, Wellington, called upon the Guards, who were still lying down to escape the fire of the French artillery, to stand exclaiming 'Now, Maitland, now's your time,' and it was then that enemy saw them rise up before them as though sprouting from the earth in what appeared to be an impenetrable barrier. The duke, as he had done so often in Peninsular battles, ordered the firing of a single volley, after which the men were to advance firing. The first thunderous point-blank discharge of a well-formed British line was irresistible and the heads of the French squares went down in one weltering mass.

As their enemy recovered and began to move forward again deliberate volleys continued until, at only fifteen yards distance, the men fired from the hip, instead of raising their muskets to their shoulders, while the rear ranks passed their loaded muskets forward so that the front rank could fire again immediately on targets that could not be missed. The survivors of this onslaught of concentrated fire broke and fled downhill. Saltoun called out to his battalion, 'Now's the time, my boys.' The brigade answered with a cheer, and led by Maitland, Saltoun, Reeve, and Gunthorpe, sprang to the bayonet charge. The advance of Maitland's brigade was only momentarily checked by the appearance of the last French *échelon*, two battalions strong, on their flank. Captain H. W. Powell of the First Guards in his journal described the incident thus:

> Immediately the brigade sprang forward. *La Garde* turned and gave us little opportunity of trying the steel. We charged down the hill till we had passed the end of the orchard of Hougoumont, when our right flank became exposed to another heavy column who were advancing in support of the former column, This circumstance, besides that our charge was isolated, obliged the brigade to retire towards its original position.
> Opportunely, Sir F. Adam's Light Brigade had in the meantime come round the knoll between the position and Hougoumont, when we had been ordered to take ground to our left, and were advancing under the hedge and blind line along the northern side of the orchard at Hougoumont. As soon as we had uncovered their front, we halted and fronted. The two brigades now returned to the charge which the *chasseurs* did not wait for, and we continued our forward movement till we got to the bottom of the valley between the positions.

As the second column of the Imperial Guard advanced up the slope, it was received by Adams' Brigade: the second battalion 95th on the left, then Colborne's 52nd and the 71st on the right, extended towards Hougomont so that they swung like a door upon its hinges. The ensuing volleys of fire tore away the whole left flank of the French battalions, which broke in helpless disorder and also rolled back down the slope. Their retreat carried with it the two battalions of the Old Guard which were crossing the valley in their support, as well as the half-formed and depleted masses of Reille's corps which were lingering under the lee of Hougoumont.

Wellington had, incidentally, been initially unaware of the existence of the threat posed by Reille's men. The duke was close to the First Brigade, and after looking carefully with his glass along the whole of the French position, turned to his staff, said, 'Well, I think they are pretty well told out now.' Saltoun, over hearing him, spoke to one of the staff officers, commenting, 'I don't know; when I was outside the wood at Hougoumont, this morning, before the action began, I watched a column of men, as far as I can guess about 5,000 or 6,000, go into a hollow opposite; I have kept my eye on this spot all day, and have never seen them come out yet.' This observation was reported to the duke, who immediately turned his telescope to investigate Saltoun's claim, and after a moment's pause said, 'By God, he is right—they are coming out now.'

The brilliantly conceived flank fire of Adams' Brigade mainly contributed to the final overthrow of the second column. The cry, '*la Garde recule*,' was already running along the whole French line, when Wellington let loose upon the wavering masses below him his last British reserves, the two cavalry brigades of Vivian and Vandeleur. They crashed down the hill-side east of Hougoumont, across the *débris* of the fight, and fell upon the retreating Imperial Guard and the exhausted and disordered remnants of Kellermann's and Milhaud's cavalry. All gave way before them, almost without resistance; and the French centre was transformed in a minute into a panic-stricken crowd.

As the Duke of Wellington saw the enemy waver, he ordered the general advance of his whole line. Adams' Brigade followed

The repulse of the Imperial Guard

this second column, while the First Guards, under Maitland followed the track of the first column, till it reached the Charleroi road, near La Belle Alliance. The Grenadiers of the Imperial Guard, attempted, after forming square, to stem the flying torrent and its pursuers, but to no avail.

General Cambronne, who commanded part of the Imperial Guard, has become famous for his apparently defiant proclamation, '*La Garde meurt, mais ne se rend pas!*' One should regard famous pronouncements with scepticism and it has been suggested that if this one was actually spoken it was by another officer who actually died in the battle, whilst Cambronne allegedly muttered a far less poetic, though undeniably emphatic *'Merde!'*. Halkett, with some degree of detail to support the authenticity of his claim, asserted that he personally, forcibly dragged Cambronne into captivity making the details of his 'surrender' speech, if he made one, academic.

However, be that as it may, Saltoun shortly appeared on the scene to place the general in the charge of a strapping guardsman, named Kent, with instructions to conduct him securely to Brussels. Other sources have Cambronne put into the care of one of Halkett's Osnabrückers. Halkett was wounded shortly afterwards, shot through the face cheeks as he was calling out orders.

At the moment when Napoleon's last attack was repulsed, Ziethen's Prussian corps had broken in between d'Erlon's and Lobau's troops at the north-eastern point of the French front. With an enemy army to the front and another pressing in from the side, the French lines caved inwards. The Prussian cavalry, pushing hard, arrived near La Belle Alliance at the same moment as the British cavalry brigades who were driving down from the ridge. Whilst Wellington's whole front line advanced, prepared to support the cavalry, it discovered there was practically no enemy before it to fight and so after reaching the crest of the French position it halted.

The continued pursuit was left to the Prussians for, having carried the burden of the battle, there was no strength left in the remnants of Wellington's shattered battalions. The First Guards, for their part, having pursued the French as far as the Charleroi road, formed into column, and continued their advance along the *chaussée*, through the whole depth of the late French position, and bivouacked for the night in the fields on the right, two miles in advance of the position of Waterloo. The second and third battalions of First Guards were commanded, after the action, by Lieutenant-Colonels Fead and Lord Saltoun respectively.

The emperor's army was no longer the pride of its nation or the scourge of the continent, but no more than a helpless horde of fugitives. Harassed through every step of its flight, it was harried through the night by the Prussian cavalry, never allowed a moment to rally nor given an opportunity to rest. The French were driven out of seven successive bivouacs, panicked by the sound of an approaching Prussian drum which was beaten by a drummer-boy mounted upon a horse to give the impression the avenging infantry were close at hand. By the following morning French soldiers were fleeing over the River Sambre, crossing the frontier in isolated groups. It had been a little more than a week since these men, now in a very different condition and simply relieved to be alive, had proudly marched in the opposite direction intent on winning another grand victory.

At Waterloo, Napoleon's army lost all its artillery, more than 250 guns, and suffered about 30,000 men in killed and wounded. French prisoners of war were comparatively few in number, probably not more than 6,000 or 7,000, but, in many units of the Imperial Army, the actual casualties tragically exceeded 50 *per cent*, of those present for they had battled like heroes. Wellington's army had lost over 13,000 men, of whom 7,000 were British. The Prussians reported losing over 6,000 men.

Wellington had encountered Blücher at La Belle Alliance where the old marshal reportedly declared, *'Quelle Affaire!'*, as he warmly took the duke's hand. Rarely had two commanders performed so well in concert, so no one could take issue with Blücher's incisive summation on that score. There was some sug-

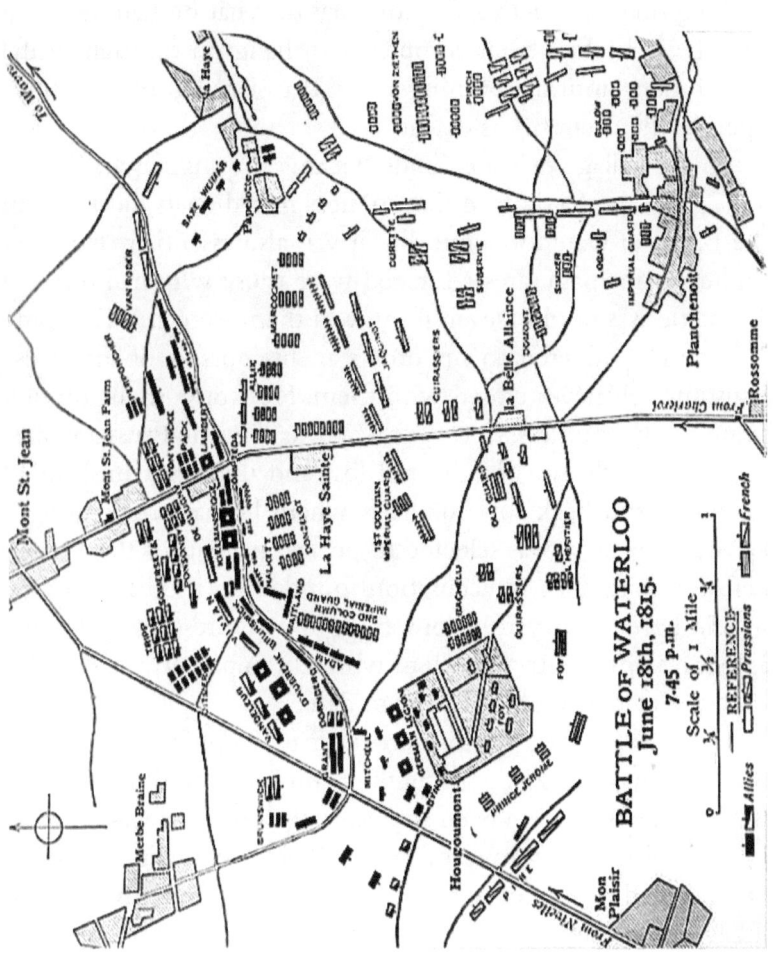

gestion that, '*La Belle Alliance*' offered an appropriate name for the battle in the circumstances, but Wellington was never going to approve of a French language title for a battle that France had so comprehensively lost to an army under his command. Furthermore, whilst it was indisputable that the victory had been won by an alliance, there was nothing 'beautiful' about it from Wellington's perspective, for contrary to what he had been led to believe, he had been compelled to hang on through brutal punishment until the evening as the Prussians left their options open in the event of his defeat.

So, the village of Water Lude became the anglicised, 'Waterloo'. It was perfectly true that soldiers in red coats did not win the Battle of Waterloo alone, but it was also essentially true that soldiers principally dressed in red were those who had ensured the battle was not lost, even if some of them were also Germans.

Grouchy adhered to his orders in his pursuit of the Prussians, though never closed with them. He won a small, though strategically pointless, victory at Wavre against the Prussians after the main battle was fought and lost and thereafter husbanded his command back towards Paris where he handed it over to Davout. Grouchy was selected to be a scapegoat for the French defeat at Waterloo; an accusation founded on the basis that he should have disobeyed his orders, prompted presumably by imagination or gallantry—both of which he apparently lacked, despite the evidence of his career to date.

In any event, that proposition, ultimately, only has credence if the consequence of his joining the main battle, at his earliest opportunity, would have been to ensure the emperor was securely positioned on the throne of France. That eventuality, even had he managed to influence a French victory of sorts on the 18th June, would have become more fantastical with the sound of every approaching resolute Russian and Austrian boot, for nothing could by then have undone the crippling losses suffered by the French Army at Quatre Bras and Waterloo.

The following day Saltoun put pen to paper to write a short note to his wife which requires no elaboration.

June 19th 1815
Field of Battle, near Water Lude.

My dear dearest Catharine

I have only just time to tell you that I have lived through two of the sharpest actions ever fought by men. We have defeated the French at all points, and they are in full retreat. Our loss has been prodigious, as the brunt of the business fell upon the Guards, and many of my best and oldest friends are gone, but these things must tarry—my favourite little horse was shot under me, and at present I have only one, but I must get another here. I have no time to write more at length, as, if I do, I fear I shall be too late for the staff-officer who is to take this. So, God bless you, my dear love, and believe me, ever your affectionate

Saltoun.

The final word on the struggle for Hougoumont will be given in this narrative to Rees Howell Gronow, of the First Guards. His words poignantly illustrated the tragedy of war on several levels, though appropriately for this narrative, from the perspective of the Guards and our principal character most particularly.

Early on the morning after the Battle of Waterloo, I visited Hougoumont, in order to witness with my own eyes, the traces of one of the most hotly-contested spots of the field of battle. I came first upon the orchard, and there discovered heaps of dead men, in various uniforms: those of the Guards in their usual red jackets, the German Legion in green, and the French dressed in blue, mingled together. The dead and the wounded positively covered the whole area of the orchard; not less than two thousand men had there fallen. The apple trees presented a singular appearance, shattered branches were seen hanging about their mother trunks in such profusion that one might almost suppose the stiff growing and stunted tree had been converted into the willow: every tree was riddled and smashed in a manner which told that the showers of shot had been incessant. On this spot I lost some of my dearest and bravest friends, and the country had to mourn many of its most heroic sons slain here.

I must observe that, according to the custom of commanding officers, whose business it is after a great battle to report to the Commander in Chief, the muster-role of fame always closes before the rank of Captain. It has always appeared to me a great injustice that there should ever be any limit to the role of gallantry of either officers or men. If a captain, lieutenant, an ensign, a sergeant or a private, has distinguished himself for his bravery, his intelligence, or both, their deeds ought to be reported in order that the sovereign and nation should know who really fight the great battles of England. Of the class of officers and men to which I have referred, there were many of even superior rank who were omitted to be mentioned in the public despatches.

Thus, for example, to the individual courage of Lord Saltoun and Charley Ellis, who commanded the light companies, was mainly owing our success at Hougoumont. The same may be said of Needham, Percival, Erskine, Grant, Vyner, Buckley, Master, and young Algernon Greville, who at that time could not have been more than seventeen years old. Excepting Percival, whose jaws were torn away by a grape-shot, every one of these heroes miraculously escaped.

I do not wish, in making these observations, to detract from the bravery and skill of officers whose names have already been mentioned in official despatches, but I think it only just that the services of those I have particularised should not be forgotten by one of their companions in arms.

In a letter from an anonymous officer of the First Guards, published in John Booth's miscellany there appears the following description of the battlefield the day after the battle:

> After our bivouac of the 18th, after the battle, we marched to Nivelles, over the terrible field; so horrible a scene, scarcely any man ever witnessed; the ground, for the space of a league was covered with bodies, absolutely lying in ranks, and horses grouped in heaps with their riders. Towards our right was a château, which during the battle took fire from the enemy's shells; and in that state it was heroically defended by Saltoun and afterwards by the 2nd brigade of Guards. The appearance brought to my mind St. Sebastian; it was equally horrid, though on a smaller scale.

Rees Gronow has left a harrowing view of the sufferings of the wounded in his reminiscences. The march had barely begun when the regiment came across numbers of their own wounded packed into farmers wagons. As the officers came close, one man cried out, 'For God's sake, Mr Gronow, give us some water or we shall go mad!'. Gronow jumped into the cart and gave the man all the water that he carried in his own flask. The report of this incident continues in Gronow's own words:

> The other wounded soldiers entreated me to fill the flask with some muddy water that they had seen in a neighbouring ditch, half filled with water from the rain of the previous day. As I thought the flask would be of little use among so many, I took off my shako, and having first stopped up with my belcher handkerchief a hole which a musket ball had made in the top of it, filled it with water several times for these poor fellows who were all too severely wounded to get it for themselves and who drank it off with tears of delight.

Chapter Thirty-Seven

The Pursuit to Paris

Napoleon's ambitions had been crushed beyond hope of recovery and on the 19th of June, he was not only a renegade, but a hunted fugitive. The great deciding battle had been fought, but resistance continued and the campaign would not be over until the capital of France was taken and occupied by the armies of the alliance. The Prussians resumed the advance immediately and Wellington likewise ordered his own army forward without delay. The Guards were on the road at day break and during the day reached Nivelles. Gronow, in his reminiscences, has left posterity an informative and amusing insight of the camaraderie of officers of the Guards on the march which is readily datable to the 20th of June.

> About twelve o'clock, on the second day after the Battle of Waterloo, when on our march to Paris, we were ordered to come to a halt. Every officer and soldier immediately set to work to get rid of the superabundance of beard which had been suffered to grow for several days. During this not very agreeable duty, a shout was heard from Lord Saltoun, who called us to witness a bet he had made with Bob Ellison, that he, Ellison, could not shave off his beard in one minute.
> Preparations were made, Ellison taking care to bathe his face for a considerable time in water. He then commenced operations and in less than a minute, and without the aid of a looking-glass actually won his bet (a considerable one) to the astonishment, and I must add, the satisfaction of his comrades. This feat appeared to us all perfectly impossible to accomplish, as his face

was covered with the stubble of a week's growth of hair, so dark that it had procured for him in the regiment the sobriquet of 'Black Bob'.

The march continued, some troops heading for Mons, whilst the Guards took the high road to Binche and thereafter, on the 21st, reaching Bavay. The frontier into France was crossed and on the 22nd the right of the army marched to Le Cateau Cambresis whilst the Guards raised their own camp at Gourmignies.

For the first time since the battle, Saltoun had sufficient time at his disposal to write a full letter to Catharine. Readers should recall that his references to 'Hove' mean modern 'Hoves' near Enghein not modern Hove near Antwerp. If Saltoun believed that Napoleon had literally led the Imperial Guard into the battle, he was mistaken. The emperor had, indeed, led the pride of his army towards the front for a short period, but then moved aside as if to review it as it marched by his position. Understandably, Saltoun's assessment of the numbers engaged and killed were optimistic.

Those details notwithstanding, readers who have arrived at this point in this narrative will appreciate that Saltoun's report (if understandably sanitized and general) substantially represented the facts.

This letter is particularly interesting as he confesses how close he had come to being wounded or killed, since he had not only had two horses shot from beneath him, but a French musket-ball had actually passed through his shako whilst he was wearing it, which is a close shave in anyone's language. Such hairs breadth escapes were not apparently unique, for Gronow also reported that whilst in the square he had a grape shot pass through the top of his shako and that one of his coat-tails had been completely shot off.

Camp, near Gourmignies,
22nd June 1815.

My dear Catharine,
I wrote you a few lines from the field of battle on the 19th, but I have just heard that letters are to go immediately to England.

I take this opportunity of telling you what has taken place since I wrote last from Hove on the 15th.

A few hours after my letter was gone, we got the alarm that Bonaparte had attacked the Prussians, and we were ordered to march at a moment's notice, and on the morning of the 16th, at 3, we marched from Hove, through Braine and Nivelles, to a place called Quatre Bras, which place we reached about 5 in the afternoon, and were immediately very hotly engaged in the Bois de Bossu, and at nightfall we had succeeded in taking the wood from the enemy, but not without very great loss. My old friends Grose and Miller fell in the affair, with many others, and about five hundred men of the regiment.

During this time Boney had attacked the Prussians at Fleurus, and had gained some advantages, so as to oblige them to retreat. Our position of Quatre Bras being in consequence exposed on the left, we were obliged to fall back, and accordingly, on the 17th, retired, and took post in position at Water Leud.

On the 18th Napoleon attacked us with the whole of his army. The action was extremely severe, and our loss much greater than in any of the battles in the Peninsula. . . . The infantry formed squares, and about five o'clock had completely repulsed and destroyed the French cavalry by their steadiness in square, and the excellence of their fire. About half-past six Napoleon made his last desperate attack, at the head of his Old Imperial Guards, upon our brigade. It was a thing I always wished for, and the result was what I have often said it would be; to do them justice they came on like men, but our boys went at them like Britons, and drove them off the field in less than ten minutes.

From that moment the day was our own, and the French were completely routed, and fled, leaving their artillery, stores, baggage, and an immense number of prisoners. We estimate the French Army before the action at about 120,000 men, and that they lost full 50,000. The Prussians are in hot pursuit, and have taken a great many prisoners.

On the 19th we marched to Nivelles, 20th, to a village near Binche, yesterday to Bavay, and today we are bivouacked here. Our baggage is a long way in the rear, and I do not know when I shall get a clean shirt. I have got my toothbrush, so I am not quite a beast.

I have this moment, my dear love, got your letter of the 15th. You little thought how near we were coming to the work. I am sure you will be sorry for poor Stables; he was killed on the 18th. In short, we have lost in the First Regiment twelve officers killed and twenty-two wounded. I was in great luck again, as I had two horses killed under me, and a ball through my cap, but the head remains as good as ever. I have been very much applauded, and so forth, and been reported for good conduct, and everyone says that I am sure of a medal. I am so glad that England had the first of it, I was always certain of the event, if he and the Duke ever met, and now we consider the whole thing over. He may perhaps make another struggle at Laon, or on the Marne, but he must be defeated in the end, and I should not be surprised any day to hear of his being deposed.

You must not now, my dear love, be in the fidgets because you do not hear every post, for situated as we are, we do not know when to write; and indeed I could not have written today had I not been in good luck enough to borrow a sheet of paper from my sergeant; but, depend upon it, I will write by every opportunity, and as I do not expect any more fighting, you may make yourself easy on that head.

I must now, my dear Kate, send this to the adjutant-general, for fear of being too late; and believe me, my dear love, that I fully expect to see you before August, and until I do, that I am your most affectionate

Saltoun.

In his letter Saltoun mentioned having had two horses killed under him; when each fell the saddle was, of course, removed and with the cloak rolled up across the pommel, was placed upon another horse. After the battle, when his servant unrolled the cloak, he discovered no fewer than seventeen French musket-balls within it, many of which, given their position, must have proved fatal had they not been stopped by the folds of thick material. Saltoun claimed that this servant, James Hughes, who had previously been a very foul-mouthed man, was so struck by the apparent providence of this occurrence, that he uttered no oath or bad language ever again.

The rain had continued to fall heavily since the battle and

it was decided to make the 23rd a day of rest for most of the army. This camp allowed stragglers to rejoin their units and ammunition and baggage to be brought up. Wellington had the practical issues inherent in taking possession of Cambrai and Peronne to consider for both places remained in enemy hands. Recent losses meant that changes had to be made with the staff of the Guards. Sir John Byng, who had commanded the Second Brigade in the battle, was now temporarily put in command of the first *Corps d'Armée*, consisting of the First and Third Infantry Divisions replacing the Prince of Orange who fortunately had urgent business elsewhere.

The command of the Guards Division went to Maitland, and William Bathurst of the First Guards went with him as *aide-de-camp*, to fill the void left by the death of young Lord James Hay at Quatre Bras. Stanhope was appointed Assistant-Quartermaster-General of the First Division, replacing Bradford, who had been wounded at Waterloo.

The first three divisions of the army were close by Le Cateau on the 24th, the First Guards being at Bussigny, where the French King, Louis XVIII., came up to them. On the 25th, the First and Third Divisions, with the Dutch-Belgic infantry, advanced and were encamped at Premont, near Serain; while the Fourth Division occupied Cambrai, which surrendered to them that evening.

Saltoun was now at liberty to write to his wife regularly once again, though his next letter covered a period of three days, so for some reason he was unable to send it on the day he began to write it. The contents of the first dated section speak for themselves and give the reader insights into the nature of the march to Paris in 1815 which do not often appear in other accounts. Additionally, this letter reported the suddenly failing health of his servant, James Hughes. It is clear that Hughes was so ill that Saltoun believed he would die, which made the necessity of abandoning him the more difficult, for despite the fact that Hughes was something of a rogue, the two men had shared many trials together and there was an undeniable bond between them. Saltoun appears at pains to reassure Catharine that there would be no more fighting and, of course, this would be a reasonable comment to make to his new wife whether, he believed it to be the case or not. However, there would be fighting ahead and he, once again, would be in the heart of it.

Camp near Serain,
25th June 1815.

I wrote you last, my dearest Catharine, from Gourmignies, giving you an account of what had taken place up to that date. We halted there the next day and yesterday we marched to a place called Boussiers short of Cateau. Today we marched through Cateau to this place. The weather is most horrible, and resembles more a winter than a summer campaign; for it has rained almost every day since the action, and the roads—for as yet we have been marching by the cross roads, and not the *chaussées*, to avoid the strong places—are up to the men's knees in mud; but as we get nearer Paris I hope it will be better.

The news of the day is very good—Napoleon retired from Laon to Soissons, and the Prussians occupied Laon this morning. They say also, and we have reason to believe it, that the two Chambers at Paris have deposed Napoleon, and have elected a Provisional Government, with Carnot and Fouché at the head, to manage the nation during the minority of the King of Rome. This will of course be rejected, and we shall advance and put Louis on the throne, I really think, without firing another shot. It is just a week since the action, which all hands, both French and others, agree as to having been the most severe and bloody that ever was fought, and since that day we have advanced about seventy miles, and we are now within one hundred and twenty of Paris. The old king came up to us yesterday, and today remains at Cateau.

I am sorry to say that poor Hughes is in a bad way. I have been obliged to leave him in the village where we halted last night, for from violent rheumatics, he was unable to sit on his horse; and the number of our wounded is so great, added to the confusion that took place in the rear, owing to the false alarm the day of the battle, that our carts for carrying sick men have never come up, so I do not know whether I shall ever see him again, indeed I much fear I shall not; this, added to the very disagreeable task, which I have just got through, of writing to the families of all our poor officers who fell an account of their death, which as Commanding Officer I am obliged to do, the loss in the action having given me the temporary command of the Second Battalion, has made me very melancholy; so I will not write to you any more at present, for fear of making you so likewise, but finish this as soon as I can get an opportunity of sending it.

Saltoun broke off writing this letter at this point and resumed it on the 27th. The number of officers present with the battalions was now much reduced, owing to so many casualties.

On the morning of the 26th of June, as Sir John Byng was passing the village of Vermand, he learnt that Wellington wanted to see him. Upon their meeting the duke announced, 'You are the very person I wish to see; I want you to take Peronne; you may as well take with you the Brigade of Guards and a Dutch-Belgian brigade. I shall be there almost as soon as yourself.'

The formidable fortress at Peronne (Peronne La Pucelle) was built in 1710 and was once considered the key to Picardy, and even to France itself, when approached from its vicinity. It was about eleven miles from the Guards' position at the time. Byng passed on his orders to both to Maitland's Brigade of First Guards, who marched towards the place immediately and also to a Dutch-Belgian brigade which was to cooperate with them. When the Guards reached Peronne, Wellington called upon the garrison to surrender, but received an emphatic refusal from the governor.

After reconnoitring the fortifications, he decided they could be taken by storm and directed the attack to be made upon a horn-work which covered the suburbs on the left bank of the Somme. The assault was allocated to the Third Battalion, First Guards, preceded by the light companies of the First Brigade which would be under the command of Saltoun, while the second battalion were to be employed carrying fascines for their comrades. Since Saltoun was by this point commanding the Second Battalion, this suggests he had resumed his previous

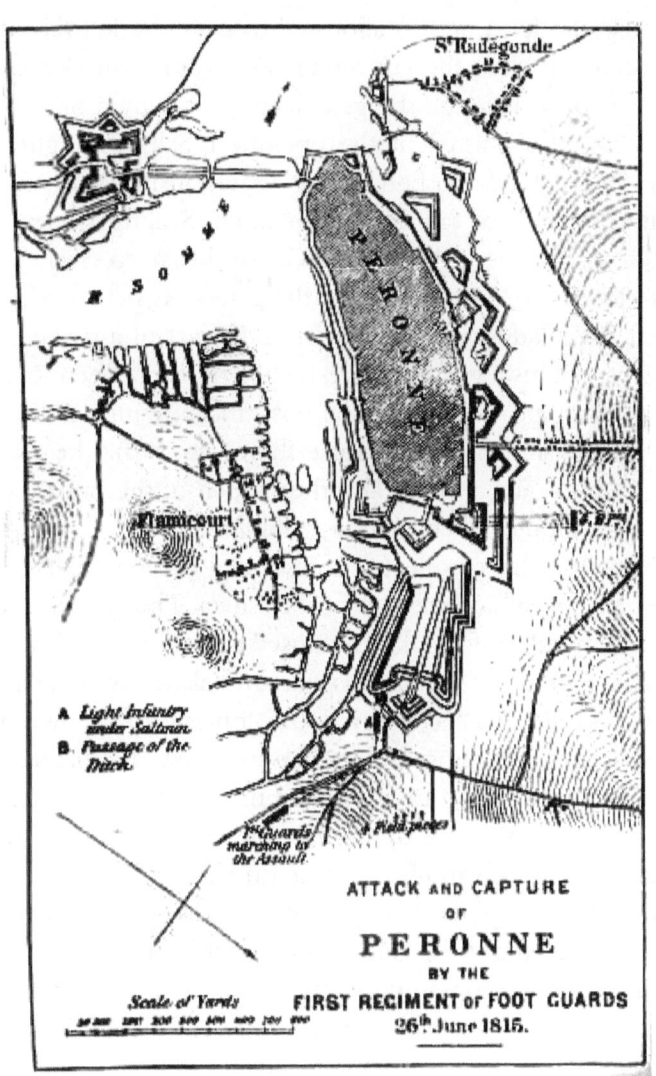

role as commander of the light companies by his own choice—presumably to ensure he took part in the action. Readers are encouraged to read the following paragraph in concert with the accompanying plan of the action.

As the Guards (E) advanced they separated into two columns of attack, the left one (C) allocated to scale the left face of the right demi-bastion; the right one (D) to force an entrance by the ravelin and through the gate, which was blown open by the engineers who assisted in the operation. Saltoun's light companies immediately rushed to the assault, losing a few men to enemy fire as they ran across the ditch. Scaling ladders were thrown against the walls and the Guards began to climb as they came under more fire from the defenders. As he was climbing one of these ladders, Saltoun felt the impact of a strike on the upper part of his leg and realised he had probably been struck by a piece of grape-shot, but his almost uncanny luck did not fail him, for the shot had hit a purse full of coins that he was carrying in his pocket which absorbed much of the impact of the blow. Saltoun described them as gold *ducats*.

Gronow in his recollections described them as 'half a dozen 5-*franc* pieces' which were probably silver. Though the impact was extremely painful, Saltoun refused to report himself wounded and the horn-work was carried. On balance we may assume Saltoun was best placed to know the contents of his own pockets, especially in these singular circumstances. That having been said, Gronow went on to wryly comment, 'Saltoun, though not very Buonapartist in his opinions, retained the mark of the emperor's effigy on his thigh for some time'.

Hamilton, the Guards regimental historian, was inclined to be diplomatic about the role of the Dutch-Belgians at Peronne, but Sir John Fortescue, who was reliable as a historian in not caring to 'pull his punches' took a different view. He reported that the Dutch-Belgian infantry did not appear on the scene until 9 p.m., an hour after the Guards had taken the place.

In fact, as General Byng was returning to Vermand to report to Wellington that the fortress had been taken, he met the

Dutch-Belgian brigade making is leisurely progress in the opposite direction, though it had been ordered to the front at the same time as the British troops. However, a Dutch brigade of four 9-pounders (A) had been brought up and established to the east of the town, to take in reverse the face to be attacked, a few shots were exchanged; while a brigade of four field-pieces (B) was placed so as to command the front of the horn-work itself.

Since it was apparent that further resistance by the defenders within Peronne was futile, Byng sent forward Lieutenant-Colonel Stanhope, his acting quartermaster-general, with a flag of truce, whereupon the garrison agreed to capitulate on condition of the men were then allowed to go to their homes. Fortescue recorded that some Belgian cavalry cut the ropes of the drawbridge after the capitulation was ratified, broke into the town and began to loot it. A British staff-officer present—who was possibly Stanhope—ordered them to leave, whereupon one of them attempted to cut him down and he was only saved by the intercession of the French governor who drew his sword in his defence. Peronne cost the First Guards, Second Battalion, one rank and file wounded, whilst third battalion had one rank and file killed, one sergeant and six rank and file wounded. Eight enemy cannon were taken in the action.

The two battalions of the First Guards encamped at Peronne that night, while the Second Brigade with its headquarters halted at Caulaincourt. Some of the Dutch-Belgian brigade, which had arrived too late to take part in the assault, were ordered to occupy it, while the First Brigade of Guards, with the balance of the Dutch brigade, marched through Nesle to the village of Crescy, and rejoined the First Corps, bivouacking at Caulaincourt. The actions at Cambrai and Peronne, and waiting for supplies, placed the army one day behind the Prussians.

Saltoun at this point had the time to finish his letter and had much to report. The anecdote concerning the little purse of money, which in all probability saved Saltoun's life, is revealed to be all the more delightful because the purse had been lovingly made for him by Catharine. Furthermore, it also contained a metallic heart (which his wife certainly placed within it before she presented it to him as a token of her devotion) which miraculously survived the damage of the shot that mangled the coins. The least romantically inclined reader would probably subscribe to the view that a young married couple would believe Saltoun had, therefore, been providentially saved by his bride's love for him.

27th.—I am now, my dear love, quite out of the blue devils; for yesterday, on the march from Serain to Caulaincourt, we were halted at Vermand, and our brigade sent to the right to attack Peronne, which we stormed yesterday evening with very little loss. I have heard an old saying that everything is made for some purpose: but I do not suspect you had the least idea, when you made my little purse, that it would ever be put to the use that it was. Yesterday, during the storm of Peronne, a grape-shot hit me full in the thigh. Fortunately, I had the little purse in that pocket, full of small gold pieces called *ducats*, which so stopped the ball, that, although it knocked me down, it lodged in the purse, and has given me a slight bruise, not half so bad as a blow from a stick. Had it not been for the purse it would have been very near a finish.

So, you see, my dear Kate, I owe you something. The purse is cut right open by the ball, but I shall not have it mended till it comes into your hands. What is rather odd, the little heart I had in it is the only thing not hurt, for all the gold pieces are bent and twisted about properly. I write this, first, because I promised to write exactly what happened; and next, because they are so fond of killing people in reports, especially if they have been hit in the slightest manner possible.

Today we marched at seven o'clock, and are just come into this place. It is about two miles nearer Paris than Nesle, and about the same distance on the left, of Roye. It is famous for a skirmish which took place here the day before the Battle of Cressy, in Edward the Third's reign, and we are now about the same distance from Paris that Portsmouth is from London.

I have this moment received yours of the 19th, and I find you at that time knew nothing about the matter. I like your quizzing about our soldiers. We have tolerable proof now of what they are worth, and the oldest French soldiers say they never saw such a battle as the one at Water Leud. I think I told you that our regiment and Napoleon's Guards came in contact, and I can assure you we handled them most handsomely, and the old Life Guards completely upset Napoleon's *Cuirassiers* of the Guard Imperial. The headquarters are today at Nesle, where a deputation has arrived from Paris to wait upon the Duke. I hope he will receive no terms till he dictates them from the Tuileries, and I rather think he will be of my way of thinking in that particular. I must send this forthwith to headquarters to wait an opportunity of its getting to England, as we now move so rapidly that we have no notice. The baggage-horses begin to feel it, especially from want of shoeing. I have lost two—one that was stolen in the row and confusion of the false alarm, and the other died yesterday; that, added to the two that were shot, has decreased my stud much. I have, however, bought two, so I can get on, and that is all, for the large horse has just fallen lame and got a sore back, but Paris is near, and the sooner we get there the sooner I get to England. So, *adieu*, my dear love, and believe me, your affectionate,

Saltoun.

Although he had many narrow escapes, the action at Peronne was the only occasion upon which Saltoun was hit during his long service. He made light of the matter to his wife, describing the bruise as slight, and, doubtless so that she would not worry, promised he had told her exactly what happened. However, the blow was, in reality, much more severe. The purse and its contents were driven into his groin, from which the surgeon, having cut the pocket away from the trousers, and gathering its edges together, pulled out the whole mass, before applying a dressing. The purse, the gold (or otherwise) coins, and heart were thereafter kept safely by Catharine, and after her death by Saltoun himself.

After he died, they were given to Mrs. Brown, wife of General Samuel Brown, and Lady Saltoun's sister, who had expressed a wish to have them. They were kept by her, together with Lord Saltoun's letter of the 27th June, and Lady Saltoun's reply of the 3rd July, which appears following. When Mrs. Brown died, the purse and the letters disappeared, probably stolen for the money. Astonishingly, the letters were picked up on the high road, near

PERONNE

to Ipswich in Suffolk, sometime later, during the time of some races near the town, and their finder kindly returned them to the family, but the purse and coins were never recovered. As a result, of the preservation of this correspondence we have rare access to one of Catharine's letters to her husband.

> 3rd of July:
> I this morning received your dear letter of the 25th and 27th. I am most thankful your life has been spared, but the many narrow escapes quite horrify me. I had hoped, from your letter of the 22nd, all the fighting was over, not that I shall, or can, feel really happy till you are returned safe; this last escape is quite frightful to think of, and most miraculous that your valuable life should hang on such a trifling thing as that little purse; lucky indeed it was you had it in your pocket. I shall value it ever more; pray don't part with any of the gold coins that were in it if you can help it, they will be invaluable to me. I want words to express all I feel at your repeated kindness and attention in writing so often, and such long letters too, when you must have a thousand other things to do and to think of; they do afford me great comfort, and as much consolation as I can receive in your absence. I immediately communicate to your mother and sisters the heads of your letters, so that they are never kept in suspense about you.... I am very sorry for poor Hughes, I read that part of the letter to your mother and sisters, so that they will use their discretion in telling his wife; she seems to love him so sincerely, that I pity her from the bottom of my heart. I trust you do not give up all hopes of his coming home safe at last, poor man! The chance is but small, I fear. I heard you were promoted, but have yet to learn what it is. ... I heard of your word of command being given through the whole line, to follow your example, and that it was the Duke who ordered them to follow the example of the Guards. I hope and trust he knew it was you who commanded them at the moment, for I long for you to have all the honours due to you; I am sure they would be pretty numerous. ... You seem to have but a scanty quantity of comforts just now with these quick movements, but you always make the best of everything.

Catharine clearly knew about and had regard for the relationship between her husband and James Hughes and believed that he would, among the chaos of the march and with no one close to him to give him care, not long survive. On the home front, the ladies of the family were preparing to break the news to Mrs. Hughes, which they knew would be the cruellest of blows.

On the 28th, the First Corps under Sir John Byng marched upon Couchy, and the next day by Estrées St. Denis along the *chaussée* to St. Martin Longeau, where the Guards encamped, just thirty-five miles from Paris. The advanced posts of the British Army were already at Senlis, ten miles further forward. The following day, Saltoun dutifully wrote to his wife. His report of the encounter between the Prussians and the French at Compiègne was perhaps more optimistic than factual. The affair is considered to be a skirmish by modern historians in which d'Erlon (rather than Soult) and the remnants of his men continued their dogged retreat. However, Saltoun was correct in his supposition that the emperor would attempt to flee across the Atlantic to America if he could and he was also in tune with common sentiment that when Napoleon was eventually captured, he might be executed.

There is ample evidence that Blücher, given his own way, would have put an end to the former emperor. Saltoun's fears concerning Edward Stables were, unfortunately, justified. He had been mortally wounded in the great battle and was taken to the former tavern of l'Etoile in Joli-Bois where he had spent the previous night. He died the following morning and, for a time, would lie buried in its garden at Waterloo.

> Camp at Choissi,
> 29th June 1815.
>
> I yesterday, my dear Catharine, received yours of the 22nd, and today the letter of the 12th, which, as it must have arrived in the country just at the time we were at work, had been delayed till now.
>
> We are going on as well as it is possible to do. Today we are encamped here, having marched from Couchy on the *chaussée* leading by the Pont St. Maxence to Paris. This is one league short of St. Martin, and about thirty-seven miles from Paris, which place we expect to reach on Sunday, if we do not halt,

and we have no idea of halting at present. The Pont St. Maxence was destroyed in the last campaign, and has not as yet been repaired; but I hope our pontoons, or some other boats, will be collected, so as to ensure our passage without loss of time.

The Prussians had an affair two days ago with Soult at Compiègne, in which Soult was beat, and suffered considerably; they say today that Bonaparte has left Paris and gone to Havre, with an intention of embarking for America, it is the best thing he can do now, for if he is taken, I do not know what the Allies will do with him, but I should think they would hang him.

We have today fallen into the line of a column of Prussians, who have been plundering at such a rate, that all the villages are entirely deserted, and I may almost say destroyed. To be sure they are only paying off old scores, but it is rather a bore for us, as we have great difficulty in purchasing any articles of provision, for the people are afraid of returning to their houses, as they do not know that they will be protected by us; however, it can't last long, and at Paris we shall be able to get anything that we want.

I find that some officers and men are immediately to be sent to us from England, and the sooner they arrive after we get to Paris the better, as I shall be superseded by some of them in command of the battalion, as they are all my seniors, and then as soon as things are a little settled I shall apply for leave to go home, which I could not do if I remained in command of this battalion, from the very small number of officers that are left to do duty. The weather has become very fine and hot, but the dust is terrible; however, anything is better than rain for our sort of life, and I now hope we shall have a continuance of fine weather.

I suppose people in England are half mad—we hear of illuminations, etc. etc.; to be sure the Victory is the greatest that ever was gained, not only by us, but by any people, but it was at the same time very dearly bought, the *Gazette* does not contain one-fifth of the officers who have suffered in this business. I send you that of our regiment, as you may hear them asked for.

Killed	Wounded
Lieut.-Colonel Stables	Colonel Askew
" F D'Oyly	" Stuart
" Thomas	Lieut.-Colonel Townshend
" Miller	" Cooke

"	Milnes	"	H. D'Oyly
Captain Grose		"	Bradford
"	Chambers	"	Hardinge
"	Cameron	"	Lord F. Somerset
Captain Brown		Captain Adair	
Ensign Pardoe		"	Streatfield
"	Lord Hay	"	Clements
"	Barrington	"	Bridgeman
		"	Ellis
		"	Simpson
		"	Luttrell
		"	Burgess
		Ensign Batty	
		"	Barton
		"	Bruce
		"	Fludyer
		"	Lascelles
		"	Mure
		"	Croft

We had 82 officers of the regiment in the field, of which 34 have been killed or wounded; so, shot, you will perceive, did not fly very thin that morning. I should have mentioned Stables in my first letter, but I did not know what had been his fate. I saw him fall, and the next morning when I wrote, I did not know what sort of a wound he had received, and I did not like sending a false report of his death, although, from the way he fell, I was much afraid of him.

I have nothing more to say at present, and will write you again in a day or two, and believe me, my dear love, your affectionate

Saltoun.

The French Army of the North had now retired into Paris, and on the 30th of June the First Corps of the Allies crossed the Oise. The advanced cavalry arrived at Louvres, twelve miles from the capital and the First Division went to La Chapelle, in the neighbourhood of Senlis. On the 1st of July the two brigades of Guards, with the Third Division, were within five miles of Paris with their right resting on Le Bourget and their left extending to the Forest of Bondy. During this march Lord Saltoun continued in temporary command of the second battalion. Wellington established his headquarters at Gonesse, halfway between Louvres and St. Denis, from the 2nd of July, and remained there for three days as allied troops, occupied Asnières, Courbevoie, and Suresnes linking with the Prussians to complete the investment of the north and west of Paris.

Saltoun's next letter was sent as the army lay in position outside Paris and opposite French defensive positions which, from his perspective, may have required an assault though, on this occasion, certainly with the assistance of the imminently expected Russian and Austrian armies as well as the Prussians with whom Wellington was already operating in concert.

Bourjet,
2nd July 1815.

I wrote you last, my dear Catharine, from Choissi on the 29th, on the 30th we marched to La Chapelle, about two miles beyond Senlis; and yesterday we came to this place, which is about two miles beyond Gonesse, on the left of St. Denis, and nearly parallel with it; and we have taken position on this ground, our right resting on the Seine, opposed to St. Denis, where the French are strong, our centre in this town, which is immediately opposite to Mont Martre, and our left resting on the canal de l'Ourcq, to the left of the road that runs through this place to Paris, which is about four miles distant; and I rather think we shall remain in this position till the Russians and Austrians come up. The Prussian Army, on our arrival yesterday, made a movement to the right, crossed the Seine at the bridge of St. Germain, and are to take post on that side of Paris, at Malmaison, St. Cloud, and Versailles.

Since we came, perpetual flags of truce have been passing between the town and the duke, but nothing has as yet been settled, and in the meantime each party is making himself as strong as possible. Nobody knows anything about Bonaparte; some say he is in Paris, but no person knows for certain. Davoust commands the army on Mont Martre, and many think that Boney is there *incog.*

We were yesterday on the advanced posts with the Prussians, supporting them, until Lord Hill's corps came up, when we took our front of the line; and they told us that they took the whole of Vandame's baggage, as well as Napoleon's. One of their officers of light cavalry fell in with his jewels, and had his pocket full of diamonds. I wish I had had the same luck; I would have put them to good account, besides the *éclat* of the thing. If I fall in with him again, I will try and buy some of them, but yesterday I was not very full of cash, as the baggage had not come up; he wanted to buy a horse, but mine had such a devil of a sore back that it would not go down, even with a Prussian. They have the greatest confidence in us. They say that the French used to tell them that we were good for nothing on land, of which, however, they had doubts; but they say they had not the least idea that our troops were so good as they are. All their troops formed and cheered us as we passed them, which we answered; and as the French posts were quite within hearing, the effect upon them could not have been very animating. I every day expect to hear from you, but our march has been so rapid that the post-office line could not have been established, but shortly I hope we shall open a nearer line. If I can get a sketch of the position, which young Nixon is making for me in the next room, done in time, I will send it in this letter; if not, by the next. I have no more news, except that we are all well and in great spirits, in hopes that the job will soon be over; and believe me, my dear love, your affectionate,

Saltoun.

On the 4th the duke, in conjunction with Blücher, concluded a military convention with the French authorities, whereby their troops were to evacuate St. Denis and Neuilly the same day, the heights of Montmartre on the 5th, and Paris itself on the 6th. Saltoun wrote a brief note to Catharine to give her the news. The house in Great Cumberland Street mentioned would become their family home in London.

Bourjet,
4th July 1815.

My dear Catharine,
I yesterday received yours of the 26th, and also the papers.
I am at this moment on the advanced posts, and we have just heard that we are to occupy Paris tomorrow, and the French

Army is to retire behind the Loire, and make as good terms with the king as they can. Our army is to encamp in the Bois de Boulogne.

As to the house in Great Cumberland Street, I most perfectly agree to everything you have done. As to the distance, it is nothing, as I always go on horseback, and I hope before long to take a look at it myself. I have no time to say any more, as the A. D. C. is waiting for this to take it to headquarters; and believe me, my dear love, your affectionate,

Saltoun.

On the 6th of July British and allied troops took possession of the barriers to the north of the Seine, while the Prussians took those in the south. Saltoun's letter to his wife revealed that his animosity towards his enemies went beyond the view that he had simply fought other soldiers who were also doing their duty. He had lost many friends, (including the lamented Edward Grose of the third battalion, who had fallen at Quatre Bras), in the recent battles against a foe which he quite correctly considered, lacked any political legitimacy. This otherwise reasonable man would have seen Paris in flames, notwithstanding it was the capital of the returning monarch, and believed that the British Army warranted a triumphal march through the city that should not be shared with troops who had not stood and suffered on the fields of Quatre Bras and Waterloo. His forecasts regarding his own future proved accurate as usual. James Hughes was still missing and prominent in Saltoun's thoughts.

Villette,
6th July 1815.

I this morning, my dear Catharine, received yours of the 29th, and I did not intend to have written before tomorrow, as I was in hopes that we should have marched through Paris with laurels in our caps, as we deserve to do; but the Heads think otherwise, and we are therefore to go tomorrow to the Bois de Boulogne to encamp, and as we march at five, and letters must be in at eight, I must write now or not at all. It does not suit my taste sneaking round a capital in this manner. I almost regret that they did not defend the heights of Mont Martre: to be sure we should have lost 2 or 3 thousand men in taking them, but then we should have burned the town, and that would have been some satisfaction, for I hate these rascals almost as much as I love you, and that is more than they can be hated by any other. Poor Grose and myself were brothers in that hatred, and if the brave fellow were alive, he would have gone half mad to suppose that we came victorious to the gates of Paris, and did not show the natives that we were so. So much for national indignation! Our chief has most probably good reasons; for my part I would not give a straw to march through it when the Russians come up.

As to your getting what you call a detailed account of the action of Waterloo from the duke, you will get no other than the one you have got already. It is rather unfortunate, and the army are sorry for it, that my name was not mentioned, and but for a mistake, which I will explain when we meet, I know that it would have been; but I have been so handsomely reported by the Prince of Orange, Generals Byng and Maitland, to the Dukes of Wellington and York, that I am perfectly satisfied, and someday I shall lead a division, perhaps a victorious army; so your moralising preamble must be postponed *sine die*, as it is the only point I think you will never gain with me. To tell the truth, I do not think you remember we always agreed that a dead lion was better than a living dog.

We came here yesterday. This is, if I may use the term, part of Paris, as much so as Connaught Place is of London, for it is the same distance from the Barriere as that is from Tyburn. Lord Castlereagh has arrived: I saw him as he passed by here, but I understand he has not gone into the town, but has gone to the duke's headquarters. Party is running very high in the town, but I think we shall have no more fighting.

I have no doubt myself that Napoleon is with the army, *incog.*, but his chance gets more and more desperate as the Allies come up, and he probably will start for America, for the army will never give him up to us; at least if they do, they will lose with me that little respect I still have for them.

Your story of ears and noses is quite morning post. They had something else to do about that time, but the Prussians treat them much the same as if their noses and ears had been cut off, and I suspect that the Russians are not far off, for the people have come in today from the country, saying that the pillage is still going on: they are perfectly thunderstruck at our men not doing the same, as their own troops plunder them, and how we prevent our men from doing it perfectly astonishes them.

As soon as things are quiet, and I am superseded in the command—which I shall be when the people from England arrive—I shall ask leave to go to England. I have as yet heard nothing of Hughes, but as soon as we are quiet, I shall send after him; and I shall now, my dear love, wish you goodnight, and believe me, your affectionate,

Saltoun

Chapter Thirty-Eight

The Occupation of Paris

The Allies entered Paris on the 7th of July, 1815. and the British troops raised their camp in the Bois de Boulogne. The Guards were, indeed, to have marched triumphally through the streets of Paris with laurels in their caps, but at the last moment the authorities directed them to march straight to the 'Bois,' 'in a quiet way' which was very poorly received by the officers or the men who not unreasonably believed they had earned their moment. It was not so long in the past that one monarch had promptly quit Paris as another came to it and on the 8th the pattern repeated as Louis XVIII. made his public entry into his capital. Napoleon covertly set sail from Rochefort in an attempt to escape his reckoning by fleeing to the United States of America where he expected to be offered refuge.

> Paris,
> 10th July 1815.
>
> Here we are, my dear Catharine, well established, and the old king as regularly crammed down their throats as anything could possibly be. He made his *entrée* yesterday at the head of the National Guards, and all the Eagles are upset, and the *Fleur-de-Lys* everywhere; not but what there is a very strong party against him, but I do not think they lean towards Boney, they are rather for a Republic.
>
> I was at the opera last night, and the people had *Vive Henri Quatre* played over and over again, and a great deal of holloaing and so forth; but I am told they did just the same when Napoleon came: if so, it all goes for nothing, they say that the

army have sent deputies to make submission. If so, the game is over, for this time at least, and I shall apply for leave as soon as I possibly can.

At present we are encamped in the Bois de Boulogne, and I suppose we shall remain there. I am in a house halfway between the Bois and the Barriere de Roule. The distance is not above two miles, so it is nothing on horseback; not that there is much to see here since I saw it last, but one rides in to dinner, as the *traiteurs* here are rather superior to our soldier cooks. I only yesterday got her Ladyship's letter, but as she had put no date to it I could not tell if it was written on the same day as your last, which I received three days back, and answered from La Villette, in a great rage at not marching through Paris.

The people here, I mean the gentlemen, are inclined to be particularly civil to us; indeed they are much struck with the strict discipline we preserve, so totally different from Continental armies nowadays, and which gives us such a decided advantage over them; and lucky for them it is so, for if our army were permitted to plunder and destroy as the Prussians and others are, they would first of all get drunk, and then they would burn down the town, or commit some horrible massacre or other.

I am going this morning to see the Louvre, and I shall afterwards ride out to Boulogne to see Lord Hill, and dine there, if he is at home. I never was a good hand at playing at soldiers, *surtout* when I wanted to get away; if not, I can do that well enough. But I now want much to cross the herring pond, and shall be with you as soon as I possibly can.

I have as yet heard nothing of poor Hughes. I mean to send a man back to the village to enquire about him, for it is rather out of the direct road. He was perfectly well in health when he was left, and therefore I am not afraid of him—at least the surgeon is not—yet I think he ought to have turned up before now.

I have not a particle of news, and in hopes to see you before I write many more letters, believe me, my dearest love, your affectionate

Saltoun.

In Saltoun's letter to Catharine of the 12th, he touched upon the unknown whereabouts of Napoleon. In fact, two days previously, the vessel conveying him had been discovered by the

Royal Navy. The deposed emperor surrendered to Captain Maitland, commanding the *Bellerophon,* a 74-gun ship of the line that had seen action at both the Nile and Trafalgar. Maitland brought his imperial prisoner to Torbay on the coast of Devon on the 24th of the month, whereupon the British Government decreed that he should be conveyed forthwith to the island of St. Helena, a forsaken rock far out into the Atlantic Ocean, bearing no comparison to the sunny Elba from which he had absconded, without landing in England. There he would end his days, dead within six years, aged just 51 years.

There can be no doubt Napoleon was possessed of a perverse genius, indomitable energy and grasping ambition which has immortalised his name and times. Much about him has remained romantic for his epoch was indisputably imbued with elegance and style. For all that, he was a self-aggrandising monster who was fortunate, on account of his duplicity alone having abdicated in 1814, not to have been put against a wall and shot. His final exile arguably remained lenient given the fates of many of those who had served him and who, during the period of the 'Second White Terror' as a consequence of their faithful though misguided devotion to him, had far less deserved their deaths, imprisonments or exiles at the hands of avenging Bourbon regime.

Naturally, given the fighting was over Saltoun's principal concern was to return home to his new wife and his family. If that was not possible, he resolved to bring her to his side in Paris. He concluded his letter with some very good news for all concerned.

Paris,
12th July 1815.

My dear Catharine,
I have not got a word of news or anything else to say, but the day being very hot, and therefore not worth slaving about seeing sights, I cannot employ it better than in writing to you.
I forget if I told you in my last that the Kings and Emperors were arrived. They are however come, and, what is worse, we have to mount guard over them, which, in our present reduced state of lieut.-colonels, comes rather sharp; and what I am most

afraid of is, that when our draft comes, they may in consequence, take it into their gracious heads to refuse me leave, which will be rather a bore, as it will fix me here till the end of the chapter. Now, if that event takes place, and they refuse me leave, you shall, if you like, come here; for, as Mahomet observed (and he is very good authority), if the mountain would not come to him, he must go to the mountain.

My only reason, next to seeing you, for wanting to go home, is that I wish to go to Scotland: now, if I can't go there, I see no reason why you should not see France. Should this be the case, I can manage to meet you at Calais, and William can escort you that far. I shall make the application as soon as our people come up, and write you the result, and if you approve of this plan, instructions how to proceed, and when to set out so as to meet me.

I think all the fighting over, but, if anything else should blow up before these grand continental matters are settled, you can only return. I do not think these things will be settled under three or four months, and if you were here, I don't care if they take as many years to debate it, for the country is a very good one to live in.

A mail has come in up to the 4th instant, but as I have had no letters or papers I suppose that you were too late, or, what is now very likely, the bag was so full, Lord Castlereagh being here now, as well as the Duke, that they did not send them, should you have sent them to the office, as they have not arrived. You had better send your letters *per* post; but if you did not send them to Barnard, you need not, as yet, make any alteration.

They talk of some generals having come from the French Army with proposals of submission; but I do not know if anything has been done. However, I suppose they must shortly come to terms.

No one knows anything certain about Napoleon, and nobody seems to care anything about him. Paris is just the same as when I was here last, and the rascals are calling *Vive le Roi* now as lustily as they last week cried *Vive L'Empereur*.

God bless you, my dear love, and believe me, your affectionate

                 Saltoun.

P. S. Your last letter that I have is dated the 29th June. Hughes came up yesterday, his rheumatism has left him, but he is very thin, as he got very little to eat on the road.

Reinforcements were now ordered out to France from the Guards battalions in England for, discounting those who were wounded, the second battalion had lost in killed, since the 15th of June, 82 of its number whilst the third battalion had lost 75 men. Detachments from the three Guards regiments, amounting to 660 men (of which 228 were for the First Guards) left England and joined their respective service battalions at Paris arriving on the 19th of July.

Saltoun's letter to Catharine continued on the subject of the concerns he had expressed in his last with regard to his desire to return to England or, failing that, his wish to bring her to France to join him. In any event, it was typical of his character that he was not enjoying, 'playing the soldier', acting as a guard for the Emperor of Russia. Not for the first occasion there is, in Saltoun's correspondence, a clear dissatisfaction concerning the Duke of Wellington's attitude in his reluctance to acknowledge exemplary service performed by regimental and corps officers. This view was by no means confined to Saltoun, for it appears regularly in accounts by British officers of the period and caused much unnecessary distress and annoyance in the army from those who believed their efforts were not fully appreciated.

In this detail of generalship, if within no other, Wellington could have taken lessons from Napoleon (irrespective of their sincerity) in his dealings with the officer corps, for whilst they knew Wellington was a superlative general, he merited little good feeling from them. Indeed, he was intransigent, high-handed and arrogantly reactionary. After Waterloo, the duke would never fight another battle and turned his attention to politics—a career for which he was, predictably, temperamentally poorly suited and one which (unlike his military career) imbued his memory with virtually no abiding credit.

It is possible that Catharine had suggested to her husband that the blow he had taken at Peronne might serve as a legitimate pretext to bring him home, but in his letter he rejected that idea as beneath his honour and, in any event, injurious to his reputation since his peers, who knew the facts of the matter, would not themselves have taken advantage of such a situation. His forecast about the future of Louis XVIII was prescient. The king died in 1824 after just nine further years of uninterrupted rule upon the throne, the last monarch of France to die whilst still reigning. He was succeeded by his brother, Charles who reigned, though with his powers much curtailed, until 1830 at which time he abdicated the throne and the country did, indeed, become a republic.

Paris,
15th July 1815.

My Dear Catharine,

You may see by the paper that I am not at home. The fact is that I am on guard over H.M. the Emperor of all the Russias, and as he gives nothing but long paper, I am obliged to manoeuvre it as well as I possibly can.

We have just done dinner, six o'clock, about an hour before you are thinking of dressing for yours; it is very well this hour for His Majesty's household, who can go out and walk in the cool of the evening, but for us, who have to remain here, rather too early. However, I will do him the justice to say that the dinner was a very good one, and by a fortunate accident we had a clean table-cloth, for the waiter, a regular ruffian of a fellow, had put such a beastly thing on the table that it was even too much for us, who of late days have not been much used to luxury.

However, I had the satisfaction to make the most unfortunate mistake in the world, just as he put some wine down, by breaking a bottle of it, which so sluiced the table-cloth, that we were perforce obliged to have another, which was clean. Some of the Emperor's household dined with us, and they were tolerably genteel fellows, and spoke very good French, and some little English, indeed most of the Russians are good linguists.

I received yesterday, my dearest girl, both your letters, one of the 6th, and the other of the 10th, but I still suspect that you wrote a letter either on the 3rd or 4th, which has not as yet turned up; it will however, I make no doubt, come to hand someday or another....

About *Gazettes*, etc., as if 500 others were not exactly in the same situation as I am, and as if I do not know that it has been the only outcry against the Duke of W. ever since he commanded an army, that he seldom or never mentioned people, excepting generals and others high up in the army; and as to being returned wounded at Peronne, it's all fiddlesticks. I do not intend that my military reputation, if ever I get any, shall have so hollow a foundation. I see a parcel of fellows figuring about who have returned themselves severely wounded when they only had scratches and bruises, who are the perfect laughingstock of their companions, and therefore not very far from being so of other people...

We expect our people up in a day or two; they were last night at Roye; today they will therefore be at St. Martin's, tomorrow at Senlis, then Bourjet, and from that here, which will bring them up on Tuesday or Wednesday at the farthest. I shall then immediately make my application, and if I find any difficulty in obtaining leave, shall apply for leave merely to bring you over, which I rather think will certainly not be refused. I shall sound the ground first, and then apply. I rather suspect you will have to come here, for General Vivian has gone to England for the same purpose, to bring his wife, and if any person could have got leave, I think he might.

Besides, if they only give me a month, it will not be worthwhile, so you may, if you feel inclined, make your mind up to soldier a little. You may continue to send letters and papers after you receive this, as my leave will take some time going through, and should they come here after I am gone they will be very well taken care of, and sent to any place I may direct, or kept till I return, as the case may be.

No news of any kind, and nothing as yet known of what the remains of Boney's army mean to do. They have not as yet made submission, nor will they, I suspect, as long as they can get anything to plunder where they are. I hope the king will cut off a good many heads, but I am told he will not, and the consequence will be that he will be deposed in less than two years, and France a Republic.

My paper begins to run short, so I shall wish you, my dearest love, goodbye for the present. I shall write you again in a day or two, and also as soon as I know how my leave goes; and I am, my dear Catharine, your affectionate,

Saltoun.

Lieutenant-Colonels Hon. Dawson West and John Hanbury assumed the command of the third and second battalions of the First Guards respectively, till the recovery of Colonels Askew and Stuart from the wounds they had received at Waterloo.

Since the fighting was now over the armies were once more engaged in the pomp and circumstance of reviews. The Prussian Guards, impressively stepped out in the presence of the allied sovereigns on Saturday, the 22nd of July. A voice on the podium was heard to remark that the Prussian Guards were the finest troops they had ever seen, though the French had beaten them, and that the British Army could not show such a splendid body of men. It is entirely possible that Wellington overheard this remark for as the Prussian Guards were marching past and all were admiring them, he turned to the lady next to him and said, 'Ah, but I will show you on Monday some men that can lick these fellows.' On the Monday in question, the 24th, the duke's army, 65,000 strong, including the two brigades of British Guards marched past the allied sovereigns in review. One hundred years later the British Army was putting the duke's claim to the test.

Saltoun, in his letter to Catharine, remained focussed on his return to England as a priority. The anecdote concerning the French Army's substitution of the number eighteen (as in Louis XVIII) for *gros cochon* (fat pig; in reference to the king's obesity) is a fascinating period detail. This letter, written on the 22nd of July, makes it clear Saltoun did not know the current state of affairs with regard the remnants of Napoleon's army.

Davout (Davoust) after a show of defending the capital had indeed withdrawn the force under his command beyond the Loire, but by the time of Saltoun's letter he had bent the knee to the returning king and relinquished authority over the troops to Marshal Jacques Macdonald, one of Napoleon's former marshals who, having given his promises of allegiance to the Bourbons at the time of the First Restoration, kept his word and fortunately did not join his erstwhile master in the great disastrous gamble of 'The Hundred Days'. Davout, for his complicity, was stripped of his rank and titles, but these were returned to him by 1817, though he died in 1823 aged just 53 years old.

Paris,
22nd July 1815.

This morning, my dear Catharine, I received yours of the 17th, and also the papers up to that date. I have put off writing from day to day in hopes of being able to say when I should set out for England. Our draft from town joined three days back, and I immediately sent in my application for leave, but as yet I have not had any answer. I am told that General Barnes meant to have made the application yesterday, but that the Duke was in such a devil of an ill-humour about something or another, that he could not speak to him on any subject with any chance of success; I expect, however, an answer in a day or two, and shall then write you further. This place is horridly stupid, and I shall be most happy to leave it.

Today we had a review of the Prussian Guards, 13,000 strong; the finest body of men I ever saw in my life, the only horrid thing is that the French have licked them like sacks. On Monday next, at ten o'clock, the Duke of Wellington's army is to be reviewed. We shall be about 65,000, and it will take up nearly the whole day marching past. We shall not be able to show such fine men as these Emperors and Kings have, but yesterday, as the Prussians, etc. were marching by, Lord Wellington said to Lady Kinnaird, 'On Monday I will show you some men that can lick those fellows.'

The remains of the French Army, under Davoust, have not as yet made submission, they say they will acknowledge the king if he will retain them as an army; but the king says they shall be disbanded, and they are at issue on that point. I think probably the end of it will be that we shall send some troops against them and give them a good licking: that army will never have the king. It is a curious fact, that during his short reign before Boney came back, the soldiers, in telling off from the right, never mentioned the number eighteen, but said, '*dixsept, gros cochon, dixneuf,*' and so on; and whatever man it fell to to be 18, he was the butt for the day; that shows how little they cared for him, and he now ought to hang every twentieth man by lot, and then, such slaves are these rascals, that he would be very much respected, and thought a very good king.

This is the most rascally pen that ever was, and I have got no penknife by me, so I much fear you will not be able to read this letter; however, as I hope soon to follow it myself, it will be of less consequence. My next will probably tell you about my leave: till then *adieu*, and believe me, my dearest Catharine, your affectionate,

Saltoun.

Saltoun's letter of the closing days of July needs no elaboration.

Paris,
28th July 1815.

I have this moment, my dear Catharine, received yours of the 25th instant, and two days back I got yours of the 20th, and as to your letter of the 4th, it was the one that came by Mr. Prince, but I did not receive it till after two other mails had arrived. I shall take this letter to the post, and forward the other, which is very likely one of mine which my servant has taken there by mistake, instead of the military post.

I have put off writing from day to day, in hopes of being able to say something about leave. Yesterday I was ordered to send in my reasons in writing, so I went this morning to Barnes, the Adjutant-General, and told him my reason was not one that could well be sent upon paper, but I would be much obliged to him to tell the Duke that I had been married a fortnight, and I wished to go home to bring you out here. I am to have my final answer tomorrow, and I shall then either write you how to proceed, or shall forthwith proceed to England, as the case may be. We expect that the army will shortly move into Normandy, as we begin to be short of forage for the cavalry, but they say the First Division is to remain in Paris, or near it; however, if I get my leave, that will make no difference to us. Hughes, I told you in one of my letters, has turned up, and he is now quite well again, and the horses consequently begin to show the improvement. I have not a word of news, and as I am always anxious as long as anything that I particularly wish for remains undecided, I shall finish this; and in hopes of following it very shortly, believe me, my dear love, your affectionate

Saltoun.

P.S.—I have not as yet got the papers, so the post is at present the most expeditious.

THE BRITISH ARMY IN CAMP AT PARIS, 1815

BRITISH OFFICERS WALKING OUT IN PARIS, 1815

Having recovered from his wound, Askew resumed the command of the second battalion in August. The British Army remained encamped all the summer and autumn in the Bois de Boulogne and its neighbourhood, and it was while quartered there, on the 29th of July, 1815 that the second and third battalions of the First Guards received the notification that 'H.RH. the Prince Regent, in the name of the sovereign had been pleased to direct that their regiment should henceforward be styled: 'The First or Grenadier Regiment of Foot Guards,' in commemoration of having defeated the French Imperial Guard at Waterloo'. The Grenadier Guards had assumed the title by which it would be henceforth known.

Epilogue

Saltoun, much to his satisfaction, and to the rejoicing of his wife and family, obtained the permission for the leave he had applied for and departed forthwith to England. Nevertheless, his duty continued with the army and in due course he returned to France, though now accompanied by his wife. Besides the Waterloo medal, which was granted to all officers and men who took part in the campaign, Lord Saltoun was appointed to become a Knight of the Order of Theresa (subsequently Grand Master-Austrian) and 4th class of the Order of St. George (Russian). He was, in due course, also appointed to the Order of the Thistle and Knight Commander of the Order of the Bath.

As the seasons advanced in 1815, the weather about the French capital became too inclement for Wellington's army, amounting to 70,000 men and horses, to remain under canvas and it was moved into more permanent billets in surrounding towns and villages. The division of Guards under Maitland, was moved into Paris itself. Since France and the political state of Europe had become generally settled a treaty was signed on the 20th of November, agreeing to send home substantial numbers of the soldiers from the various foreign armies which were on French soil. Those remaining formed an Army of Occupation which would serve for three years and which would come under the command the Duke of Wellington. Cambrai was fixed upon as the headquarters of the British Army.

Among the troops selected to return home without delay were the second battalions of Grenadier and Third Guards which left for England at the beginning of December. Among those remaining was one brigade of Guards, consisting of the Third Battalion, Grenadiers, and of the Second Battalion, Coldstreams, under Major-General (now Sir Peregrine) Maitland, as the First Brigade of the First Division. As a fitting termination to the year 1815, on the 23rd of December, the Prince Regent announced he was 'pleased to approve of the Grenadier Guards being permitted to bear on their colours and appointments the word 'Waterloo,' in commemoration of the distinguished services of the second and third battalions of that regiment on the 18th of June, 1815'.

The Second Battalion, Grenadier Guards, under Colonel Askew, returned to England in the middle of January, 1816. After spending nearly three months of the winter in Paris, the Guards and the rest of the British Army of Occupation marched to the country quarters allotted to them about Cambrai. The Brigade of Guards, under Sir John Lambert, continued to perform garrison duty at Cambrai until the 17th of November, 1818, three days before the expiry of the term fixed by the 1815 treaty, at which time it executed its orders to leave the continent.

From February 1816, with the exception of temporary annual leaves of absence, Saltoun served in France with the Army of Occupation at Cambrai. During this time, he was able to enjoy the company of his family for his mother, the Dowager Lady Saltoun, together with his sisters Eleanor and Margaret, joined him and his wife, living in France for some time. He also received flying visits from his brother William, who was a partner in a West Indian mercantile house.

On the 23rd of November, 1818, the departing Grenadiers completed their march to Calais, and embarked immediately aboard their transport vessels. Colonel Henry D'Oyly in command of the Third Battalion, Grenadier Guards—the last of the Guards remaining in France who had fought Napoleon's armies—brought them home at last to England. It would be nearly 40 years before the regiment would be called upon to fight again. When the time came, it would be against their former allies, the Russians in the Crimea, though some of soldiers who had fought Napoleon, (including Fitzroy Somerset, Wellington's secretary at Waterloo and by then, Lord Raglan) would still be following the colours. Raglan, as it transpired, would forever be associated with the, 'Charge of the Light Brigade' and would die, aged 66 years, on service in the Crimea.

Upon the return of his battalion to England, Lord Saltoun, as his military duties were principally within London, lived with Catharine, Lady Saltoun at their house at No. 1 Great Cumberland Street. Leaves of absence were generally spent in Scotland, at his house of Philorth, where he enjoyed the traditional pursuits of a Scottish gentleman.

While campaigning in Spain he had learned to play on the guitar, and at his house in Great Cumberland Street held afternoon concerts in which he always took a part with his guitar, though its notes were often lost amid those of the more powerful instruments. In fact, on one of these occasions a lady said to him, 'Lord Saltoun, I can't hear your guitar at all,' to which he replied, 'Oh! that doesn't matter; I hear it myself, and that's enough for my pleasure.'

Shortly after the return of the Grenadier Guards from France, an amusing incident occurred, which is worth recording as an illustration of the eccentricities of soldiers of the period, and which is here given in the manner habitually related by Lord Saltoun.

> There used to be a sentry placed at Storey's Gate, between Birdcage Walk and Great George Street, Westminster. About noon, on a hot summer's day, the sentry then on that post saw a round-about, ruddy little man carefully examining his sentry-box, and, though it was against orders, entered into conversation with him, which turned on the merits of the said article. 'Lord bless me!' said the little man, 'I never saw anything so nice and convenient. When I'm at home I lives out to the east, and has a little garden right down to the river, and I'm blowed if I don't have one like it made, and put a seat in it, and then when work's done, I can sit of evenings and smoke my pipe in it, and look at the ships going by.'

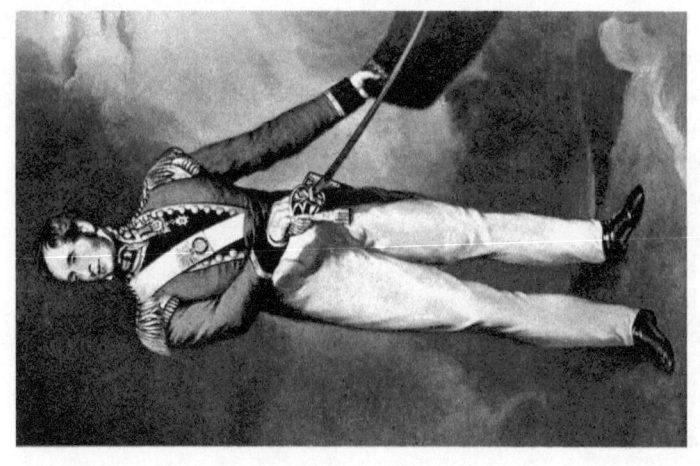

Lord Saltoun in Grenadier Guards uniform

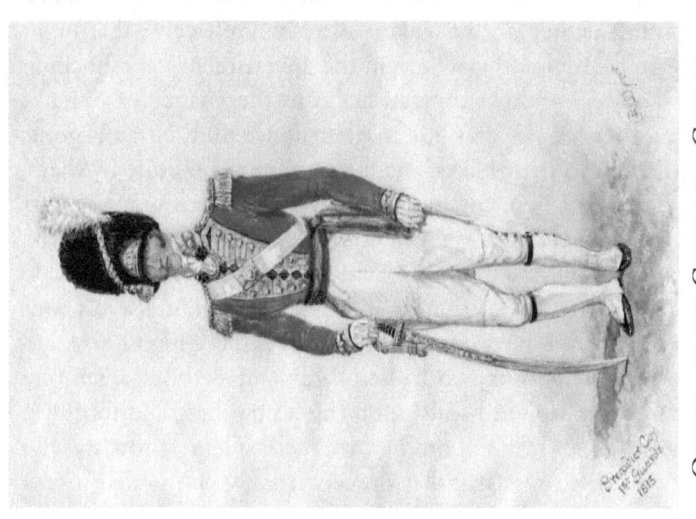

Officer of the Grenadier Guards, 1815

'Why,' said the sentry, 'why should you go to the expense of having a new one made, which will cost you a matter of three or four pounds, when you can have this one for a guinea.'

'How can I have this one?' exclaimed the little man.

'Why, what day is this?'

'It's his gracious Majesty's birthday, God bless him! to be sure, and that's the reason I'm out for a holiday.'

'Well, that's just it (taking a confidential tone). We soldiers is treated very hard, you see; but we has our privileges, and one is that we has new sentry-boxes every year, and they are changed every king's birthday, and the man that's on sentry in them at the end of that day has a right to sell the old one. Now, what o'clock is it?'

'Close upon twelve o'clock,' says the little man

'That's it! and I shall be on sentry here again tonight at twelve o'clock, so it's my right to sell the box; now it's yours for a guinea; say done!'

'Done!' said the little fellow, and paid his guinea; 'but how am I to get it away?'

'I'll tell you all that. You see, there's a rule that the old boxes stand till noon the next day, and that then they may be taken away; but if they are not taken away before twelve that night they go on for another year, and the government is so shocking mean and stingy that they always runs the chance of our not selling them, and won't put another down till the first is gone; but I'm up to their tricks, and ain't going to be done by them. So, you just be here any time after twelve tomorrow with a cart and ropes and carry it off. No one will stop you, and there'll be a new one put down directly.'

So they parted good friends, on this understanding; and about one o'clock the next day the little man came with a horse and cart, and a friend or two to help him, and without ceremony began to lay violent hands upon the sentry-box, and to pull it down, in order to put it on the cart. A considerable row was the result of these high-handed proceedings, which ended in the dispersion of the little man's friends at the point of the bayonet, and his own capture by the sentry then on duty at the post, by whom he was penned up in his much-coveted sentry-box, while the guard was alarmed, and a party being sent from it, he was brought in a prisoner. I happened to be there at the time, and he came before me, and on being questioned unfolded his pitiful tale of how he had been duped and done by the unscrupulous sentry of the day before.

None of those present could refrain from shouts of laughter as he went on; but I soon got the guard report, and seeing in it who was the sentry on that post at twelve o'clock, ordered him to be sent for from the barracks. In a short time, he arrived, and was brought in to answer the charge.

When the complainant had again told his story, 'Now,' I asked, 'what have you got to say in answer to this?'

'Well, my Lord,' he replied, 'I'm very sorry; but, first of all, I'm willing to give him back his guinea and here it is. Thank God I hadn't time to spend it! and, my Lord, you knows me; I haven't been a bad soldier; you've seen me in Spain and at Waterloo, and I hope you'll look over it; but—he was such a damned fool, I couldn't help it!'

The last plea was acknowledged in all our hearts to be a valid one, and with a good wigging he got off; but I really believe he would have considered it a tempting of Providence had he failed to use the opportunity which meeting such an inconceivable idiot threw in his way.

The name of the canny sentry has been recorded for posterity and it was Stephen Gagin.

Saltoun was appointed a Knight Grand Cross of the Prince Regent's, Royal Guelphic Order in 1821 and became a major in the Guards, and full colonel in the army, on the 17th of November 1825. He succeeded to the command of the third battalion of his regiment, which he held until the 12th of February, when, in consequence of changes and promotions, he became senior major, and was transferred to the first battalion, which he commanded so long as he remained in the regiment.

In February 1826, when marching into the barracks at Windsor, he had a very severe accident. He was riding a young, spirited horse, which, on passing through the gate, was so startled by the guard presenting arms, that it plunged violently, and slipping on the causeway, fell upon its side, crushing its rider's right leg between its body and the kerb-stone of the foot-pavement. The fracture was very serious and had to be re-broken after it had been originally set, causing a slight shortening of the leg which caused Saltoun to limp a little when tired, but was otherwise imperceptible. Unfortunately, the year 1826 would, for Saltoun, transpire to be an *annus horribilis*.

In July, Lord and Lady Saltoun, as usual, set out to visit Scotland, when on the journey disaster overtook them. Lady Saltoun was suddenly attacked by illness-according to the original document—at Bramby Moor Inn, in Leicestershire (Barnby Moor in Nottinghamshire is, in fact a midway point between London and Edinburgh on the Great North Road which offered at least one coaching inn), and after a short, but severe period of suffering, tragically died there upon the 9th of that month. Their married life, having so often seemed tenuous by the perils of war, had lasted a little over eleven years and they had no children. Catharine's body was taken to Edinburgh, and interred in Holyrood Chapel.

Promotion in the army advanced him to the rank of major-general on the 10th January 1837, which ended his connection with the Grenadier Guards. Saltoun served in the First Opium War in China, where he commanded the First Brigade at the Battle of Chinkiang in 1842, which was the first major engagement of the campaign. The army was at that time under the command of Hugh Gough, another Peninsular War veteran though after 1843, Saltoun became the overall force commander in his stead. He was promoted to lieutenant-general in 1849.

Alexander George Fraser, Lord Saltoun died of dropsy (the archaic term for oedema) at his shooting lodge in Auchinroth near Rothes, Banffshire, Scotland on the 18th of August, 1853, in his sixty ninth year. In the opinion of his family his body had become worn out by his service in the army and that, most especially, he continued to suffer from maladies he had contracted at Walcheren. Catharine's body was removed from Holyrood and laid beside her husband forever in the mausoleum at Fraserburgh. His brother William had pre-deceased him in 1845 so the title of the 17th Lord Saltoun passed to his eldest son, Alexander.

Appendix No. 1

THE SIBORNE-SALTOUN CORRESPONDENCE CONCERNING THE BATTLE OF WATERLOO

Letter from Captain W. Siborne to Lord Saltoun.

Dublin, January 4th, 1838.

Dear Lord Saltoun,

As rumour assigns to you the command of a Brigade of Guards for service in Canada, I am anxious to avail myself of the only opportunity which time may allow, to beg you will, with your usual kindness, favour me with your recollections of Quatre Bras, as also with a few particulars concerning the French attacks upon Hougomont during the *earlier* part of the day. I enclose a rough sketch of that portion of the former field upon which the Guards were principally engaged, as also a plan of Hougomont and its immediate vicinity.

It appears that during the interval between the commencement of the Battle of Waterloo—half-past eleven—and the attack upon Picton's division about two o'clock, the action was, with the exception of a general cannonading along both lines, confined to Hougomont; but in drawing up my history of the battle, I find considerable difficulty in giving a clear and satisfactory view of the *progressive* course of the contest at the latter post during the above interval, and I should feel truly grateful for any hints with which your Lordship may be kind enough to favour me on that point, including the remainder of the period during which you remained at Hougomont. I am also anxious to learn whether any artillery were brought to bear against the orchard or the garden from the rising ground on our left of the long outward eastern hedge, which I have marked *a*, *b*, and

THE HONOURABLE SIMON FRASER,
SECOND SON OF ALEXANDER, FIFTEENTH LORD SALTOUN.
BORN 1787 - DIED S.P. 1811.

THE HONOURABLE WILLIAM FRASER
THIRD SON OF ALEXANDER 15TH LORD SALTOUN.
BORN 1791. DIED 1845.

of which the highest point was at c. I think I heard you mention your having at one time attempted to get possession of a French gun, which was worked *à la prolonge*.

I am rather doubtful as to an attack by the 1st Brigade of Guards upon French *Infantry previously* to that of the Imperial Guard. I am aware that a strong column of French infantry, flanked by *Cuirassiers*, advanced against a part of our line more to your right, sweeping by the outward north-east angle of the orchard of Hougomont, and that they were driven back,—perhaps another column made a simultaneous attack against the 1st Brigade of Guards; of the time and circumstances of the latter attack I know literally nothing.

Should I be warranted in stating that when your Lordship discovered the mistake caused by the passing of the word "form square" immediately after the defeat of the *first* column of the Imperial Guard, you gave the order, as well as your voice at such a moment would admit, for every man to retire to the original position, that the brigade accordingly retired, though in considerable confusion, re-formed in line four deep, and brought up its left shoulder to meet the attack by the *second* column? Such a circumstance as their accidentally retiring in confusion, and then re-forming for another attack, redounds so highly to the credit of our Guards, that I should wish particularly to notice it, if such actually occurred: for certainly none but British troops would have halted to re-form, aware as they must have been that a second immense column was rapidly moving against them; foreign troops would not have stopped until they had fairly crossed the main ridge of the position.

The model, I am happy to say, proceeds very satisfactorily though slowly, and I am now fagging with all my might to bring it out in London on the 18th of June, as also my history of the whole campaign at the same time.—I remain, my dear Lord Saltoun, yours very faithfully,

W. Siborne.

P.S.—I have just this moment heard that you are to command the Light Division in Canada, upon which I take the liberty of congratulating both your Lordship and the service.

May I ask if it be true that the Duke of Wellington made use of the expression, so often attributed to him, of, "Up, Guards, and at them," at the attack of the first column of Imperial Guards?

An officer belonging to the battery on the immediate right of the Guards informs me that he heard the Duke say, "Look out, Guards—ready;" perhaps these were the precise words—a point, however, of very little consequence.

W. S.

Letter from Lord Saltoun to Captain W. Siborne.

London, 19th January 1838.

My dear Sir,

Your letter of the 4th reached me on my way to town, but I have not had time to answer it sooner, and by this time you know that one of your generals from Ireland goes instead of me with the Brigade of Guards to Canada.

I can give you little or no information regarding Quatre Bras. On that day I commanded the Light Companies of the First Brigade of Guards, and the post we occupied was in and about the wood on the right of the field of battle; but from the circumstance of your plan of the ground not being shaded, I am unable at this distance of time to trace our operations upon it. When we debouched from the wood (which we had cleared of the French light troops), we had on our right a deep ravine, or perhaps I should rather call it a hollow, and about 150 yards to our left, and about half that distance to the rear, was a low scrubby hedge, behind which the 33rd Regiment was posted.

This point I cannot make out on your sketch of the ground, but as far as information goes it is not of much importance. That was the extreme point we advanced to, as did also the Brigade; and although we were driven back from it, we recovered it again, and held it till the firing ceased at dark. I perceive you have a small brook or marshy bottom running through the wood. But as far as my recollection serves me, we met with an obstruction of that description much nearer the Nivelle road, from which we commenced our advance, than it appears to be in your plan, but I most likely am wrong in this; for hurried into action as we were into a large, and in some parts thick wood, without any instructions, and nothing to guide me in my advance but the fire of the enemy, it is not likely at this distance of time that I should retain a very clear recollection of distances. Next with respect to Hougomont. From the first attack to the period mentioned in your letter (till about two o'clock), during the whole of which time I was at that post, *(he omits to mention that he had to retake the orchard first of all)*, the whole was a succession of attacks against the front of that post, attended with more or less partial success for the moment, but in the end always repulsed. And it was in one of these attacks, when I had been driven from the front hedge of the orchard to the hollow way in the rear of it, that they, occupying the outward side of the front hedge with infantry, brought a gun along the line marked by you *a*, *b*, to a point I have marked *d* on that line. This gun I endeavoured to take, but failed. I however regained the front hedge of the orchard, from which I never was again driven. Whether the enemy had artillery at the point marked *c*, I am unable to state. We suffered very little from artillery on the post, but it is quite clear that the house and farmyard of Hougomont was set on fire by that arm.

Your next point is the attack (as you call it) of the First Brigade of Guards against a body of infantry previous to the attack of the Imperial Guard, etc. You seem to have mistaken the advance not of that brigade, but of one battalion of them, *viz.*, the Third Battalion Grenadier Guards, and have concluded that this was an attack against a regular body of infantry, but that was not the case. The circumstances were as follows:—

During the cavalry attacks on the centre, a great number of the enemy's sharpshooters had crept up the slope of the hill, and galled the Third Battalion, who were in square, very severely. At that time the Second Battalion Grenadier Guards (the other battalion of the brigade) was likewise formed in square, about 100 yards in rear of the Third Battalion. The Third Battalion, who suffered severely from this fire, wheeled up into line, and drove them down the hill, and advanced to a point I have marked *E*. and there, re-formed square. A small body of Rifles were at a point I have marked with a *X*, and the 52nd Regiment in line at *F G G*.

In this position we received the first attack of cavalry I saw that day, who, refusing us, passed between us and the *inward rear angle of the orchard*, and receiving our fire, did not pass between us and the left of the 52nd, where the Rifles were, but rode along the front of the 52nd, with a view of turning their right flank, and were completely destroyed by the fire of that regiment. After this, we, the Third Battalion, retired to our original position in square, as I conclude the 52nd did also, as the next I saw of them was their attack, with the rest of General Adam's Brigade, on the second column of the Imperial Guards. As to any attack made about that time by the outward angle of the orchard of Hougomont, I could not from my position see or know anything about it.

Your next point is with respect to what took place towards the close of the action, and during the momentary confusion that took place in the First Brigade from the cry of "form square."

It will not do, in an account such as yours, to put down any order that was not given, however scientific it might be, still less to make me give an order to retire, when that was the last thought that came into my head at that moment. The word of command passed was—"Halt! Front, form up;" and it was the only thing that could be done—any other formation was impossible; and as soon as this order was understood by the men it was obeyed, and everything was right again. To prove this, I must take you a little into the drill-book. The original information of this brigade at the commencement of the action was in contiguous column of battalions, at quarter-distance, right in front. From that they formed squares on their respective leading companies.

When they were ordered towards the end of the day to form line of four deep, instead of being deployed into line to either flank, they were wheeled up into line from square (in order that they might get the quicker back into square should that formation be required again). It followed from this that when in line the Grenadier Company and No. 1 formed the centre of each battalion, and the right sections of each company formed the right wing, and the left sections formed the left, thus completely separating the companies, and rendering any formation upon our principles of drill utterly impracticable, except the one before mentioned of wheeling back into square.

From this you will at once, I should think, see that any such account as you suggest would, to any soldier acquainted with the circumstances of the formation of that brigade, prove its own inaccuracy, and do your account more harm than good. For such person would at once know that no fresh formation was practicable with those battalions, until one of two things had been done.

Either they must have been re-formed into square, from that to column, and then deployed in the regular way; or they must have been ordered to fall out, and formed again as at the beginning of a parade to their respective covering sergeants, when all the process of a fresh telling off would become necessary. You had better therefore, I think, have it as I have given it to you, *viz.*, that as soon as the men were made to understand they were not to form square, but to *Halt, front, and form up*, they did it; the left shoulders were then brought forward, and we advanced against the second column of the Imperial Guards, but which body was defeated by General Adam's Brigade before we reached it, although we got near enough to fire if we had been ordered so to do; and, as far as I can recollect at this distance of time, we did fire into that column.

Your last point is, whether the Duke made use of the words, "Up, Guards, and at them!" I did not hear him, nor do I know any person, or ever heard of any person, that did. It is a matter of no sort of importance, has become current with the world as the cheering speech of a great man to his troops, and is certainly not worth a controversy; if you have got it, I should let it stand. I have endeavoured to answer your queries to the best of my ability, and I hope I have made them intelligible to you, and as I am not going with this army, I hope to see your model on the 18th of June next, and that the result will be of use to you.

I remain, my dear Sir, yours very truly,

Saltoun.

Appendix No. 2

THE CHARLEY ELLIS ANECDOTE

Although the following anecdote does not relate to Lord Saltoun personally, yet as he used to tell it of his old brother officer and intimate friend, the late Lieutenant-Colonel Charles Ellis, and as it shows great presence of mind and cool observation in a young officer under difficult circumstances, it is worthy of being placed on record.

> You know Charley Ellis. He is not very big now, and when a young man he was still smaller; but he is the pluckiest fellow I ever met, and I don't think he knows what fear means.
> We were skirmishing in a thickly-wooded bit of country, and Charley had somehow got separated from his men, and lost his way for a time. Trying to rejoin them, he dived through an opening in the bushes, and found himself in a little clearing, just as a tall French soldier entered it through a similar opening on the opposite side, about twenty paces from him. Charley was staggered for an instant, but his eyes and wits were as keen as ever, and he noticed that the hammer of the Frenchman's musket was down, and the pan open.
> Rushing at him with his sword drawn, he cried in French, 'Down with your arms, and surrender! My men are all round, in a moment you'll be cut to pieces!' The soldier, taken by surprise, threw down his musket. 'Now, off with your cartouche-pouch,' cried Charley. The man obeyed; and Charley, before his adversary had time to think, had loaded the weapon. 'Now,' said he, 'I don't know where my men are any more than you do, but I know the way to find them, so you march on quietly before me, if you try to escape, I'll blow your brains out.'

When he appeared with the Frenchman, some six foot two or three in height, before him, the men all cheered him; and when they heard how the capture had been made, they were still more pleased, for he was a general favourite with them, from his kindness to them, and from his invincible courage joined to so small a frame.

Appendix No. 3

Information from the Regimental History
by F W Hamilton, 1871

Losses of the First Guards at Quatre Bras and Waterloo

The officers of the First Guards wounded at Quatre Bras were:—

Second Battalion

Colonel H. Askew, Commanding.

Captain James Simpson.

Ensign George Fludyer.

Ensign T. E. Croft (severely).

Third Battalion

Colonel Hon. William Stuart, Commanding.

Lieut.-Colonel Hon. H. T. P. Townshend.

Captain T. Streatfield.

Ensign William Barton.

The officers of the First Guards killed at Quatre Bras were:—

Lieut.-Colonel William Miller, 3rd battalion, died on 19th, at Brussels.

Captain E. Grose, 3rd battalion.

Captain R. Adair, 3rd battalion, died on 23rd at Brussels.

Captain T. Brown, 2nd battalion.

Ensign Hon. S. P. Barrington, 2nd battalion.

Ensign Lord James Hay, A.D.C., 2nd battalion.

(Lord J. Hay was acting as adjutant to Lord Saltoun, mounted on a very fine horse, nearly, if not quite, thorough-bred. In its excitement at being put at a fence it refused, reared, and tried to wheel round. As Saltoun was proceeding down a path, after passing through the wood at Bossu, a body fell across his horse's neck and rolled off. It was that of Lord Hay, who had just been shot by a cavalry skirmisher, who was in his turn shot by a grenadier close to Saltoun.)

Total casualties of British troops at Quatre Bras, on the 16th of June, 1815, were:—

```
Guards 1st Div., 1st Brig., 2nd battn., 1st Guards    279)
   "           "       3rd     "          "           255)=   534
   "        2nd Brig., 2nd battn., Coldstreams          0)
   "           "       3rd     "   3rd Guards           7)=     7
5th Div., 8th Brig., four battalions                         781
   "      9th   "    four battalions                         705
                                                           ——————
                                          Total             2027
General Staff, Royal Artillery Lieutenants                   362
                                                           ——————
                                                            2389
```

The officers of the First Guards killed at Waterloo were:

Second Battalion,
Sir F. D'Oyly, K.C.B., lieutenant-colonel

★★★★★★

Lieutenant-Colonel Sir Francis D'Oyly, K.C.B., of the First Guards, third son of the Rev. Mathias D'Oyly, archdeacon of Lewes, was only thirty-nine at the period of his death. He was present throughout the action at Quatre Bras, and till towards the close of the action of the 18th, when, in the last charge, he received a musket-ball in a vital part of his body, and fell dead from his horse.

★★★★★★

Lieutenant-Colonel W. H. Milnes, wounded, since dead.

Third Battalion.

E. Stables, Lieutenant-Colonel (Lieutenant-Colonel Stables, of Great Ormead, Hertfordshire), died the following day.

Charles Thomas;

Ensign E. Pardoe.

And serving on the staff there were killed—Captain Newton Chambers, (Captain Newton Chambers, *aide-de-camp* to Sir Thomas Picton, by whose side he fell a few minutes after his general), and Captain Cameron.

The officers wounded were:—

Second Battalion.

Lieutenant-Colonel Sir Henry Bradford, K.O.B., assistant-quartermaster-general, severely;

Lieutenant-Colonel R. C. Cooke, severely;

Captain F. Luttrell, severely;

Captain S. W. Burgess, severely;

Ensign H. Lascelles, slightly.

Third Battalion.

Lieutenant-Colonel Henry D'Oyly, severely;

Lieutenant-Colonel George Fead, slightly;

Captain Hon. Robt. Clements, severely;

Captain C. P. Ellis, slightly;

Ensign R. Batty, slightly;

Ensign R. Bruce, severely.

And serving on the staff there were:—

Lieutenant-Colonels Cooper, Hardness, and Lord Fitzroy Somerset; Captain Hon. Orlando Bridgeman; Lieutenant George Mure.

The total loss of the Second Brigade, Third Guards in the two days was 500 men; but that was sustained almost entirely at Hougoumont, as they had but few casualties at Quatre Bras.

Out of eighty-two officers of the First Guards in the field

at Quatre Bras or Waterloo, thirty-five were either killed or wounded—for casualties at Quatre Bras see list earlier.

The losses of the two battalions of First Guards, both at Quatre Bras and at Waterloo, during those two days, in killed and wounded, were 1034 men.

List of Killed & Wounded Quatre Bras and Waterloo

Killed

2nd Batt. 1st Guards

Officers	Sergts.	Drmrs.	R. & F.	Total	
2	1	—	22	25	Quatre Bras
1	—	—	50	51	Waterloo

3rd Batt. 1st Guards

Officers	Sergts.	Drmrs.	R. & F.	Total	
1	2	1	17	21	Quatre Bras
3	2	—	79	84	Waterloo
—	—	—	—	—	
7	5	1	168	181	Grand Toatal

Wounded

2nd Batt. 1st Guards

Officers	Sergts.	Drmrs.	R. & F.	Total	
4	6	—	250	285	Quatre Bras
5	7	—	89	152	Waterloo

3rd Batt. 1st Guards

Officers	Sergts.	Drmrs.	R. & F.	Total	
6	9	1	225	262	Quatre Bras
6	7	—	238	335	Waterloo
—	—	—	—	—	
29	1	802	853	1034	Grand Total

ALSO FROM LEONAUR
AVAILABLE IN SOFTCOVER OR HARDCOVER WITH DUST JACKET

OFFICERS & GENTLEMEN *by Peter Hawker & William Graham*—Two Accounts of British Officers During the Peninsula War: Officer of Light Dragoons by Peter Hawker & Campaign in Portugal and Spain by William Graham.

THE WALCHEREN EXPEDITION *by Anonymous*—The Experiences of a British Officer of the 81st Regt. During the Campaign in the Low Countries of 1809.

LADIES OF WATERLOO *by Charlotte A. Eaton, Magdalene de Lancey & Juana Smith*—The Experiences of Three Women During the Campaign of 1815: Waterloo Days by Charlotte A. Eaton, A Week at Waterloo by Magdalene de Lancey & Juana's Story by Juana Smith.

JOURNAL OF AN OFFICER IN THE KING'S GERMAN LEGION *by John Frederick Hering*—Recollections of Campaigning During the Napoleonic Wars.

JOURNAL OF AN ARMY SURGEON IN THE PENINSULAR WAR *by Charles Boutflower*—The Recollections of a British Army Medical Man on Campaign During the Napoleonic Wars.

ON CAMPAIGN WITH MOORE AND WELLINGTON *by Anthony Hamilton*—The Experiences of a Soldier of the 43rd Regiment During the Peninsular War.

THE ROAD TO AUSTERLITZ *by R. G. Burton*—Napoleon's Campaign of 1805.

SOLDIERS OF NAPOLEON *by A. J. Doisy De Villargennes & Arthur Chuquet*—The Experiences of the Men of the French First Empire: Under the Eagles by A. J. Doisy De Villargennes & Voices of 1812 by Arthur Chuquet.

INVASION OF FRANCE, 1814 *by F. W. O. Maycock*—The Final Battles of the Napoleonic First Empire.

LEIPZIG—A CONFLICT OF TITANS *by Frederic Shoberl*—A Personal Experience of the 'Battle of the Nations' During the Napoleonic Wars, October 14th-19th, 1813.

SLASHERS *by Charles Cadell*—The Campaigns of the 28th Regiment of Foot During the Napoleonic Wars by a Serving Officer.

BATTLE IMPERIAL *by Charles William Vane*—The Campaigns in Germany & France for the Defeat of Napoleon 1813-1814.

SWIFT & BOLD *by Gibbes Rigaud*—The 60th Rifles During the Peninsula War.

AVAILABLE ONLINE AT **www.leonaur.com**
AND FROM ALL GOOD BOOK STORES